# The Good News
# of the Kingdom

*Alice and Arthur Glasser*

# The Good News
# of the Kingdom

*Mission Theology for the Third Millennium*

**Edited by**
**Charles Van Engen**
**Dean S. Gilliland**
**Paul Pierson**

*Wipf and Stock Publishers*
EUGENE, OREGON

Wipf and Stock Publishers
199 West 8th Avenue, Suite 3
Eugene, Oregon 97401

The Good News of The Kingdom
Mission Theology for the Third Millennium
Edited by Van Engen, Charles, Gilliland, Dean S. and Pierson, Paul
Copyright©1993 by Van Engen, Gilliland, and Pierson
ISBN: 1-57910-278-6
Publication date 9/17/1999
Previously published by Orbis Books, 1993

*Essays in Honor of Arthur F. Glasser*

# Contents

*vii*

## PART 2
## THEOLOGICAL REFLECTIONS

## PART 3
## ECUMENICAL RELATIONSHIPS

## PART 4
## EVANGELICAL CONCERNS

## PART 5
## MISSIOLOGICAL ISSUES

## PART 6
## CONTEXTUAL CONSIDERATIONS

## CONCLUSION

# Foreword

## DAVID A. HUBBARD

This is an important book. Its authors are a *Who's Who* of mission scholars and practitioners. Their experiences and insights from lifetimes of study and service combine to bring credibility and cogency to their chapters. The variety of Christian traditions and the range of cultural and geographical backgrounds enhance the vigor of the book. Their participation and obvious delight in doing so are a splendid contribution to Christian movements of many kinds as they head into the challenges and opportunities of century twenty-one. The illustrious list of contributors is, furthermore, a high tribute to the ministry of Arthur Glasser. Few persons in the post World War II era have done as much to encourage interest in missions worldwide, to train and retrain missionaries, and to stimulate sound and courageous thinking about the task of global evangelization.

More than a Festschrift, this book will become a standard handbook on mission theology for its decade. Tackling the pressing issues of our times — pluralism, syncretism, church-state relations, the urban sprawls on every continent, the role of women in missions, the ways and means of updating our theologies without distorting their biblical messages — the essays form a veritable textbook for all who care about Christ's great commission and its implementation in our day.

The trio of editors have rendered us all a fine service. They have done their work on this project well from its conception to its birth. The topic is the right one for the times and the field: the Kingdom of God is the overarching subject under which Christians of all stripes must gather, worship, study, and work. The contributors are the right group, each one chosen to share the unusual competence for which each is distinguished. The brief comments of continuity and interpretation add measurably to the usefulness of the chapters. Many thanks are due Charles Van Engen, Dean Gilliland, and Paul Pierson for their fruitful labors.

Arthur Glasser had long been one of my heroes before he became my

David Allan Hubbard is President of Fuller Theological Seminary, where he serves also as Professor of Old Testament. Born of missionary parents, he has gained special joy from the School of World Mission founded at Fuller under his leadership in 1965.

colleague at Fuller. His passionate heart, his arms ever-extending to embrace the world, his ready tongue and artful pen, his level head when others are rattled, his shoulders broad in support of all whom he loves — these all have become examples of Christian leadership and resources of spiritual maturity to me. I welcome the opportunity to join the editors and contributors in saying thanks to Arthur Glasser for his remarkable half-century of service to the cause of Christ.

# Preface

## CHARLES VAN ENGEN

Because much missiology of the last twenty-five years took an action-oriented and pragmatic direction, there has been less reflection on the theology of mission during this time. The volume edited by Gerald Anderson in 1961, *The Theology of the Christian Mission* is still primary. Although there have been overview texts by a number of people regarding the historical development of theology of mission, no one-volume work has drawn out the major global issues facing theology of mission today. Hopefully, this volume will fill a void felt by many of us who teach theology of mission and will become an important reference work that illustrates the state-of-the-art thinking on the subject. I, for one, will use it as a required text in my courses.

It has been twenty years since I first sat under the teaching of Arthur Glasser. Although I was studying at the same time with G. E. Ladd and Geoffrey Bromiley, it was Glasser who introduced me to the radically creative implications of Kingdom-of-God theology for missiology. The last two decades have been filled with pleasant surprises as I have begun to understand the depth of wisdom Glasser has offered us. By means of this volume, I and the other editors want to show our gratitude and debt to Arthur Glasser.

The purpose of this volume is to gather some of the best thinking on theology of mission available to the Christian church today. As such, it presents reformed, ecumenical, evangelical, strongly missiological, and critically contextual perspectives. The volume's richness may be found in the breadth of perspective, the depth of consensus around a trinitarian kingdom-oriented missiology, and the height of the challenges facing the church in mission into the next millennium.

The book has been designed for use by teachers and students of missiology, mission practitioners, and mission-oriented pastors of churches all over the world. Bible schools and seminaries with missions courses will find

Charles Van Engen was born and raised in Mexico, where from 1973-1985 he also served the National Presbyterian Church of Mexico in theological education, evangelism, youth ministries and refugee relief. He is presently Associate Professor of Theology of Mission and Latin American Studies at Fuller Seminary's School of World Mission.

the volume very useful as a tool to gain a broad familiarity with the people, thoughts, and issues facing mission theology.

We have attempted to design and compile this book without intentional bias, knowing that differing views would be presented. The opinions expressed in it are those of each author. Likewise, the overall perspective of the book should not reflect either positively or negatively on Arthur Glasser, since it is the responsibility of the editors. Any sins of omission or commission in the preparation of this volume are our responsibility, for which we beg forgiveness.

I cannot adequately express my deep appreciation to my coeditors for their help with this project. As Dean of the School of World Mission during most of the time this volume was being prepared, Paul Pierson has been wonderfully supportive, personally, theoretically, and administratively. He was intimately involved in the selection of those who were invited to contribute and has been strongly encouraging of the issues being pursued. Without his encouragement and support I would not have begun this project. His infectious enthusiasm about writing the biographical sketch inspired us all.

Every step of the way, Dean Gilliland has been my advisor, friend, encourager, and partner. His masterful introductions to each section will show the reader the depth of his own scholarship in theology of mission, along with his profound understanding of Arthur Glasser's thought. His wise counsel helped us make some difficult editorial decisions. I could not have completed this project without his help. Professor Gilliland's "introductory overviews" at the beginning of each new part of the book will help orient readers to the dynamics of the project.

I am forever indebted to those who were willing to contribute to this volume. Given their busy schedules, their joyful and enthusiastic acceptance of one more writing project was witness to their friendship and appreciation of Arthur Glasser — and their willingness to trust the editors. As the reader can appreciate, the stringent limits on the length of each chapter meant that we often tried the patience of the contributors by asking them to accept shorter versions of what they had submitted. I want them to know how deeply I appreciate their cooperation in this regard.

I well remember the day that I danced into Dean Gilliland's and Paul Pierson's offices to show them the contract I had just received from Bill Burrows and Orbis Books. The careful, sensitive, and thoughtful approach that Bill brought to our discussions, along with Orbis's willingness to risk on a type of work that is becoming less common, were sources of great encouragement to us. Initially we thought of Orbis for the publication of this work due in part to Orbis's connection with the American Society of Missiology — an organization that includes many close friends of Arthur Glasser. After our conversations and our close cooperation on this project, we are happy for many additional reasons that Bill Burrows and Orbis Books were willing to accept the project.

I want to thank four very special people who helped compile this volume. Betty Anne Klebe spent hundreds of hours doing the mailing for the congratulatory list, and communicating all over the world with the various authors. She inspired me with her timely suggestions, willingness to do more than was required, and spirit of loving service.

Rob Gallagher gave us his time and ingenuity to help us compile the Glasser Bibliography. Attempting to do this without Art knowing about it was a very tricky enterprise, but Rob was sufficient for the challenge.

The word processing and manuscript formatting would have been nearly impossible for us without the help of David Sielaff and the staff of the Word Processing Office at Fuller Theological Seminary. We express our deepest gratitude to them. They approached the book as if it were one of their personal pet projects and dedicated many hours to helping us with it.

Lastly, I want to thank Gerald Anderson for his enthusiastic support for the project. His encouragement was deeply moving to me and especially meaningful because of the connection that I see between this volume and the one Gerald edited thirty years ago. It was icing on the cake when Gerald offered to check the Glasser bibliography against his data. This kind of friendship and loving support has made the compilation of this volume a very enjoyable task.

May we all be led by the Spirit to understand more profoundly, and participate more fully in, what it means to pray, "Your Kingdom come."

# INTRODUCTION

# Arthur F. Glasser:
# Citizen of the Kingdom

## PAUL E. PIERSON

Arthur Glasser was born into a Christian home with German Brethren roots in New Jersey, but by his own admission was nominal in his faith until just before he went off to Cornell University. That summer at a Keswick Bible conference through Donald B. Fullerton, founder of the Princeton Evangelical Fellowship, he became a committed Christian. At Cornell, Arthur studied engineering and rowed on the crew. Marked by an aptitude for solving unusual technical problems, Art was offered a scholarship for postgraduate study. However, after graduation he began his career with an engineering firm in Pittsburgh, visualizing himself as a layman, eager to serve Christ in his chosen profession.

But gripped by the vision of making Christ known wherever He was not being named, he resigned from his firm and prepared to enter Faith Seminary to study theology with the goal of becoming a missionary. The seminary had been formed out of the fundamentalist-modernist controversies in the Presbyterian Church, a movement in which first Westminster Seminary had split off from Princeton and then Faith from Westminster. Thus his early theological training took place in an institution that was ultra separatist and, as he would put it later, hoped "to make the world safe for the Reformed faith." Glasser thoroughly embraced the importance of biblical authority and the centrality of Christ advocated at the seminary. But precisely because of his constant grappling with Scripture through the years he would be led beyond its separatism to a genuinely evangelical ecumenism.

His concern that all should hear the gospel led him in two directions during his seminary years. He became involved in the Foreign Missions Fellowship, which would soon merge with InterVarsity Christian Fellowship. Through the FMF he came into contact with people such as J. Christy Wilson, Jr., and Samuel Moffett, who had remained in the broader Pres-

Dr. Paul E. Pierson is Dean Emeritus and Professor of History and Latin American Studies in the School of World Mission at Fuller Theological Seminary. He served as missionary and professor with the United Presbyterian Church (USA) in Brazil and Portugal from 1955-1973.

byterian Church and would have a strong impact on the North American missionary movement.

"To the Jew first" became a second focus as he walked the streets of New York, handing out gospel tracts and talking with Jews on weekends and during the summers. This concern, against the background of events in Nazi Germany, led him to study ardently the Old and New Testaments to discover God's purpose for the Jews.

Graduating from seminary in 1942, he married Alice Oliver, the lovely, gracious woman who became his life's companion. Shortly thereafter Arthur entered the navy to become a marine chaplain. This led him to service in areas of heavy fighting in the South Pacific, where he was an evangelist, leading a number of marines to personal faith in Jesus Christ. At the same time, he continued his theological reflection on the nature of the church and the Christian mission. Seeing a New Testament lying beside the headless corpse of a Japanese soldier deeply affected his growing concern for the body of Christ worldwide and spurred his questions about the relationship between Christ and Caesar.

After the war, the Glassers were accepted as missionaries under the China Inland Mission and arrived in Shanghai on the last day of 1946 to begin their missionary career. They were eventually sent to southwestern China, where they worked with tribespeople in a church that had been the result of a large people movement. Even though the Han Chinese and some missionaries looked down on this tribal people, the Glassers found great joy in working with them and having them as frequent guests in their home.

Membership in the China Inland Mission further broadened Arthur's understanding of the church, since the mission included among its personnel men and women from a variety of Christian traditions, from Brethren to Anglican. In this very evangelical mission he began hearing more positive views about certain European theologians, especially Karl Barth, whom he had been taught to fear at Faith Seminary. But the Glassers' missionary career was cut short when they, along with other missionaries, were expelled from China by the Communists in 1951.

The experience in China, building on his wartime chaplaincy, led Arthur to further reflection. Not content simply to condemn Communism and lament the expulsion of missionaries and the apparent demise of the church in China, he began to reflect on why so much of the church had collapsed and why so many Christians he had known were easily captured by the Communist ideology. This reminded him that some of his own family members, pious and separatist Brethren in Germany, concerned about a type of worldliness that focused on matters of conduct and a purely future anti-Christ, had failed to see the anti-Christ under their very nose in Adolph Hitler and had been blinded by a far more demonic kind of worldliness which led to the Holocaust and World War II. What was the proper relationship between the church and Caesar, whether a Caesar of the right or of the left? And what of a democratic center? Why had the church in

Germany failed to resist Hitler or speak against the extermination of the Jews? Why had Communism triumphed in China? Had the missionaries prepared the church adequately to face that ideology? Had the church and the Christian mission been genuinely biblical and holistic as they attempted to fulfill the missionary task? What did the Bible have to teach about these issues? These were questions swirling around his mind in those immediate post-China years.

When they returned to the United States, Arthur taught at Columbia Bible College in South Carolina for four years. Recognized as one of the younger leaders in the China Inland Mission, now without a country, Arthur was one of a group of men invited to meet in London as the mission restructured itself and chose a new director. At that time he was invited to become North American director of the mission that would later be known as the Overseas Missionary Fellowship. This led to a move to Philadelphia, where the Glassers lived for fifteen years. During this period he also taught missions at Westminster Seminary.

These were years of reflection. In *Missions in Crisis*, written with Eric Fife in 1961, Arthur went far beyond most evangelicals in raising key issues for Christian missions. Writing in a spirit of humility, wanting to hear God speak to the church through its apparent defeat in China, he said that missionaries should reject any lingering paternalism and strongly encourage national leadership. Secondly, while he affirmed the necessity of communicating the center of the gospel, criticizing liberals for their one-sided social gospel, he also scolded evangelicals for failing to teach the "whole counsel of God contained in Scripture," for erecting a false antithesis between the material and the spiritual worlds, and for failing to transmit the deeply rooted social concerns of both the Old and New Testaments. Anticipating a number of emphases that would receive attention in subsequent decades, he called for a greater focus on the unreached, more concern for the urban centers, emphasis on non-Caucasian missionaries, a more positive approach to Chinese culture, and greater recognition of the Pentecostal movement. Missionaries had been far too naive about Western imperialism, he said, but he still expressed his confidence in the sovereignty of God, working in China and the church there.

The Philadelphia years also led to growth in ecumenical contacts. Through his friend Russell Hitt, editor of *Eternity* magazine, Arthur participated in a series of consultations on mission which included evangelicals and conciliar Protestants. Together they attempted to discover future directions of missions and as colonialism ended, some called for a "moratorium," and pessimism grew.

In 1969, anxious to continue his study and reflection, Arthur resigned from the Overseas Missionary Fellowship and went for a year to Union Seminary in New York. There he studied under Hans J. Hoekendijk, the Dutch theologian who came from a radically different theological perspective. He did additional study at Columbia University on Chinese culture and at the Jewish Seminary, following two of his earliest interests.

At that time David Allan Hubbard, President of Fuller Theological Seminary, approached Arthur to join the faculty of the School of World Mission and Institute of Church Growth at Fuller and, as he put it, "to put some theology into this church growth business." The School of World Mission had been founded in 1965 under the leadership of Dr. Donald McGavran, the father of the church growth movement. The movement, led by McGavran in reaction to the institutionalization of the Christian mission and the neglect of evangelism and the planting and multiplication of the church, was fiercely pragmatic. Both Hubbard and Glasser affirmed the core values of the movement but saw the need for greater theological reflection. Thus in 1970 Arthur joined the School of World Mission faculty to teach theology of mission and related subjects and to serve as its dean from 1971 to 1980. To this task he brought his wealth of experience as a missionary practitioner and mission administrator, coupled with his constant reflection on the Scriptures and the missionary task as defined by them. The school saw considerable growth in students, faculty, and programs during Glasser's years as dean.

The courses he taught at Fuller indicate a number of his concerns and the fruit of years of reflection and study. His Biblical Foundations of Mission went beyond the exegesis of a few favorite passages and sought to understand the whole of Scripture as a book about mission. The goal was to lead students to understand and live out the whole biblical agenda wherever they engaged in mission. The church in Hostile Environments recognized that we engage in mission in a world which is fundamentally hostile to the Christian faith, and that consequently the church must often live under persecution. The parallels to China and its lessons were important. Theology of Religious Encounter recognized that the key issue facing the church everywhere is the uniqueness of Jesus Christ as the only way to God's salvation. Arthur continually sought new ways to affirm this while being sensitive to other cultures and non-Christian religions. His course in Ecumenics and Mission examined mission documents of conciliar Protestants, Roman Catholics, and evangelicals, taking students beyond the stereotypes which many brought to the classroom, encouraging them to engage in the theological debate and learn from traditions different from their own. Since 1980 Glasser has served as Dean Emeritus, Senior Professor of Theology of Mission, and friend, encourager, and mentor to his faculty colleagues and students.

During the Fuller years his leadership in the broader missiological community grew. Arthur was present at the historic evangelical gathering in Wheaton in 1966 and helped draft the "Wheaton Declaration." This led to continued leadership in evangelical missiology at Lausanne (1974), Pattaya (1980), Wheaton (1983) and Manila (1989). In 1972, Arthur took part in the establishment of the American Society of Missiology and served as editor of its journal, *Missiology*, from 1976 to 1982. He also served a one-year term as president of the Society (1982–1983). Arthur's contacts through the American Society of Missiology developed into deeper participation in missiological discussions with ecumenical missiology at Bangkok (1973), Melbourne (1980) and Vancouver (1983). During this time Glasser's participation with the International Association for Mission Studies (IAMS) at Dreybergen (1973), Maryknoll (1978), and Rome (1980) led to close friendship with, and appreciation for, a large number of Catholic missiologists as well.

As an outgrowth of the 1974 Lausanne Conference he took part in and provided the summation statement for a Consultation on Muslim Evangelism in Glen Eyrie, Colorado, in 1978. Recognizing the failure of most Western missions among Muslims, he rejected any "gimmick methodology," adding, "we must face the cross and enter into the trauma of conflict with 'the powers' while seeking to witness simply and lovingly of Jesus Christ" (Glasser 1979, 46). The consultation led to the establishment of the Samuel Zwemer Institute, which would encourage research and preparation for ministry among Muslims.

His growing ecumenical concern led to attendance at the "Salvation Today" meeting of the Division of World Mission and Evangelism of the World Council of Churches, held in Bangkok in 1973. In the midst of strong currents of theological relativism, he focused on the "Lamb Slain, whose resurrection affirms the triumphant power of God," and quoted William Temple, "Our message is Jesus Christ. We dare not give less, we cannot give more. This is salvation today" (Glasser 1973, 147–149).

After participation in a Presbyterian mission consultation in 1978, he wrote that the only starting point for mission had to be the Word of God. Affirming his desire for ecumenical dialogue and concern for social change, he insisted there could be "no compromise on the fact that all peoples need to hear and respond to the gospel." He added, "Our God-given responsibility . . . is to baptize in the name of the triune God all those who turn to Jesus Christ in repentance and faith. Should we not anticipate that God would call many to Himself through the gospel, and that they should be incorporated by baptism into fellowship with those who bear His name?" (Glasser 1978, 279).

Continuing his ecumenical contacts he attended the Vancouver Assembly of the WCC, urging evangelicals to be more involved in the ecumenical movement, while in conciliar circles he insisted on the centrality of Jesus Christ and the essential task of communicating the gospel to the whole world.

His early interest in China has continued. He was one of the architects of the program of Chinese studies and evangelism in the School of World Mission at Fuller, and has been active on the board of Kairos, a largely Scandinavian-sponsored agency that has supported and encouraged training programs in the Peoples' Republic of China done by Chinese through cassette tapes and radio.

To the Jew first! In recent years he has returned to his concern that the gospel be proclaimed to the Jews, coming full circle from his seminary days. Instrumental in establishing the program of Judaic Studies and Jewish Evangelism in the School of World Mission, he has encouraged those movements designed especially to present the gospel in culturally sensitive ways to our Jewish friends. His most recent research and writing have been focused on that issue.

I believe Glasser's pilgrimage can be summarized by examining briefly his understanding of the nature of the gospel, mission, and the church.

His conversion took place in a warmly pietistic context which focused on the importance of personal faith in Jesus Christ as the only way to personal salvation, coupled with a high view of Scripture. These concepts have continued to be central in his thought, even as his understanding has grown that the gospel must be seen as good news for the poor and the oppressed in this life as well. His experience, beginning in China, and his continued study of Scripture, have led him to the conviction that because God is concerned about poverty and injustice in human society, Christians must be also, even while our ultimate focus is on eternity.

The call to make Christ known where the gospel had not yet been heard led him into mission and then to China, only to suffer apparent defeat and expulsion after five years. No less committed to his original call, he was led to reflect on the nature of that mission. He wished that his mission — and others — had shown greater love for Chinese culture and traditions, had moved more aggressively to build up the Chinese Church and its leadership, and been more holistic in its approach. Thus he longed to see missionaries better prepared. This would become an important aspect of his ministry at Fuller.

His broadening understanding of the church has been remarkable. Graduating from a seminary on the extreme edge of the separatist movement, he has discovered and affirmed Christians in a variety of traditions without compromising his own deeply held evangelical convictions. His ecumenical relationships have not only extended to conciliar Protestants and Roman Catholics. He has encouraged and mentored Pentecostals and Seventh Day Adventists. One of the latter wrote of how amazed he was at Glasser's warm welcome, which in turn made him much more open to cooperation with Christians of other traditions.

Glasser's pilgrimage eventually led to what he would term a "Copernican revolution" in his theology, the rediscovery of the biblical motif of the Kingdom of God. Secularized by the social gospel movement, pushed safely into the future by fundamentalist dispensationalism, and ignored by most others, the Kingdom of God provided a unifying framework for the understanding of conversion and the Christian life, of mission, and the church. Glasser also believed it could provide a common meeting ground for evangelical/ecumenical discussions. For some years he has been polishing a manuscript on the theology of mission around this theme, and his many admirers and colleagues are looking forward to its publication. Thus it is most appropriate that the theme of this book which honors Arthur should focus on the Kingdom.

One of the privileges of being a member of the faculty of the School of World Mission at Fuller is that of sitting with one's colleagues every Wednesday for two hours, to eat lunch, to share personal concerns, to pray, and to reflect together on the missionary task. Having done that with Arthur Glasser for twelve years has been an inestimable privilege for this writer.

How to characterize such a unique individual? Central to his life's pilgrimage has been the desire to be a thoroughly biblical Christian, and such a person never fits into neat categories. His focus on the incarnation, the cross, the resurrection, and the lordship of Christ are central to his faith and life. That is accompanied by a strong conviction regarding the authority of Scripture and his desire to study, reflect, understand, and live out its mandates. With this goes a passionate concern that men and women everywhere, of every race, language, and culture, have the opportunity to know Christ and become His disciples.

The security of these convictions and the breadth of his experience have allowed, indeed impelled him, to range widely in his ecumenical contacts and social concerns. Strong and secure at the center, he has not been afraid to relate to those with whom he differed theologically, nor has he feared to examine any number of issues in the light of the gospel. In his eagerness to continue to learn and discover new aspects of the truth, and in his refreshing humility and contagious enthusiasm, Arthur Glasser has been a constant stimulus and friend to his faculty colleagues. We will forever be in his debt.

# Bibliography of Arthur F. Glasser's Works

## DEAN S. GILLILAND

**1946**

*And Some Believed: A Chaplain's Experiences with the Marines in the South Pacific.* Chicago: Moody Press.

**1950**

"Three Counties Our Field" (with Alice Glasser). *The Millions* 58 (May): 77.

**1951**

"Swlowu Bible School." *The Millions* 59 (March): 43–44.

**1955**

"Hastening Day." *HIS* 15, no. 8 (May): 8–13, 29–31.

"Our Over-All Strategy." *The Millions* 63 (September): 115–17.

"If Paul Had Prayed for You." *The Millions* 63 (December): 163–64.

**1956**

"Our Brothers Are Engaged in War with the Beast." *HIS* 16, no. 9 (June): 1–3.

**1957**

"This Malaya 1957." *HIS* 17, no. 9 (June): 6–9.

"Vocational Witness." *HIS* 18, no. 2 (November): 9–12, 18.

**1959**

"Communism." *Religion in a Changing World.* Howard F. Vos, ed. Chicago: Moody Press, 297–337.

"In What Sense Is the China Inland Mission 'Interdenominational'?" *The Millions* 67 (January): 2.

"Heritage of the Lord." *The Millions* 67 (July): 99–100.

**1960**

"Mary." *HIS* 21, no. 3 (December): 4–6, 25–26.

**1961**

*Missions in Crisis: Rethinking Missionary Strategy* (with Eric S. Fife). Chicago: InterVarsity Press.

"Our Muddy Thinking About Communism, Part I." *Eternity* 12, no. 2 (February) 10–12, 30.

"Our Muddy Thinking About Communism, Part II." *Eternity* 12, no. 4 (April) 20–22, 28–30.

"February Theses." *East Asia Millions* 69 (May): 67–68.

"Laos Facing the Hard Questions Raised by the Present Crisis." *East Asia Millions* 69 (July): 99–100.

"What About Our Children?" *East Asia Millions* 69 (August–September): 114.

"Literature Issue." *East Asia Millions* 69 (October): 130.

"Our Literature Strategy." *East Asia Millions* 69 (October): 134.

"Student Issue." *East Asia Millions* 69 (December): 162.

"Current Strategy in Missions." *HIS* 22, no. 1 (October): 8, 10–12.

"Current Strategy in Missions (Continued)." *HIS* 22, no. 2 (November): 3, 5, 21–23.

**1962**

"Commission: Nineteen Centuries of Missionary Work, A General Survey." *Commission, Conflict, Commitment. Messages from the Sixth International Student Missionary Convention* (University of Illinois, Urbana-Champaign, December 1961). Chicago: InterVarsity Press, 113–21.

"Conflict: The Church and External Pressures, The Mission Board and the Church." *Commission, Conflict, Commitment. Messages from the Sixth International Student Missionary Convention* (University of Illinois, Urbana-Champaign, December 1961). Chicago: InterVarsity Press, 164–72.

"Conflict: The Church and Internal Pressures, Marxist Ideology." *Commission, Conflict, Commitment. Messages from the Sixth International Student Missionary Convention* (University of Illinois, Urbana-Champaign, December 27–31, 1961). Chicago: InterVarsity Press, 145–53.

"Commitment: The Demand of the Hour, The Urgency of the Hour." *Commission, Conflict, Commitment. Messages from the Sixth International Student Missionary Convention* (University of Illinois, Urbana-Champaign, December 1961). Chicago: InterVarsity Press, 200–10.

"Lord, Thrust Them Forth." *East Asia Millions* 70 (January): 3.

"Partners in Obedience." *East Asia Millions* 70 (February): 18.

"Tribal Issue." *East Asia Millions* 70 (March): 34.

"Training Nationals." *East Asia Millions* 70 (June): 83.

"Of Course This Man Is Important!" *East Asia Millions* 70 (July): 99.

"Taiwan: Its Church and Our Mission, Cooperation Unlimited?" *East Asia Millions* 70 (August–September): 115–18.

"Denis Clark Takes a Look at Literature Overseas: Interviewed by Dr. Glasser." *East Asia Millions* 70 (October): 131–32.

"2 Messages." *East Asia Millions* 70 (November): 147.

**1963**

"Candidate School." *East Asia Millions* 71 (January): 5–6.

"New Recruits." *East Asia Millions* 71 (January): 8–10.

"Helping Asians in the Missionary Task." *East Asia Millions* 71 (February): 19.

"Central Thailand." *East Asia Millions* 71 (April): 51–52.

"Hudson Taylor as a Young Missionary and His Counterpart Today." *East Asia Millions* 71 (May): 67.

"Advance Inevitable with God." *East Asia Millions* 71 (June): 83.

"Indonesia." *East Asia Millions* 71 (July): 99.

"Is There a Case for Medical Missions?" *East Asia Millions* 71 (November): 147–48.

**1964**

"Dr. Irwin Moon Talks Our Language." *East Asia Millions* 72 (January): 3.

"Wintertime in Japan." *East Asia Millions* 72 (February): 19.

"Has the Day of Missions Passed?" *East Asia Millions* 72 (April): 51–52.

"Our Foster Child." *East Asia Millions* 72 (April): 60–61.

"Opportunities Unlimited!" *East Asia Millions* 72 (May): 67–68.

"Christian Obligation." *East Asia Millions* 72 (June): 82.

"One Billion Souls Really Lost?" *East Asia Millions* 72 (July): 99.

"Is Today God's Time in the Far East?" *East Asia Millions* 72 (August–September): 115–16.

"Culture Shock." *East Asia Millions* 72 (August–September): 123–24.

"At The Crossroads—Two Young Workers Face Disappointments in the First Months on the Field." *East Asia Millions* 72 (August–September): 125–26.

"Missionary Candidate Called Home." *East Asia Millions* 72 (October): 130.

**1965**

"Witness Unashamed, The World Scene." *Change, Witness, Triumph. The Seventh InterVarsity Missionary Convention* (University of Illinois, Urbana-Champaign, December 1964). Chicago: InterVarsity Press, 103–10.

"Interdenominational Foreign Mission Association." *Christianity Today* 9 (January 29): 19–21.

"1865." *East Asia Millions* 73 (January): 2.

"The Propagation of Christianity." *Church Growth Bulletin* 2, no. 2: 1–2.

"1865–1875." *East Asia Millions* 73 (February): 18.

"1875–1885." *East Asia Millions* 73 (March): 34.

"Men of God." *East Asia Millions* 73 (March): 35.

"Mao, a Basket of Eels, and the Church." *Eternity* 16 (March): 32–34, 36.

"1885–1895." *East Asia Millions* 73 (April): 50.

"1895–1905." *East Asia Millions* 73 (May): 66–67.

"Our Esteemed Brother, and Our Friend." *Latin American Evangelist* (May–June): 13.

"1905–1915." *East Asia Millions* 73 (June): 82.

"Hudson Taylor: An American Tribute." *Christianity Today* 9 (June 18): 11–13.

"1919–1925." *East Asia Millions* 73 (July): 98.

"1925–1935." *East Asia Millions* 73 (August–September): 114.

"An Almost Unbroken Decade of War: 1935–1945," *East Asia Millions* 73 (October): 130.

"Darkness and the New Day: 1945–1955." *East Asia Millions* 73 (November): 146.

"1955–1965." *East Asia Millions* 73 (December): 162.

**1966**

"Unevangelized Fields Mission Loses Leader." *East Asia Millions* 73 (February): 31.

"Why the Reds Failed in Indonesia." *Eternity* 17 (April): 12–14, 47 (Interview by Arthur Glasser).

"Servanthood." *Reformed Presbyterian Reporter* (May): 8–12.

**1967**

"4 November 1966, Kongresshalle Berlin." *East Asia Millions* 74 (January): 2–3.

"Bangkok." *East Asia Millions* 74 (February): 18–19.

"The World Needs a Message." *Eternity* 18 (July): 11–13, 34.

"Getting the Horse to Drink!" *East Asia Millions* 74 (October): 131.

"From the Editor." *East Asia Millions* 75 (November): 146.

"From the Editor." *East Asia Millions* 75 (December): 162.

"A Critical Look at the Wheaton Congress–From a North American Perspective." *Evangelical Missions Quarterly* 3 (Fall): 1–5.

**1968**

"Confession, Church Growth and Authentic Unity in Missionary Strategy." *Protestant Crosscurrents in Mission: The Ecumenical-Conservative Encounter.* Norman A. Horner, ed. N.Y.: Abingdon, 178–221.

"My Life to Give – Motivation: The Lord's Return." *God's Men from All Nations to All Nations. Eighth InterVarsity Missionary Convention* (University of Illinois, Urbana-Champaign, December 1967). Chicago: InterVarsity Press, 168–76.

"Church-Planting." *God's Men from All Nations to All Nations. Eighth InterVarsity Missionary Convention* (University of Illinois, Urbana-Champaign, December 1967). Chicago: InterVarsity Press, 222–29.

"Maybe We're To Blame!" *East Asia Millions* 76 (February): 18.

"Achievement at Nongbua." *East Asia Millions* 76 (February): 26–28.

"Our Task – Broader Than You Think!" *East Asia Millions* 76 (April): 50–51.

"Your Move." *East Asia Millions* 76 (May): 66.

"I Have A Dream." *East Asia Millions* 76 (June): 82.

"Look at this Picture: Sanburi." *East Asia Millions* 76 (October): 134.

"May We Introduce ... " *East Asia Millions* 76 (November): 154.

"Fellowship and Mergers as Demonstrations of Evangelical Unity." *Evangelical Missions Quarterly* 4 (Winter): 94–101.

"Dropout." *HIS* 29, no. 3: 16–18, 23.

**1969**

"Paul's Right Hand Man." *HIS* 29, no. 4 (January): 3–6.

"What Has Been the Evangelical Stance, New Delhi to Uppsala?" *Evangelical Missions Quarterly* 5 (Spring): 129–50.

"The Man Who Loved Revenge." *HIS* 29, no. 8 (May): 4–7.
**1970**
"Who Says the Missionary Movement Is Dead?" *Eternity* 21 (November):
11–12, 24–27 (Interview with Arthur Glasser before he became Dean
of the School of World Mission, Fuller Theological Seminary).
**1971**
"Introduction." *Crossroads in Missions.* A. F. Glasser, ed. Pasadena, Calif.:
William Carey Library, vii–xxi.
"The Evangelicals: World Outreach." *The Future of the Christian World
Mission: Studies in Honor of R. Pierce Beaver.* William J. Danker and Wi
Jo Kang, eds. Grand Rapids, Mich.: Eerdmans Publishing Company, 99–
113.
"Mission and Cultural Environment." *Toward a Theology of the Future.*
Clark H. Pinnock and David F. Wells, eds. Carol Stream, Ill.: Creation
House, 293–319.
"Theology: With or Without the Bible." *Church Growth Bulletin* 7, no. 3:
111–14.
"Thinking About Jericho in Ethiopia—What Would You Do?" *Church
Growth Bulletin* 7, no. 3: 116–17.
"Since We Are Growing Older, Let's Grow Bolder!" *Church Growth Bul-
letin* 7, no. 6: 153–55.
**1972**
"Red China." *Eternity* 23 (November): 12–13, 28.
"Salvation Today and the Kingdom." *Crucial Issues in Missions Tomorrow.*
Donald McGavran, ed. Chicago: Moody Press, 33–53.
**1973**
"Church Growth and Theology." *God, Man and Church Growth.* A. R.
Tippett, ed. (A Festscrift in Honor of Donald Anderson McGavran).
Grand Rapids, Mich.: Eerdmans, 52–68.
"What Key 73 Is All About." *Christianity Today* 17 (January 19): 12–13.
"Deep Feelings of Ambivalence." *World Vision* 17, no. 3 (March): 16–17.
"What Evangelicals Can Learn from Bangkok." *Eternity* 24 (April): 27–29,
75–78.
"Salvation—Yesterday, Tomorrow and Today." *Evangelical Missions Quar-
terly* 9 (July): 144–49.
"Timeless Lessons From the Western Missionary Penetration of China."
*Missiology: An International Review* 1, no. 4 (October): 445–64.
"What Evangelicals Can Learn From Bangkok." *The Evangelical Response
to Bangkok.* Ralph D. Winter, ed. Pasadena, Calif: William Carey
Library, 86–93.
"Deep Feelings of Ambivalence." *The Evangelical Response to Bangkok.*
Ralph D. Winter, ed. Pasadena, Calif: William Carey Library, 99–102.
"Salvation—Yesterday, Tomorrow, and Today." *The Evangelical Response
to Bangkok.* Ralph D. Winter, ed. Pasadena, Calif: William Carey
Library, 103–8.

"Epilogue." *The Evangelical Response to Bangkok.* Ralph D. Winter, ed. Pasadena, Calif: William Carey Library, 147–53.

**1974**

"What Is 'Mission' Today? Two Views." *Mission Trends No. 1.* Gerald H. Anderson and Thomas F. Stransky, eds. New York: Paulist Press, and Grand Rapids, Mich.: Eerdmans, 5–11.

"Bangkok: An Evangelical Evaluation." *Themelios* 10, no. 1: 26–32.

**1975**

"China." *The Church in Asia.* Donald Hoke, ed. Chicago: Moody Press, 131–79.

"Success and Failure in the China Mission." *International Reformed Bulletin* 18, no. 61: 2–21.

"What Does God Want Us To Do?" *A World To Win — Preaching World Missions Today.* Roger S. Greenway, ed. Grand Rapids, Mich.: Baker Book House, 50–60.

**1976**

"The Missionary Task: An Introduction." *Crucial Dimensions in World Evangelization.* A. F. Glasser, Paul Hiebert, C. Peter Wagner, and Ralph Winter, eds. Pasadena, Calif.: William Carey Library, 3–10.

"Jesus Christ Making Disciples: A Study in Method." *Crucial Dimensions in World Evangelization.* A. F. Glasser, Paul Hiebert, C. Peter Wagner, and Ralph Winter, eds. Pasadena, Calif.: William Carey Library, 11–22.

"The Apostle Paul and the Missionary Task: A Study in Perspective." *Crucial Dimensions in World Evangelization.* A. F. Glasser, Paul Hiebert, C. Peter Wagner, and Ralph Winter, eds. Pasadena, Calif.: William Carey Library, 23–33.

"Mission in the Early Church: From the Apostle John to Constantine, A.D. 90–313." *Crucial Dimensions in World Evangelization.* A. F. Glasser, Paul Hiebert, C. Peter Wagner, and Ralph Winter, eds. Pasadena, Calif.: William Carey Library, 34–40.

"Timeless Lessons from the Western Missionary Penetration of China." *New Forces in Missions — The Official Report of the Asia Missions Association.* David J. Cho, ed. Seoul, Korea: East-West Center for Missions Research and Development, 178–202. (The complete official documentation, letters, speeches, and resolutions, both of the All Asia Mission Consultation, Seoul '73 and the Inaugural Convention of the Asia Mission Association held at Seoul, Korea, in 1975.)

"I Give You My Word." *Missiology: An International Review* 4, no. 1 (January): 7–11.

"Ecumenics and Missions: Crumbs from Nairobi." *Missiology: An International Review* 4, no. 2 (April): 131–44.

"Is Friendly Dialogue Enough?" *Missiology: An International Review* 4, no. 3 (July): 259–66.

"Africa, 1976, and the Gospel." *Missiology: An International Review* 4, no. 4 (November): 387–94.

"An Introduction to the Church Growth Perspectives of Donald Anderson McGavran." *Theological Perspectives on Church Growth.* Harvie M. Conn, ed. Nutley, N.J.: Presbyterian and Reformed Pub. Co., 21–42.

**1977**

*Understanding World Evangelization: Cultural Dimensions in International Development.* Pasadena, Calif.: William Carey Library.

"Bangkok: An Evangelical Evaluation." *The Conciliar-Evangelical Debate: The Crucial Documents, 1964–1976.* Donald McGavran, ed. Pasadena, Calif.: William Carey Library, 297–305.

"1977: The Year of Crisis for Southern Africa—and the World." *Missiology: An International Review* 5, no. 1 (January): 3–12.

"Culture, the Powers and the Spirit." *Missiology: An International Review* 5, no. 2 (April): 131–39.

"Clues to Mission (in Colossians)." *Missiology: An International Review* 5, no. 3 (July): 259–64.

"Blessed Be Egypt My People." *Missiology: An International Review* 5, no. 4 (October): 403–9.

**1978**

"Missiology—What's It All About?" *Missiology: An International Review* 6, no. 1 (January ): 3–10.

"Reflections on Training for Missions." *Missiology: An International Review* 6, no. 2 (April): 131–38.

"Can This Gulf Be Bridged? Reflections on the Ecumenical/Evangelical Dialogue." *Missiology: An International Review* 6, no. 3 (July): 275–82.

"One-half the Church–and Mission." *Missiology: An International Review* 6, no. 4 (November): 403–8.

"Evangelicals and the WCC." *Ecumenical Trends* (June): 90–92.

**1979**

"Report of a Happening." (4th International Association for Mission Studies. Conference at Maryknoll, N.Y., August 21–26, 1978.) *Missiology: An International Review* 7, no. 1 (January): 2–3.

"Reflection from Pasadena (Reader Response to New Religious Movement)." *International Review of Mission* 68 (January): 68–70.

"Dialogue and/or Conversion." M. L. Fitzgerald and A. F. Glasser (Workshop 7: IAMS Conference at Maryknoll). *Missiology: An International Review* 7, no. 1 (January, 7): 96–100.

"Encounters of the Best Kind—A Sabbatical Report." *Missiology: An International Review* 7, no. 2 (April): 131–38.

"Missiological Events: Report of the North American Conference on Muslim Evangelization." *Missiology: An International Review* 7, no. 2 (April): 233–45.

"Efforts at Puebla to Clarify the Role of the Church in Revolutionary Latin American Society." *Missiology: An International Review* 7, no. 3 (July): 274–75.

"Help from an Unexpected Quarter or, the Old Testament and Contextualization." *Missiology: An International Review* 7, no. 4 (November): 403–10.

"Reconciliation Between Ecumenical and Evangelical Theologies and Theologians of Mission (PCUS Montreal Consultation)." *Missionalia* 7, no. 3 (November): 99–114.

"Conference Report on Muslim Evangelization." *The Gospel and Islam: A 1978 Compendium.* Don M. McCurry, ed. Monrovia, Calif.: MARC, 38–57.

"Power Encounter in Conversion from Islam." *The Gospel and Islam: A 1978 Compendium.* Don M. McCurry, ed. Monrovia, Calif.: MARC, 129–42

"One-half the Church — and Mission." *Women and the Ministries of Christ.* Roberta Hestenes and Lois Curley, eds. Pasadena, Calif.: Fuller Theological Seminary, 88–92.

**1980**

"Handing on the Torch." *Theology, News and Notes* 27, no. 1: 3–5.

"Robinson Crusoe Had it Easy." *Missiology: An International Review* 8, no. 1 (January): 5–12.

"Liberation Is In, The Unreached Out in Melbourne View of the Kingdom." *Christianity Today* (June 27): 48, 50.

"Two Rubrics: 'Your Kingdom Come' vs. 'How Shall They Hear?' " *Missiology: An International Review* 8, no. 2 (April): 133–40.

"The Church Encountering Totalitarianism." *Missiology: An International Review* 8, no. 3 (July): 259–68.

"Archival Alert–Rome 1980." *Missiology: An International Review* 8, no. 4 (November): 389–94.

"Foreword." *Christian Conversion in Context.* Hans Kansdorf. Scottdale, Penn./Kitchener, Ontario: Herald Press, 11–12.

**1981**

"1980 — Where Were the Students?" *Missiology: An International Review* 9, no. 1 (January): 4–14.

"China Today — An Evangelical Perspective." *Missiology: An International Review* 9, no. 3 (July): 261–76.

"A Paradigm Shift? Evangelicals and Interreligious Dialogue." *Missiology: An International Review* 9, no. 4 (October): 393–408.

"The Missionary Task: An Introduction." *Perspectives on the World Christian Movement — A Reader.* Ralph D. Winter and S. C. Hawthorne, eds. Pasadena, Calif: William Carey Library, 100–3.

"The Apostle Paul and the Missionary Task." *Perspectives on the World Christian Movement — A Reader.* Ralph D. Winter and S. C. Hawthorne, eds. Pasadena, Calif: William Carey Library, 104–12.

"Response to Stanley Samartha's 'The Lordship of Jesus Christ and Religious Pluralism'." *Christ's Lordship and Religious Pluralism.* Gerald H. Anderson and Thomas F. Stransky, eds. Maryknoll, N.Y.: Orbis Books, 37–45.

**1982**

"Problem: 'The End' or the 'End.' " *Missiology: An International Review* 10, no. 1 (January): 5–12.

"Missiology: At the Cutting Edge." *Missiology: An International Review* 10, no. 2 (April): 131–40.

Report on the Proceedings of the 5th International Association of Mission Studies Conference, Bangalore, January 1982. *Missiology: An International Review* 10, no. 3 (July): 258.

"Creative Tension." *Missiology: An International Review* 10, no. 4 (October): 386–88.

**1983**

*Contemporary Theologies of Mission* (with Donald A. McGavran). Grand Rapids, Mich.: Eerdmans.

"Should Evangelicals Cooperate with the WCC? Yes." *Christianity Today* 27, no. 17 (November 11): 82.

"The Mission of Missiology and the ASM." *Missiology: An International Review* 11, no. 1 (January): 4–8.

"Convergence and the ASM." *Missiology: An International Review* 11, no. 4 (October): 511–26. Presidential address.

**1984**

"Missiology." *The Concise Evangelical Dictionary of Theology.* Walter A. Elwell, ed. Grand Rapids, Mich.: Baker Book House, 319.

**1985**

"The Evolution of Evangelical Mission Theology Since World War II." *International Bulletin of Missionary Research* 9, no. 1 (January): 9–13.

"Vatican II and Mission, 1965–1985." *Missiology: An International Review* 13, no. 4 (October): 487–99.

**1986**

"An International Perspective." *Entering the Kingdom.* Monica Hill, ed. Southampton, England: MARC Europe/British Church Growth Association, 22–38.

"The Conciliar Debate." *Entering the Kingdom.* Monica Hill, ed. Southampton, England: MARC Europe/British Church Growth Association, 84–97.

"Truth as Revealed in Scripture." *Religion and Intellectual Life* 3, no. 4 (Summer): 65–71.

"Defining Tomorrow's Missionary Challenge." *Missions Tomorrow* 1, no. 1 (Fall): 3.

"Church Growth at Fuller." *Missiology: An International Review* 14, no. 4 (October): 401–20.

Book Review of *Third World Liberation Theologies, an Introductory Survey and a Reader* by Deane William Ferm. *Missions Tomorrow* 1, no. 1 (Fall): 29.

Book Review of *Chinese Theology in Construction* by Lam Wing Hung. With

Samuel Chao. *Missiology: An International Review* 14, no. 1 (January): 107–9.

**1987**

"The Evolution of Evangelical Mission Theology Since World War II." *Evangelical Review of Theology* 11, no. 1 (January): 53–64.

"Religious Pluralism, Civil Religion, and the Antichrist: A Suggested Explanation." *Mission Focus* 15, no. 4 (December): 56–58.

**1988**

"Ecumenism: Signs of Hope?" *Theology, News and Notes* 35, no. 1 (March): 15–17, 27.

"Christian Ministry to the Jews." *Presbyterian Communique* 11, no. 2 (March/April): 6–7.

"One Spirit, Many Traditions." *Global Consultation of World Evangelization 2000 Newsletter* (December): 4.

"Conversion and the Kingdom." *World Evangelization* (July–August): 14–17.

Book Review of *All For Jesus* by Robert L. Niklaus, John S. Sawin, Samuel J. Stoesz. *International Bulletin of Missionary Research* 12, no. 2 (April): 79–80.

**1989**

"The Jewish People." Part I, The Jewish People: Issues and Questions. *Missionary Monthly* (April–May): 3–4.

"The Holocaust: How Should Christians Evaluate Anti-Semitism?" Part II, The Jewish People: Issues and Questions. *Missionary Monthly* (June–July): 3–4.

"How Are Christians to Regard the State of Israel?" Part III, The Jewish People: Issues and Questions. *Missionary Monthly* (August–September): 19–20.

"The Synagogue: What Attitude Should Christians Adopt Toward Rabbinic Judaism?" Part IV, The Jewish People: Issues and Questions. *Missionary Monthly* (October): 12–13.

"Should Christians Evangelize Jews?" Part V, The Jewish People: Issues and Questions. *Missionary Monthly* (November): 3–4.

"The Encounter: Should Christians Respond to the Call for Jewish-Christian Dialogue?" Part VI, The Jewish People: Issues and Questions. *Missionary Monthly* (December): 6–7.

"Mission in the 1990s." *International Bulletin of Missionary Research* 13, no. 1 (January): 2–8.

"Old Testament Contextualization: Revelation and Its Environment." *The Word Among Us: Contextualizing Theology.* Dean Gilliland, ed. Dallas, Tex.: Word Books, 32–51.

"The Churches and the Jewish People: Towards a New Understanding." *International Bulletin of Missionary Research* 13, no. 4 (October): 158–59.

"A Friendly Outsider Looks at Seventh-Day Adventists." *Ministry — International Journal for Clergy* (January): 8–10.

"That the World May Believe." *Mission Handbook*, 14th ed. W. Dayton Roberts and John A. Siewert, eds. Monrovia, Calif: MARC, 33–48.

Book Review of *Memoirs* by W. A. Visser't Hooft. *Missions Tomorrow* 2, no. 1 (Spring/Summer): 63.

**1990**

*Christianity and Judaism.* Tacoma, Wash.: Evangelical Theological Society.

*Spiritual Conflict: 6 Studies for Individuals or Groups.* Downers Grove, Ill.: InterVarsity Press.

"The Palestinians: How Shall Christians Respond to the 'Intifada,' the Palistinian Uprising?" Part VII, The Jewish People: Issues and Questions. *Missionary Monthly* (January): 9, 27.

"Is Christian Zionism Legitimate?" Part VIII, The Jewish People: Issues and Questions. *Missionary Monthly* (February): 8–9.

"The Apostates: How Should Gentile Christians Regard Hebrew Believers?" Part IX, The Jewish People: Issues and Questions. *Missionary Monthly* (March): 6–7.

"What of the Silence of God? The 'Question of All Questions.' " Part X, The Jewish People: Issues and Questions. *Missionary Monthly* (April–May): 3–4.

"My Last Conversation With Dr. McGavran." *Missionary Monthly* (August–September): 3–5.

"Thoughts on Messianic Jewish Congregations." Part I of a Series. *Missionary Monthly* (November): 12–13.

"Did Jesus Teach the Rejection of Israel?" Part II of a Series. *Missionary Monthly* (December): 9–10.

"Conversion of the Kingdom." *The Best in Theology*, Vol. 4. J. I. Packer, ed. Carol Stream, Ill.: Christianity Today, 275–84.

"The Evolution of Evangelical Mission Theology Since World War II." *Practical Theology and the Ministry of the Church, 1952–1984.* Essays in Honor of Edmund Clowney. Harvie M. Conn, ed. Westminster Theological Seminary, 1985. Phillipsburg, N.J.: Presbyterian and Reformed Publishing Co., 235–52. Reprinted from *IBMR*, January 1985.

"Training To Go Now!: Missionary Training Today and Tomorrow." *Mission Training.* Pasadena, Calif.: U. S. Center for World Mission, 31–33.

"My Pilgrimage in Mission." *International Bulletin of Missionary Research* 14, no. 3 (July): 112–15.

**1991**

"The Jewish Remnant." Part III of a Series. *Missionary Monthly* (January): 13–15.

"Messianic Jewish Congregations: Indispensable." Part IV of a Series. *Missionary Monthly* (February): 17, 30.

"The Significance of Messianic Jews." Part I of a Series. *Missionary Monthly* (April–May): 6–7.

"The Non-Negotiable: Getting Stories Straight!" Part II of a Series. *Missionary Monthly* (June/July): 21–22, 30.

"Messiah's Coming: A Vivid Hope." Part III of a Series. *Missionary Monthly* (August–September): 10–11.

"What of the Kingdom of God?" Part IV of a Series. *Missionary Monthly* (October): 10, 29.

"Anti-Semitism in the New Testament?" Part V of a Series. *Missionary Monthly* (November): 9–11.

"The Evangelicals: Unwavering Commitment, Troublesome Divisions." *Mission in the Nineteen 90s.* Gerald H. Anderson, James M. Phillips, Robert T. Coote, eds. Grand Rapids, Mich.: W. B. Eerdmans, 6–13. Reprinted from *IBMR*, January 1989.

"Biblical Basis for Jewish Evangelism." Part I, Evangelical Objections to Jewish Evangelism. *Missionary Monthly* (December): 11–13.

"Foreword." *God's Missionary People: Rethinking the Purpose of the Local Church.* Charles Van Engen, ed. Grand Rapids, Mich.: Baker Book House, 11–14.

Book review of *Our Father Abraham: Jewish Roots of the Christian Faith* by Marvin R. Wilson. *International Bulletin of Missionary Research* 15, no. 2 (April): 83–84.

**1992**

"Make Disciples of All the Gentiles." Part II, Evangelical Objections to Jewish Evangelism. *Missionary Monthly* (January): 12–14.

"What Right Do Gentiles Have to Evangelize Jews?" Part III, Evangelical Objections to Jewish Evangelism. *Missionary Monthly* (February): 8–9.

"Jewish Evangelism Is Biblical." Part IV, Evangelical Objections to Jewish Evangelism. *Missionary Monthly* (March): 10–11.

"Jacób Jocz, 1906–1983." Part I, An Outstanding Christian Theologian and Missiologist. *Missionary Monthly* (April/May): 6–7, 30.

"Jacób Jocz, Scholar and Writer." Part II, An Outstanding Christian Theologian and Missiologist. *Missionary Monthly* (June/July): 14–16.

"The Rabbinic Conception of Humankind." Part III, An Outstanding Christian Theologian and Missiologist. *Missionary Monthly* (August/September): 9–10, 30.

"Jocz' View of Hebrew Christianity." Part IV, An Outstanding Christian Theologian and Missiologist. *Missionary Monthly* (October): 15–18.

**1993**

"Evangelical Missions." *Toward Century 21 in Christian Mission.* Festschrift in honor of Gerald H. Anderson. James M. Phillips and Robert T. Cole, eds. Grand Rapids, Mich.: W. B. Eerdmans.

"The Legacy of Jacób Jocz." *International Bulletin of Missionary Research* (forthcoming).

# PART ONE

# BIBLICAL FOUNDATIONS

# Introductory Overview

## DEAN S. GILLILAND

For Arthur Glasser the Bible is the first and last reference for Kingdom issues. Since the volume before us is in his honor, there is no better way to begin than with the Bible. Art leaves no doubts about his stand on Scripture. His teaching becomes eloquent preaching when it comes to the Bible. Students hear something like this in the very first week of class: "The Bible constitutes for the church and the Christian the sole ground of religious authority. It has the force of law. God has not given his people any other rule of faith and practice" (Glasser 1990a).

Holding this high view of Scripture, Arthur does not allow the superficial use of Scripture or the glossing over of textual problems. Reciting "proof texts" makes him very uncomfortable. He is always willing to take that second look so that the text can "speak for itself." The result is that he can turn corners of interpretation that surprise and motivate. For Glasser, the whole canonical text speaks to the Kingdom theme. While some sections are less germane, there is no "canon within the canon." Rather, as Art would say, "Use *all* of Scripture but use it without distortion."

For example, Glasser insisted very early that the mandate for mission, biblically speaking, does not begin with the Great Commission. Far from mission as God's "afterthought," God is already seen in mission at creation. This was a departure from traditional conservative thinking which began with the negative consequences of the fall.

Obviously, this volume should begin with a chapter from our chief editor, Charles Van Engen. Readers need to know that Art Glasser holds Chuck Van Engen in highest regard. It was Glasser's personal choice that Van Engen be invited to join the faculty. He recognized that Chuck's missiological convictions were grounded on issues which he, Art, firmly holds, such as scriptural authority, broad ecclesiology and a positive view of God's actions in human history. And, for the record, Chuck conceived of the idea

---

Dean S. Gilliland, author of all the Introductory Overviews in this volume, was a United Methodist missionary to Nigeria for twenty years. He began teaching at Fuller Theological Seminary in 1977, having served as Principal of the Theological College of Northern Nigeria. He is currently Professor of Contextualized Theology and African Studies at Fuller's School of World Mission.

for this Festschrift and did most of the work, by far.

Van Engen shows that the Bible is related to mission through a careful integration of the biblical text and the particular missionary situation. Glasser would agree fully that critical hermeneutics, which Chuck describes, is absolutely essential when taking the Word into any missionary context. The whole of Scripture must be allowed to disclose its own truth; that is, the biblical text must be "self definitive" as it interacts with cultural themes.

Glasser's own Reformed background builds in him a tradition that is deep and wide. At this point, he has common ground with Roman Catholic scholars. Arthur has shown that it is a great and loving service to one's own tradition to criticize without malice. Steve Bevan's conclusions on *Redemptoris Missio* carry that spirit of the loyal critic. It is not enough to use Scripture profusely. When the Bible is the ground for mission theology, it cannot be forced to prove the past or simply buttress old doctrines. Bevans' work shows there is a certain superficiality about the use of the Bible in the Pope's encyclical, *Redemptoris Missio*. While taking an uncompromising position on the authority of the Bible, Glasser would be the first to say that we do not bring our sectarian dogma to the text.

Chapters three and four both center on the Apostle Paul and both are written by scholars with Latin American connections. Tim Carriker demonstrates that revelation must be grounded in the real human situation. He traces the apocalyptic idea as that which motivates and shapes Paul's theology. When we work with revelation it must be in the real human situation. The contextual realities of the biblical text are important to Art Glasser. He does not accept a revelation that has no connection to human experience. Carriker illustrates that Paul's message was formed against the reality of an imminent *parousia*. The point for mission is that the force restraining the return of the Lord Jesus (2 Thess. 2:6–7) is the necessity of preaching the gospel to the Gentiles (Matt. 28:19–20). The divine priority given to the apostolic mission of the church and, indeed, the missionaries themselves, is something about which Art speaks with eloquence. Themes such as the *parousia* do not stand alone but lead directly to the mandate to spread the gospel to every creature.

Samuel Escobar's sermonic approach to Romans 15:14–33 is especially appropriate when the dedication is to Arthur Glasser. For one thing, Art often crafts his teaching material in three or four homiletical points. (When he does, he will likely clear his throat and say, "Now here is something for your Sunday morning sermon.") A second reason Escobar's approach is appropriate is because it is one of Glasser's strong points to make Romans 15 the climax of Paul's hope and appeal for mission. Escobar's Latin American "reading" carries an appeal for prophetic evangelism, grounded in applied spirituality and a visible commitment to human need. These are Kingdom assumptions that are close to Glasser's heart. Art might add that these Kingdom convictions were there from Israel's beginning when God mandated the principles of Shalom as a life-style for his people.

# 1

# The Relation of Bible and Mission
# in Mission Theology

## CHARLES VAN ENGEN

One of the most basic aspects of mission theology has to do with the relation of the Bible to mission theory and practice. Initially, one would think this would be obvious. Such is not the case. In each generation there is a need to reflect again on the way the Church uses or abuses Scripture with reference to its understanding of mission.

### The Need to Approach the Bible as a Whole

According to David Bosch,

> We usually assume far too easily that we can employ the Bible as a kind of objective arbitrator in the case of theological differences, not realizing that (all) of us approach the Bible with (our) own set of preconceived ideas about what it says . . . This means that it is of little avail to embark upon a discussion of the biblical foundations of mission unless we have first clarified some of the hermeneutical principles involved (David Bosch 1978, 33).

Senior and Stuhlmueller end their otherwise magnificent work on *The Biblical Foundations of Mission* with a rather strange note stating that they did not mean to "imply that the biblical style of mission is absolutely normative for mission today. There is no definite biblical recipe for proclaiming the Word of God . . . Nevertheless there is a value in reflecting on the biblical patterns of evangelization" (1983, 332).

Biblical scholars and mission practitioners have contributed to the confusion by ignoring each other for too long. Lesslie Newbigin (1986 and

1989a) demonstrated that Western culture's preoccupation with the *origin* of the created order and human civilization brought with it a degree of blindness to questions of *purpose, design,* and *intention.* To a large extent biblical scholars have followed this same path in their examination of the biblical text. With notable exceptions, their analysis of Scripture has seldom asked the missiological questions regarding God's intentions and purpose.

On the other hand, the activist practitioners of mission have too easily superimposed their particular agendas on Scripture, or ignored the Bible altogether. Thus Arthur Glasser calls for a deeper missiological reflection on the biblical message.

> All Scripture makes its contribution in one way or another to our understanding of mission ... In our day evangelicals are finding that the biblical base for mission is far broader and more complex than any previous generation of missiologists appears to have envisioned ... In our day there is a growing impatience with all individualistic and pragmatic approaches to the missionary task that arise out of a proof-text use of Scripture, despite their popularity among the present generation of activistic evangelicals (1990a, 26–27).[1]

Johannes Verkuyl advocates a similar change in hermeneutical approach. "In the past," he says, "the usual method was to pull a series of proof-texts out of the Old and New Testaments and then to consider the task accomplished. But more recently biblical scholars have taught us the importance of reading these texts in context and paying due regard to the various nuances. ... One must consider the very structure of the whole biblical message" (1978, 90).[2]

The basic contours of a broader hermeneutic were explored thirty years ago in Part I of *The Theology of the Christian Mission,* edited by Gerald Anderson (1961, 17–94). Here G. Ernest Wright, Johannes Blauw, Oscar Cullmann, Karl Barth, Donald Miller, and F. N. Davey surveyed a wide range of biblical material, deriving from the Bible what the Church's mission ought to be.[3] Interestingly, at about the same time, the role of Scripture in the missiological reflection of the Second Vatican Council (for example, in *Lumen Gentium* and *Ad Gentes Divinitus*) closely followed this model as well (Flannery 1975, 350–440, 813–62). Subsequent papal encyclicals like *Evangelii Nuntiandi* and *Redemptoris Missio* have appealed to Scripture; though this appeal has at times appeared like elaborate proof-texting to buttress predetermined ecclesiastical agendas. Meanwhile, Orthodox missiology has also begun to draw from an overarching approach to the whole of Scripture.

So, over the last several decades a significant global consensus has emerged with regard to the Bible and mission. As David Bosch explains it,

> Our conclusion is that both Old and New Testaments are permeated with the idea of mission ... (But) not everything we call mission is

indeed mission ... It is the perennial temptation of the Church to become (a club of religious folklore) ... The only remedy for this mortal danger lies in challenging herself unceasingly with the true biblical foundation of mission (1978, 18–19).

## Ways to Approach the Bible as a Whole

Although we may agree that it is important for missiologists to deal with the whole of Scripture as a diverse unity, we are in need of a hermeneutical method that enables us to do that. We cannot have mission without the Bible, nor can we understand the Bible apart from God's mission. The *Missio Dei* is *God's* mission. Yet the *Missio Dei* happens in specific places and times in our contexts. Its content, validity, and meaning are derived from Scripture; yet its action, significance, and transforming power happen in our midst. Even when we affirm that we will take the whole of Scripture seriously, we still need a basis on which to link the Bible, in its numerous contexts, with the here and now of the context of our missionary endeavor today. In what follows, I will review four ways that others have suggested the connection be made, and then add a fifth for the reader's consideration.

### From Above

One of the most common linkages between the Bible and theology of mission involves a "theology from above." In Roman Catholic and mainline Protestant denominational mission alike, this has often involved the use of *church tradition* as the link between Bible and mission. The church interprets Scripture and through its teaching authority or its denominational mission structures it derives missional action from what it sees in Scripture. This has tended to mean that the extension of the institutional church and its agendas becomes the heart of mission.

But there is a second method that falls in the "from above" category. This involves seeing the Bible as a source of *commands* for mission. William Carey was a champion of this method, basing most of his link with the Bible on the Great Commission of Matthew 28:18–20. This imperative type of biblical support is common in "evangelical" Protestant missiology, and especially in Church Growth Theory, as popularized by Donald McGavran's continual appeal to Matthew 28:18–20.

The basic problem with both these approaches is that the Scriptures themselves are not allowed to interact with the present contexts of our mission. They are mediated, reduced, and filtered either by the agendas of the institutional church or by the guilt-based appeal of the one who expounds on the commands. Curiously, this approach causes Protestants that would avidly defend a Gospel of grace to fall into a pit of legalism when it comes to mission. When we place church tradition or missional command between the Bible and our mission context, we reduce the impact that Scripture can have in transforming the way we understand, exercise, and evaluate our missional action.

### From Below

After World War II many Protestant churches and missions, especially those associated with the World Council of Churches, became concerned with relevance. Although commendable in many ways, a hermeneutic of relevance pushed much mission reflection to an almost purely "from below" perspective. This hermeneutic has dominated the World Council of Churches, exemplified most recently in the 1989 San Antonio meeting of the Commission on World Mission and Evangelism, with its heavy emphasis on "acts of faithfulness." The starting point is not the Bible, but rather particular contextual agendas.[4] Once these agendas have been determined, *exemplary cases* are sought in the Bible to illustrate and validate the pre-determined activity.

But evangelicals should not judge the ecumenical stance too harshly. When evangelicals need to find justification for doing mission activities involving development, health, church planting, education, or urban ministries, they invariably scramble around the pages of the Bible to find illustrative cases (sometimes oddly-chosen minute texts read in a literal and biblicist fashion) to legitimize their already-determined agendas.

Although the positive side of this approach is its contextual commitment, the downside is its loss of the normativity of Scripture. The Bible is not allowed to critique the assumptions, motivations, or rightness of the action itself—it is used only as a justification for what has been predetermined. This mission is not God's. It belongs to the practitioners. The text is used primarily as a justification of the activity.

### The Hermeneutical Circle of Liberation Theology

The idea of "the hermeneutical circle" has been around since the early 1800s and is often associated with Friedrich Schleiermacher, along with others such as Wilhelm Dilthey, Edmund Husserl, Martin Heidegger, Rudolf Bultmann, and Georg Gadamer.[5] But Latin American liberation theologians transformed the concept into an intentional, creative, and revolutionary methodology.

Perhaps the best liberationist articulation of the hermeneutical circle to link Bible and mission may be found in Juan Luis Segundo (1976).[6] Segundo outlined four decisive steps in the process of the hermeneutical circle. First, we experience reality, which leads us to ideological suspicion. Secondly, there is the application of our ideological suspicion to our understanding of reality in general and to Scripture and theology in particular. Third, we experience a new way of perceiving reality that leads us to the exegetical suspicion that the prevailing interpretation of the Bible has not taken important pieces of data into account. This calls for re-reading the biblical text. Fourth, we develop a new hermeneutic, that is, we find a new way of interpreting Scripture with the new perceptions of our reality at our disposal. This leads us to look again at our reality, which begins the process all over again.

Through their intentional and positive formulation of the hermeneutical circle, and by adding particular contextual data to the equation, Latin American Liberation theologians offer missiology a very creative way of linking Bible and mission (cf. Guillermo Cook 1985). But Latin American Liberation Theology tends to reduce this new hermeneutical method to narrow socioeconomic and political agendas, due in part to the heavy borrowing of European and Marxist sociopolitical theory (cf. Rebecca Chopp 1986). This in turn shrinks the basis on which the Bible is being read. The method would look different if the analysis of the reality were itself governed by biblical perspectives.

### Critical Hermeneutics Through Mission Paradigms

We all mourn David Bosch's untimely and deeply unfortunate death. Prior to his going, David Bosch was able to finish what will be considered his opus magnum: *Transforming Mission*. One of the most helpful parts of Bosch's monumental work is the hermeneutical methodology he illustrates.

Bosch begins by affirming, "We cannot, with integrity, reflect on what mission might mean today unless we turn to the Jesus of the New Testament, since our mission is 'moored to Jesus' person and ministry' " (Bosch 1991b, 22: quoting from Hahn 1984, 269). But Bosch goes on:

> To affirm this is not to say that all we have to do is to establish what mission meant for Jesus and the early church and then define our missionary practice in the same terms, as though the whole problem can be solved by way of a direct application of Scripture ... (Due to both historical and socio-cultural gaps between then and now), a historico-critical study may help us to comprehend what mission was for Paul and Mark and John but it will not immediately tell us what we must think about mission in our own concrete situation (1991b, 23).

Bosch, then, offers a new approach to the problem by drawing from the theory of paradigm construction that Hans Küng and David Tracy (1989) adapted from the philosophy of science.[7] Bosch's suggestion is to recognize that there are several self-definitions being offered both in the biblical text as well as in our modern contexts. Thus, "the approach called for requires an interaction between the self-definition of early Christian authors and actors and the self-definition of today's believers who wish to be inspired and guided by those early witnesses" (1991b, 23). This in turn would move us to re-read the biblical text, incorporating the newer sociological analysis of the Bible in its various contexts, then going beyond them to a series of self-definitions of mission for today's contexts. Bosch calls this "critical hermeneutics."

> The critical hermeneutic approach goes beyond the (historically inter-esting) quest of making explicit early Christian definitions, however. It desires to encourage dialogue between those self-definitions and all subsequent ones, including those of ourselves and our contempo-raries . . . The challenge to the study of mission may be described . . . as relating the always-relevant Jesus event of twenty centuries ago to the future of God's promised reign by means of meaningful initiatives for the here and now (1991b, 23–24).
>
> The point is that there are no simplistic or obvious moves from the New Testament to our contemporary missionary practice. The Bible does not function in such a direct way. There may be, rather, a range of alternative moves which remain in deep tension with each other but may nevertheless all be valid (1991b, 23–24).[8]

Following this method, Bosch examines what he calls the "missionary paradigms" of Matthew, Luke, and Paul. Bosch does not try to reconcile the distinct paradigms of mission he finds in the New Testament. Although he demonstrates the internal coherence and consistency of each paradigm within itself, he shows no compulsion to develop coherence or consistancy between paradigms. In fact, he seems to feel that the breadth of their differences is precisely what may offer new linkages between the New Tes-tament paradigms and the other five paradigms of mission that Bosch traces throughout the mission history of the church.[9]

In the end, Bosch tantalizes us by suggesting a host of "elements of an emerging ecumenical missionary paradigm," but he does not help us con-struct it. Thus we need to find a way to build on Bosch's work and go a step further.

### The Bible as a Tapestry of God's Action in the World

One way to build on Bosch's hermeneutical method is to approach Scrip-ture from the perspective of a number of themes and sub-themes (or motifs) of God's action in the world. As seen in the diagram below, this approach would view the Bible as a tapestry, with the woof (horizontal) threads of various themes and motifs interwoven in the warp (vertical) of each con-text's historical situation. This yields a perspective simultaneously involving a view from above and from below.

The themes may be approached from above because they are the action of *God* in history. They are from below because they occur in the midst of *human* history in the stories of men and women in context. Maybe this is what Johannes Verkuyl had in mind when he suggested the Universal Motif, Rescue and Liberation, the Missionary Motif, and the Motif of Antagonism as the place to begin formulating a biblical foundation for mission (Verkuyl 1978, 91–96).[10]

### The Bible as a Tapestry of Missional Themes and Motifs in Context

By viewing the Scriptures as an interwoven tapestry, we can affirm the Bible as a unified whole and also deal intentionally with the diversity of the history and cultures of the Bible (cf. Glasser 1990a, 9; Van Engen 1981, 160–66). This is not an allegorical approach, nor is it purely literalist or literary. We are not advocating a simple one-to-one correspondence of biblical response to perceived felt-needs, nor is it strictly a matter of discovering "dynamic equivalence" (cf. Charles Kraft 1989). Rather, we are seeking an intimate interrelationship of text and new contexts through the vehicle of particular themes or motifs that bridge the text's initial context with today's contexts of mission. This, then, provides a creative interaction of word and deed throughout the history of God's missionary activity. Such

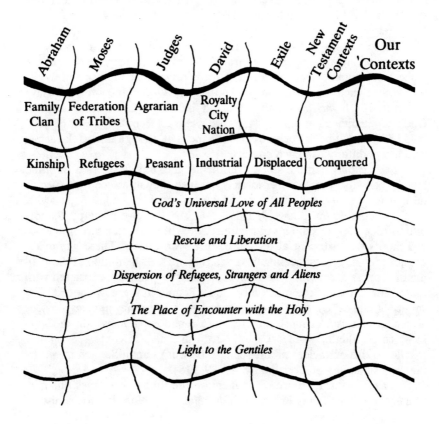

a critical hermeneutic helps us get away from finding a few proof texts or isolated nuggets in the Bible to buttress our missional agendas. It goes beyond the search for a few "keywords" of the Gospel that might lend themselves for missiological reflection. (See, for example, H. Berkhof and P. Potter 1964). And it is broader and deeper than a set of commands that may be external to the People of God and to their contexts.

This approach calls us to take seriously the uniqueness of each biblical context in terms of its history, sociology, anthropology, and grammatical peculiarities. We must be able, therefore, to use all that we have learned so far from source, form, redaction, history, rhetoric, and canon criticism (cf. Richard Muller 1991, 194–96). But we must go beyond these to ask the missiological questions of God's *intention* in terms of the *Missio Dei* as that occurs in word and deed in each particular context (see Bosch 1991b, 21). This method involves a critical hermeneutic that attempts to discover the particular "self-definition" (Bosch 1991b, 23) of God's people in a particular time and place — and then challenges all subsequent self-definitions, including our own.

Daniel Shaw demonstrated from anthropology that the various contexts in biblical history can be described through the use of a "three cultures model" of kinship, peasant, and industrial societies (Shaw 1988, 31–33). Yet interwoven throughout these radically different contexts are clearly identifiable themes and motifs in a word-deed conjunction of God's self-definition of missional revelation throughout human history. To do this, the biblical data must be broken down to focus on specific themes and motifs that course their way through the tapestry of God's mission. As I have shown in *The Word Among Us* (Gilliland 1989b, 74–100), the concept of God's covenantal relationship with God's chosen People ("I will be your God and you will be my people") is a theme that, though always the same, is radically different in each context.

But this is only half the story. The themes and motifs selected from the biblical narrative are chosen precisely because they interface with specific deep-structure themes or motifs of the worldview of the people in a specific missional context (cf. Shaw 1988, 193–94). As we delve more profoundly into the deep-level meanings of a culture, we will encounter certain themes and motifs that are central to that culture's worldview. These worldview themes provide the connecting links whereby the self-definition of the People of God at a particular time in biblical history can be associated with the self-definition of the mission of God's People in the new context. The variety of biblical contexts where the theme or motif may appear provides a number of closer or more remote contextual comparisons with the ways in which the theme may work itself out in the modern context. Such new manifestations of ancient motifs seem to be what Lamin Sanneh meant by the "translatability of Christianity" (1989, 215).

By way of illustration, we could mention the following themes: the mission of the remnant; mission through dispersion of refugees; God's mission as a "tree of life" whose leaves are for the healing of the nations; the place of human encounter with the divine; mission and washing, forgiveness, refreshment, water; mission and wholistic healing; mission and true (or false) prophets; mission and God's rule over all nations; mission and monotheism (versus poly- and henotheism); mission and wealth and poverty; mission and the stranger in our midst; mission as light/illumination in darkness/blindness; mission as "a light to the Gentiles"; mission and food, eating, table fellowship; mission as reconciliation, return, re-creation.[11]

In selecting only certain themes as threads out of both the biblical tapestry and the contextual worldview, we may narrow the Gospel too much. On the other hand, if we end up with too large a list of seemingly unrelated themes, we cannot achieve a cohesive and consistent missiology. But neither of these problems need necessarily arise. Rather, if we are able to discover an integrating idea that holds together a number of these themes and motifs, we may be able to construct a truly biblical basis of mission for a particular context (cf. Van Engen 1987, 524–25). Bosch's concept of the missionary God of history and God of compassion that radically transforms humanity was for him just such an integrating central idea that allowed biblical missiology to impact the South African context (1978, 44; see also J. G. Du Plessis 1990). For Verkuyl and Glasser, along with many others, the Kingdom of God provides the necessary unifying idea. The concept of covenant or the glory of God might also serve as viable integrating ideas. The point is that the themes selected, their mutual interaction, and the particular integrating idea that may hold them together—all these must arise from the interaction of the themes as self-definitions both in their biblical contexts and in the new missionary context. As Arthur Glasser has said it, "We have rather deliberately chosen the Kingdom of God as the particular diachronic theme most seminal to understanding the variegated mission of the people of God touching the nations" (1990a, 9, 13).

Bible and mission? May all of us involved in missiological reflection continue to explore new methods whereby we may preserve the unique authority of Scripture as our only rule of faith and practice—yet allow it to question, shape, direct, and deepen our understanding of, and commitment to, our ongoing participation in God's mission.

## Notes

1. See also David Bosch (1980, 42-49) and J. Verkuyl (1978, 89-100), J. Scherer (1987, 243), and Andrew Kirk (1987).

2. Verkuyl points to two works as exemplifying this approach: Johannes Blauw (1962), and A. de Groot (1964). We could add the works of Harry Boer (1961), Berkhof and Potter (1964), Georg Vicedom (1965), Bengt Sundkler (1965), Richard de Ridder (1971), John Stott (1975b), J. Verkuyl (1978), David Bosch (1980, 42-49; 1991b, 15-178), Senior and Stuhlmueller (1983), Harvie Conn (1984), Dean

Gilliland (1983), Rene Padilla (1980, 1985), Arthur Glasser (1990), and Ray Anderson (1991).

3. Their approach to the Bible represents a step forward from older attempts to give a "Bible basis" for mission, like those of Robert Glover (1946) and H. H. Rowley (1955).

4. This perspective was also dominant at the recent meeting of the International Association of Mission Studies in Hawaii in August 1992 — due, in part, to the strong influence exerted at that gathering by conciliar missiologists from the older Protestant mainline churches of Europe and North America.

5. See, for example, Kurt Mueller-Vollmer (1989), Richard Muller (1991, 186-214), and Mark Branson and Rene Padilla (1986).

6. See also Gustavo Gutiérrez (1974), Guillermo Cook (1985), Leonardo Boff and Clodovis Boff (1987), Rene Padilla (1985), Mark L. Branson and Rene Padilla (1986), Samuel Escobar (1987), José Míguez Bonino (1975), and Roger Haight (1985).

7. See, for example, Ian Barbour (1974), Thomas Kuhn (1962, 1977), Imre Lakatos (1978), Stephen Toulmin (1977), and Nancey Murphy (1990).

8. Bosch's thought in terms of theology of mission seems to echo what Paul Hiebert has called "critical contextualization" from an anthropological perspective.

9. For a friendly critique of Bosch's approach, see J. G. du Plessis (1990).

10. Donald E. Messer recently followed this method when he pointed to five Old Testament mission motifs and eight New Testament themes of mission. He then synthesized these into four new contemporary "images of Christian mission: A Covenant of Global Gardeners, A Collegiality of Bridge Builders, A Company of Star-throwers, A Community of Fence Movers." Together, Messer argues, these new images represent a "Conspiracy of Goodness." See Donald E. Messer (1992).

11. An exploration of this method in the South African context was recently suggested by B. Wielenga (1992).

## 2

# The Biblical Basis of the Mission
# of the Church in *Redemptoris Missio*

### STEPHEN B. BEVANS

The publication of Pope John Paul II's eighth encyclical, *Redemptoris Missio*, was undoubtedly one of the most significant missiological events of 1991, equaled in importance only by the long-awaited appearance of the late David Bosch's *Transforming Mission* in the spring and the publication of the Roman document Dialogue and Proclamation in the early summer.[1] A massive document of one hundred fifty-three pages in the official English edition, the encyclical covers a wide variety of topics, and could even be described as a concise *summa* of official Roman Catholic thinking on mission today (cf. Laverdiere 1991, 373). Nevertheless its most distinctive contribution to current missiological thought might well be its properly theological "first part,"[2] which consists of the first three chapters and focuses on the Christological (Chapter I), ecclesiological (Chapter II) and pneumatological (Chapter III) foundations of the church's universal mission. Because of their fundamental importance, therefore, I will limit myself in this essay to reflection on these three chapters.

The chapters are not easy reading, filled as they are with quotations of and references to both scripture (138, two-thirds of the biblical references in the entire document) and Roman Catholic magisterial teaching (more than fifty). They are foundational, however, to the whole encyclical, because as Cardinal Josef Tomko insists, they "reconfirm the Church's faith in truths which have been endangered by sketchy theories" (Tomko 1991). Tomko indicates three such "sketchy theories" which are targeted in the encyclical's first three chapters. The first of these is a Christology which places so little stress on Jesus' unique mediatorship that it can acknowledge that the

Stephen B. Bevans, SVD, was a missionary to the Philippines from 1972 until 1981. He is Associate Professor of Doctrinal Theology at Catholic Theological Union at Chicago and is an Associate Editor of *Missiology: An International Review*.

founders of other great religions are "almost an incarnation of God, or mediators or saviors equal to Jesus Christ" (Tomko 1991); Chapter I therefore speaks of "Jesus Christ, the Only Saviour," in whom and only in whom is found the fullness of God's salvation (cf. RM 11). The second "sketchy theory" is a pneumatology which stresses so much the universal work of the Spirit that it tends to deny the unique role of Jesus in the world's salvation; this question is taken up in Chapter III. In the third place, Tomko points to a notion of the Kingdom or Reign of God which too easily separates this reality from the reality of Jesus and the church; this is the concern of Chapter II.

These three "temptations" of contemporary theology (cf. RM 11; 4) seem to have as a common element the weakening of the role of Christ as God's and humankind's *unique mediator*, and the pope interprets such contemporary tendencies as endangering the very enterprise of mission itself. It is because of this keenly felt danger to the integrity of the faith and of the church's mission that John Paul provides a thoroughly Christocentric answer to the question "why mission?" "We reply with the Church's faith and experience that true liberation consists in opening oneself to the love of Christ. In him, and only in him, are we set free from all alienation and doubt, from slavery to the power of sin and death. . . . *Mission is an issue of faith*, an accurate indicator of our faith in Christ and his love for us" (RM 11). While such a statement is quite in tune with the basic affirmations of Vatican II's *Ad Gentes* (1965) and Pope Paul VI's *Evangelii Nuntiandi* (1975), *Redemptoris Missio*'s Christocentrism as the primary motive for mission represents a significant departure from *Ad Gentes*'s more trinitarian starting point (AG 2) and *Evangelii Nuntiandi*'s more Reign-of-God-centered approach (EN 6–16).[3]

*Ad Gentes* and *Evangelii Nuntiandi* — especially their first chapters — are documents that have deep roots in the biblical tradition, even though the former seems to be more directly nourished by patristic sources. The language of paragraph 2 of *Ad Gentes* "attempts to bring the Pauline *mysterion* (cf. Ephesians 1:3-22: Colossians 1:11-28) motif to the modern understanding of mission" (Burrows 1986, 185); *Evangelii Nuntiandi* starts with a reflection on the ministry of Jesus, especially as it is recorded in the synoptic gospels, and goes on to show how "the Church is born of the evangelizing activity of Jesus and the Twelve" (EN 15). Can we say, however, that *Redemptoris Missio* is grounded in the same way? Does the pope base his Christocentric starting point on an adequate understanding and use of scripture? These are the questions which have prompted the writing of this essay.

At first blush the answers seem obvious. The encyclical, particularly the section on which I am focusing, is rife with scriptural quotations, references, biblical imagery and language.The answer, however, may not be that simple, for the question of an adequate biblical foundation is more complex than just a lavish use of biblical illustrations and proof texts (cf. Müller 1987,

19–22; Bosch 1991b, 15–189). "The Bible," says David Bosch, "is not to be treated as a storehouse of truths on which we can draw at random" (Bosch 1991b, 9); rather "one must consider the very structure of the whole biblical message" (Verkuyl 1978, 90).

Pursuing the question, then, this essay will proceed in two steps. A first step will ask a fundamental question of the encyclical: how does it "construe" the Bible as *scripture*? Why, in other words, does it take the Bible as an authority? Then, in a second step, I will reflect on how scripture is actually used in the text. These two moves should produce a fairly clear picture of the encyclical's biblical basis for the church's universal mission.

## Why Is the Bible "Scripture"?

In what has become a standard source on the use of scripture in theology, David Kelsey argues quite convincingly that "there is in actual theological practice no one standard concept of 'scripture.' Scripture is not something objective that different theologians simply use differently. In actual practice it is concretely construed in irreducibly different ways" (Kelsey 1975, 2). Although he in no way claims to present an exhaustive survey, Kelsey distinguishes three basic ways of "construing" scripture by analyzing the works of seven theologians. An analysis of a book by B. B. Warfield and an unpublished essay by Hans-Werner Bartsch yields a notion of scripture as doctrinal (Warfield) or conceptual (Bartsch) content: the Bible is scripture because it teaches what is to be believed. Quite different is the position of G. W. Wright and Karl Barth, who understand scripture (although in different ways, to be sure) as "a self-manifestation by God in historical events, and not information about God stated in divinely communicated doctrines or concepts" (Kelsey 1975; 32). A third way of understanding the Bible as scripture is revealed in Kelsey's analysis of L. S. Thornton, P. Tillich and R. Bultmann, all of whom regard the Bible as containing symbols, images or myths which become the Word of God as they "express the revelatory and saving 'Christ event' and occasion contemporary saving and revealing events" (Kelsey 1975; 74).

I would suggest that John Paul II's "construal" of scripture is similar to that of the first notion in Kelsey's analysis. For *Redemptoris Missio*, scripture contains certain teachings, certain doctrines, which must be faithfully safeguarded by the church. With regard to the reasons for the church's mission, scripture clearly teaches that Jesus is the only way by which men and women can come to God; therefore the church is missionary by its very nature, especially in terms of mission *ad gentes*.

Several intimations of the pope's understanding of the nature of scripture are present in the three chapters on which we are focusing. In the opening lines of paragraph 5, for example, we read that from the very origin of the church "we find a clear affirmation that Christ is the one Saviour of all, the only one able to reveal and lead to God." To back up this statement the pope quotes Acts 4, verses 10 and 12, a text which proclaims that "there is no other name under heaven given among men and women by which we must be saved." Then—and I believe this move is crucial—the pope asserts that the statement not only had meaning in its immediate context as a faith-statement made to the Sanhedrin; it also "has universal value, since for all people—Jews and Gentiles alike—salvation can only come from Jesus Christ." Whatever one might think of the logic of this statement, what is the issue here is that the pope seems to presuppose that there is a truth in scripture which needs to be taught—Jesus' uniqueness—and that this passage is teaching it. Indeed, the pope goes on to say, "the universality of this salvation in Christ is asserted throughout the New Testament," and he then cites Paul (1 Cor. 8:5–6), John (Jn. 1:9, 18; Jn. 14:6) and the author of Hebrews (Heb. 1:1–2) to prove his point.

In Chapter II, the pope's concern is to preserve what Paul VI called the "profound link between Christ, the Church and evangelization" (EN 16; cf. RM 19)—preaching, serving and witnessing to the Reign of God does not exclude either Christ or the church, but must necessarily include them. But this is not how some theologians are understanding the Reign of God, says the pope: "they are silent about Christ: the Kingdom of which they speak is 'theocentrically' based. ... Furthermore, the Kingdom, as they understand it, ends up either leaving very little room for the Church or undervaluing the Church in reaction to a presumed 'ecclesiocentrism' of the past" (RM 17). This, he counters, is not the Reign of God "as we know it from Revelation." Revelation teaches, the pope implies, that "the Kingdom cannot be detached either from Christ or from the Church" (RM 18). Revelation—of which scripture is at least a part—is not ultimately a series of events or contained in a set of pregnant symbols; it is rather a teaching, a content, a set of doctrines.

A third illustration of the encyclical's construal of scripture is found in Chapter III, paragraph 23. As I will point out more fully in the next section, this paragraph contains one of the encyclical's most sophisticated uses of scripture—it is remarkable in its admission of a pluralism of viewpoints and theology in the New Testament. Nevertheless, the *point* of the discussion is the basic *unity* of gospel teaching on the universal task of the church's mission and the continuing presence of Jesus through the power of the Spirit. Implied, it seems to me, is that despite the pluralism of the sources, the *message* is clear: "Mission . . . is based not on human abilities but on the power of the Risen Lord."

Because the encyclical construes scripture as a source of doctrine, it tends to use scripture in the ways described in the next section. And it is the *use* of scripture in the encyclical which will reveal whether or not it is written out of a firm scriptural base.

## How Is Scripture Used?

In his study on the use of the New Testament in several documents of the Second Vatican Council, John W. Nyquist concludes that the Council's use of scripture was limited to the citation of texts, for the most part at least, "as the basis and authority for stating and using a particular doctrine of the Catholic Church" (Nyquist 1991, 25; cf. 200). Ultimately, Nyquist says, scripture is really "not the norm . . . the Magisterium is the final court of interpretation as the Scripture is applied within the Catholic Church" (Nyquist 1991, 191). I would suggest that scripture is employed in the same way in *Redemptoris Missio*. By and large, its use of scripture reflects a "proof-text method" rather than one that considers context, literary nuances and basic structure (Verkuyl 1978, 90); even this method breaks down, however, as the chapters are developed.

This is evident in the first paragraphs of Chapter I. The chapter begins with three citations from the Magisterium, the most important being a line from the Nicene-Constantinopolitan Creed: "I believe in one Lord, Jesus Christ, the only Son of God, eternally begotten of the Father" (RM 4). Scripture is then used—in great abundance—to bolster what is clearly a dogmatic claim. Consider how scripture is used in the following excerpt from paragraph 6:

> To introduce any sort of separation between the Word and Jesus Christ is contrary to the Christian faith. Saint John clearly states that the Word, who "was in the beginning with God," is the very one who "became flesh" (Jn. 1:2, 14). Jesus is the Incarnate Word—a single and indivisible person. . . . The Church acknowledges and confesses Jesus as "the Christ, the Son of the living God" (Mt. 16:16): Christ is none other than Jesus of Nazareth; he is the Word of God made man for the salvation of all. In Christ "the whole fullness of deity dwells bodily" (Col. 2:9) and "from his fullness we have all received" (Jn. 1:16).

As the chapter continues and the claims of some contemporary theologians are refuted, evidence is cited less and less from scripture itself and more and more from the Roman Magisterium. Scripture is quoted or referred to some thirteen times in paragraphs 6 to 11, but there is only one reference in paragraphs 7 to 10; the Magisterium (mostly documents from Vatican II) is quoted or referred to fifteen times in the same paragraphs.

The same thing happens in Chapter II. The beginning of the chapter sketches the image of the Reign of God as it is manifest in the ministry of Jesus, and here scripture is used quite liberally in order to give the emerging picture more definite shape: over forty out of fifty-some quotations or references are found between paragraphs 12 and 16. In the next three paragraphs the encyclical zeroes in on the fact that "nowadays the Kingdom is much spoken of, but not always in a way consonant with the thinking of the Church" (RM 17). In these paragraphs only six quotations or references to scripture appear (largely illustrative), and all nine of the chapter's references to the Magisterium are cited.

As I have pointed out above, the beginning of Chapter III contains what is perhaps the best use of scripture in the encyclical. Rather than basing his development on a doctrine or a few texts, the pope speaks in paragraph 22 of how all four gospels conclude with a "missionary mandate." Furthermore, as is clear from both John and Luke, this mandate is a sending forth in the Spirit. While each gospel includes different emphases, there can be distinguished two common elements—the universal dimension of the mission and the continuing presence of Christ through the Spirit. In what may well be the most important statement in the encyclical, and the one that provides its most adequate biblical basis for the church's mission, the pope concludes:

> The four Gospels therefore bear witness to a certain pluralism within the fundamental unity of the same mission, a pluralism which reflects different experiences and situations within the first Christian communities. It is also the result of the driving force of the Spirit himself; it encourages us to pay heed to the variety of missionary charisms and to the diversity of circumstances and peoples. Nevertheless, all the Evangelists stress that the mission of the disciples is to cooperate in the mission of Christ: "Lo, I am with you always, to the close of the age" (Mt. 28:20). Mission, then, is based not on human abilities but on the power of the Risen Lord.

Unfortunately, however, the same problem that emerged in the first two chapters when the pope begins to deal with the "sketchy theories" cited by Cardinal Tomko (cf. Tomko 1991) surfaces in this chapter as well. In paragraph 29 the pope makes the point (citing his fifth encyclical *Dominum et Vivificantem*) that the Spirit "leads us to broaden our vision in order to ponder his activity in every time and place" (RM 29; cf. DeV 53); nevertheless, he cautions—and here is his point—the Spirit is "not an alternative to Christ, nor does he fill a sort of void which is sometimes suggested as existing between Christ and the Logos. Whatever the Spirit brings about in human hearts and in the history of peoples, in cultures and religions serves as a preparation for the Gospel and can only be understood in reference to Christ." Reference is made here to Vatican II's Constitution on the Church and to its Pastoral Constitution on the Church in the Modern World, but there is no appeal to scripture nor any indication that such a position has a basis in scripture.

I can only conclude from a reading of these three foundational chapters that, despite the plethora of biblical citations, the basis for John Paul II's strong Christocentric motive for Christian mission seems to be more magisterium/doctrinally based than really rooted in the Bible. In saying this I do not in the least want to deny that the pope did not *intend* to develop a biblical foundation; nor do I want to deny that such a biblical foundation is possible. My point is only that, given the pope's *understanding* of scripture as basically doctrinal content and given his *use* of scripture in the encyclical, he has not provided much of a biblical basis other than an appeal to scripture to illustrate his retelling of the biblical stories or to confirm prior dogmatic beliefs. In comparison to *Redemptoris Missio*, the Vatican paper "Dialogue and Proclamation," issued a few months after the encyclical, has a much more subtle and sophisticated approach to scripture (it seems to construe scripture in the second sense explained above) and so provides a far more satisfying biblical basis for the necessity of proclaiming the Lord (cf. DP 55–65). It should be studied along with the encyclical.

*Redemptoris Missio*, however, remains an important document. It rightly defends the Church's faith in the centrality of Jesus Christ; it upholds the necessity of continuing the mission *ad gentes*, even in the face of the need for a "new evangelization" in countries that have long been considered fully evangelized; and it expresses no hesitation about the church's relationship to human culture and other religious ways. Somehow, perhaps simply because it is in pursuit of its truth, *Redemptoris Missio* is possessed by the Bible's Spirit.

### Notes

1. The encyclical is dated December 7, 1990, in order to commemorate the twenty-fifth anniversary of the publication of Vatican II's Decree on Missionary Activity, *Ad Gentes*; it was presented to the public, however, at a press conference on January 22, 1991. In Roman Catholic theology, an encyclical is a document written by the pope to the bishops of the world in the first place, but also to the entire Catholic faithful and sometimes as well to all "people of good will." The practice is to name the encyclical after the first two or three words of the official Latin text, and to number the various paragraphs. It is commonly referred to by the initial letters of these first two or three words, followed by the paragraph number—e.g.: the fourth paragraph in *Redemptoris Missio* is referred to as "RM 4." Encyclicals do not per se proclaim teachings that Roman Catholics consider infallible, but they nevertheless claim a high level of authority and require at the least a deep respect from the entire church membership. Cf. Stravinskas, ed. (1991) and Liégé (1956).

2. The encyclical itself is divided into eight chapters and not into "parts." Nevertheless, even a cursory reading will reveal that the first three chapters form a more theological "first part," and that the following five form a more practical "second part." Such a division is also intimated in Tomko (1991).

3. This is not to say that a trinitarian and reign-of-God-centered approach is not

present. In Chapter III, in the middle of #23, the "ultimate purpose of mission" is defined as enabling people "to share in the communion which exists between the Father and the Son." And Chapter II develops the relationship between Christ, the Reign of God and the church. My contention, however, is that these starting points are not *central* to the encyclical's basic argument.

## 3

# Missiological Hermeneutic and Pauline Apocalyptic Eschatology

## C. TIMOTHY CARRIKER

Eschatology, an essential element of the Kingdom of God theme, offers one of the primary points of contact between biblical studies and contemporary missiology. That mission and eschatology are inseparably related biblical concepts is widely recognized from a theological perspective (Braaten 1977, Wiedemann 1963, Kramm 1979). However, apart from some lesser known works of Oscar Cullmann (1936; 1938; 1956; 1963; and J. N. D. Anderson 1970) and his then student David Bosch (1959), there has been little discussion of the relation of eschatology to mission from the perspective of formal biblical studies. While major paradigm shifts have occurred since the publication of these works both within the area of biblical hermeneutics and missiology, they nevertheless have not been adequately reckoned with or built upon. This study seeks to do that through a focus on Pauline apocalyptic eschatology.

The following discussion serves as a case study in biblical and missiological hermeneutics. In particular, to use the language of biblical studies,[1] it concerns the relation of contingency to coherence. Or, to use the language of missiology (cf. Gilliland 1989), it concerns the relation of contextualization to theological consistency. My thesis is this: Paul's apocalyptic mission shapes his apocalyptic gospel, which, in turn, finds its contingent expression in the particular settings of Paul's letters. Or to say it a little differently, Paul's missionary call and ministry are fundamentally shaped by an apocalyptic perspective that influences the theological expression of Paul's gospel. The principal characteristics of that expression are crucial

C. Timothy Carriker, church planter and evangelist, is Academic Dean of the Brazil Evangelical Missions Center and President of the Association of Professors of Mission. He is a Ph.D. candidate at Fuller's School of World Mission, and his forthcoming dissertation will deal with Pauline apocalyptic eschatology and missions.

to a kingdom-oriented theology of mission as that is eschatologically expressed.

To illustrate the above thesis concerning the essentially apocalyptic nature of Paul's mission, we will examine 2 Thessalonians 2:6–7.[2] This passage treats Paul's end-time orientation. Careful examination, however, will reveal its apocalyptic content coupled with its missionary orientation. By way of this case study I will attempt to clarify the hermeneutical relation of the coherence-contingency scheme and the apocalyptic framework of Paul's gospel.[3]

### 2 Thessalonians 2:6–7

For nineteen centuries, commentators have been baffled by 2 Thessalonians 6 f.,[4] particularly by the apostle's reference to the "restraining": *tò katécon* of 2:6 and *ho katéchōn* of 2:7.[5] Almost any review of the exegetical literature reveals the wide diversity of interpretations presented.[6] The major difficulty involves the identity and purpose of the restraining activity and the restrainer.

My treatment will be limited to a review of some of the major interpretations given for *tò katécon* and *ho katéchōn*. This must include an examination of the text within the wider context of the 2 Thessalonians letter as it relates to other New Testament passages. This examination will serve as a case in point for a deeper understanding of Paul's apocalyptic mission.

One of the difficulties involved in interpreting 2 Thessalonians 2:6–7 is its typical apocalyptic terminology. Ridderbos (1975, 508–11) points to the expression *en tō eautoû kairō* as one such example. Just as the "fullness of the time" can refer to Christ's first coming in the flesh (Galatians 4:4; cf. Ephesians 1:10) as a fulfillment of the divine plan of salvation "in its own time" (1 Timothy 2:6; Titus 1:3; Romans 5:6), so also "in their own times" (2 Thessalonians 2:6) refers to the parousia of the Lord as a specific fixed time and particularly in a specific order.[7] Paul's use of "must" (*dei'*, cf. 1 Corinthians 15:25, 53) reflects the idea of an order of events established in God's plan of salvation. Romans 11 (first, the fullness of the Gentiles and then all Israel will be saved) also illustrates this sequential perspective. Other apocalyptic passages in Paul's letters which relate to the future of the Lord include 1 Corinthians 15:51ff and 1 Thessalonians 4:13–18. This apocalyptic outlook does not imply *computation* or *speculation* of the precise time of the parousia (see 1 Thessalonians 5:1ff.). So Paul is in accord with the prophecies and teaching of Jesus that the day of the Lord is unknown and has a sudden and surprising character (cf. Isaiah 13:6–8; Matthew 24:38; Luke 21:34; Acts 1:7; Luke 12:39ff; 2 Peter 3:10 and Revelation 3:3; 16:15). On the other hand, it does imply *sequence and delay* of the event. Some things cannot happen before something also "first" occurs.[8] Any interpretation of 2 Thessalonians 2:6f then should take account of the terminology as apocalyptic.[9]

Not all of the interpretations given for *tò katéchon* and *ho katéchōn* are mutually distinct. Some, in fact, are relatively compatible with others. I will list five of those interpretations.

In the first place, throughout the centuries a large group of interpreters believed that *tò katéchon* referred to the Roman emperor.[10] That interpretation is supported by Paul's positive attitude toward government (Romans 13:4; 1 Timothy 2:1–7) and his appeal to Roman law for protection as *civis Romanus*. This interpretation explains the alternate masculine and neuter uses of the *katechein* terms and even alleges an allusion to the name of the then-reigning emperor, Claudius (*claudio* means "to shut, to close, to prevent").

A variant of this view considers the opposite pairing[11] of the *katechein* and *anomías* phrases as a reference to "law" and "lawlessness." In this case, *tò katéchon* would refer to the general order of law and good government.[12] Neither of these views reckons with the imagery of Antichrist in Daniel, upon which this reference depends, whereby the Antichrist is the Syrian empire. Would Paul sketch the Antichrist as the state and then suggest that the restrainer is also the state? For the Thessalonian Christians, probably the state was the source of harassment and persecution rather than protection.[13]

A second interpretation views *tò katéchon* as the binding of Satan or evil and *ho katéchōn* as an angel or God himself.[14] Appeal is made to Luke 8:31, Revelation 20:2 and also to a similar situation in Daniel 10 and 12. Bauer (1957, 423f.) refers to a late Egyptian prayer where *katechein* is employed to describe the restraint of the mythological dragon by Michael. However, as H. Berkhof (1966, 130) pointed out, any reference by Paul to a supernatural or mythical power would still demand some earthly correlate. If this "earthly reality" was Paul's apostolic ministry, the mission to the Gentiles, then this interpretation, too, would be related to Cullmann's. As evidence we refer to Daniel 12:1–4, where the binding of Satan (10:13, 21) by Michael is in fact related to the proclamation of the gospel (12:3, cf. Ephesians 3:10; 6:10–16). Roger Aus demonstrates that Daniel, as well as Isaiah 66, is the background for Paul's argument here.

A third interpretation understands the *katechein* phrases as referring to a "seizing force" and to an (unknown) individual incorporating this force (Giblin 1967 and Coppens 1970). In this case, *tò katéchon* would translate as "seizing power" and *ho katéchōn as* "the Seizer." However, the antitheses in verses 6 and 7 between God and the man of lawlessness and the similar antithesis in verse 8 rules out any identification of *katechein* and *anomias* phrases.

A fourth interpretation takes the *katechein* phrases in reference to God's will and plan. The root for *tò katéchon* is related to the verb in Isaiah 66:7–9, "to shut up." Just as the subject of the verb there is God, so too, according to this argument, *ho katéchōn* must refer to God. Parallels to the idea of God as the one who closes a woman's womb include Genesis 2:18 and examples from rabbinic and Jewish apocalyptic literature (Aus 1977, 546–48). Among the patristic writers who expressly stated or assumed that it is God "who restrains" are Theodore of Mopsuestia and Theodoret of Cyrus (Aus 1977, 548).

Following this viewpoint, a case can be made that *tò katéchon* refers to God's will regarding the mission to the Gentiles. There is, in fact, no effectual difference between use of *tò katéchon* as referring to the mission of the Gentiles and to its referring to God's will or plan that the gospel first be preached to all people before the parousia. Aus himself cannot clearly distinguish between the two. They are, in fact, one and the same. Although this may not necessarily imply the use of *ho katéchōn* as either referring to the preacher or to God himself, these two also are closely linked. Aus's effort to distinguish between the two only ends in frustration when he himself points to the reference by Paul in the following verses (13–14) to "our gospel" as the vehicle of salvation among the Thessalonians. By this he does not imply that salvation has its origins in his gospel. Rather it is God himself who calls (verse 14). The role of the preacher and the one whom he represents are inseparably linked, yet in no way confused.[15]

With this we come to our fifth and final interpretation: *tò katéchon* as the preaching of the gospel and *ho katéchōn* as the preacher, prototypically the apostle Paul himself. This view is defended by Cullmann on the basis of the question asked in Jewish apocalyptic literature concerning the reason for the parousia's delay. The most frequent response referred to Israel's lack of repentance. That answer firmly sets the stage for the Christian view of the apocalyptic necessity of preaching the gospel to the Gentiles, a view expressed most clearly in Matthew 24:14 and Mark 13:10. These texts in turn highlight the chronological order of events preceding the end: "first" (Mark) the gospel must be preached to all the Gentiles and "then" (Matthew) shall the end come. It is important to note that in these passages the Antichrist's appearance follows the preaching of the gospel, just as in our view of 2 Thessalonians 2. Other possible parallels include Revelation 6:1–8; 19:11ff. and 11:3, where Cullmann interprets the first horseman as being the preacher of the gospel throughout the world who immediately precedes the End. Acts 1:6–9, too, relates the proclamation of the gospel worldwide to the question of the kingdom's delay, also illustrating the early Christian view of missionary activity as the prelude for and apocalyptic sign of the coming new age.[16]

The immediate context further strengthens this interpretation. Verses 9–12 refer to the perdition of those who will not receive the love of the truth. The audience in verses 13–15 is contrasted with those who reject the apostle's preaching. Even the whole preceding chapter treats the relation of apocalyptic events to persons accepting or rejecting the gospel.

These internal, contextual, grammatical[17] and source considerations all favor the view that the *katechein* phrases refer to the preaching of the gospel and to the preacher himself.[18] Thus we can affirm that 2 Thessalonians 2 should be read against a background of political pressure[19] and social deprivation,[20] conditions highly favorable for the rise of millenarian expectations, and in a context of Paul's own apocalyptic framework. Not surprisingly, then, we find all the usual apocalyptic themes present:

- *vindication* (The triumph of the "Lord Jesus" over the power of "lawlessness" and the "lawless one," verses 4–8, is assured!)
- *dualism* (The forces of evil war against the forces of God, the wicked over against the faithful.)
- *cosmic universalism* (All kinds of counterfeit miracles, signs and wonders will be unleashed by the work of Satan.)
- *imminence* (In spite of the clear sequence of events, the spreading of the gospel is a task demanding urgency.)

As can be seen in 2 Thessalonians 2:6, 7, Paul views the Gentile mission as the chief apostolic task for the period preceding the End. His own vocation as apostle to the Gentiles (Romans 15:15ff) is particularly critical in God's plan of salvation, for only when that task is "complete," will "all Israel" be saved (Romans 9–11). With that sense of apocalyptic urgency, Paul ambitiously yet carefully sets out to circle the Mediterranean world, with one eye always back on Jerusalem (Romans 15:15ff), in the hope that the obedience of the nations will provoke some of the Jews to jealousy (Romans 9–11). The proclamation to the Gentiles reaches such apocalyptic intensity that only its removal will allow for the final judgment and inauguration of the messianic kingdom (2 Thessalonians 2:6–7).

Such an apocalyptic framework gave Paul the strongest possible motivation for his missionary activity of preaching the gospel to the nations. Here we find his keenest incentive to action. Nowhere else does apocalyptic motive have such positive significance for the present task of the apostle. Such motivation could but only spur Paul on by the disquieting realization that the gospel proclamation must be speedy and that time is always to be viewed as short in light of the uncertainty of the time of Messiah's return.

### Paul's Apocalyptic Framework

Paul thought, wrote and ministered within an essentially apocalyptic framework, albeit radically modified in its details by his own encounter with the risen Lord and by his sense of call which arose from this event. On the one hand, then, to understand the apostle Paul, one must attempt to identify the details of framework and consider the manner by which their various themes and components function together to form an essentially apocalyptic worldview. In this study we have not attempted, as many scholars are now doing, to specify and qualify further these crucial details. Rather we have tried to demonstrate that to understand the apocalyptic framework of Paul's theology or gospel, one must *first* come to grips with the apocalyptic nature and self-understanding of Paul's ministry and mission. Here the clues to unravel Paul's most fundamental convictions are found.

## Paul's Apocalyptic Mission

Beker has aptly demonstrated, along with others, that before one sees Paul as theologian and in relation to his theology, one must first see Paul as interpreter and contingent contextualizer in relation to his gospel and its coherent, apocalyptic core. While this insight, extensively developed by Beker, has greatly furthered the debate concerning the interpretation of Paul, it does not go far enough. For before one sees Paul as interpreter of a gospel revealed to him, one must see Paul in his purposive context, Paul the apostle in relation to his apocalyptic mission. Here we see Paul not only before the specific pastoral challenges of his congregations, but also in the context of his life's call and drive, an intent based and radicalized by his past encounter on the Damascus road and now essentially governed by deep anticipation, even passion, for the Lord's return. Thus Paul's apocalyptic and purpose-oriented call shapes him, according to his specific pastoral situations, to be the interpreter of the gospel, the missionary apostle we encounter in his epistles.

## Paul's Contextual Hermeneutic

An appreciation of Paul's apocalyptic mission can shed some light on Paul's hermeneutic, which is both missional and apocalyptic.

### Missional

Paul's hermeneutic is missional in that he addresses the specific situations of his churches, applying the "coherent core of the gospel" to the varied challenges of different churches facing diverse problems. Beker's coherence-contingency scheme is of great help here. In this regard, both the wording and structure of Paul's arguments are shaped by contingent situations which he addresses in his letters. This may well be the case of 2 Thessalonians where Paul's arguments are developed against the background of the Thessalonians' millenarian piety. While the contextual nature of Paul's gospel is usually related to the specific pastoral problems of the churches which he established, at least in one case, the letter to the Romans, the specific situation may be the larger context of Paul's call and mission. Here contingency is best seen against the background of the conflicts which Paul encountered during his previous ministry in Corinth and Galatia as well as his missionary aspirations for his forthcoming trip to Spain and Jerusalem. Martin Hengel (1983, 50) stated this succinctly: "the *Sitz im Leben* of Pauline theology is the apostle's mission."[21]

### Apocalyptic

Paul's hermeneutic is also apocalyptic, in terms of Paul's interpretation of his life's call and present ministry. This apocalyptic framework enabled Paul conceptually and radically to modify the fundamental Jewish convictions he had previously held. Paul understood his mission as part of the "age to come" which Christ's death and resurrection had radically inaugurated. A radically new age demanded radical theological reformulations. While Paul's call explains the existential premise for such changes, it was his apocalyptic framework that gave him the conceptual and passionate paradigms by which radical modifications of formerly cherished doctrines were made possible.

The apocalyptic nature of Paul's mission also explains and qualifies the interfacing of Beker's coherence-contingency scheme. That is, the contextual nature of Paul's gospel is limited ultimately by its apocalyptic framework. Paul understood his mission not only within the context of specific historical and cultural circumstances, but within the broader, overriding retrospect of the new age inaugurated by Christ and consequential prospect of Christ's return. It is this view that best explains the background of Paul's letter to the Romans. As chapter 15 indicates, the background to this letter is to be found not so much in Paul's trip to Rome, but his trip to Spain and Jerusalem and the consequential apocalyptic role of his own mission in relation to the parousia.

### Conclusion

Paul's apocalyptic framework for mission presupposes a goal toward which God's plan of salvation is moving. That is, it assumes a purposive view of history. Such apocalypticism, at least Pauline apocalypticism, is no flight from this world of events. Like Jewish apocalypticism, Paul's apocalyptic framework presupposes conflict and discontinuity as the manifestations of "this age." In this respect, an apocalyptic framework qualifies structuralism's basic presupposition of stability and gradual change in societies. An apocalyptic framework will take account of those points of sin and conflict within social networks as manifestations of the rebellion of this current evil age.

While an apocalyptic framework presupposes conflict and discontinuity with this age, it also presupposes an overriding continuity with the unfolding of God's salvific plan since creation. A theology of history and the diachronic view of the world which this brings will then qualify the otherwise synchronic view which underlies the social sciences. This should clarify the task of contextualization as to its historical goal and its change-oriented character.

An apocalyptic frame could shed new light on the theologies of liberation. While the latter rely heavily on a view of the manifestation of the kingdom of God within the structures (especially social) of this world, the former stubbornly hopes for God's ultimate intervention from outside the structures of and at the end of history. This does not imply an attitude of passive resignation. To the contrary, present history is to be filled up by the churches' constant preparation for that kingdom through the establishment of beachheads of the coming of the kingdom. Signs of that coming age are to be established in the here and now. Such was Paul's understanding of his mission.

Paul understood his mission as related to the parousia. His own special call as apostle to the Gentiles becomes the *conditio sine qua non* between the inauguration of the "age to come" through the crucified and resurrected Christ and the parousia of the exalted Christ (Stendahl 1977, 51). Paul himself, then, is none other than a "precursor of the parousia" (Käsemann 1980, 307). His mission must be seen within the context of the "divinely willed conclusion of salvation history" (Käsemann 1980, 307). In this regard, apocalyptic fervor and missionary strategy must be seen to be intimately connected in Paul's mind, providing him the deepest motivation and broadest hermeneutic through which he viewed God's mission, his apostleship, and the end of history.

## Notes

1. Beker (1980; 1982, 29-53) posits that two related components govern Paul's writings. The first concerns Paul's hermeneutic as characterized by an interaction between the coherent center of the gospel and the contingency of the particular situations which this gospel addresses. The second elaborates the character of Paul's contingent hermeneutic as being shaped by apocalyptic motifs and pointing to God's imminent but future cosmic triumph. Accordingly, four basic Jewish apocalyptic motifs are central to the basic structure of Paul's apocalyptic gospel: vindication of God's salvific promises to Israel and the nations, universal cosmic expectation, historical dualism and the imminent end of the world.

New Testament scholars have assessed Beker's theses, calling for some adjustments and further clarifications, especially in regard to Paul's dependence on apocalyptic categories from Pauline to Deutero-Pauline literature and also from the earlier to the later Gospels. Vincent P. Branick (1985) challenges Beker's thesis that the apocalyptic framework is the one consistent core of Paul's theology. Mary Ann Getty (1983) confirms Beker's central theses through her exegesis of "Christ is the end of the law" within the larger context of Romans 9:30-10:13. Robert Jewett (1986a) exemplifies more extensively the implications of Beker's theses (while not addressing Beker directly) by presupposing Paul's apocalyptic framework as well as millennial motifs in Thessalonica as the background to Paul's letters there. Leander E. Keck (1984) contends that Paul's theology (rather than gospel, as Beker insists) is apocalyptic not because it includes vindication, universalism, dualism and imminence (against Beker), but because of the perspective of discontinuity which also characterizes apocalyptic theology in general. And E. P. Sanders (1983, 5 and 12) agrees that Paul's worldview and ministry were crucially conditioned by the nearness of the end.

2. Dean Gilliland (1989a) recently teased out some of these same implications in 1 Corinthians 15:20-27 and 1 Thessalonians 4:13-5:11 with reference to an unpublished Ph.D. seminar paper which I presented in 1987 at Fuller Theological Seminary (Carriker 1987). David Bosch (1991b, 123-78), too, has recently addressed the missiological implications of this subject.

3. The history of research on Pauline eschatology and apocalyptic is both long and complex. The current debate concerning a delimitation of the concept of apocalyptic (genres, motifs and movements) and its distinction from eschatology defies any concise treatment. Nevertheless, both demand careful discussion for a more definitive defense of this paper's thesis. Therefore, due to space limitations, we will confine our discussion, at least initially, to the definitions which Beker works with as mentioned above.

4. Opinion concerning the authenticity of the letters to the Thessalonians is divided, many questioning especially the authenticity of 2 Thessalonians. Some allege a stylistic change in language (Townsend 1980), while others indicate that the expectation of an imminent parousia is here given up.

Differences in writing style as well as differences in content may be due simply to differences in the occasions of the two letters, even while written to the same audience by the same author within a relatively short period. Even the difference in eschatological expectancy is more readily understood against the background of a misunderstanding which had not arisen when 1 Thessalonians was written.

Robert Jewett (1986a, 16-18), against Christopher Mearns's (1981) developmental theory of Pauline eschatology and most of current critical opinion, masterfully demonstrates the very high probability of 2 Thessalonians' Pauline authorship by comparing the style and vocabulary of both letters and reconstructing the religious and political occasions which gave rise to the differences in tone and emphases. In support of Pauline authorship, F. F. Bruce (1982) points out the inclusion of Paul's name five times (1 Thess. 2:18; 3:5; 5:27; 2 Thess. 2:5; 3:17), twice with the first person singular pronoun (1 Thess. 2:18; 2 Thess. 3:17), and especially his signature at the end of the second letter. This argument could also be used to support the forgery hypothesis, but particularly in light of Jewett's study, the difficulties surrounding this hypothesis are much greater than those concerning authenticity.

Along with these refutals to objections against Pauline authorship on the basis of internal evidence, we cite strong external evidence in favor of the authenticity of 2 Thessalonians. That is, the letter is included in the Canon of Marcion and the Muratorian List and was mentioned by Irenaeus by name, and apparently was known also to Ignatius, Justin and Polycarp. Therefore, we consider 2 Thessalonians as authentically Pauline.

Beker's argument against the Pauline authorship of 2 Thessalonians follows a different path than the forgery hypothesis or difficulties concerning the relation between this letter and 1 Thessalonians. In reference to 2 Thessalonians 2, the specific apocalyptic program, a program which he considers predictive and calculable, Beker (1980, 161; 1982, 48-49) contends that the letter could not have been written by Paul, who expected an imminent end, not based on human disclosure. This observation seems rather odd, in light of the no less specific and calculable apocalyptic program of Romans 9-11, which Beker considers foundational for Paul. Here Beker errs by equating calculability with the presence of a given order or progam.

For a more thorough treatment of the subject, see Bailey (1979).

5. Cf. E. E. Schneider (1963).

6. A thorough list of current literature is found in Jewett (1986a, 193-213).

7. Compare the sequence which the term "order," *tágmati*, denotes in 1 Corinthians 15:23f in relation to the accompanying terms: *aparché*, *épeita* and *eîta*.

8. For the idea of sequence, see Michaelis (1968) and O. Cullmann (1967a, 1967b, 57ff). That process, sequence and chronology are important elements in Paul's apocalyptic framework is commonly recognized. Cf. C. K. Barrett (1962, 42-46), Vos (1949, 83, 91), and Schoeps (1961, 105).

9. Concerning sources in Jewish apocalyptic literature, Townsend (1980) affirms that no parallels exist, although concerning attempts to find parallels, he cites Betz (1963) and M. Barnouin (1976/77). We add, however: Schippers (1961), and particularly the references by Cullmann to apocalyptic ideas in Strack-Billerback III, where the question is asked concerning what is "holding back" or "retarding" the coming of the Messiah. Schoeps (1961, 99) also affirms, "if we are to understand the eschatology of Paul aright ... we must make its apocalyptic presuppositions more central in his thought than is usually done."

Roger Aus (1971; 1976, 252-68; 1977) suggests that Isaiah 66, Daniel 11:36 and Ezekiel 27:10-25 and 28:2 are sources for 2 Thessalonians 2 and that the Hebrew verb for "to shut" (the womb) in Isaiah 66:9 forms the background for the term *katéchōn* in 2 Thessalonians 2:7. LaRondelle (1983) also sees here allusions to these Old Testament passages.

Robert Jewett (1986a) also affirms Paul's debt to Jewish apocalyptic here, but points to the setting of the church in Thessalonica as heavily influenced by a budding millenarian movement.

10. Such as Claudius, Vitellius, Vespasian, Titus Trajan, or even Nero's tutor, Seneca. This view was held by Tertullian, Lactantius, Chrysostom, Luther, Stauffer and more recently by G. E. Ladd. Cf. the review of interpretations by F. F. Bruce (1982, 170-72).

11. Vos (1949, 130f.) notes that the two pairs of phrases are usually interpreted by the principle of oppositeness.

12. Ladd (1974a) seems to hold to this variation of the historical interpretation. We should add, in favor of this view, that it best employs the principle of oppositeness mentioned above. As well, if one understands *tò katéchon* as God's order and *ho katéchōn* as either God himself or one of his ambassadors, possibly Paul would still be in view. That is, God's order is not incongruous with the idea of the Gentile mission. Indeed, the "lawlessness" and consequential "rebellion" of 2 Thessalonians 2:3 (note the type of rebellion, that is, against all that is called God or is worshiped) are also a part of the context of Isaiah 66 (for the idea of rebellion, note the improper worship mentioned in verses 3-4 and the defiance of God men-

tioned in verses 5-6; for the idea of order, note verses 7-9 and 22) and there they are also related to mission (verses 18-24).

We are not suggesting, however, that *tò katéchon* refers both to the preaching of the gospel and to God's order while *ho katéchōn* refers both to the preacher and to God. Rather, we maintain that *tò katéchon* refers primarily and fundamentally to the preaching of the gospel to the nations and *ho katéchōn* refers to the preacher and probably to Paul himself as the prototype missionary. Nevertheless, the mission to the Gentiles is by no means unrelated to the furtherance of God's order; much to the contrary. Neither is the preacher to the Gentiles nor Paul, as the prototype preacher and apostle to the Gentiles, unrelated to God as the retainer. Certainly Paul's understanding of his call as representative and even ambassador of God justifies this view. Yet, we here suggest that only in a secondary manner is *tò katéchon* to be understood as God's order and *ho katéchōn* as God himself. This is not to suggest that God is second to Paul qualitatively, but rather that in Paul's argument at this point in the text, the preacher is the essential factor in the proclamation of the gospel (cf. Romans 10:14, 15). Strong contextual evidence for this view is found in 2 Thessalonians 2:14, "He (God) called you to this (salvation, verse 13) through *our* gospel" (NIV, emphasis mine). That *Paul* is God's instrument in God's plan of salvation in no way minimizes divine omnipotence.

13. Cf. K. D. Donfried (1985), Robert Jewett (1986b), and Bruce (1982, xxiii).

14. Ridderbos (1975, 524f.) and Vos (1949, 131ff.).

15. Compare Romans 10:13-15 and the use of *leiturgòn* in Romans 15:16 as comparing Paul's ministry to that of a Levite, as a subordinate or auxiliary to that of Christ the Priest.

16. Elsewhere in Paul's writings the missionary preaching of the gospel to the Gentiles is viewed in closest connection to the End. Besides Romans 9-11 and 15:14-33, note Paul's apocalyptic sense of "compulsion" to preach (1 Corinthians 9:16) as a "debtor" (Romans 1:14) to and "prisoner" for the Gentiles (Ephesians 3:1). To do otherwise would be to call upon himself an apocalyptic "woe" (1 Corinthians 9:16).

17. We add here one observation concerning the use of the third person in reference to *ho katéchōn*. Paul elsewhere refers to himself in the third person rather than the first (e. g., 2 Corinthians 12:2). Therefore the use of the third person for *ho katéchōn* would not eliminate the possibility that Paul may be referring to himself.

18. The view that refers *tò katéchon* to mission preaching and that *ho katéchōn* refers to some instrument of God was expressed previously by Theodore Mopsuestia, Theodoret of Cyrus and later by John Calvin (Cullmann 1938).

19. Cf. Donfried (1985).

20. Cf. Jewett (1986a).

21. Cf. Stendahl (1977, 12): "Again and again we find that there is hardly a thought of Paul's which is not tied up with his mission."

# 4

# A Pauline Paradigm of Mission

## *A Latin American Reading*

### SAMUEL ESCOBAR

Third World Christianity has emerged as a new decisive factor for Christian mission in the twenty-first century. Young thriving churches grow in the midst of complex processes of uneven modernization and social change. The fall of the Berlin wall smashed the hopes that revolutionary class struggle would bring the just and free society envisaged by socialist manifestos. However, awareness of failed utopias in itself will not bring Third World societies ahead on the road to radical transformation, if a minimum of human dignity is going to be preserved for the poor masses. Within this scenario Christian missiology in Latin America is challenged to grasp the significance of unexpected changes in the religious map of the region[1] as well as the challenge to mission from Latin America in the next century. It will have to be a transformational missiology, the outcome of faithfulness to the Gospel where "if anyone is in Christ there is a new creation: everything old has passed away; see, everything has become new!" (2 Cor. 5:17, NRSV).

## Theory and Practice in Pauline Missiology

The Apostle Paul was the great hero and patron saint of Evangelicals in Latin America during the initial decades of their presence in this vast

Samuel Escobar, a native of Peru, has been a missionary among university students in Argentina, Brazil, and Canada. A founder and past president of the Latin American Theological Fraternity, he is also involved in the International Fellowship of Evangelical Missions Theologians. Currently he teaches missiology at Eastern Baptist Theological Seminary in Philadelphia, Pennsylvania.

continent. Their evangelistic enthusiasm, within nominally Catholic societies, was the source of the emphasis of Evangelical preaching on the Pauline
foundation for the basic tenets of the Reformation, such as justification by
faith. Paul's missionary strategy, in open tension with the synagogue, was
seen as an adequate paradigm for Evangelical missionaries confronted with
the rejection and opposition of a highly institutionalized Church that was
part of the feudal establishment. However, during the 60s and the 70s, two
decades of great theological ferment, Paul's popularity decreased signifi-
cantly, and in some forms of liberation discourse there was not much room
for him. There was a certain embarrassment about Paul because of his
alleged social conservatism and dualistic spirituality.

More recently, a significant amount of Pauline scholarship has gathered,
especially about his missionary practice and teaching.[2] One of the consequences of current research has been to question the picture of the apostle
as the provider of an ideology to buttress conservative attitudes in his own
society. As E. A. Judge, one of the pioneers of the shift, points out, "One
basic reason for suspecting that Paul was not a conservative person in his
ideas on society is that he deliberately abandoned the security of established
status in his own life" (Judge 1974).

Paul's missiology is often expressed as theological exposition, interlaced
with references to his own missionary practice. I find Romans 15:11–33
illustrative of Paul's methodology and uniquely relevant to missiological
reflection in Latin America. This passage presents an interaction between
theory and practice, between facts of life in obedience to God and reflection
about those facts. Rather than a speculative exercise, missiology is a reflection of God's people as they engage in acts of obedience to God's missionary
call, under the light of God's word. This passage is permeated by an intense
personal tone. It is the expression of deep and living affections from the
heart of a man who lives and shares not only "everything he has" but even
"himself as well" (2 Cor. 12:15). This is not the dry, institutional, impersonal language of time charts, job descriptions and management schemes
which in some circles today constitutes the image of the missionary enterprise. Isn't this Pauline style in itself filled with suggestions?

A careful reading of Romans 15:11–33 shows a fourfold structure of
Paul's missiology. In each section we find a central "fact" related to Paul's
practice, followed by pastoral and missiological reflection that stems from
the fact and moves around it. First, *Proclaiming*: "I have fully proclaimed
the Gospel of Christ" (vv. 17–22); second, *Envisioning*: "I plan to see you
when I go to Spain" (vv. 23–24); third, *Completing*: "Now, however, I am
on my way to Jerusalem" (vv. 25–29); and fourth *Struggling*: "I urge you
... to join me in my struggle" (vv. 30–33).

## Proclaiming

Paul begins by stating a *fact*: "So from Jerusalem all the way around to
Illyricum, I have fully proclaimed the Gospel of Christ" (Romans 15:19).

His life as an apostle has been spent proclaiming the gospel of Christ in a vast region of the Mediterranean world. This proclamation is described with an element of fulfillment and completion, as the New English Bible renders v. 19: "I have completed the preaching of the Gospel of Christ." In his trips from city to city, from synagogue to marketplace, in houses, ships or along the road, Paul's main concern has been this proclamation of the Gospel. Luther was within this Pauline tradition when he stated that he wanted to be known only as a "servant of the Word." Many Evangelical pioneers in Latin America, like James Thomson in the nineteenth century or Francisco Penzotti in the twentieth century, wrote about their apostolic work along the lines of adventures as they moved along "with the Word" or "with the Book" in Latin America. It is an encouraging sign of new times that in some Latin American countries where a measure of biblical renewal has touched the Roman Catholic Church, the catechists are nowadays called "agents of the Word."

This proclamation of the Gospel among the Gentiles and in places where it has not been known before is Paul's ambition and specific task. He sees himself as contributing to fulfill what the prophets announced (v. 21). As the earlier part of this chapter shows, "he sees *testimonium* of the Gentile mission in the Law, the Prophets and the Psalms" (Bruce 1985, 243). His life is the practice of obedience which brings to reality what was announced in the Word. As Leon Morris says: "Paul is saying that his constant aim was the lowly one of being a pioneer evangelist" (Morris 1988, 515). Such proclamation is central for mission. Latin Americans of my generation who have been described as "radical Evangelicals" because of their struggle for a holistic approach to mission have never questioned or denied the centrality of the proclamation of the Gospel for mission. The practice and the theology of people such as Rene Padilla, Orlando Costas, Rolando Gutierrez and Pedro Arana confirm this commitment.

In this passage Paul's proclaiming activity is seen within a wider, more comprehensive frame which clarifies the nature of the missionary proclamation. At least two aspects of that wider frame are worth considering. In the first place Paul sees himself as nothing but an agent of an active triune God who is really the one who has the initiative. Paul's ministry is presented as an accomplishment of Christ for obedience to God in the power of the Spirit (vv. 17–19a). Because of that, glory is to be given to God alone. In 15:16 Paul has compared his apostolic ministry to the priestly ministry of the Old Testament, and as Leenhardt says:

Just as the priest at the altar merely obeyed the prescription of Moses, so that his individuality was effaced behind the divine institution which alone gave to his actions their value, so the sacerdotal ministry of the Apostle does not give rise to any personal vanity (1 Cor. 15:10–31; 2 Cor. 10:13). It is Christ who is the unseen actor who imparts to this ministry its astonishing fecundity (2 Cor. 3:5; 4:7; 13:3). (Leen-hardt 1961, 369)

Thus, though the Apostle states his specific call, he also acknowledges the particular calls of others and the complementarity of tasks within a holistic view of mission (1 Cor. 3:5–15). Paul does not need to use marketing techniques to prove that his own call is the best and the most urgent in order to attract donors from competing agencies.

In the second place, through the proclamation of the Gospel, God is "leading the Gentiles to obey God" (v. 18). The Gospel involves a clear call to repentance, faith and obedience. The truth of Christ is an engaging truth. To use the image forged by John A. Mackay, a great missionary to Latin America, the Gospel is a call to follow Christ on the road, not to contemplate him from the detached distance of a balcony: "It is ever he who does the will of God that knows the doctrine." This is another way of saying that truth, as it relates to God, is always existential in character, involving a consent of the will as well as an act of understanding. "Assent may be given on the balcony, but consent is inseparable from the road" (Mackay 1942, 50).

This point has been pursued consistently by Rene Padilla, an evangelist, pastor and theologian in Argentina. His missiology has been an effort to work out the consequences of the notion of "obedience of faith" for mission in Latin America. In a continent that proclaimed itself "Christian" since the sixteenth century there has been a need to come to terms with a form of mission that reduced the Gospel to a minimum in order to keep within the fold the maximum number of people. I agree with Padilla that within Evangelicalism there are today some forms of missiology that espouse precisely that principle. "As a result the church far from being a factor for the transformation of society, becomes merely another reflection of society and, what is worse, another instrument that society uses to condition people to its materialistic values" (Padilla 1985, 55). This sort of missiology separates faith from repentance, the announcement of God's indicative of salvation in Christ from God's imperative of a new life, salvation from sanctification. "On its most basic level, it entails distinguishing between Christ as Savior and Christ as Lord. This produces a Gospel that permits a person to maintain the values and attitudes prevalent in a consumer society and at the same time enjoy the temporal and eternal security that religion provides" (Padilla 1985, 55).

As Orlando Costas once said, "If present-day Christianity is not to be reduced to a museum piece, a historically insignificant religion, a topic of the past, a corpse or a free-floating religious club, it will need to recover the urgency of proclaiming three things: the name of Jesus, the radical nature of God's Kingdom and the call to repentance and faith" (Costas 1979, 12).

## Envisioning

From the beginning of this epistle, Paul is very explicit about his intention of visiting Rome (1:16). What he now makes clear is that Rome will be only a station on his way to Spain. "I hope to visit you while passing through and to have you assist me on my journey there" (v. 24). The Iberian peninsula was the western extreme of the empire, and the eyes of this visionary are set on it. "He had long placed in his agenda a campaign to Spain. For that trip it was necessary to travel through Rome, for obvious geographical reasons as well as for less obvious logistic reasons (1:8–15; 15:14–33). However his projected trip had been frustrated time after time" (Minear 1971, 2). In this section the central fact was this definite plan for which possibly the whole epistle is a preparatory stage. Luke has given us a brief insight into the single-mindedness of Paul's purpose when in Acts 19:21 he alludes to the decision the Apostle made while he was in Ephesus: "Paul decided to go to Jerusalem, passing through Macedonia and Achaea. 'After I have been there,' he said, 'I must visit Rome also.'" F. F. Bruce has pointed out that while for Luke the city of Rome seems to be the culminating point in the way he tells his story in Acts, it was not so in the case of the Apostle himself. "Rome in his mind was a halting place, or at best an advance base, on his way to Spain, where he planned to repeat the programme which he had just completed in the Aegean world (Rom. 15:23)" (Bruce 1977, 314).

Paul's single-mindedness in terms of the direction of his trip matches his firm determination as to the type of ministry in which he would engage. Knox has said it with great precision: "No one can doubt that Paul had a peculiar sense of vocation and a sense of peculiar vocation—that he thought of himself and his work as having extraordinary importance of some kind in the working of God's purpose in Christ. Over and over again in reading his letters, one is impressed, and sometimes repelled, by signs of what may appear to be an almost morbid sense of his own importance" (Knox 1964, 5). The same could be said of missionaries of every age. Just think of Ramón Lull, Bartolomé de las Casas, Francis Xavier, William Carey, Henry Martyn, Robert Moffat, Allen Gardiner, and some contemporaries that we know! This sense of personal call is matched by the conviction about the obligation implied in the nature of the Gospel and the Christian faith itself. It is only in relation to this basic sense of personal vocation, dramatically lived out in practice, that the theological material of the Epistle to the Romans makes sense. Here is absolute certainty about a God who wants to bring salvation to every human being, to the ends of the earth, and has chosen Paul as an instrument.

Who could deny today the right of Latin American Evangelical churches to exist and proclaim the Gospel in Latin America? Who then would deny the effects that the proclamation of the Gospel during the last two centuries has had, not only in giving birth to thousands of thriving Evangelical communities, but also contributing to shake Roman Catholicism out of complacency, into a renewed sense of mission? Decision makers at the famous missionary conference of Edinburgh in 1910 denied the right of Evangelicals to missionize in Latin America. Eighteen years later, in the meeting of the International Missionary Council at Jerusalem, John A. Mackay said: "Sometimes those who are interested in Christian service in South America are apt to be regarded as religious buccaneers devoting their lives to ecclesiastical piracy, but that is far from being the case. The great majority of men to whom we go will have nothing to do with religion. They took up this attitude because religion and morality had been divorced throughout the whole history of religious life in South America" (Mackay 1928, 121). The Ecumenical Movement eventually corrected its mistake of 1910. But I am afraid that the old misconceptions are still there in the minds of many ecclesiastical leaders.

All along missionary history there is evidence of this tension between single-minded visionaries on the one hand and dormant churches or hardened institutions on the other. God's Spirit moves in this tension in order to revitalize his church and accomplish his mission. But there is another side presented in this passage of Romans 15. Paul does not want to go alone about his mission. "Some think that Paul was looking for prayers and good wishes only and this indeed may be the case. But it seems somewhat more likely that he hoped to have Rome as his base for his work in the western regions. Until now Antioch had functioned as his base but this was too far from places like Spain. It would be a very great help for Paul if the Christians at Rome could see their way clear to acting as his home church, so to speak, while he went forward into unknown territory . . . " (Morris 1988, 518).

Where is the unknown territory, where are the frontiers to cross as we enter into a new century? In the case of Latin America, increasingly the new martyrs of mission are not among the Aucas of the jungle anymore, but in crowded cities like São Paulo or Lima, where inflation, drugs, and traditional corruption are making life a very risky adventure for missionaries. The single-mindedness of pioneers such as Viv Grigg in the urban inferno of Manila is offering all of us a new missionary approach (Grigg 1990).

One of the marks of our time is the ascent of the masses, the irruption of the poor as a disturbing presence, alongside luxury and affluence. I see it in Philadelphia as I see it in Lima. They include the masses of refugees in some Asian countries, the migrants to the cities in Latin America, the masses of illegal aliens in the United States, the foreign workers in some European countries.

### Completing

The third section in our passage is introduced by a sentence that sounds like an interruption in the flow of the discourse. "Now, however, I am on my way to Jerusalem in the service of the saints there ... " (v. 25). The central fact in this section is that in spite of his plan to evangelize Spain and the sense of urgency he has about it, Paul finds himself in the midst of another missionary trip to which he ascribes a special importance. The expression "service of the saints" points to a financial collection that Paul had organized among the Gentile churches of the vast region he had evangelized. He was taking the money for the poor in Jerusalem. The language of the passage is revealing. He has expressed his single-minded purpose to go to Spain via Rome, but here comes a "however." As Bruce says: "It would be difficult to exaggerate the importance which Paul attached to this work and to the safe conveyance of the money to Jerusalem in the hands of delegates of the contributing churches" (Bruce 1977, 319).

Paul Minear has called our attention to the fact that the very idea of succor for the poor was a complete novelty for the Gentile churches. "Financial drives," says Minear,

> are so routine in our modern churches that we readily overlook the strategic importance of this first drive. It was a startling innovation. *Gentile* Christians in Macedonia and Achaea had been asked to send money to poor *Jewish* Christians in Jerusalem. Earlier appeals had been resisted; Paul's authority had been rejected. There were rumours that the whole business was graft. (Minear 1971, 3)

Unlike the Jews, Gentiles were not used to almsgiving. The resistance of some Jewish Christians to the missionary methods of Paul among Gentiles, in which they were not asked to become judaized, may have been the source of resentment against Jerusalem. Probably it was at Corinth where Paul found more resistance, and that explains the long and careful explanations given by Paul in his second letter to Corinthians. However, Minear's conclusion is illuminating: "Money was thus the root of church conflicts then as now. The heat of conflict, however, had not induced the Apostle to withdraw his request for funds. He had in fact made the gathering of his fund one of the tests of loyalty of the Gentile congregations. He had spent several years at it and had shaped his itinerary to facilitate it. References in five of his letters prove how carefully he planned the solicitation" (Minear 1971, 3).

In these verses Paul uses theological language to refer to the financial transaction and theological arguments to explain its meaning. Paul refers to the money in question as a *koinonia* (vv. 26, 27), a word with deep spiritual connotations. As Morris says, this is an indication "that the money was not a soulless gift, but the outward expression of the deep love that binds Christian believers in one body, the church (it is used similarly in 2 Cor. 8:4; 9:13)" (Morris 1988, 520). We notice also Paul's insistence on the voluntary nature of this offering. Twice he uses the verbal form "were pleased" to refer to the attitude of the believers in Macedonia and Achaea

(vv. 26, 27). It would not be totally out of place to suppose that some Jewish believers in Jerusalem may have misunderstood the nature of the offering, thinking of it as a kind of tribute that the Gentile churches were obliged to pay to the mother church in Jerusalem. The thrust of Paul's teaching about this offering emphasizes its voluntary nature: it had to be prepared "as a generous gift, not as one grudgingly given" (2 Cor. 9:5).

In the context of God's saving purpose for humankind, Paul establishes a sense of mutuality and reciprocity between those who first received the Gospel and those who later on were evangelized by them. Paul's own sense of compulsion to evangelize came from the deep source of Christ's love: "Christ's love compels us" (2 Cor. 5:14). In the same way, spontaneous gratitude to God for the gift of salvation received was to be the source of the Gentiles' offering to the poor in Jerusalem. Such is the frame within which we are to understand how the mutual sharing of blessings places on the same plane the spiritual blessing shared by the Jews and the material blessings shared by the Gentiles. A cultural barrier was broken along the way. "The collection" — says Leenhardt — "is a manifest sign of the unity of the Church. It shows in concrete fashion that the young shoots were firmly linked to the old trunk" (Leenhardt 1961, 375).

Notice also that in v. 28 Paul refers to a completion of his task, to the maturation of a fruit. The images could well point to the fact that as Paul finalizes one stage of his apostolate, this trip to Jerusalem was the crowning point of it. Paul was delivering not only the money but also a group of Gentile believers, as representatives of the donor churches. In line with the image of priesthood (v. 16) Paul's intention has been described by Bruce, "The Gentile delegates were to bring their offerings to Jerusalem, but the Gentile delegates themselves were Paul's own offering, presented not so much to the mother church as to the Lord who many years before had called Paul to be his apostle to the Gentiles" (Bruce 1977, 323). So there are two elements in this holistic view of mission: one is the empirical fact of an amount of money given, sacrificially in many cases, as an expression of concern for the poor in other lands. The other is the sign of maturity, of completion of the process of evangelization, that the act of offering in itself expresses. In giving, the giver grows and receives a blessing, and the receiver is blessed by the practical help provided for his distress. The transaction itself acquires a "eucharistic" dimension (2 Cor. 9:12).

"The basic notion here is not almsgiving but reciprocity" (Bassler 1991, 94). Dieter Georgi finds that v. 27 provides a clearer understanding of the significance that Paul attributes to the very existence of the economically impoverished ones, who would themselves be representatives of "the spiritual blessings" that Jerusalem offered. Georgi says that "There is a gift, a witnessing quality in their lives, ideally but also practically, even economically. They point to poverty as the basis for human societal existence; they remind the society of its constant fringe" (Georgi 1992, 164).

This matter is especially significant as a frame of reference for the many

missionary efforts from rich to poor societies in our time of growing dis-
parities at national and global levels. By paying attention to Pauline principles we might be able to correct some of the negative aspects that have
developed along the way. To begin with, Christian contribution to relief of
the poor and even to elimination of the causes of poverty should be channeled within the frame of reciprocity and mutuality that can come only
from a common commitment to faith in Christ. It should contribute to
strengthen the ties of Christian unity across cultural, political and even
ideological barriers. Rather than a paternalistic approach, patterned more
after the bureaucratic welfare system of the secular state, we could say that
a "eucharistic" approach needs to be forged. The helpers and the helped
must become partners and agents of their own development and liberation.
This would express a true holism in which the proclamation of the Gospel
and the service of the needs of the saints go hand in hand, without embarrassment or apologies.

The relief operation organized by Paul was something new for the Gentile churches. His missiological creativity is a good example for the kind of
creativity that our times demand as we look to a future of missionary partnership on a global scale.

## Struggling

This section of the epistle ends with an urgent request for solidarity in
prayer. "I urge you brothers by our Lord Jesus Christ and by the love of
the Spirit, to join me in my struggle by praying to God for me" (v. 30).
That is the fact: the Apostle asks his brothers and sisters in Rome to pray
for him. This is an "agonic" request, if I may remain close to the Greek
root and use that word in the sense in which Unamuno used it: "agony"
as struggle. In fact, as the great Spanish philosopher said, life, even Christian life, is to be lived as an agony, a struggle. To the famous dictum of
Descartes, *cogito ergo sum* ("I think, therefore I am"), Unamuno opposed
his *pugno ergo sum*, ("I fight, therefore I am"). Very Spanish indeed! But
we could say also very Pauline. The Apostle saw his mission as part of a
cosmic struggle, and it is very important to notice how in this request for
prayer there is a trinitarian element that accompanies the request for help
in his struggle.

Prayer for Paul was not just a perfunctory action to keep in line with
tradition. His epistles are filled with a prayerful attitude, as well as with
advice about the central place of prayer in the life of the Christian. In v.
18 of his chapter, Paul acknowledged with humility that his fruitful apostolic
efforts in that vast region were really "what Christ accomplished." This
theological perception is expressed as a confession in the practice of constant and disciplined prayer.

Again, as we look back at the history of missions, we find the same pattern repeated century after century. Great missionary movements are born in the cradle of a life of prayer. Great missionaries were also "mystics" in this sense, people of deep spirituality. That single-mindedness to which we referred above is also single-mindedness in relation to prayer. John R. Mott, whose outstanding ecumenical career started when he was a college student, said something most eloquent about this. Referring to the vitality of the Student Volunteer Movement thirty-three years after its foundation, Mott, one of the founders, said: "The true source of the vital energy of the Movement has been its relation, through the exercise of prayer, to the source of all life and power. The streams that turn the machinery of the world rise in solitary places—in the lives of individual students in communion with the Living God. The movement assumed visible, corporate expression in the never-to-be-forgotten gatherings for united prayer of the undergraduates at Mount Hermon" (Mott 1946, 199). Personally, I owe an immense debt to the Evangelical student movements, where I grasped for the first time the joyful experience of tasting the universality of the Church and the beauty and logic of Evangelical doctrine. But not only that. With them I learned the deep significance of commitment to a disciplined life of prayer.

I feel it is necessary here to qualify what I have said thus far about prayer. A few years ago I had to be an interpreter for a popular Korean pastor who in one of his sermons spoke about prayer and numerical church growth. To my astonishment he established an almost mechanical and mathematical correlation between the hours spent in prayer and the number of conversions added to his church. I understand that some missiologists are now doing the same in a more systematic manner and with the use of computers. This is not what I mean, and it is not what Paul says in this passage. Some of the missionaries who had a deep life of prayer and devotion and a unique commitment to their missionary task were not successful by numerical standards. Let me point, however, to a fact: regardless of statistics, I have seen in Korea, North America, Latin America and Europe, many churches and movements where a life of intense prayer is closely linked to missionary vitality.

Paul prepares to mobilize the church in Rome for mission by getting them to pray for him as he approaches critical days in Jerusalem. Similarly, it is interesting to observe in the Third World how total congregational participation in proclamational and service missions of the church is usually connected with mobilization in prayer. When I am in Mexico I try always to worship at Horeb Baptist Church, a lively congregation of some eight hundred Christians, where the ministry is carried on by a council of twenty deacons. The minister is Dr. Roland Gutierrez, lecturer in Philosophy at the Metropolitan University of Mexico and President of the Latin American Theological Fraternity. It is a missionary church that has set a goal of two thousand new churches for the year 2000. It is a church where people are mobilized for prayer!

Paul wanted the Roman Christians to pray for the problems he expected outside and inside the Church as he approached Jerusalem. Consistent with his theology of evangelism, he refers to those outside as "the disobedient," (a more literal translation than "unbelievers"), from whom he expected opposition and even persecution. He was going, like Daniel, to the lions' den, and he would need to be rescued. The record in Acts tells us the rest of the story (Acts 23:12–35). We do not know much about his success with the "saints" in Jerusalem. Morris makes the observation that probably he did not succeed. "Paul was regarded by some members of the Jerusalem church as a dangerous innovator, a man who was disobeying God by taking lightly the obligation to obey the law that God had given through his servant Moses ... The church at Jerusalem as a whole does not appear to have been very helpful and, for example, no assistance of any sort is recorded after the apostle's arrest" (Morris 1988, 524).

God answered Paul's prayer in an unexpected way. Eventually he arrived in Rome as a prisoner of the emperor, in the hands of the soldiers. But his desire to meet the believers in Rome with joy and be refreshed with them (v. 32) was still a joy that his Lord gave him in answer to their prayers (Acts 28:14–16). His mission there took another direction, even the penetration of the palace guard (Phil. 1:13), but probably he was not able to go to Spain. God had other plans for him. And Paul as a good servant was ready for whatever the Master wanted.

Today's surprises offer the Church in Latin America a host of new missiological challenges. Yet Paul's missionary vision remains a trustworthy guide. On the road into the next millennium the Church in Latin America needs to find new ways of proclaiming the Gospel of Jesus Christ, envisioning its calling, completing its task, and struggling for radical transformation of its reality.

## Notes

1. For a missiological reflection about new conditions in Latin America, see the special issue of *Missiology* 20, no. 2 (April 1992), about the theme "Columbus and the New World: Evangelization or Invasion."

2. An excellent summary of recent Pauline scholarship can be found in Bosch (1991b, 123-78).

# PART TWO

# THEOLOGICAL REFLECTIONS

# Introductory Overview

Where theological issues in missiology are raised, we are definitely on Glasser's turf. In 1970, when the ship of church growth at Fuller was listing heavy with anthropology, Art Glasser was brought on to give theological balance. One afternoon at a faculty meeting Art asked for a moment to make what he called a "theological observation." With a wry smile, President David Hubbard reminded Arthur that he is always theological, even when he is not thinking about it. But Glasser's theology is neither a spin on theory nor a game for the guild. Art is the incurable missionary, so his theologizing is habitually and by first love grounded in the missionary vision.

With this as his inspiration, Arthur works on a broad canvas. He finds his work difficult to finish because new ideas and fresh mediums of expression postpone that "final touch." His theological painting is always in process. The brushes are carefully chosen and expertly introduced. The Calvinistic strokes are strong but not overbearing. They blend beautifully with his love for Wesley and the Anabaptists. The ecumenical shades are exquisite in color and texture. It is rare, indeed, for one whose roots grew in a more separatistic tradition to learn from and share with both World Council and Roman Catholic thinkers. The ecumenical contributions in this volume are ample testimony to the consistent way he has interacted with the whole church.

The respect Arthur has for Johannes Verkuyl is transparent to us who work alongside him. Verkuyl shows how exacting it is to embrace an open approach to the religions when revelation through Jesus Christ and the scriptures are the uncompromisable authority. Human religious systems are at least indicators of common grace. But it is inconceivable that Christian missiologists could idealize about what is patently wrong in the "other religions" simply for the sake of dialogue. Art has done a lot of writing on this.

James Scherer shows how the ancient and reformation communions have reacted strongly against the current drift toward relativism in the WCC, especially with respect to the Trinity. Glasser and Scherer both would agree that any slant toward universalism, however benign, must be rejected in kingdom theology. Art would support fully the way Orthodox and Lutheran churches have pushed the WCC on issues concerning the Trinity. Glasser places the King high above all other allegiances, so he would also reject, with Scherer, any haziness around the lordship of Jesus Christ.

As I was reviewing David Bosch's chapter in April 1992, Arthur broke into my office with the awful news of David's death. I shall never forget how startling that coincidence was. Art wanted to read the Bosch chapter immediately, because in my initial shock I let it slip that this may be the last piece David published before his death. (Now Art knows why I kept him from reading it!) Bosch and Glasser had spent a lot of time together, which includes a memorable year when Art studied at UNISA in the late 70s.

David Bosch's straightforward analysis of church-state models is "Glassarian" in style, and Bosch's conclusions fit Art beautifully: Let the church's relationship to the state be catholic in its substance, evangelical in its principles, socially active and prophetic in witness.

All who know Harvie Conn appreciate his personal involvement in the city. The Bible is replete with reflections on the good and the evil of the city. Appropriately, Conn sees missiology and theology coming together in urban missiology. Conn's careful biblical work on the city recalls how eloquently Glasser utilizes the Old Testament in developing the motif of Babel as a far-reaching missiological component of kingdom theology. At no time has the city so impacted our missiology. The city, as place, process and power, leads to the ultimate question, "Who is the Lord of the city?"

D. S. G.

# 5

# The Biblical Notion of Kingdom

*Test of Validity for Theology of Religion*

## JOHANNES VERKUYL

A well-known American sociologist has written recently that nowadays both evangelicals and ecumenicals in America and Europe are fully aware that the place they presently occupy is squarely located within the pluralistic "pressure cooker" of the modern Western world. I find this to be an apt metaphor and suspect, moreover, that the pressure involved in this situation will continue to mount. Next year will mark the 100th anniversary of the World's Parliament of Religions, which was held in Chicago in connection with the Columbian Exposition in September of 1893. In his 1992 book, *Pilgrimage of Hope: One Hundred Years of Global Interfaith Dialogue* Marcus Braybrooke rings in the celebration of this centennial and surveys a large number of historical and contemporary models of what today is often termed *theologia religionum*. The theme of the 1993 centenary, interfaith dialogue, figures strongly in present discussions within theology of religion and is being elaborated along the lines of both very old and very new projects of interreligious mutuality.

Clearly, the subject is of great theological interest. Its timeliness is not, however, solely of a theoretical nature. One need only call to mind the myriad eruptions of religiously inspired fanaticism, conflict and violence pervading our present world to realize that this theme has an extraordinarily direct bearing on the events of everyday global news. Within the limits of the scope of this essay I can, of course, do no more than delineate a number of fundamental considerations that in my view must be taken

Johannes Verkuyl, missionary and theological professor in Indonesia 1939-1963, was Professor and Department Head of Missiology and Evangelism at the Free University of Amsterdam 1968-1978. He has authored a great many books, such as *Contemporary Missiology: An Introduction* (1978). This chapter was translated by Jerald Gort.

account of in any theological formulation respecting the proper relationship between Christianity and other religious faiths. Before moving on to the main part of this composition — a consideration of the implications the biblical notion of Kingdom bears for *theologia religionum* — I should like to give a brief account of my understanding of the concepts *Gospel of the Kingdom* and *Kingdom-centered theology*.

## The Gospel of the Kingdom

The heart of the message of the Old and New Testament is that God, the Creator of the universe and all earthly life, is actively engaged in the reestablishment of His liberating dominion over the cosmos and all of humankind. In seeking out Israel, He sought all of us and our entire world, and in Jesus Christ He laid the foundation of the Kingdom. Jesus Christ, the Messiah "promised to the fathers," is the *auto basileia*: in Him the Kingdom has both come and is coming. In the person, the words and deeds of Jesus, in His life, His death, and His resurrection, the Kingdom of God has come, is present, and is coming in an absolutely unique way and with exceptional clarity. In His preaching Jesus divulges the riches, the *thesaurus* of that Kingdom: reconciliation, the forgiveness of sins, victory over demonic powers. Standing within the tradition of Mosaic law, He expounds the core message of the *Thora* and the prophets; He accomplishes the reconciliation of the world to God; He opens the way to the present and future Kingdom which demands decisions of us in all aspects of life.

## Kingdom-Centered Theology

A Kingdom-centered theology worthy of the name is concerned with every aspect of life and society. Often in the history of the Church and theology Jesus has been — and in some cases continues to be — proclaimed *without* His Kingdom. In the face of that kind of proclamation, it should not come as a surprise to discover people attempting to find the Kingdom and salvation without Christ. A truly Kingdom-centered theology is a thoroughly trinitarian one; it is a theology which has God the Creator, the Redeemer, and the Comforter at its very heart. This kind of theology may never disregard the biblical message of the forgiveness of sins and thus can never neglect the call for the conversion of persons among all peoples and religious communities. To everyone of whatever religious persuasion the message must be repeated: "The Kingdom of God is at hand; repent, and believe in the Gospel." In no circumstances may the Evangel be proclaimed in a neutral way. The Gospel always involves decision. The pearl of great value must be sought with singlehearted diligence and is obtained, like the treasure hidden in the field, at the cost of all else. Kingdom-centered theology entails a call to recognition of the lordship of the King and new orientation to the constitution of His Kingdom. In the absence of this aspect, proclamation of the good news of the Gospel is impossible. A theology and missiology informed by the biblical notion of the rule of Christ will never fail to identify personal conversion as one of the inclusive goals of God's Kingdom.

The good news of the Kingdom also has to do with the formation and in-depth growth of the Body of Christ throughout the world and to the end of time. As the World Council of Churches publication, *Mission and Evangelism: An Ecumenical Affirmation* (World Council of Churches 1983a) rightly avers, the planting, upbuilding and extension of churches among all peoples and amid all religious and secular communities must always be viewed as one of the ongoing inclusive aims of missionary activity. The Kingdom is, of course, far broader than the Church alone. God's Kingdom is all-embracing in respect of both point of view and purpose; it signifies the consummation of the whole of history; it has cosmic proportions and fulfills time and eternity. Meanwhile, the Church, the believing and active community of Christ, is raised up by God among all nations to share in the salvation and suffering service of the Kingdom. The Church consists of those whom God has called to stand at His side to act out with Him the drama of the revelation of the Kingdom come and coming.

The Church constitutes the firstling, the early harvest of the Kingdom. Thus, though not *limited* to the Church, the Kingdom is unthinkable *without* the Church. Conversely, growth and expansion of the Church should not be viewed as ends but rather as means to be used in the service of the Kingdom. The Church, in other words, is not a goal in and of itself; but neither is it — as some at present would seem to imply — a contemptible entity that should feel ashamed of its calling and seek its redemption in self-destruction. The keys of the Kingdom have been given to the Church. It does not fulfill its mandate by relinquishing those keys but rather by using them to open up the avenues of approach to the Kingdom for all peoples and all population groups at every level of human society. It makes no biblical sense whatever to deny, as many do, that the upbuilding of the Church everywhere in the world is a proper concern of the proclamation of the good news of the Gospel; and it is high time for a forthright repudiation of such nonsense.

Finally, the gospel of the Kingdom addresses itself to all immediate human need, both physical and mental. It aims to right what is wrong on earth. It enjoins engagement in the struggle for racial, social, cultural, economic and political justice. Kingdom-centered missiology frees us from the sham dilemmas responsible for much of historical and present evangelical-ecumenical divarication, delivers us from the theological zero-sum game involving false, unbiblical dichotomies between individual and corporate *shalom*, vertical and horizontal reconciliation, word proclamation and comprehensive approach, witness and service, micro- and macro-structural concerns, and so forth. The good news of the Kingdom has to do with all of these things. For that reason missiology must bend its efforts to the erection of a multiplicity of visible signs of God's Kingdom throughout the length and breadth of this planet. That is, it must commit itself to the task of equipping the new humanity for the journey to its final destination. It is against the background of the foregoing that I will attempt to outline the implications of a truly Kingdom-centered missiology for theology of religion. Unfortunately it is beyond the scope of this essay to give an overview of the various models of *theologia religionum* that prevail today. The reader may consult the extensive literature produced lately on the subject. In 1978 I made an attempt to develop the parameters of a trinitarian theology of religion in *Contemporary Missiology: An Introduction* (Verkuyl 1978, 341–372) but it would be useful to give a new overview of the prevailing models. In the following pages I will try to write only *some notes* for a kingdom-centered theology of religion within the scope of this essay.

## Notes for a Kingdom-Centered Theology of Religion

The late M. A. C. Warren, one of the most keenly sensitive missiologists of the post-Second World War period, often wrote of the great need for a "theology of attention." My purpose here is simply to call attention to a number of issues that need to be taken into account in any attempt to formulate an appropriate, that is to say, biblically responsible, *theologia religionum*.

### General Revelation: God the Creator

Most of the churches of the Reformation hold to creeds that profess belief in God the Creator who has revealed Himself in every age and place in divers ways in both nature and history, the God who is engaged in a love affair with every human person and the whole of humanity. What Paul wrote down in Romans 1 and 2 establishes this as a primeval fact, a given with which we must reckon when reflecting on the divine-human encounter and the totality of the spiritual history of humankind. I count myself among those who owe much to the person and theology of Karl Barth, but I cannot accept everything he taught in his magisterial *Kirchliche Dogmatik*. One of his serious weaknesses was that for most of his working life he turned a blind eye to what Calvin and all the other Reformers called *general revelation*. It was only toward the end of his days that his thinking on this matter began to evolve in a different direction. In this regard Hendrik Kraemer, it should be noted, was by no means a Barthian; he always recognized and espoused the concept of God's general revelation.

Among other things, religions are, in one way or another, echoes of, answers to, God's general revelational activity. That is, of course, by no means the same as saying that such echoes and answers are *deposits* of this revelation, which would represent a total vitiation of the teaching of Romans 1:19–23. There we read that although God has enlightened us humans from the beginning by plainly showing us what can be known about Him, we suppress the truth in our reaction to this divine self-disclosure, whereby our minds become darkened: we exchange contact with the living God for the worship and service of idols. Paul's words in this passage ring strikingly true. The history of religions is the history of God seeking people and people fleeing God. This analysis, however, in no way releases us from the obligation, both in our study of the religions and in our personal contacts with people of other faiths, to be open to the discovery of signs of the divine-human relationship.

Whenever we enter the domain of another religious community, whether through study or in actuality, we must be fully conscious of the fact that God has been there long before our arrival and that we find ourselves in the arena of divine-human encounter. J. H. Bavinck, whom I was privileged to succeed at the Free University, provided a profound demonstration of such openness in his classic study, *Religieus Besef en Christelijk Geloof* (1949). Notwithstanding this, however, we ought never to lose sight of the equally important fact that there is no continuity between the religious traditions of the human race and God's revelation, but rather only between the revelation of God the Creator and that of God the Savior in Israel and in Jesus Christ. This given may not be ignored in any discussion of continuity and discontinuity.

### Common Grace: God's Patience

It has been and still is not uncommon in certain Christian circles to judge the religious life of others solely in terms of the wrath of God. Certainly, Paul does speak of God's wrath in connection with human religiosity, and the Old Testament witnesses repeatedly to the trials of prophets caught in the middle of the struggle between the true God and the false gods. But this same Bible also teaches the patience and forbearance of God in His dealings with humanity in all of its activities and with individual people in their every circumstance. Who could fail to see evidence of the clemency of God in the fact that the great religions have created forms of human community that have provided for a certain amount of regularity and order in the lives of whole peoples? Who could fail to recognize the presence of God's compassion in the humanizing of social relationships brought about by the great religious systems of the world? Who would dare to deny the workings of God's mercy in the development of ideas and the refinement of human thought inspired by these religions? Who would not view it as a proof of God's grace that the peoples of the world, though ignorant of the law of God, accept and do things that are in accordance with that law?

### The Light of the World: Jesus Christ

Jesus Christ, and He alone, is the Light of the world. That Light cannot be compared with anything or anyone (cf. Isaiah 40:18), nor can it be combined, mingled or blended with other so-called light. It is not susceptible of etiolation or attenuation by putative rival lights. It is surpassingly incandescent and can be outshone by no other light, whether in terms of the quantity or the quality of the leniency, the grace, the love that has been and shall be revealed in it. Jesus Christ is not a light but *the* Light. And we must be fully prepared to discover radiant beams of that Light in the religious life of people of other faiths. Melchizedek and Job and Balaam and a host of others who—far beyond the borders of Israel—saw the light of Israel's God, witness to the fact that through the working of the Holy Spirit all religions everywhere are shot through with efficacious shafts of the light of Christ. Never in my life have I met a single missionary from any continent who has not experienced something of this. In every inter-religious encounter and on every occasion of witnessing, at all times and in all places it behooves us to be sharply watchful for the presence and activity of *Christus Prolongatus*, not excluding those times and places when and where we might least expect to meet Him. For His light knows no bounds and fears no obstacle, not even the profundity of darkness, the hellish pit itself.

### Autosoteriology and Spurious Saviors

People everywhere are irrepressibly religious. Throughout its history humankind has been engaged in a quest for the restoration of the broken relationship with God. The Bible, for example Romans 1–3, speaks of the results to which a solely human quest inevitably leads: the fashioning of idols, the attempt to achieve self-deliverance (*autosoteria*), the creation of fantasized mythical saviors, a blind casting about in search of the Divine. Any Christian thinker who wishes to deal appropriately with the other religions, however, will make a genuine effort to understand something of the mystery of this uncertain religious groping on the part of the peoples of the world, in the humble acknowledgment that each one of us tends toward the worship of false gods and often succumbs to the lure of self-redemption. Processions of idols move through the streets of all places of human habitation, whether they be found in areas informed by the traditions of the great religions or in those shot through with secularism or postmodernism.

### The Cross of Jesus Christ

A truly Kingdom-centered theology of religion will be a *theologia crucis*, a theology of the Cross. What Paul writes in 1 Corinthians 1:18–20 can only be understood as an unequivocal judgment of the autosoteriological strivings of humankind. And this clear biblical teaching cannot but constitute one of the central themes of any Kingdom-centered approach to other religions. The way of the Cross as the way of reconciliation between God and people may never be muted in interreligious encounter in a misguided attempt to "give no offense." The paramountcy of Jesus Christ the crucified and risen Lord may never be called into question. He may never be shunted aside, never be deposed from his position as the only Way leading to God's Kingdom. It should be made clear that we are not advocating a reductionistic Christo*monism* here, which would fly in the face of all three main articles of the Apostle's Creed. What is being argued is the need for solid trinitarian commitment in theology. A theocentric theology that is not simultaneously Christocentric simply cannot be termed Christian theology. Any *theologia religionum* that is ashamed of the name of Jesus ought to be deeply ashamed of *itself*. There is no Kingdom without the King: no other gods, no other name.

### The Holy Spirit, Church, and Eschatology

A theology of religion informed by the biblical concept of the Kingdom will also include room for explicit reflection on the work of the Holy Spirit, who "blows where he wills" in the world and in the Church. In this kind of *theologia religionum* the Church will be viewed rightly as the Spirit-imbued Body of Christ, the provisional ingathering of the people of God from among all nations, the servant of the coming Kingdom, and therefore as a celebratory, diaconal and missionary community. Moreover, any truly Kingdom-centered theology of religion will be suffused by *expectant eschatology*, a childlike trust in the realization of God's salvific purposes, and consequently will not fail to draw out the implications of this surety for human justice *in concreto* here and now.

### Communication of the Gospel

The subversion of the missionary mandate one encounters in various contemporary missiologies and models of theology of religion must simply be called what it is: betrayal of Jesus Christ. It is incumbent on every Christian to give assent to the ongoing necessity of the missionary task. Of course, the definition and interpretation of mission is never an indifferent matter. It is surely obvious that the understanding of this vocation must always be biblically qualified. According to the New Testament, the mission of the Church can only be mission *in Christ's way*, as the San Antonio conference so strikingly put it. But if such calls to Gospel communication are not attended by factual missionary activity reaching unto the ends of the earth, they are more vain than vanity itself. It is important to heed the pleas of those who advocate an interpretation of the Gospel in terms of the cultural-linguistic idiom of a given context, but if appeals of this kind are not accompanied by active witness to Christ, they are less than useless.

It goes without saying that Christians must be fully prepared to be enriched and even transformed by those to whom they communicate the Gospel. Likewise, the fact that other religions, too, claim uniqueness and finality must be kept in mind and seriously taken to heart. But this may never lead to feelings of shame or discomfiture with respect to the truth claim of Jesus of Nazareth or to resignation of our calling as ambassadors of God in Christ. In my handbook on missiology I have dealt with each of the missionary mandates found in the four gospels and the Acts of the Apostles, and these biblical commissions have been examined even more extensively and with far greater exegetical and hermeneutical skills by the late David Bosch in his magnum opus entitled *Transforming Mission: Paradigm Shifts in Theology of Mission* (1991b). Proponents of a genuinely Kingdom-centered theology of religion will be filled with a yearning to encourage young people to be obedient to the King and His mandate, for the gospel of the Kingdom must be proclaimed to all nations throughout the entire earth, and then the end will come (cf. Mt. 24:14).

## Kingdom-Oriented Dialogue with People of Other Faiths

In his book referred to at the beginning of this paper, Marcus Braybrooke lists a number of organizations that advocate a renewal of emphasis on the parliamentary style of dialogue. It is encouraging that already some years ago Diana Eck, the former moderator of the WCC Commission on Dialogue, rejected this form of dialogical encounter on the grounds that it proceeds on the assumption that truth can be determined by majority vote and that it implies that all religious faiths are branches or variations of one universal basic religion (World Council of Churches 1987, 5ff.). Dialogue between adherents of differing faiths for the purpose of removing prejudice and misinterpretation is both valuable and necessary as a catalyst of greater mutual understanding and fair, honest representation of the various religious convictions involved. Also of great importance is dialogue that has as its aim cooperation in social, economic, cultural and political matters that are or ought to be the common concern of all people of good will. But in addition to this, Kingdom-oriented theology of religion requires the type of dialogue in which a true exchange of information regarding deeply held convictions takes place, one in which each of the partners *listens* most attentively to the other's articulation of beliefs concerning the fundamental questions of life and death and tries, in turn, to *convince* the other of the worthiness and truth of the core message to which he or she has given assent. I prefer to call this *trialogue*, that is to say, interreligious conversational encounter and confrontation in the holy presence of God, the third partner. Any theology of religion that fails to abet this third kind of dialogue can only be characterized as hopelessly impoverished.

With an eye to the centenary of the Parliament of Religions in 1993, many global organizations have been making a plea for a "year of understanding," a "year of cooperation." But dialogues to promote understanding or cooperation do not have the capacity for penetrating to the existential roots of human life and the depth dimensions of human society. One gains access to these fundamental areas only by addressing the deepest questions and tapping the most profound sources. There are some today who call for a "dialogue of life," and indeed this is what is needed. Successful encounters of this nature, however, require a great deal of careful, patient and dedicated endeavor. They will always be difficult to achieve within the context of institutional dialogues such as those between the Vatican or the WCC and international Jewish, Muslim or Buddhist organizations, for gatherings of this sort are in the very nature of the case elitist. They constitute occasions for the meeting of highly educated people whose participation in such discussions is wholly determined by their identity as official representatives of a given religion.

In my experience only those interreligious encounters founded in deep, personal and lasting friendships, only those contacts that take place at the level where heart meets heart are worthy of the name "dialogue of life," because only they are capable of touching the deepest levels of human existence. This conviction is unmistakably corroborated by the witness of veteran practitioners of dialogue such as Kenneth Cragg, e.g., in *The Call of the Minaret* (1956) and *Sandals at the Mosque* (1959); George Appleton, who worked in Burma for many years and became that country's first postindependence minister of education; and Lamin Sanneh, who as a young man converted from Islam to Christianity. Eugene R. Borowitz, too, argues cogently in his important book, *Contemporary Christologies: A Jewish Response* (1980), that it is only by means of direct encounter and confrontation at the level of our deepest differences that we come to know each other fully and thus establish the basis for authentic reciprocal friendship. I know evangelical Christians who are totally opposed to dialogue of whatever stripe. Aversion to certain kinds of dialogue seems reasonable; but it remains a great mystery to me as a missionary how one could reject each and every form of dialogue. Fortunately, most evangelicals do not acquiesce in that wholesale rejection; some, in fact, have been and are masters of dialogical exchange.

Missiological students and others preparing themselves for work in mission must be provided with specific training to help them prepare for participation in dialogues of mutual witness. And such pedagogues for dialogue must be underpinned by an evangelical-ecumenical *theologia gloria, gratiae et oboedientiae.* In other words, it must be undergirded by a theology in which the Father and the Son and the Holy Spirit are accorded the full honor due to them, in which the Reformation insight "by grace alone" takes permanent pride of place, and in which obedience to the missionary mandate figures prominently. With regard to this latter aspect, it behooves us to take careful note of the trenchant observation made by Gerald H. Anderson in the *International Bulletin of Missionary Research* (1991b) that the explosive growth in the number of missiological publications in recent years has unfortunately not been accompanied by a corollary increase in actual missionary involvement. It is my fond hope that institutions such as the School of World Mission in Pasadena will continue to produce large numbers of graduates who, by the quality and intensity of their participation in dialogical encounter (and, if necessary, confrontation with adherents of other religious faiths and ideologies throughout the length and breadth of the earth) prove themselves to be well-equipped, ardent servants of the Kingdom of God.

### Religious Freedom and Kingdom-Oriented *Theologia Religionum*

Fulfillment of the calling to communicate the Gospel of the Kingdom in word and deed is not dependent on national or international legal systems guaranteeing freedom of conscience, expression, and worship, or the freedom to engage in missionary activity and to change religious affiliation. The history of Christian mission is replete with striking examples which prove that even without the protection of law and in the face of persecution, ostracism and martyrdom, the proclamation of the Gospel amid religious, ideologically determined and indeed atheistic communities was, is and will continue to be possible. Nevertheless, governments and international authorities have an obligation to promote and protect full religious freedom. The First Amendment to the Constitution of the United States is a bright monument to past and present struggles to achieve such protection, as is the Universal Declaration of Human Rights adopted by the United Nations in 1948. My impression is that in the period immediately following World War II the churches and the international community were much more active than they are now in the pursuit of universal religious freedom. Meanwhile, in many parts of the world, threats to this fundamental right are gaining force day by day.

The realization of human rights is at one and the same time a goal of and an important aid to the communication of the Gospel of the Kingdom among all nations. With regard to the latter a clear distinction must be drawn between essential and peripheral conditionality. The spread of the Gospel does not *depend* on the existence of religious liberty. Nevertheless, freedom of conscience and expression obviously do constitute a significant precondition for unrestricted witness, unimpeded trialogue and the formulation of a truly Kingdom-centered theology of religion. John Milton, one of those who fought for freedom of conscience, wrote that the crown of reward for the establishment of human liberty is sought in vain on the head of emperors, kings and popes but readily found positioned above the constitutions drawn up by free citizens. What the world stands in need of today is an open, receptive and active evangelical-ecumenical Christianity, which seeks by all legitimate means to influence the creation of adequate room for the untrammeled advance of the Gospel of the Kingdom among all peoples, sufficient space for mission in, to and from all six continents. Concern to maintain an open door for the Gospel is just as needful in the present period as it was in the years immediately subsequent to the Second World War. The battle against fanaticism and coercion, on the one hand, and *pro libertate et religione*, on the other, must be joined or continued unabated in every part of the world. The time for attentive wakefulness is here, the *kairos* for committed action has arrived.

## A Brief Concluding Remark

My purpose in this essay was to argue the essential importance of a Kingdom-centered approach for any *theologia religionum* that is meant to be both relevant to the context of the present world and consistent with the biblical message concerning the salvation offered by God, wrought by Christ, and made operative by the Holy Spirit. Appropriate theology of religion will take full account of existing religious realities, on the one hand, and the universal significance of the Gospel of God's Kingdom in Christ Jesus, on the other.

## 6

# Church, Kingdom, and *Missio Dei*

*Lutheran and Orthodox Correctives to Recent Ecumenical
Mission Theology*

## JAMES A. SCHERER

One of the crucial missiological problems of the second half of the twentieth century has been how to accomplish a successful transition from an earlier *church-centered* theology of mission to a *kingdom-oriented* one without loss of missionary vision or betrayal of biblical content. It can scarcely be denied that we are in the midst of such a transition. It is equally clear that we have not yet fully grasped the meaning of a move toward the *kingdom* orientation, which closely correlates with the trinitarian *Missio Dei* viewpoint that gained currency in the 1950s. The fuller implications of this changeover for our missionary practice still lie in the future.

The latter half of the nineteenth century and the first half of the twentieth were largely dominated by the church-centered concept as the practical goal for what were then called "foreign missions." Church-centrism replaced earlier individualistic mission theories derived from pietism and evangelical revivalism that focused on personal conversion (*conversio gentium*) and "soul-saving." The new church-centered view, prominent around the middle of the nineteenth century through the work of Henry Venn and Rufus Anderson (cf. Warren 1971; Shenk 1983; Beaver 1967), set forth the view that "church planting" — especially the planting of local "three-self" churches with their own autonomy and indigeneity — should be considered, alongside personal conversion, an important goal of missions. The acknowl-

James A. Scherer, a missionary in China and Japan, later became Professor of World Mission and Church History at the Lutheran School of Theology at Chicago and is now Professor Emeritus. He has served in various capacities with the American Society of Missiology.

edged "father" of mission science, Gustav Warneck, could declare that mission activity was "the road from [existing] church to church [in the mission field]" (cf. Duerr 1947). By 1900 foreign mission work came to be understood more and more as church extension overseas.

The World Mission Conference at Edinburgh (1910), echoing the report of the Shanghai Missionary Conference (1907), declared prophetically in its commission report on Christian unity that the goal of missionary activity was the planting in each nation of a single united church representing the best elements of that society's culture.[1] It did not say, and could not really imagine, how this ecumenical vision was to be achieved. By the time of the Tambaram-Madras Meeting of the International Missionary Council (1938), it was widely accepted that the local church, and not the foreign mission, was the single most important instrument in world evangelism (International Missionary Council, 1939). Accordingly, mission agencies were called on to lend their support to the growth and missionary outreach of the "younger churches" they had helped to create.

The Whitby IMC Meeting (1948) put its stamp of approval on this global church-centered mission development with its slogan "partnership in obedience" between older and younger churches in fulfilling the unfinished evangelistic task (Ranson 1948). A few years later, however, at the Willingen IMC Meeting (1952), the report on the "Missionary Obligation of the Church" declared that "God sends forth the Church to carry out His work to the ends of the earth, to all nations, and to the end of time" (*The Missionary Obligation of the Church* 1952, 1–5). The church-centered perspective was being challenged at Willingen by other viewpoints, as we shall see, but within the IMC it still held center stage.

In the period between the Second World Assembly of the WCC at Evanston (1954) and the Third World Assembly at New Delhi (1961), the WCC and the IMC were moving steadily and in concert, despite some opposition, toward the integration of the International Missionary Council into the WCC as its Commission on World Mission and Evangelism (CWME). The merger was formally consummated at New Delhi. This act of structural integration and the theological arguments advanced in support of it (viz. that missions would now fully receive the support of the churches, and that churches would take their missionary vocation more seriously) represented the culmination, but also the beginning of the end, of the church-centered missionary view. Lesslie Newbigin's IMC staff paper entitled "One Body, One Gospel, One World" (1958), and the "six continent mission" slogan of the first CWME Consultation at Mexico City (1963), represent a kind of watershed between the older church-centered mission framework and the emerging kingdom-oriented pattern.[2]

Before exploring the kingdom-oriented philosophy of mission, let us examine some deeper reasons for the decline of the church-centered pattern. From 1860 to 1960 the church-centered goal of mission served a very useful purpose in replacing the earlier missionary pattern of individual conversions, in that it clearly defined the necessary steps toward planting churches among all nations. But as the task of church-planting advanced in all six continents, it was rapidly becoming obsolete as a missionary goal. Moreover, as political emancipation from western colonialism occurred in newly independent countries of the third world, local church autonomy was a foregone conclusion.

Additionally, the church-centric pattern of mission work did not fully reflect the biblical witness about Christian mission as found in the New Testament. The "three-self" formula for church autonomy accurately mirrored western Protestant, middle-class, democratic and capitalist values of self-government, self-support and local responsibility. However, it was silent about Jesus' love for the poor and his identification with the marginal and the oppressed. Such persons were viewed more as candidates for missionary charity than as potential members of local "three-self" churches.

Again, the church-centered model espoused by western mission theorists opened the door to fierce (though unintended) denominational competition and rivalry between western missions in seeking converts and planting churches.[3] Unfortunately, it was not seen until much later that naming the name of "one Lord" and proclaiming "one faith" and "one baptism" in the mission situation involved stark contradictions between the missionary ideal and actual practice. In time these contradictions would demand correctives in terms of missionary cooperation and common witness.

The church-centered model also suffered from a serious theological flaw: it possessed no clear *eschatological* perspective. It soon became clear that it was not enough to plant churches where they did not already exist. What was the *purpose* of these churches, and what was their function in the mission of God? For if newly planted mission churches had no real vision of their purpose except as outposts of foreign religious agencies — dependent on them for nurture, maintenance, and inspiration — planting them in all nations could hardly be justified. The third of the three "selves" — *self-extension* (sometimes "propagation") — received far too little actual attention. Moreover, the emerging issue of contextuality was only primitively discerned in this period.

The ongoing pursuit of the unfinished missionary task by churches in the whole world — "Calling the Whole Church to Take the Whole Gospel to the Whole World," as Lausanne II at Manila rightly put it — demanded clear answers to several questions: the meaning of the "whole gospel," the scope of the "whole world," and the urgent issue of how the "whole church" might carry out its mission in unity.[4] None of these concepts could properly be resolved apart from the eschatologically grounded *kingdom* context of the mission of the Triune God. For it is the pressure of God's coming kingdom which impels the Christian community to define the content and method of its gospel invitation, to identify the frontiers for its witness and service, and to coordinate its resources for authentic and credible common witness in the "time between."

"Proclaim Christ Until He Comes," declared Lausanne II. This eschatological context belongs to the very nature of biblical mission—viz. that the gospel of the kingdom must first be proclaimed throughout the whole world as a witness to all nations (Matt. 24:14), and this not tied to any particular view of dispensationalism. Lausanne II aroused expectation that this crucial eschatological theme would be fully explored, but in the end it said little that was not already stated in the *Lausanne Covenant*.

The gospel proclaimed by Jesus at the start of his ministry was the "gospel of God," a gospel about the "fulfillment of time" and the approach of the "kingdom of God," calling human beings to repent and believe (Mark 1:15). It was not a gospel created by and owned by the *church* or its mission enterprise, but a gospel which called the church into being and gave it, in and through Christ, a spirit-filled missionary existence. It is, therefore, impossible to speak of the *church's* mission apart from the mission of the Triune God—*Missio Dei*—or apart from a fully trinitarian theological standpoint. After Willingen (1952), the church-centered mission framework—largely the creature of nineteenth-century western mission agencies—was no longer adequate for dealing with the problems facing churches engaged in mission *in*, *from* and *to* all six continents in the post-colonial era. Those problems required a *Missio Dei* response, with a clearer understanding of the trinitarian basis and nature of the church's mission, and an openness and sensitivity to the eschatological character of the kingdom, and the church's subordinate relationship to it (cf. "Missio Dei" 1971 and "Missio Dei" 1991).

Abandoning the church-centered framework in no way implies forsaking the church's mission, but rather a revisioning of that mission from a fresh biblical, missiological, and above all, eschatological point of view. This remains a priority task for the theology of Christian mission today.

Despite earlier favorable signs pointing toward a successful transition from the church-centered to a fully trinitarian understanding of mission after Willingen, above all the brilliant work done by the Advisory Committee on the theme of the Second WCC Assembly at Evanston (1954)—"Christ—the Hope of the World"—the goal was not easily attained. The road forward proved to be strewn with traps and mine fields, partly connected with wrong interpretations of *Missio Dei*. For in the decade of the 1960s, *Missio Dei* was to become the plaything of armchair theologians with little more than an academic interest in the practical mission of the church but with a considerable penchant for theological speculation and mischief making.

Following the Mexico City CWME meeting (1963), armchair mission strategists from Western Europe and the United States, operating under a mandate to examine the "missionary structure of the local congregation" in the period before Uppsala (1968), came forward with a radically different and fundamentally nontrinitarian understanding of *Missio Dei*.[5] This new view was actually a secular reworking of the trinitarian *Missio Dei* concept.

God was seen to be working out the divine purpose in the midst of the world through immanent, intra-mundane historical forces, above all secularization. The trinitarian *Missio Dei* view was replaced by a theory about the transformation of the world and of history not through evangelization and church-planting but by means of a divinely guided immanent historical process, somewhat analogous to deistic views of the Enlightenment. This secular view of God's mission made the empirical church virtually dispensable as an agent of divine mission, and in some cases even a hindrance.

The underlying philosophy of the ecumenical study, published in a report bearing the beguiling title *The Church for Others*,[6] was that the *world* set the agenda for the church, and that the real locus of God's mission was no longer the church but the world. Accordingly, the church must now receive its marching orders from the world. At the 1968 Uppsala Assembly of the WCC, the section report on "Renewal in Mission" declared that the mission of God was "the invitation to men to grow up into their full humanity in the new man, Jesus Christ." Humanization was the new keyword, and the new mission fields were described as being centers of power, revolutionary movements, the university, and so forth (World Council of Churches 1968a, 27ff.).

Lutherans had initially given their support to the *Missio Dei* view, seeing it as a way of moving beyond the *church-centered* framework toward a more comprehensive basis for mission. A Lutheran missiologist, Georg Vicedom (1965), helped to popularize the idea of *Missio Dei* in a book bearing that title. God's mission was, after all, not coterminous with the work of the church but included other important dimensions, especially those related to divine creation, order and justice. However, when the secularizing, horizontalist interpretation of *Missio Dei* in the *Church for Others* was put forth, Lutherans felt obliged to critique it theologically and practically at a consultation organized by the Lutheran World Federation just prior to the Uppsala assembly. The Lutheran response to the ecumenical report on missionary structures criticized the theological basis underlying *The Church for Others* as being one-sided and excessively negative in its attitude toward the church.[7] Some twenty years later a 1988 Lutheran statement on the theology of mission set forth a firmly trinitarian line, affirming the mission of God the Creator as providing "the foundation and promise for our world and all its peoples," "the sending of Christ for the salvation of the world [as] the center point of God's mission in history," and the "Holy Spirit [who] sends and enables God's people in every age for participation in mission."[8]

The decisive turning point in the development of ecumenical mission theology was only reached, however, with the entry of Eastern Orthodox theologians into that discussion early in the 1970s.[9] Orthodox tradition had always demonstrated a firm commitment to trinitarian theology, and it possessed an implicitly *Missio Dei* view of mission. Unfortunately, however, Orthodoxy's important contribution to ecumenical mission theology was

delayed because of the widely held Orthodox view that western missions —
both Protestant and Roman Catholic — represented foreign incursions into
traditional Orthodox areas for the purpose of proselytizing Orthodox
believers. Aggressive mission efforts were condemned as unspiritual and
inimical to Orthodoxy. Mission theology in the ecumenical movement was
viewed as a Protestant preoccupation, slighting Orthodox teaching and
holding little interest for Orthodoxy, which opposed the integration of the
International Missionary Council into the World Council of Churches at
New Delhi (1961).

Beginning after the Mexico City meeting (1963), but especially in the
1970s and 1980s, Orthodox theologians carefully and methodically brought
the force of their tradition to bear on the discussion of missiological issues.[10]
Orthodoxy's previous neglect of the "forgotten commandment" — the Great
Commission — now became a matter of profound concern, as Orthodox theologians carefully prepared theological statements on major themes of mission theology. An Orthodox desk was created within the CWME, along
with an Orthodox Advisory Commission that met annually to formulate
Orthodox responses to announced themes of ecumenical missionary conferences and WCC assemblies.

A dramatic change in the tenor of ecumenical missionary statements was
first observable in the report of Section I at the 1975 Nairobi WCC Assembly, which reflected an important Orthodox contribution (World Council
of Churches 1975). Nairobi 1975 also reflected the influence of the 1974
Lausanne Congress and the 1974 Roman Bishops' Synod on "Evangelization in the Modern World," followed in 1975 by the Apostolic Exhortation
of Paul VI known as "Evangelii Nuntiandi." Orthodox influence was again
clearly seen in drafts of the 1980 CWME Melbourne World Conference on
Mission and Evangelism, on the eschatological theme "Your Kingdom
Come" (World Council of Churches, 1980). Section III at Melbourne, "The
Church Witnesses to the Kingdom," accurately reflects Orthodoxy's view
of the church as a sign and instrument for witness within the purpose of
*Missio Dei*. The 1989 San Antonio CWME Conference, on the theme "Your
Will Be Done: Mission in Christ's Way," became an ideal vehicle for setting
forth enduring Orthodox concerns in the four conference section reports
dealing with conversion and witness, suffering and martyrdom, creation and
care of the earth, and the Christian community gathered for Eucharist and
scattering for mission in the world (World Council of Churches 1990).

The most important Orthodox contributions to recent mission theology
are gathered up in a small booklet entitled *Go Forth in Peace* (World Council of Churches 1986).[11] In these essays the value of Orthodox theology as
a corrective to weaknesses in ecumenical mission theology is readily apparent, especially with regard to the comprehensive trinitarian framework of
*Missio Dei*. The Orthodox vision of God's mission sees the salvation of the
world as the "program" of the holy trinity for creation. The kingdom of
God is the eschatological goal. Attention always focuses on the central act

of confessing the incarnate, crucified and risen Christ as the one who restores our broken communion with God. Such Orthodox perspectives can be enormously enriching for evangelical mission. The contention of this essay is that the special Orthodox contribution to ecumenical mission theology, at a decisive moment in the history of the ecumenical missionary movement, has helped to save ecumenical mission theology from serious aberration by bringing it back to solid moorings in scripture and apostolic tradition.[12]

## Notes

1. Cf. China Centenary Missionary Conference Records, Shanghai (1907). This recommendation had a strong impact on the 1910 Edinburgh World Missionary Conference.

2. Newbigin (1958), Orchard (1958), and Orchard (1964) also point to the transition from an older church-centric paradigm to a newer one.

3. This was incisively pointed out by Johannes C. Hoekendijk in several seminal essays, among them "The Call to Evangelism" (1950) and "The Church in Missionary Thinking" (1952). Hoekendijk brought his critique of church-centric missionary work to the 1952 IMC meeting but was not successful in overturning the conventional view at that time. See also J. C. Hoekendijk (1966).

4. Lausanne II in Manila, *Proclaim Christ Until He Comes: Calling the Whole Church to Take the Whole Gospel to the Whole World,* 1989 (1990) reflects a similar transition in the evangelical missionary movement from an individualistic toward an ecclesiological and kingdom-oriented understanding of mission.

5. This development is competently surveyed by Dietrich Werner (1991).

6. See World Council of Churches (1967) and Wieser (1966). Viewpoints expressed in both volumes strongly reflected the church-centric critiques of Johannes Hoekendijk noted above.

7. Cf. the devastating theological critique by East German Bishop Werner Krusche of positions taken in the missionary structure study found in the Lutheran response in World Council of Churches (1968b).

8. *Together in God's Mission: An LWF Contribution to the Understanding of Mission,* LWF Documentation no. 26 (Geneva: LWF 1988). The LWF statement, while echoing a trinitarian view of *Missio Dei,* unfortunately stopped short of exploring the implications of the kingdom for mission theology.

9. Cf. James A. Scherer and Stephen Bevans (1992a) and a parallel article by the same authors in *International Bulletin of Missionary Research* (1992b).

10. See the previous note for references to the sources of this change.

11. Essays deal with trinitarian foundations, the relation of church and mission, eucharistic liturgy as the focal point of mission, scripture, forms of evangelism, and mission as "liturgy after the liturgy."

12. Although not referred to here, the WCC's "Ecumenical Affirmation: Mission and Evangelism" (1983a) is another excellent illustration of the balancing and stabilizing influence of Orthodox theology within the ecumenical movement.

# 7

# God's Reign and the Rulers of This World

*Missiological Reflections on Church-State Relationships*

### DAVID J. BOSCH

From the moment of its birth, the Christian mission has had to deal with civil authorities and find ways of coexisting with them without compromising its very nature. It has done so in at least five different ways.

In drawing the contours of these five traditions, I will, sometimes, illustrate what I say with reference to my own country, South Africa—not only because this is the situation I know best, but also since specificity in one instance may also help us relate what we hear to other situations.

## Christian Missionary Attitudes toward the State

The five traditions may be termed "Constantinian," "pietist," "reformist," "liberationist" and "anabaptist." It is not possible to divide them neatly between the different ecclesiastical traditions. Although a specific denomination may reveal a penchant to one particular model, it has to be remembered that individuals and groups *within* denominations may adhere to different models. I am therefore using the categories *sociologically* rather than theologically. In addition, the models are rarely found in pure form; in most situations one encounters a mix of two or more.

The *Constantinian* model presupposes a *close alliance between a particular religious organization and the state*. Metaphorically speaking, a liaison develops between "throne" and "altar," as happened after Constantine legalized

---

The late David Bosch was a missionary in the Transkei (South Africa) for 17 years before accepting an appointment as Professor in Missiology at Unisa in 1971. He authored numerous books, including *Witness to the World* (1980) and *Transforming Mission* (1991b).

the Christian religion in the fourth century C.E. This model is to be found wherever there is a tendency to regard the *task* of church (or mission) and state to be almost identical, their *enemies* to be the same people and powers, and the church as *partner* of the state and *champion* of its interests.

The Kairos Document—prepared by a group of South African theologians and released in 1985—calls this "state theology" and defines it as, "simply, the theological justification of the status quo with its racism, capitalism and totalitarianism. It blesses injustice, canonises the will of the powerful and reduces the poor to passivity, obedience and apathy" (G. Gutiérrez 1985b, 3).

The document detects this approach particularly in the White Dutch Reformed Church which, it claims, actually subscribes to a heretical theology (1985b, 7). It also points out (1985b, 3–7) that in the Christian groups adhering to this model there is a tendency to appeal to Romans 13:1–7 for one's attitude toward the state, particularly sayings to the effect that every person must "be subject to the governing authorities" (vs. 1), since they have been instituted by God (vs. 2) and are therefore "God's servants" (vs. 6). It is logical—at least in extreme cases of Constantinianism—that mission agencies would try not to embarrass the state and refrain from challenging it on issues of justice.

In the *pietist* model, throne and altar, religious organization and powers that be, are completely separated from each other.[1] Here mission is strictly interested in people's spiritual needs and steers clear of any involvement in the social, political or economic order. Those who subscribe to this model indeed exert themselves—often at the cost of almost incredible sacrifices— to provide health services, education, orphanages, etc., but such projects are not regarded as impinging upon the structures of society. These remain intact, even sacrosanct. Pietist missionaries thus regard curative and preventative measures as falling within their province, not however any measures aiming at restructuring society. That would, after all, be "politics," and the domains of religion and state should be kept neatly separate.

The third, or *reformist*, model manifests itself where mission is viewed as involving more than soul-saving and church planting. It includes social and moral uplift and aims at introducing structural changes that would lead to greater justice, freedom and prosperity for all.

Most so-called mainline churches—particularly those standing in the Calvinist tradition—tend to be reformist. They seem to argue that change in the areas of justice and freedom has to come from the top, from those in power. There is, by and large, an aversion to revolution in these circles and a tendency to believe that moral appeal to the powers that be will bring results.

There is something very attractive about the reformist position. It also has its weaknesses, however. For one thing, if they wish to be heard, reformists remain dependent on the goodwill of the government. Secondly, and because of this, they operate best in contexts where they belong to the privileged section of the population. They frequently attempt to remake the world into their own image and often fail to think through how they might live together with those with whom they disagree (Wolterstorff 1983, 22).

The Kairos Document (Gutiérrez 1985b, 8–14) refers to this approach as a manifestation of "church theology." It says, "The assumption seems to be that changes must come from . . . people who are at the top of the pile. The general idea appears to be that one must simply appeal to the conscience and the goodwill of those who are responsible for injustice . . . and that once they have repented of their sins and after some consultation with others they will introduce the necessary reforms" (Gutiérrez 1985b, 10).

Our fourth model is the one I termed *liberationist*. This is also the model the Kairos Document promotes (it calls it "prophetic," however). It rejects both "state theology" (Constantinianism) and "church theology" (reformism). As a matter of fact, the second is really more sinister than the first. After all, Constantinianism, as everybody ought to know, is so manifestly wrong that it hardly needs refutation. The reformist position, however, *looks* so convincing and so thoroughly Christian that one does not immediately detect its intrinsic evil. In rejecting it, the Kairos Document (Gutiérrez 1985b, 8f.) argues:

> not all cases of conflict are the same. . . . there are . . . conflicts in which one side is right and the other wrong. There are conflicts where one side is a fully armed and violent oppressor while the other side is defenceless and oppressed. There are conflicts that can only be described as the struggle between justice and injustice, good and evil, God and the devil.

Liberationists therefore advocate the adoption of what they call "a biblical theology of direct confrontation with the forces of evil rather than a theology of reconciliation with sin and the devil" (Gutiérrez 1985b, 10). They do not deny that the reformists can indeed book some successes, but they add, "can such reforms ever be regarded as real change, as the introduction of a true and lasting justice?" (Gutiérrez 1985b, 11).

In the liberationist model, then, mission primarily means exercising "a preferential option for the poor." More than that, the principal agents of mission are the poor and the oppressed. The Latin American Catholic Bishops Conference meeting in Puebla, Mexico (1979), referred in this respect to the "evangelizing potential of the poor," a theme later developed more fully by Gustavo Gutiérrez in *The Power of the Poor in History* (1985a, 148–50). Their activities are "missionary" or "evangelistic" not so much in the sense of winning over non-Christians to the Christian faith and church, but in the sense of restoring the credibility of the gospel among the poor and marginalized and mobilizing them for the struggle against injustice.

It follows that liberationists tend to regard incumbent rulers as beyond the pale. It would be a sheer waste of time to try to persuade them to change their evil ways, as the reformists are doing. This attitude emerges clearly in the Kairos Document, which has the following to say about the South African government and the National Party, "the apartheid minority regime is irreformable. We cannot expect the apartheid regime to experience a conversion or change of heart and totally abandon the policy of apartheid (Gutiérrez 1985b, 19).

Our fifth model is the one I called *anabaptist*, after the Anabaptist or "radical" branch of the sixteenth-century Reformation. Here the primary task of the church is simply to *be* the church, the *true* community of committed believers which, by its very existence and example, becomes a challenge to society and the state. Mission means planting churches that embrace this pattern of conduct.

In this model there is no attempt at any form of cooperation with the state. One might even get the impression that the state is *ignored*. In reality, however, the church is understood to be an implicit or latent *critical factor* in society.

It is important to note the difference between this model and the other four. In contrast to Model 1, the church is critical of the status quo, indeed *very* critical of it. There is, moreover, no attempt at withdrawing into a kind of apolitical stance (Model 2). Neither does the church try to persuade the government to introduce reforms (Model 3). Nor does it, as in Model 4, either confront and denounce the state or empower and liberate the oppressed. The church simply exists in society in such a way that people should become aware of the transitoriness, relativity and fundamental inadequacy of *all* political programs and solutions. The believing community is a kind of antibody in society, in that it lives a life of radical discipleship as an "alternative community."

One group that has consistently followed this model in recent centuries has been the Mennonites. It was, of course — broadly speaking — the model adopted by the church in the Roman Empire before Constantine, particularly during periods of persecution and opposition. In more recent times it has been and still is found among religious communities who live in oppressive states where they are barely tolerated. They cannot openly confess or proclaim their faith. They can only exhibit an exemplary life which, by its very integrity, becomes a challenge to the status quo and thus invites people to embrace the Christian faith.

### The Modern State

Having noted these five models, it may be of some importance to reflect briefly on the different political systems we may encounter in our missionary enterprise today. These range from democracies to one-party states, military dictatorships, states where one racial or ethnic group rules over all other groups, a few remaining doctrinaire Marxist states, and some countries that have sunk into chaos and anarchy.

Still, almost all contemporary governments share one characteristic: they are all, in varying degrees, *totalitarian*. The totalitarian state is a recent phenomenon. There were no real totalitarian states until the twentieth century. Only modern technology, communications media, and the like have made totalitarianism possible. Often, of course, this totalitarianism is benevolent rather than malevolent, so that people are unaware of the fact that they are being managed. Totalitarianism manifests itself in the state assuming wide responsibilities for virtually all areas of society: the economy, education, health, social security, policing, the military, mass media, and so forth. The modern state is, in effect, omnipresent. Its tentacles reach into the most remote village.

Sometimes, however, totalitarianism can become malevolent. This normally happens where the state feels threatened. It then musters all those forces that could have been employed for justice and freedom to usurp those very values and to keep its citizens under control. One example of this is the modern "national security" state, of which Latin America, in particular, has had more than its fair share. Frequently this leads to nothing but a permanent state of revolution, where one oppressive regime is replaced by another.

It will be impossible to devise a blueprint that Christian mission agencies could follow in all cases. Circumstances differ, and so must our strategies. There are, even today, situations where Christians will be forced to adopt the "anabaptist" model: situations of extreme oppression and dictatorship, or where any form of public Christian worship or witness is proscribed, for instance, in some Islamic countries. Of course, there are also countries where Christians are free to do mission work and witness prophetically, without any danger to them. It has to be remembered, however, that where we are free to challenge the state, it may easily happen that the state is equally free to ignore our challenge.

## Some Guidelines for Christian Mission

It should be clear that we ought to adopt an extremely flexible attitude toward civil authorities, improvising according to the circumstances in which we find ourselves. This does not suggest that we are without compass. So let me risk giving some guidelines we might be able to follow under most circumstances.

I submit that Models 1 and 2 are both unacceptable. In spite of the apparent differences between them, both assume the *otherworldliness* of the Christian faith, that is the assumption that what happens in government is of little concern to the church. All that really matters is what happens in and to the church, since only that has to do with eternity. The physical world is not our home, merely an anteroom of our ultimate destiny. We are aliens here, just passing through. The *real* world is the eternal, the immutable, the incorruptible. This tradition has been profoundly informed by Augustine's enormously influential *The City of God*, according to which believers should keep their gaze fixed on "the everlasting blessings that are promised for the future, using like one in a strange land any earthly and temporal things, not letting them entrap him or divert him from the path that leads to God" (quoted in Wolterstorff 1983, 5).

Glasser criticizes this approach from the perspective of the reign of God and of the conviction that God is concerned about the totality of human life and reality. His views on this are of crucial importance for the way we conduct our mission. He says, "If God's tomorrow means the end of exploitation, injustice, inequality, war, racism, nationalism, suffering, death, and the ignorance of God, Christians must be 'signs' of God's conquest of all these 'burdens and evils' through the cross and resurrection of Jesus Christ" (Glasser 1985, 12).

Glasser thus views the Christian faith not as *otherworldly*, as Models 1 and 2 do, but as *world-formative*, as Models 3, 4, and 5 do (cf. also Wolterstorff 1983, 3–22). I would therefore suggest that, in spite of very real differences between the reformist, liberationist and anabaptist models, they are closer to each other than may appear at first glance. And it is gratifying to note that more and more scholars are detecting the fundamental affinity between them. De Gruchy, for instance, proceeds from the conviction that Reformed theology is best understood as a liberating theology that is catholic in its substance, evangelical in principle, and socially engaged and prophetic in its witness (de Gruchy 1991, xii; cf. Bosch 1991a).

This kind of perspective is, in fact, increasingly embraced, in various degrees, in all Christian traditions—including Roman Catholics who, for centuries, had subscribed to the Constantinian model, and evangelicals who, for a long time, had a penchant toward the pietist model. As examples of a shift in the latter tradition, let it suffice to mention two recent documents from my own country, the *Evangelical Witness in South Africa* (de Gruchy 1986) and *Towards a Relevant Pentecostal Witness* (G. Gutiérrez 1987), both of which reveal clear reformational and liberational tendencies in their attitudes toward the state.

On the wider international scene, the same is happening. Quite apart from the fact that Third World evangelicals and pentecostals have, by and large, never really shared the dualistic thinking of their counterparts in the West, one could refer to a consultation sponsored by the World Evangelical Fellowship and held in Wheaton in 1983. The *Wheaton '83 Statement* (Samuel and Sagden 1987), released by the consultation, states in paragraph 26, "Evil is not only in the human heart but also in social structures. . . . The mission of the church includes both the proclamation of the Gospel and its demonstration. We must therefore evangelize, respond to immediate human needs, and press for social transformation."

None of the three documents just referred to can really be termed ana-baptist, in the strict sense of the word. They all presuppose a situation in which the church's prophetic voice is still being listened to, where it has not yet been silenced or completely suppressed. They are therefore reform-ist *cum* liberationist. There are, however, still situations in which the church is not able to witness publicly or protest injustice audibly. This is where the anabaptist model remains valid. Millions of people still live under repressive governments or in countries where rulers adhering to other religions do not grant them any meaningful religious freedom. In these situations the church has no public face. In such cases there is a temptation to withdraw into the privacy of the soul. Those standing in the authentic anabaptist tradition would, even in these trying circumstances, not abandon the world-formative thrust they share with persons representing the reformist and liberationist models. We cannot, even in the most oppressive situation, amputate polit-ical ethics from theology or from our faith. The doctrine of common grace teaches us that God uses not only Christians to execute his will, but all of humanity. We should therefore, even in the hour of trial, adopt a basically positive but sober attitude toward the civil realm. We should neither view any particular manifestation of the civil order as God's kingdom on earth nor regard what we consider to be falling short of the ideal as a manifes-tation of the Beast.

Finally, in our mission to Caesar we should remember that, in the long run, a society, any society, can only survive if it can rely on the assumed virtue of its citizens. It can only succeed if certain controls and morals have been implanted into its citizens. This means that even a pluralist or secu-larist society will *remain* dependent upon the witness and existence of believers, that is, of persons whose integrity and good conduct can be relied upon. It is only a shared moral vision that can hold society together (cf. Walzer 1966, 302f). If we can continue to contribute to this vision, our mission will be a blessing to all. Since we know of the reality of sin in individual and corporate life, we will remain anti-utopian, sober, and watch-ful, not fooling ourselves into believing that we shall build the ideal society here on earth or losing hope when there are setbacks and when the social and political fabric remains fragile and under pressure. In this way we will be doing our utmost for the peace of the city, calling people to true con-version—a conversion that includes social responsibility and a moral vision for society.

### Notes

1. I should add that I am using *pietist* here as a general sociological category, without identifying it with the eighteenth-century Christian movement called Pie-tism, which was a much more complex phenomenon (cf. Bosch 1991b, 252-55, 276f.).

## 8

# A Contextual Theology of Mission
# for the City

## HARVIE CONN

The title of this essay links mission theology with two topics of recent concern in missiological studies: contextualization and urban missiology.

### Contextualization and Mission Theology

In the last two decades especially, contextualization has assumed increasing prominence in understanding the process of Christian reflection. More and more evangelicals have begun to recognize that " 'contextualizing the faith' has been a part of the mission of the church from the beginning" (Stackhouse 1988, 4). Theologians and exegetes also are coming to see that contextualization has been part of the theological and hermeneutical task of the church throughout the ages (Muller 1991, 202). Recognition of these realities has been stimulated by churches in Africa, Asia, and Latin America as they have wrestled with understanding and communicating the Gospel in their own contexts (Schreiter 1985, 1).[1]

In the last two decades especially, a second group of questions has appeared in relation to the church's mission in the city. Statistically alone, the city demands our attention. "Today the number of people living in cities outnumbers the entire population of the world 150 years ago" (Palen 1987, 5). A second reason for our Christian commitment to the city involves the significant drop in the percentage of urban Christians in the world. In 1900, David Barrett tells us, Christians numbered 68.6 percent of urban dwellers. By 1992, that figure had dropped to 48.4 percent (Barrett 1992). Evangelism remains a high priority in the light of this reality.

Harvie M. Conn was a missionary in Korea 1960-1972 and currently is Professor of Missions at Westminster Theological Seminary. He edits the quarterly journal *Urban Mission*.

Third, Christian integrity demands new links between justice and compassion, and compassion with evangelism in the "urban anguish" of the world's cities. How does one proclaim the reconciliation of Christ, for example, in a riot-torn south-central Los Angeles, polarized by racism, oppression and violence?

Fourth, the city has become the global stage on which the world's religions, once isolated by place of origin or ethnicity, now increasingly dialogue. For some it is an essential part of what we call modernization. So missiologist Roger Greenway speaks of the city as "the modern frontier of Christian mission" and predicts that if we fail to win this frontier "we shall have failed indeed" (Greenway 1976, 6).

Thus contextualization requires that we connect the normative biblical horizon that provides divine meaning with our contemporary urban horizons. It calls for "a critical discernment of the text's inner meaning and then a translation of it into our own culture" (Stott and Coote 1980, 315). A contextual mission theology then, by definition, adds a third horizon to the task—that of the one to whom we translate the text in gospel witness. Out of this linking of three horizons (message or text, messenger and responder-in-context) comes a theology of mission for urban missiology.

### Urbanism, Religion, and Contextualization

Recent evangelical mission studies have depended heavily on seeing the urban as primarily a place, some even making wide use of antiquated studies of industrial urbanization in interpreting the pre-industrial city. This has resulted in gaps between the urban then and now that short-circuit the contextual linking needed for a better understanding of mission theology.

A better way to look at the city may be to re-open earlier discussions of urbanism as a way of life. But, rather than focusing that study narrowly, as in the past, on the sociocultural and often negative consequences of the urban as simply a place, we need to see it also as a process and a religious process, at that. We need to underline not so much its form as its function in shaping faith responses to the mission of God and His church. And in doing this, we may find the more appropriate bridges between cities then and now.[2]

This opens an agenda for study that has been seldom explored. Current sociological and anthropological research, in reaction to past studies molded by the thinking of people like Louis Wirth, is shifting to an interest in the city as both place and process (Press and Smith 1980, 1–14). Urban research, as a result, is entering a new stage of self-inquiry and tentativeness. Adding immensely to this time of redefinitional instability is the massive inattention to the topic of religion and the city.[3] And complicating this is the compartmentalized view of religion characteristic of such se studies.

By contrast we see religion as integral to understanding urbanism, as integral, in fact, as it is to understanding selfhood and culture. As the human response to the divine revelation of God, religion is more than a functionalist, isolated response to a basic human need (Conn 1992a, 118–20); it is the holistic response of the whole human self made in the image of God (Gen. 1:26–28). It is the voice of the "heart" (Prov. 4:23, Matt. 12:34) as it shapes a creaturely worldview either for or against the Creator, either building a city in defiance of God (Gen. 11:4) or out of covenant obedience seeking the welfare of the city and praying to the Lord on its behalf (Jer. 29:4–7). The life-style of the city is religion made visible in different ways. We list a minimum of at least three.

1. Religion is made visible as it is manifest in urbanism's role as the creator, shaper, and stabilizer of cultural continuity and innovation. Cities ancient and modern are protectors of society and culture; they maintain and transmit a society's cultural character to the regions around them. They house those institutions and spin off those systems that stabilize, maintain, and transmit a previously developed worldview. Their laws, their politics are exhibition showcases of how they see themselves, God, and their neighbor.

With this, though they share with rural areas a high degree of conservatism and commitment to stabilization in their roles, they are also the source of cultural and ideological changes. The image of the city is one of shift, of mobility, of new ideas, new methods, new life-styles. Life changes, and it changes more rapidly in the city.

Both these characteristics appear early in the biblical narrative and are tied to religious commitments. Cain's building a city (Gen. 4:17) would appear to be an attempt to find urbanism's guaranteed security and stability; he builds his own "city of refuge" in order to escape from the divinely ordained blood-revenge (Ellul 1970, 7). So too the Babel history exemplifies humanity's effort to find security and stabilization through city building (Gen. 11:4), and the recorded response of the Lord to that effort recognizes in Babel its potential as a center of cultural continuity, in this case the transmission of a worldview built out of human pride (Gen. 11:6–8).

Urban i⌐    ⌐tion is reflected in this early record also. The city that flows from ⌐   Cain is the place of human achievement, the center of ⌐t and technology (the invention of harp and flute, the ⌐ iron tools) begin their developments within the city's

⌐cal category, cities are provisions of God's common ⌐l role in human life. Through their twin attributes ⌐od restrains the development of evil, blesses his out his sovereign purposes in both judgment the city is an instrument of God's preserving vay and Monsma 1989, 7).

As the provision of God's common grace, the city is a benefit, serving mankind as at least a partial, interim refuge from the wilderness condition into which the fallen race, exiled from paradise, has been driven ... Functions that would have been performed by the city apart from the Fall are now modified by being turned to the new purpose of offsetting, to an extent, the evils arising through human sinfulness and as a result of the common curse on the race. (Kline 1983, 25)[4]

2. Religion is also displayed in urbanism's capacity for centralization and integration. Cities structure activity, beliefs, and knowledge. They are not hopelessly chaotic, but consist of organizing networks and systems. And these systems provide guidelines, cues that allow a person to move through the city as if on automatic pilot (Krupat 1985, 70). In the cities of the Ancient Near East this unifying role was more explicitly religious and more tightly regulated around religion. The closest contemporary parallel might be that of the traditional Muslim city.

The city was a community drawn together by a common religious commitment. It was that area dedicated to the service of a local deity. Each national territory centralized in its urban orbit had its divine patron and became a divine estate (Block 1988, 72–74). Among the Canaanites, so prominent in the Old Testament, each city bore the name of its particular Baal god or "lord" of the city—Baal-Gad (Joshua 11:17), Baal-Meon (Num. 32:38), Baal-Peor (Num. 25:3). The life of the city as a whole found its organizing center in its locally empowered deity. Urban worship was intimately linked with good crops and the productivity of its land and citizenry, the security provided by its walls. The defeat of the city in war meant the defeat of its gods (Joshua 2:10–11, Isa. 36:9–10). Justice was a local benefice usually limited exclusively to the city's ethnic people and defined in terms of the arbitrary will of its deity expressed by the city's ruler.

Though less tightly regulated overall by religion's integrating demands, the Hellenistic and Roman cities continued this centralizing role initiated by religious commitments. The empire became a commonwealth of self-governing cities, "full of gods" (Acts 17:16) and sometimes quick to expect power epiphanies of deity in their midst (Acts 14:8–12) (Grant 1986, 54–57). Its common Greco-Roman culture provided in Greek a universal urban language for the eastern Roman provinces.

The early church quickly learned to capitalize on the empire's urban laws (Acts 16:37, 21:39) and its common language, while rejecting the religious idolatry that spawned them. Jehovah was no local urban deity; his territorial claims were bounded not by one ethnic city but by "the heavens and the earth" (Acts 14:15, 17:24–26). In the eschatological shadow of the urban heavens and earth soon to come (Rev. 21:1–2), the church proclaimed itself as the true city and its "city-zenship" (Eph. 2:19) in Christ, the cosmic, beneficent "tyrant"/*kurios* of the city.

3. Linked to the integrating characteristic of urbanism as a religious

movement is that of power. Folk culture in a rural area is more regional, power shared along somewhat autonomous, but interconnected, lines. Urbanism tends to centralize power in itself; the city tends to take control and authority in matters such as knowledge, education, and communication. Where power dominates, there is the city as a magnet, to pull it to itself.

John Gulick suggests that this may be the very feature that enables archaeology to differentiate between cities (very small sites by modern standards) and peasant villages among the oldest remains of settlements. "The single most important presumed difference is that among the inhabitants of the earliest cities were people who wielded power over others, including others living beyond the settlements themselves, while the earliest peasant villages had no such powerful people" (Gulick 1989, 68).

In the urbanism of the Ancient Near East that power was closely linked to the myths of religion and the arbitrary will of its city gods. The city-states were oppressive regimes given to violence (Gen. 6:4–5, 11, 13; 10:9), and their gates were symbols of a power structure of society as fearsome, playful, and bloodthirsty as the baal lords from which that power came (Judges 5:8). At the center of urbanism's self-understanding was cosmic *mispat*, understood as "calling the shots," "having the say" (Walsh 1987, 2–4, 13–28).

By contrast, Israel's urban calling was to unite *mispat* with *sedeq* or "rightness." In that process, pagan definitions of *mispat* would change. Power was to be exercised in covenant exhibitions of "justice (*mispat*) and righteousness (*sedeq*)" (Gen. 18:19; 2 Sam. 8:15; Prov. 21:2–3). Her mission theology was to imitate the justice and righteousness of the only cosmic Lord Jehovah (Ex. 20:1–17; Ezek. 45:9), and when she failed in that mission, the people of God would feel the tyrannical exercise of power in captivity to the political and economic structures legitimated by the gods before which she had fallen (Isa. 59:1–4; Jer. 22:13–19).

In the shadow of the Roman Empire, what has been called the product of a single expanding urban power center, this new definition of power as "justice and righteousness" took on flesh and bone. Jesus, the inaugurator of the promised Kingdom of God (Ps. 89:14; Isa. 9:6–7), through his death and resurrection for those outside the circle of *sedeq* (Phil. 2:6–9), overcame the "principalities and powers" (Eph. 6:12). And the old call to covenant power, defined in terms of justice and compassion (Micah 6:8; Matt. 23:23; James 1:27), became the new sign of the Holy Spirit's fruit exercised in a new kind of urban citizenship (Gal. 5:22–23; Phil. 1:27).

### Implications for a Contextual Mission Theology

What effect could this holistic view of urbanism have on our mission? A few features are very clear, and a study agenda for our theological reflection may be emerging.

1. Urbanism will demand a closer link between theology and missiology. Current evangelical discussions, as rich as they are, largely orbit around a missiology of the city more than a theology of the city. We study and strategize "for the evangelization of the city generally and for church renewal and church expansion in particular. Urban theology requires a larger lens and asks different kinds of questions" (Bakke 1989, 8). Our missiological vision *for* the city must also be a theological vision *of* the city.

This link is already being forged in the two-thirds world where the context of massive and rapid urbanism is pressing again for a union of missiological and theological demands characteristic of the early church. In that world evangelical scholars are finding it easier to describe themselves not simply as theologians but as mission theologians. Theology there appears to be regaining its missiological cutting edge as reflection on the road, and missiology is recognizing the need for a reflection that handles theological issues (Costas 1990, 235–50). This bridging vision could be a great corrective for Anglo-Saxon thinking long used to the isolation of mission and evangelism from theology.

2. Understanding urbanism as a "common grace" instrument of God may also help in responding to two misunderstandings of the city prevalent today. On the one hand, it can speak powerfully against the western anti-urban mentality that describes urbanization as a great brass monster that is said to pollute, impoverish, disorient, and secularize (Shorter 1991, 137–43). Such a perspective in the past has denuded western scholarship and "popular Christianity" of its missiological hope for, and its theological interest in, the city. Seeing the city as God's provision for human welfare (Deut. 6:10–12) and God's systems of justice and compassion for the needy as prototypes of its urban laws (Goldingay 1989, 6–8) can help change that perception.

On the other hand, this same perspective on urbanism as an exhibit of common grace may also help in bringing realism to the romantic urban bias of the two-thirds world. Members of the younger generation flock now to the cities of Africa, Asia, and Latin America with overblown expectations soon to be frustrated and disillusioned. Churches and Christians are soon overwhelmed.

In the face of this frenzied optimism, urban common grace is there to remind us that it is needed because of urban sin; cities are not always what God wants. The humanitarian cycle of Sabbath days/years/jubilee legislation provides one such sampling. Intended, among other reasons, to restructure urban social imbalances (Lev. 25; Deut. 15:1–18), the cycle could be forgotten in the rush for profit and power (Amos 8:4–6; 2 Chron. 36:21). Urbanism's centralization of power could be curse (1 Sam. 8:10–18) as well as blessing. The difference depends on whom we ask to reign over the city (1 Sam. 8:5–7).

3. Urbanism's integrating nature will demand we look again at the relationship between evangelism and social transformation, between the gospel

call to *shalom* (Isa. 65:17–25) and the urban needs of the community in which the church is placed. It is no coincidence that this question has emerged again in the world evangelical community over the last twenty years of rapid global urbanization (Escobar 1990, 21–29). Word and deed, proclamation and demonstration, doing justice and preaching grace (Conn 1992a), go together in the city (Greenway 1990, 3). "Our faith," Lesslie Newbigin reminds us, "is that the Word of God is in truth the power of God unto salvation—not just the rescue of each one of us separately, but the healing, the making whole of the whole creation, and the fulfilling of God's whole will" (quoted in Pannell 1992, 33).

It is a whole gospel that must speak to the needs of a whole city. Poor and wealthy, powerful and powerless must hear the gospel in the context of their own needs. A reductionism that attempts prioritizing, turning either to the right and evangelism or to the left and social concerns, does injustice to the integrating character both of the gospel and the city (Conn 1992a, 41–56).

A growing number of urban case studies affirm this call to integration. Dale Cross, in a 1989 study, analyzed four models of urban Southern Baptist Churches spread across the United States. His conclusions are typical of similar research elsewhere (Ramsay 1992; Stair 1988, 3–7). Some churches, he noted, were more intentionally evangelistic than others, while some had more visible and consistent ministries of authentic compassion. But all displayed an "effectiveness indicator" marked by "evangelistic commitment wrapped in authentic compassion."

His conclusion? "There are two kinds of churches that fail in the city. The church that thinks their ministry is words only will leave the city because they won't pay the price of incarnation. Also, the church that thinks their ministry is deeds only will die or be spiritually impotent because they have no word about Jesus, whom to know is life and hope and peace" (Cross 1989, 137).

## A Theological Study Agenda for Urban Mission

Out of our missiological concern for the city are emerging our research issues for a theology of the city. Some have begun to be studied; others are waiting in the wings. Some are old issues made new by the urban twist. Many have been researched outside a narrow evangelical orbit but still await solid evangelical reflection. Here are a few I see on the top of my exploration list.[5]

1. What are the theological paradigms created by the evangelical church in the history of its dialogue with the city? How do these paradigms affect our image of the city and model our mission to it? In what way can our anti-urban and pro-urban biases be traced to them? The still strong evangelical differences over the relationship of evangelism to social transfor-

mation would indicate they play a prominent role in shaping our pre-understanding of urbanism.

2. What shape should the church take in the city? The massive presence of the poor and marginalized in the world's cities has prompted an intense search in the Roman Catholic Church for a new understanding of ecclesiology oriented around a discussion of God's alleged bias for the poor. Charges of racism, sexism, and oppression in the United States are motivating similar questions and producing new church models such as the Women's Church movement among minorities in the northern hemisphere churches. How should evangelicals respond to this new agenda for ecclesiology?

In areas of religious freedom, the mega-church phenomenon is being heralded as a model for urban mission (Chareonwongsak 1990, 25–35; F. Smith 1992, 6–13; Towns 1990). Whereas in countries limiting church planting activity such as the Peoples Republic of China, household churches are shaping new models of the church. Is the "house church" discussion simply an issue of strategy? Or does our understanding of the nature of the church itself demand reinvestigation?

3. What is the role of the church or the Christian in the public, urban arena of social and personal ethics? Across the globe, denominations and national councils of churches have spoken out against the political abuse of human rights, against government corruption, poverty, sexism, and oppressive laws and systems. Mainline voices call for a partnership of theology, politics, and urban policy (Pasquariello 1982; Stackhouse 1972). Evangelicals and their churches have been extremely reticent to speak in these areas. Is this a legitimate role for the church as an institution or for Christians exercising what we have called, since the Reformation, the general office of the believer? The question is not simply one of ethics or even strategy planning; once again, the issue of ecclesiology arises.

4. How do we understand the work of the Holy Spirit in the city? The worldwide growth of Pentecostal and charismatic churches in the city has placed issues of spiritual warfare, of signs and wonders, on the church-growth front burner of evangelicals (Wagner 1991, 130–37). A large body of literature, most of it oriented to missiological concerns, is already appearing pro (Kraft 1989; Wagner 1988a, 1988b; Wimber 1985) and con (Coggins and Hiebert 1989). Full theological reflection is still scarce (Smedes 1987; Williams 1989), but much needed. And beyond this area is still another set of untouched issues now promoted outside the evangelical community: what is the role of the Spirit of Jesus in the promotion of urban justice and humanitarianism outside the Christian community?

The exploratory list will grow, each reader of this essay adding his or her priority items. But all our lists, each drawn from our own urban contexts, turn in the end to the same reality: urbanism is one of the great missiological and theological challenges of our day.

## Notes

1. See, for example, Richard D. Love II (1992).

2. For recent literature dealing with related issues, see Frank Frick (1977), Karp, Stone, and Yoels (1991), R. E. Blanton (1976), Eames and Goode (1977), R. L. Rohrbaugh (1991), H. Conn (1985, 1987, 1992a), Don Benjamin (1983), and Press and Smith (1980).

3. A recent study by Robert Kemper, for example, surveyed trends in urban anthropological research over the last twenty years by examining the 688 articles appearing in the journal *Urban Anthropology*. The highest area of study was in economics (182 articles), followed by ethnicity (140) and by family/kinship questions (108). Only thirteen articles on religion appeared during the twenty-year history of the journal. Consult: Robert Kemper (1991).

4. Kline also suggests that God's promise of the preservation of Cain (Gen. 4:15) is "a virtual city charter."

5. Ray Bakke (1989, 8-19) provides a very useful beginning for such a list.

# PART THREE

# ECUMENICAL RELATIONSHIPS

# Introductory Overview

The mold from which Arthur Glasser was made is of a very special kind. Over the past fifty years he has not sidestepped the twists and turns of ecumenical developments. He was young when the rigid lines were drawn between fundamentalism and liberal ecumenism. This included also a very cool distancing from anything Roman Catholic. But rather than staying with the closed position of his right-wing background, Art not only showed tolerance to the World Council of Churches during the fifties and sixties, but became a friendly critic.

The decade of the seventies greatly increased his relational opportunities. Beginning twenty years ago, his writing shows greater involvement in the debates between evangelicals and ecumenicals. Then as relationships between evangelicals and Roman Catholics became more open, Art found a still wider dimension to express his oneness with all those who love Jesus Christ as Savior and Lord.

From among his numerous articles touching on these matters, there are two events about which he wrote while he was editor of *Missiology*. Both show the integrity Art brought to ecumenical relationships. They also reveal two sides of the real Art Glasser.

On one side is the tenacity with which he stands for the basic principles of evangelical Christianity as he sees them. In 1978 he needed to express the frustration he felt after a mission consultation which was billed as an Ecumenical/Evangelical Mission Dialogue. It led him to write an editorial in *Missiology* bearing the title, "Can This Gulf Be Bridged?" At hand were his strong feelings of unallowable differences with positions taken by the Presbyterian Church (USA) and the World Council on such issues as scriptural authority, the meaning of Jesus as Lord and "witness as presence" or conversion of (in this case) Muslim people. The discussion at the conference became so blurred that Art lodged a protest. His correctives were voted down. Resulting from this, Art observed that, ironically, evangelicals hold certain mission convictions that are closer to Roman Catholic than to Protestant ecumenical thinking (July 1978).

The other side is the way in which Arthur is always ready to recognize true spirituality and to celebrate fellowship in Christ. In his "Report of a Happening," an editorial written just six months after the above case (January 1979), we see his equally affirming spirit in ecumenical consultations. It was the first time ASM members met with missiologists of the IAMS.

The gathering took place at Maryknoll. At the time Catholic and Protestant missiologists still felt somewhat inexperienced about their new relationships. Art was enthusiastic in his review of the Maryknoll community. In describing the meeting itself he used such words as "stimulating," "a happy mixture of prayer and spirituality," "encounter" and "true dialogue," while admitting that in some areas the "differences were deep and wide."

Because of Art's support for women in ministry, he will be glad that this section contains contributions from two women missiologists. Dana Robert's thesis is congenial to the strong emphasis Glasser gives to *shalom* as life-style for the Kingdom. This demands love and care for the powerless and the weaker members of society. Evangelism for conversion is not enough. The Kingdom does lift up the state of women. Art will be excited about this as well as Dana's caution that contextualization is a faulted discipline if it simply "fits" the situation and does not prophetically seek to change what is less than biblical.

Mary Motte also sounds the note for women and the poor; but, on a broader theme, she sees the foundational principles of mission as the call to greater cooperation between Protestants and Roman Catholics. As we have seen, Arthur holds fast the Word that adheres us in unity and with Motte and Robert, he also sees the Kingdom as a challenge, yea warning, to the status quo. The Church must be fully engaged in her mission against culture while she is within culture.

Emilio Castro's evaluation of the CWME gathering at San Antonio (1990) and the seventh Assembly of the WCC (Canberra 1991) leads us into issues such as Christian witness in a pluralistic world, the inculturation of the gospel and the meaning of the Trinity for mission. Art Glasser would vigorously support the council's call for discernment in this sensitive process. He would, however, just as vigorously contend that this discernment allows only what glorifies the Word and the Trinity, so any appropriation of rituals and spirits from natural religion, as was advocated by one plenary speaker at Canberra, is unacceptable syncretism.

Tom Stransky has been one of the early and honored bridge builders between Protestants and Catholics. He traces the generally optimistic trends in Catholic thinking since Vatican II. Art has been an interpreter of these developments for evangelical missiologists, both in and out of the classroom. Themes raised by *Ad Gentes* and *Redemptoris Missio* emphasize the Trinity, the sending God in Jesus Christ, the missionary nature of the Church, distinction between Church and Kingdom and a greater openness to local human situations with the one eternal saving message. Art will take much satisfaction in the Pope's idea of "a new springtime for Christianity" but will not accept that the corollary to this is "the waning of missionary activity to the nations."

D. S. G.

# 9

# Revisioning the Women's Missionary Movement

## DANA ROBERT

Although women have constituted a majority of the American foreign mission force for the past century, their roles in mission practice and policy have barely been acknowledged. In some ways, women involved in mission today face greater barriers than they did in the early twentieth century. Whereas in the early twentieth century a mass movement of forty women's missionary societies supported thousands of single women missionaries, today women mission leaders in denomination after denomination privately lament how much more difficult it is to get a single woman appointed as a missionary than it was 25 years ago.[1] Whereas a century ago deaconess and missionary training institutes were founded and run by women, now the number of Protestant women professors of mission in the United States can be counted on two hands. While in the founding years, faith missions often had women in leadership positions, today many evangelical denominations and independent mission organizations have a "glass ceiling" above which women cannot rise in policy making roles, even though the vast majority of experienced missionaries are women.[2] Missionary wives return to face a lack of status even as their husbands receive appointments in the home base organization.

At the forty-fourth General Council of the Assemblies of God held in Portland in 1991, Paul Yonggi Cho, pastor of the largest church in the world, with 350 missionaries in 60 countries, said that the reason the church is not growing in the United States is because the American Church restricts the leadership roles of its women. Calling American society a male chauvinist one, Cho remarked that "The American church must set women free

Dana Robert is Associate Professor of International Mission at Boston University School of Theology. A mission historian, she is writing *American Women in Mission: A History of Mission Theory.*

if they expect to grow. .... If the American church doesn't wake up to lay ministry, especially among women, they need not expect revival" (Cho 1991, 23, 27).[3] The irony of a male Korean Christian berating the American church for restricting its women cannot be lost on anyone familiar with mission history. After all, it was an American Methodist woman missionary, Mary Scranton, who launched the liberation of Korean women when she began the Ewha School for girls in 1886.

## "Woman's Work for Woman," A Missiological Heritage

Any reflection on a constructive missiology for women in the next century must take into account the rich but largely unrecognized history of American women's involvement in mission since the nineteenth century. Of the first group of American foreign missionaries who departed in 1812, three were accompanied by their wives. The missionary wife thus became a distinctive feature of American Protestant missions in the antebellum period.

By the middle of the nineteenth century, missionary wives were finding it increasingly difficult to supervise the mission work expected of them and they began to press the churches to appoint more single women to the field. Continued resistance to appointing more single women, however, caused women's groups in many denominations to found women's missionary organizations whose purpose was to support the growing number of single women called to missionary service.

The late nineteenth and early twentieth centuries were the heyday of the women's missionary movement. Church women at home raised funds through sacrificial and regular giving of small amounts of money. Publicizing their projects through women's missionary magazines, they nickeled and dimed their way into building hospitals and schools across Asia and in appointing single women as missionary doctors, teachers, and evangelists. Local chapters of women's missionary societies sprang up across the United States and initiated their own projects, such as the support of an indigenous woman evangelist or scholarships for girls to attend mission schools. By the turn of the century, Patricia Hill notes that there were three million American women involved in over forty denominational women's mission societies, thus making the women's missionary movement the largest women's movement in nineteenth-century America (Hill 1985, 3).

The women's mission societies were united by their central missiology of "Woman's Work for Woman." They saw their work as separate from that of the denominational boards, necessary to correct the failure of the church to take into account fully the needs of women and children, and of special urgency in sex-segregated societies where male missionaries had little access to women. The promoters of "Woman's Work for Woman" had a strong sense of their own destiny in contributing to the salvation of women everywhere. Said Mrs. E. F. Chilton in the *Woman's Missionary*

*Advocate*, "It remains for the women of the nineteenth century to do that which has never been undertaken before—that is, through the organization of her own sex into societies, to procure the means to begin the work of Christianizing the women in heathen lands" (Chilton 1880).[4]

"Woman's Work for Woman" argued that the insoluble unity between mother and child meant that work for women automatically meant work for children, and work for children was central to the well-being of the larger society. Thus a major goal of the mission theory was the conversion of mothers. The key issue of modern missions was how to reach "the mothers and home." When Mrs. Moses Smith represented the Congregationalist Woman's Board of Missions at the Ecumenical Conference held in New York in 1910, she stated,

> In all the Orient, and largely in all uncivilized lands, only a woman can break the Bread of Life to woman. Logically, it follows that the agency through which this can be done is the most far-reaching and certain force the Church has for the redemption of the race. Thus is demonstrated the value of the Women's Boards of Missions among redemptive forces (Hill 1985, 115).

By 1910, when the American woman's missionary movement celebrated its golden anniversary, it could look with pride on nearly 2,500 missionaries and over 6,000 indigenous women workers being supported around the world. Women's mission societies supported 3,263 schools, 80 hospitals, 11 colleges, and other institutions such as orphanages, dispensaries, and kindergartens. (See fold-out statistical chart in Helen Barrett Montgomery 1910.) Jointly, the women's missionary societies produced annual study material for the membership, held summer schools for mission education, and sponsored the Interdenominational Conference of Woman's Boards of Foreign Missions. In 1921, the women's boards raised three million dollars to support seven union women's colleges in India, China and Japan. United by clear goals and a common mission theory, the woman's missionary movement was a major reason why mission remained a top priority for American Christians during the early twentieth century.

Yet even as the movement was celebrating its golden anniversary in 1910, leading spokeswoman Helen Barrett Montgomery was warning of the need to maintain separate women's mission organizations if the gains of the movement were to be preserved. "There is always a danger that in the pressing demands of the wider work the women's interest might be overlooked, unless there were organizations specifically formed to care for them" (Montgomery 1910, 271). Her worst fears were realized as, beginning in 1910, one by one the women's organizations were absorbed into broader denominational structures.

The decline of the women's mission organizations was the institutional manifestation of the larger decline of "Woman's Work for Woman" as an effective missiology. By the 1920s, sex-segregated ideologies seemed old-fashioned. As denominational women began to work toward the larger goals of world peace and ecumenical cooperation, separate women's work lost its cutting edge.[5]

By the 1960s, the women's missionary movement had largely lost its power and its motivating missiology. Some speculate that the overall decline of missions commitment in the mainline churches caused the collapse of the women's mission movement. But evidence suggests it may have been the other way around—the eradication of the women's mission movement made women less interested in mission and thus hastened the overall decline of mission in the mainline Protestant churches.[6] Whatever the complex reasons for the decline, the fact remains that in the older American Protestant denominations, the commitment of the entire denomination to mission was related to the strength of its women's mission organization: the stronger the women's group, the greater commitment to mission by the denomination. Despite the theological advantages of all a denomination's mission work being united and channeled directly through the church, once women lost control over women's missionary work, the commitment of the entire denomination to mission plummeted. Since the women's mission organizations traditionally educated and recruited their own children to support the work, the decline of women's groups affected not only the current generations but the future ones as well.

That women are now having to struggle to do what they took for granted 75 years ago signifies a monstrous failure of the collective mission memory. As new parachurch mission organizations reinvent the wheel, and as the mainline churches see women's involvement in the church through the prism of ordination, the broad-based involvement of American women in Christian mission continues to decline. In the mainline churches, the decline of the women's mission movement partly reflects the failure of mission interest as a whole and cannot be separated from it. In the evangelical churches, continued struggles over the role of women serve to squeeze women out of leadership roles. All churches are affected by the need of women to work for a living and the consequent decline of free time available for mission interests. But most importantly, instead of leading the secular society in providing opportunities for women, as it did for much of American history, the church now lags behind.

### The Current Need for a Missiology for Women

The time has come for a new vision of the role of women in the mission of the church. The collapse of "Woman's Work for Woman," coupled with the increasing needs of the world's women, means that the Church must deliberately incorporate women's issues into current missiological reflection.

In the fall of 1990, *Time* magazine published a special issue on "Women: The Road Ahead." Among the articles were a few on sexist oppression faced by women in nonwestern cultures: the burning of brides by Indian men who want higher dowries, abortion of female fetuses in China, forced clitoridectomy in northern Africa, and oppression of women under Islam.[7] These pages in *Time* could have come from a woman's missionary magazine of a hundred years ago, except that the missionary magazines would have concluded that the solution of such problems was the conversion of women to Christianity. Although the existence of oppression of women in non-Christian cultures is no longer a prima facie case for the American public to support world mission, sociological evidence of the past twenty years suggests that Christian churches have too blithely abdicated their missional responsibilities toward the world's women and children. Instead of improving, since World War II the plight of the world's women relative to that of men has worsened.

In a trend called "the feminization of poverty," scholars have discovered that an increasing percentage of the world's poor since World War II are women. One cause for the feminization of poverty has been mistaken development policies. In 1970, women sociologists began to argue that postwar development policies in Africa had ignored the traditional role of women in agriculture and had thus contributed to a drop in food production during the very years of the "Decade of Development." Another cause for the feminization of poverty is the subordinate status of women in many cultures, which confines them to marginal occupations. According to Ruth Sivard, in the three major fields of employment—agriculture, industry and services,

> Women are clustered in unskilled, dead-end jobs with low pay and little potential for training or advancement. In agriculture, if cash crops are grown, women tend to do the back-breaking planting, weeding and harvesting; men to operate whatever mechanical equipment is available. In the services, women are largely in menial jobs, primarily as domestics, or in the informal sector, selling food and home-grown crops. In industry, they provide cheap assembly-line labor for the rapidly growing multinational operations in textiles, apparel, and electronic products. (Sivard 1985, 15. See also Bernard 1987 and Helmore 1985)

Women's responsibilities for child care further reduce their ability to produce income.

The feminization of poverty can be proven by indicators of well-being, such as nutritional intake, infant mortality rates, and work load, that show that women are at an increasing disadvantage. In India, the greater value placed on boys means that they get better food and medical care and are nursed longer, resulting in a mortality rate for girls 30 to 50 percent higher than for boys. Anemia is endemic among the world's women who must bear and nurse children on low caloric intakes. The majority of the world's hospital beds are occupied by men, despite women's reproductive functions.[8] Famine and war have created 15 million refugees, 70 to 80 percent of whom are women (Badaracco 1992). The poorest people in the United States today are single mothers and their children. In terms of work load, the women of the world carry two-thirds of the world's work hours, although they constitute only one-third of the world's official work force.

If one accepts that the basic cause of feminization of poverty is the subordinate status held by women in most cultures in the world, then it becomes clear that an effective mission theory for the next millennium must take into consideration not only urbanization, environmentalism, militarism, hostility to Christianity, and other trends already identified by missiologists, but must also concern itself with the role of women. As the percentage of the world's children continues to increase in the Third World and decrease in the First World, a faithful and effective mission theory for the next century must also take into account the special needs of the world's children. Just as Jesus embraced children and elevated the role of women by conversing with them as equals, so must Christian mission once again deliberately put women and children at the top of its list of priorities.

That the time has come again for a new proactive women's missionary movement can be seen in the convergence of needs and opportunities facing Christian mission today. Perhaps the seeds of a new movement were planted when, after Vatican II, Roman Catholic sisters found themselves freed for mission work in a way that they had never experienced before. The Second Vatican Council permitted Catholic sisters to go into the world rather than restricting them to traditional educational and priest-directed, parish-centered work. Pope John XXIII's call for religious orders to send 10 percent of their personnel to Latin America meant that even the "non-missionary" congregations became involved in cross-cultural mission. Many Catholic sisters embraced liberation theology's "option for the poor" and begin to see themselves in relationship with the poor people of the world, rather than in ministry to the middle classes. By the mid-1970s, Catholic women missioners were discovering that poverty had a female face. To believe that God has a special concern for the poor, the marginalized, and the oppressed means that God has a special concern for women and children.

In evangelical circles, the embracing of kingdom theology since Lausanne I in 1974 by missiologists like Arthur Glasser has created a new awareness of the needs of the world's poor as well. As long as mission work is directed solely toward evangelism, there is little motivation for special work with women, except for the pragmatic reason of reaching them and their families. After all, souls are equal regardless of sex. But as soon as missiology concerns itself with this world as the place where God's kingdom has broken in and where Christians gain a foretaste of the full reign of Christ, then missiology must make a special place for the poor and marginalized women and children of this world. In the words of the Manila Manifesto, affirmed at Lausanne II in 1989, "We affirm that we must demonstrate God's love visibly by caring for those who are deprived of justice, dignity, food, and shelter. We affirm that the proclamation of God's kingdom of justice and peace demands the denunciation of all injustice and oppression, both personal and structural; we will not shrink from this prophetic witness" (Douglas 1990, 26).

### Current Challenges for a Missiology for Women

Although the needs and opportunities seem ripe for a new women's missionary movement, involvement of women in mission today must differ from the earlier women's movement in certain key respects. The most important change from the earlier women's mission movement is that paternalism must be left in the past. The late-nineteenth-century mission movement was marred by the idea that western women knew what was best for the rest of the world's women. Western women were not always sensitive to cross-cultural realities and believed that western education was a direct path to liberation for nonwestern women. Although careful historical analysis reveals a surprisingly high degree of cooperation between western missionaries and local women such as Bible women and indigenous pastors' wives, nevertheless this cooperation was characterized by a "big sister, little sister" mentality. The global nature of the church today and the existence of women leaders in such groups as the Ecumenical Association of Third World Theologians means that a new women's missionary movement must work without paternalism, "calling the whole church to take the whole gospel to the whole world."

A second missiological issue relevant for a women's mission movement today is the implication of contextualization for women's issues. "Woman's Work for Woman" was unashamedly interested in social change and the "uplift" of women everywhere. It did not hesitate to attack social realities deemed oppressive to women in other cultures and religions. Today's movement toward contextualization, however, often emphasizes that Christianity must utilize the structures already present in a given culture. But if the goal of a women's missionary movement is spiritual and physical "liberation," then how does a women's movement grapple with cultural indigenization that may in fact leave women in the same oppressive social situation as before they were Christians? The tensions within contextualization, so aptly described by Robert Schreiter as the "liberation" versus the "ethnographic" approach, become particularly acute when it comes to the place of women in society (Schreiter 1985, 12–16). Missiologists need to put women's issues at the top of the agenda in ongoing discussions of the theories of contextualization.

A third missiological issue of importance for a women's mission movement is the meaning of evangelism and conversion. In the earlier women's missionary movement, conversion was assumed to be essential to mission, partly because Christian culture was assumed to be superior to non-Christian culture. Evangelism was not only the solution to sin, but to the social oppression of women. Today, even if one takes the evangelical/exclusivist position and believes that only conversion to Christ endows eternal salvation, one must admit along with the Manila Manifesto that conversion is not the sole priority for Christian mission. Certainly conversion to Christianity can strengthen woman's self-worth and ability to challenge her oppression, but "Christian" society can oppress women as well as non-Christian society. In terms of kingdom theology, what is the deeper meaning of evangelism and conversion for women who are caught in oppressive situations?

A fourth but certainly not final issue relevant to a new women's missionary movement is the unleashing of the Holy Spirit that has occurred over the past decades. In all religions of the spirit, from Korean shamanism to African religions, women have played large roles as healers and messengers of the spirits. In Christianity, movements of the Holy Spirit from Montanism to Methodism have used and empowered women. The growth of pentecostalism around the world is connected with the freeing of women for leadership roles in the church. In his sociological study of pentecostalism in Central America, for example, David Martin shows that the majority of pentecostals are women (D. Martin 1990a). Of the 50,000 cell group leaders in Paul Yonggi Cho's church, "all but 3,000 are women" (Cho 1991, 23). Just as the holiness movement of the late nineteenth century empowered American women for mission service and ministry, so is the pentecostal/charismatic movement of the late twentieth century empowering nonwestern women for mission and ministry. If missiologists today are serious about the Holy Spirit, as was affirmed by Lausanne II, are they prepared to accept the leadership of women that most certainly accompanies the third person of the trinity? Is the mission community prepared to provide the theological education for discernment needed by "daughters who prophesy"? Is the western church ready to listen not only to African, Asian, and Latin American brothers, but to African, Asian, and Latin American sisters called by the Holy Spirit?

## Conclusion

When Paul Yonggi Cho remarked to the forty-fourth General Council of the Assemblies of God that the American church was not experiencing revival because it was restricting its women, the male reporter to the council paper chose not to include these remarks in the report on Cho's speech. Such an oversight reflects both an ignorance of the important role that women have played in mission and revival movements and an insensitivity to the multiple needs of women in the church and world. But as the church moves into the twenty-first century, the time is right once again to encourage women to participate in mission and to put the needs of women and children at the top of the list of "kingdom" priorities. When the Holy Spirit saves women's souls and frees their spirits, is it not an act of faithlessness when the mission of the church ignores their oppression in the name of "contextualization"?

The revisioning of a women's missionary movement brings to the surface knotty missiological problems. Burying these problems and declaring them dead will not make them go away. Rather, with the power of the Spirit, the mission of the church must face women's issues head-on. Only as women are enlisted in the service of Christ through the *Missio Dei* will the earth "be full of the knowledge of the Lord as the waters cover the sea."

## Notes

1. Interviews with mission leaders in the Assemblies of God, United Methodist Church, Episcopal Church, Southern Baptist Convention, and Roman Catholic Church confirm the generalization that it is more difficult for single women to obtain mission appointments in the 1990s than it was in the 1960s, although reasons for the difficulty vary from denomination to denomination.

2. Examples of women who held important administrative positions in the emerging faith and independent evangelical mission movement of the late nineteenth and early twentieth centuries include Mrs. E. M. Whittemore, founding council member of the Africa Inland Mission; Mrs. Lettie Cowman, co-founder of the Oriental Missionary Society; Mrs. A. B. Simpson, longtime member of the Board of Managers, Financial Secretary, and Secretary of Missionary Appointment and Equipment of the Christian and Missionary Alliance; Mrs. Luy Peabody, founder of the Association of Baptists for Evangelism in the Orient; and Eliza Davis George, founder of the Elizabeth Native Interior Mission. Today, however, evangelical and parachurch missions are seldom aware of the leadership roles played by women in their founding years. For the stories of evangelical missionary women pioneers, see *Guardians of the Great Commission* (Tucker 1988). For an historical analysis of the decline of women's ministries in evangelical churches from 1880 to 1930, see Hassey (1986), *No Time for Silence.* The best one-volume overview of the history of the American women's missionary movement is the dated but helpful Beaver (1980), *American Protestant Women in World Mission: History of the First Feminist Movement in North America.*

3. The term *male chauvinist* did not appear in the article, but did in the actual interview.

4. See also Jennie Fowler Willing (1869).

5. For information on the loss of women's mission organizations in various denominations see, e.g., R. W. Macdonell (1928), Elizabeth Howell Verdesi (1973), Ian T. Douglas (1992), and Patricia Hill (1985).

6. For information on attempts to limit the power of women in the mission structures of the United Methodist Church, see Theressa Hoover (1983), especially 29-30, 49-56. See also Barbara Campbell (1983), 68.

7. "Life behind the Veil," "Africa: A Ritual of Danger," "India: Till Death Do Us Part," "Asia: Discarding Daughters," *Time* (Fall 1990), 37-40.

8. For statistics on the feminization of poverty, see Sivard (1985). Princeton demographer Ansley Coale calculates that there are 60 million women "missing" worldwide, 29 million of them in China and 23 million in India. The causes of the "missing" women stem from cultural practices that value boys over girls in such countries as Libya, China, and Pakistan (Sege 1992).

# 10

# Issues in Protestant-Roman Catholic Discussions of Theology of Mission

## MARY MOTTE

### Introduction

There are several perspectives from which one can examine issues emerging in discussions of mission theology between Protestants and Roman Catholics. I have chosen that which perceives how these discussions are leading to increased collaboration, looking especially at directions emerging for a future ecumenical agenda in mission. I make this choice because the last several years have provided a number of occasions for significant missiological discussion between Protestants and Roman Catholics at international as well as national and local levels. Experience leads one to conclude that ecumenical discussions that start from missionary engagement are providing a new place to begin. The general orientation emerging from such experiences concurs with Bosch's description of an emerging ecumenical paradigm in mission theology reflecting a growing consensus about a new understanding of mission, and especially about the relation between mission and church (Bosch 1991b, 368–510; cf. Scherer 1987, 126–63, 190–95, 227–32, 233–45). Biblical and theological concerns which have undergirded separations among Christians, are more easily being identified and discussed, rather than debated (cf. Whiteman 1990 USCMA/DOM-NCCC 1987). This has certainly been the experience in a number of consultations, such as the ecumenical consultation on mission co-sponsored by the then Division of Overseas Ministries of the National Council of Churches of Christ USA and the United States Catholic Mission Association, and the annual meeting of the American Society of Missiology in 1990, which explored the issue of joint witness. The Gospel and Culture

Mary Motte (F.M.M.) is director of the Mission Resource Center, United States Province—Franciscan Missionaries, engaged in missiological research, consultation and education.

Network, set up after the ecumenical consultation mentioned above, is also providing this kind of forum, as was evidenced in the consultation it sponsored in February 1992.

## Signs of Growing Missiological Collaboration

Two general considerations provide the framework for these ecumenical missiological discussions: one concerns topics discussed and the other, attitudes growing out of actual experiences of being together. Considerable consensus appears on the topics around which missiologists gather, as well as about methodologies, although there is more evidence of variance in the latter, as well as in the content of the topics. Such variance often reflects historical developments from within particular Christian traditions, especially in the areas of Christology, eschatology and ecclesiology. At times, however, the variance reflects differences which are more socio-political. For example, one generally meets more unity among Protestant and Catholic liberation theologians in Latin America than might be found with either relating to members of their own denominations in a North-South framework. Increased commitment to common or joint witness in mission is expressed not only in concrete willingness to reflect together on missiological issues, but is likewise expressed in pursuing a wider ecumenical participation.

The Evangelical-Roman Catholic Dialogue on Mission (ERCDOM), held between 1977 and 1984, while not resulting in an agreed statement, did issue a final report which describes "some areas in which Evangelicals and Roman Catholics hold similar views . . . and other ideas on which both sides seriously differ" (Stransky 1991, 392). Having provided a basis for greater mutual understanding, the ERCDOM report offers a way to further discussion (Wilson 1990, 452). The world mission conferences in Melbourne 1980 and in San Antonio 1989, sponsored by the World Council of Churches, along with the effort of the Joint Working Groups between the World Council of Churches and the Vatican Secretariat for Promoting Christian Unity to develop a study document on Common Witness in 1980, are some further examples of this effort to reflect together and to seek a wider ecumenical participation (cf. Meeking 1984, 62–65; Delaney 1987). John Paul II's urging that Christians find a way of giving common witness in mission, even while not experiencing perfect unity, can find a response in the witness borne by these many common searches to articulate mission theology ecumenically (RM 1991 no. 50).

Christian missiologists generally agree that proclamation of the Good News about God's Reign contained in the Gospel and a reaching out to others in a way increasingly influenced by deeper theological insight into the mystery of the Incarnation are key elements in mission today. Particular issues are: concern about those made poor in society, interaction between

Christian faith and culture, announcing God's message of love to those who follow other religious traditions, and the meaning of the now and not yet of God's Reign. Exploration of each of these issues in the context of today's world poses a number of critical questions for further ecumenical investigation in Christology, soteriology, ecclesiology, and eschatology. It is important to note a growing ecclesial awareness which is not always in the forefront of discussion agendas but is real in actual relationships formed. This awareness is rooted in the community gathered around the Word of God. Bible study and worship are generally essential, even primary in discussion schedules. These moments often result in an experience of communion together in God, and this koinonia gives strength, sustaining vision to get beyond inevitable moments of struggle and disagreement.

Protestants and Catholics, bringing the varied richness of their traditions, have been approaching missiological discussions at the service of concrete realities calling them to a working unity, under the guidance of the Holy Spirit. It is important to recognize that traditions, although not the starting point, are not ignored. At times differences arise and make genuine claims on a given participant's fidelity to a particular tradition. However, willingness to listen to one another with openness and fidelity provide a creative tension which gradually, through perseverance and patience, appears to be leading to new insights.

Missionary commitment is inherent in genuine acceptance of baptismal engagement. This experience of God's life within oneself moves toward sharing and community (World Council of Churches 1982b, no. 15), a movement noted from earliest Christian times to the present. Today ecumenical discussion among Christian missiologists is proceeding toward greater theological agreement about the essentially missionary nature of the Church and mission as primarily belonging to God, being God's expression of love for people (cf. Bosch 1991b, 392). Christian participation in God's mission is directed toward the coming of God's Reign. Seeing the Church as servant of that Reign, participating in God's mission is a major new orientation, especially among Roman Catholics (cf. Amaladoss 1990b, 212). At the same time, there remain deep differences among some missiologists, as was the case in the Evangelical-Roman Catholic dialogues concerning the nature and purpose of the Church (Stransky 1991, 393).

The emerging ecumenical missionary paradigm suggested by Bosch (1991b), reflects significant shifts toward consensus and is resulting, I believe, in a greater liberation for both Protestants and Catholics seeking common witness in mission. Gathering for worship and Bible study while discussing and exploring missiological issues, participants experience what it means to be a baptized community gathered around the Word of God, continually called to conversion by that Word, then reaching out to the larger community, not with their own message, but with the good news of God's love for all people (cf. Paul VI 1975, nos. 15, 78; Shenk 1991).

## Difficulties

Evidence of increasing consensus should not blind us to those areas
where collaboration and discussion come up against obstacles. Five hundred
years of Christianity in the Americas has enlivened consciousness about
how ambiguous communication of the Gospel has been at times. Good
News has in fact been proclaimed and received; the Gospel has also been
made subservient, consciously or unconsciously, to other powers. Developments in incarnational theology have opened the way to a deeper understanding of the importance of human relationships as a basic medium
through which to communicate the message of salvation. Contexts define
human relationships to a large extent, and increasingly, ecumenical discussions about mission reflect this awareness. Potential for human community
is the ground of salvation, for community is the place where the Word of
God becomes operative in human relationships and transforms sinfulness
into grace. Whatever inhibits potential for community is unjust and oppressive. Communication of the gospel message is, therefore, also directed to
those sinful elements in society. In any given situation, discernment is
needed to seek out signs of sin and grace. This kind of discernment can be
difficult, as each one brings to the process his or her Christian tradition
and gospel experience as tools for discernment. It is in this arena that the
process of common witness often breaks down. A case in point is that of
the World Council Assembly at Canberra, during which both ecclesiological
and missiological understandings, and especially the relation between Gospel and culture, themes represented by a wide range of positions, became
too diverse to enable deeper conversation, and in some instances continues
to jeopardize further collaboration (Kerr 1991; Mutiso-Mbinda 1991, 7–
11).

Witness together by Christians is not facilely or cheaply achieved. Membership in a Christian community is recognized by most as essential to
baptismal commitment; selection of a particular community by a new member can be an obstacle for collaboration (cf. Amaladoss 1990a, 159). Eucharist, recognized ecumenically as "bread for the missionary journey" (World
Council of Churches 1982c, 205–6; 1982b, 26), cannot be shared ecumenically. So many participants in ecumenical consultation have experienced
the poignant pain of not being able to share Eucharist together. Fully aware
of the profound difficulties we experience in respect to this matter, I believe
we must consciously choose to keep the Eucharist present in our discussions
about mission. Divisions among Christians expressed in their inability to
come together in Eucharistic celebration are the most profound divisions
in Christian society. Although speaking primarily of political and social
situations, Schreiter's (1992a) description of the process of reconciliation
is helpful in this context. Although, as he points out, one may indicate
concrete tasks, a spirituality is at the basis of successful reconciliation, i.e.,

"a view of the world that recognizes and responds to God's reconciling action in the world"(1992a, 60). In a time when so much of missionary experience is lived out in contexts of violence, in a time when there are so many Christian martyrs, the moment when we can together remember and celebrate how Jesus called us to celebrate his memory by giving ourselves completely for the people God loves is urgently needed as a sign in the world (cf. Schreiter 1992a, 76; World Council of Churches 1982b, 20).

As incomprehensible as it is at times that certain traditions, because of their understandings of Eucharist, cannot allow all to sit at the same Eucharistic table, this restriction challenges us to move toward a more powerful understanding of Eucharist as bread for the missionary journey. As one speaker remarked recently, "the table is God's table." It does not belong to any particular tradition, denomination, race or class. The consensus achieved in the Baptism, Eucharist and Ministry Document reminds us we are in process of becoming one people, "sharing the meal of the one Lord" (World Council of Churches 1982b, 26). In this state of our missionary pilgrimage, we are becoming the eucharistic assembly and "must be concerned for gathering also those who are at present beyond its visible limits, because Christ invited to his feast all for whom he died" (World Council of Churches 1982b, 20). To the extent that any one of us refuses to enter into this process and "cannot unite in full fellowship around the same table to eat the same loaf and drink the same cup," our "missionary witness is weakened at both the individual and the corporate levels" (World Council of Churches 1982b, 26).

## Directions for the Future

While there are still many challenges underlying convergence in the missiological issues, a new focus appears to be emerging which provides possibilities for a breakthrough to a more pervasive insight about ecumenical mission. In 1987 a number of Protestants and Catholics met in a consultation to probe issues in the United States concerning divided churches and common witness in relation to mission (USCMA/DOM-NCCC 1987). Central to their perception of the issues was the view that this constituted an unfinished task for United States Christians in mission. Actual topics dealt with were those indicated above as reflecting issues of common concern to Protestant and Catholic missiologists: the poor, interfaith dialogue, Church-Mission-Kingdom, and Gospel in Western Culture. This was the first time that such a group had convened officially in the United States to explore their common or joint witness in mission. Equally important, but not so readily recognized, was the fact that this consultation constituted a significant step toward connecting mission with local reality. It was not someone else's local reality; it was United States local reality, and up until this time missionaries had not seen themselves as particularly related to this local reality.

Influenced by Newbigin's (1986) analysis of the critical lack of Gospel challenge in western society, a sector of the consultation worked on the theme "The Gospel and Western Culture." Newbigin's presence at the consultation possibly reinforced the development of this theme and its conclusion at the end of the consultation: "Crucial for the mission of the Church of Christ in this age is the call to challenge certain assumptions of western society" (USCMA/DOM-NCCC 1987, 2). It goes on to call for theological dialogue among different Christian groups—Protestant, Orthodox, Catholic—in a discussion focusing on mission in western culture. Here we can perceive an underlying agreement about the essentially missionary nature of the Church and the concomitant recognition that we are engaged in mission from within a local Church. It points to the need that mission move out from the experience of a local Christian community directed toward local reality and then beyond. At the conclusion of its report, the sector signals the intimate relation between local and universal: "We also need to learn from and include other than Christian believers as well as Christians from other cultures in our analysis and critique" (USCMA/DOM-NCCC 1987, 3).

Recognizing the relation between Gospel and western culture as a missiological issue is more than saying mission is present on six continents, or even that mission is everywhere. Challenging certain assumptions of western society from the perspective of the Gospel identifies a critical interpretation of mission, especially as this is seen in the religious historical context of the United States. Such an encounter between Gospel and culture in a given situation is much more than inculturation. As Amaladoss (1990a, 121–30) notes, the Gospel is intended to be counter-cultural. Inculturation arising as response to colonial importations of Christianity in many parts of the world can lead to the opposite relation between Gospel and society, if the Gospel becomes so absorbed by the culture and its values that it can no longer question its cultural setting (cf. Hunsberger 1991, 407–8).

From a missionary perspective, Christians in the United States are perhaps in a situation where the Gospel has been so adapted to the cultural-societal demands that it no longer raises any questions. As one tries to understand mission in a postmodern world, this recognition of how critical the relation between Gospel and culture is for mission is an important indicator of how the missionary conversations between Protestants and Catholics are likely to evolve in the immediate future.

Much critical debate in recent years has dealt with sending missionaries overseas and seeing everything as mission. As Scherer notes, "the bewildering reality of change" makes "missionary terminology of the older missionary era obsolete" (1987, 245). We are still in a transition from a colonial understanding of the missionary mandate. These ambiguities are present in all discussions about mission, ecumenical and within specific traditions. Scherer states that "mission theology should assist with the task of creating a fresh vocabulary for missionary function in the new missionary era, taking into account that mission is the task of the Church in all six continents" (1987, 245).

Both Protestants and Catholics are moving to a more vital understanding of the missionary nature of the Church. Historical experience of those who have traditionally carried the mission mandate both among Protestants and Catholics makes it difficult to perceive what mission looks like as it emanates from the local Christian community. Approaching the question of encounter between Gospel and western culture opens up insights into this way of being in mission. Increasing commitment among Protestant and Catholic missiologists to take this starting point in their discussions about mission is encouraging. Elements present in this discussion are:

- questions posed by the context of a given society
- analysis of co-optation of the Gospel message by particular values in a given society
- recognition of the need for missiological proclamation in a given place
- the reception of missionaries who profess faith in Jesus Christ, but from a different perspective, e.g., the role of the "foreigner" as one who awakens and helps to call for transformation, conversion by their faith stance
- willingness to enter into a situation and walk with those there
- concern for opening the local Christian community to relations toward other Christian communities throughout the world.

Central to this perception is the missiological recognition of the need for missionaries to come to western peoples, and consequently a need to know how one prepares for mission in postmodern postenlightenment society.

## Conclusion

There has been a significant growth toward consensus in Protestant-Roman Catholic missiological discussions. Developments in ecclesiology, and especially in the area of mission-church relationship, have enabled participants in these discussions to move toward greater agreement, and appear to be fostering an ecumenical mission paradigm (cf. Bosch 1991b, 368–89).

While historical difficulties continue to accompany these discussions (cf. USCMA/DOM-NCCC 1987, 7, 19–20), common recognition of the need to take up the question of Gospel and western culture from a missiological perspective indicates an important path for future developments of an ecumenical mission paradigm. This question of Gospel and western culture focuses discussion on the central reality as the basis of a new missionary era, namely the relation between mission and the local church (cf. Bosch 1991b, 378–81; Scherer 1987, 197–200; *Redemptoris Missio* 1990, no. 2). To take this question up ecumenically, as has already been done on more than one occasion (cf. USCMA/DOM-NCCC 1987; Montefiore 1992), is to move beyond the time of transition from a colonial understanding of mission. The deep stirrings of God's love is mission operative at the heart of every Christian community which calls, sends and receives persons touched by that love to move beyond whatever barriers are present. Participating in such a mission means listening to God's Word together, being continually converted by that Word, and speaking that Word to others in a language they can understand, but which is sufficiently different to challenge their assumptions.

# 11

# Themes in Theology of Mission Arising Out of San Antonio and Canberra

## EMILIO CASTRO

World conferences and assemblies are moments in the ecumenical movement when churches gather to share out of the richness and diversity of their experiences. It is not a time when systematic theological work is done; but serious biblical and theological reflection, as well as analysis of the world scene, takes place. And in the forum nature of these meetings certain issues are highlighted. Dr. Arthur Glasser has attended many of these world events. He could never remain simply an observer. His passion for the world mission of the church made of him an active participant. He is a good illustration of the value of these ecumenical occasions: reciprocal caricatures break down and the engagement in prayerful search for clarity in obedience becomes a common concern. Out of the World Conference on Mission and Evangelism, held in San Antonio, Texas, USA, 1989, and the Seventh Assembly of the World Council of Churches in Canberra, Australia, 1991, I have chosen to highlight the following themes, not because they are new—they have all been with us in our mission discussions since the early church—but because the reflections in these meetings suggest new impulses and new challenges as we enter the last decade of this century.

### Gospel and Culture

The relationship of gospel and culture has been a permanent, if ambiguous, concern for mission reflection and practice. The San Antonio conference recalls that history:

Emilio Castro, pastor and onetime president of the Evangelical Methodist Church of Uruguay, served for eleven years as Director of the WCC Commission on World Mission and Evangelism. Until recently he was the General Secretary of the World Council of Churches, and he has authored several books.

Cross-cultural evangelization has often entailed the imposition of cultural norms on the evangelized, besides bringing the good news of salvation. In some situations it is an ideological distortion of the gospel that has been imposed. In other places evangelization has been a means of breaking cultures. Precisely because of this, some communities have resisted the gospel. Other communities have received the gospel, and their cultures have been renewed and strengthened by the dynamic of the Holy Spirit working in them. The gospel has been experienced as a liberating force, breaking the power of oppressive aspects of culture. Culture as such does not constitute an absolute value — it has positive and negative aspects. (World Council of Churches 1990, 44)

Discussions of gospel and culture have focused on the need for the inculturation of the gospel "so that it may be heard, understood and accepted in all cultures" (World Council of Churches 1991a, 237). The Canberra assembly affirmed that the "gospel of Jesus Christ must become incarnate in every culture" (World Council of Churches 1991a, 252), and suggested, as criteria for the "handing on of God's truth . . . faithfulness to the apostolic faith of the church, creative application of the gospel to contemporary issues and situations, and self-criticism of efforts to communicate the gospel in fresh ways" (World Council of Churches 1991a, 237). During the assembly itself the sharing of concepts and images from particular cultures as vehicles for Christian truth brought new force to the search for a common understanding of how to live out these criteria in the various cultural contexts.

The drama of the encounter of cultures came to the assembly not only as a call to recognize ancient cultures, but also as a polemic confrontation about the way in which the gospel of Jesus Christ relates to the particular history of people and finds expression in our spirituality and in our theology. His Beatitude Patriarch Parthenios, introducing the main theme, "Come, Holy Spirit, Renew the Whole Creation," called us to recognize the mystery of the action of the Spirit, and that in the Spirit's freedom we should be ready for surprises.

All things are sanctified by the Holy Spirit, from the beginning of creation, when he hovered over the abyss, and now in nature, in heaven and on earth, in humanity, in all beings, in every living soul . . . Our witness is one of mission and dialogue. All tongues, nations, races, sexes, all kindreds, tribes and people are God's. . . . Our goal is the unity of the world. Such unity is not alien to the work of the Holy Spirit and the church. The Spirit blows where he wills, and we have no right, nor is it an act of love, for us to restrict his movement and his breathing, to bind him with fetters and barbed wire. (World Council of Churches 1991a, 31 and 36)

Professor Chung from Korea began her presentation, accompanied by a group of dancers, by invoking the spirits of the men and women of God from the Old and New Testaments, but also of many of the nations represented in the assembly. She reminded us of the cloud of witnesses coming to see our wrestling with the Spirit in the search for faithfulness to the gospel. But she also invited us to bolder actions — to recognize the manifestation of the Holy Spirit of God, the Triune God, in the spirits of the poor people of her country who, during millennia of suffering, were giving expression to spiritual values that need to be recognized.

> The spirit of this compassionate God has been always with us from the time of creation. God gave birth to us and the whole universe with her life-giving breath (*ruach*), the wind of life. This wind of life, this life-giving power of God is the Spirit which enabled people to come out of Egypt, resurrected Christ from death and started the church as a liberative community. We also experience the life-giving Spirit of God in our people's struggle for liberation, their cry for life and the beauty and gift of nature. (World Council of Churches 1991a, 40)[1]

For many, the two presentations seemed to indicate a contrast or even a contradiction in the way in which we perceive the Spirit of God. How do we recognize the Holy Spirit among other spirits? The assembly responded: "Spirits must be discerned. Not every spirit is of the Holy Spirit. The primary criterion for discerning the Holy Spirit is that the Holy Spirit is the Spirit of Christ; it points to the cross and resurrection and witnesses to the Lordship of Christ. The biblical list of 'fruits' of the Spirit, including love, joy, and peace, should also be applied (Gal. 5:22)" (World Council of Churches 1991a, 256).

I think the intellectual problem before us is both old and new. It is new in the sense that the church of Jesus Christ, having now become a reality in most parts of the world, is reflecting on the actual as well as past experience of respective peoples. It is coming to expressions of the faith that cannot be measured with yardsticks produced by other encounters of the gospel with other cultures in Europe or in any other parts of the world.

While the assembly spoke of the limits of diversity and need for clear criteria to be found in the confession of Jesus Christ, the problem remains. How are we accountable to one another? How do we relate to the tradition that comes from the gospel of Jesus Christ? Inculturation of the gospel is a must in any missionary approach. Faithfulness to the gospel is our only contribution to the common treasure of humanity. To bring those two together in permanent and creative tension, to learn from each other, is the basic mission challenge of the assembly. We need to explore our belonging to a community of faith which implies an accountability that is not simply setting limits to diversity, but an enlarging of the horizons, an understanding that other diversities are signs of new possibilities that may challenge us.

## Christian Witness in a Plural World

In 1983, the Vancouver assembly, after much debate, rejected a statement that claimed to "recognize God's creative work in the religious experience of people of other faiths." After numerous suggestions for rewriting, the statement was finally accepted in the following form: "While affirming the uniqueness of the birth, life, death and resurrection of Jesus, to which we bear witness, we recognize God's creative work in the seeking for religious truth among peoples of other faiths" (World Council of Churches 1983b, 40). It was only in the *seeking* for religious truth, not in the religious experience itself, that delegates were prepared to recognize God's creative work among peoples of other faiths.

When the participants at the conference in San Antonio faced the crucial issue of the theological significance of other faiths, they affirmed that though "We cannot point to any other way of salvation than Jesus Christ," nevertheless, they could not "set limits to the saving power of God" (World Council of Churches 1990, 32).

> In reaffirming the "evangelistic mandate" of the ecumenical movement, we would like to emphasize that we may never claim to have a full understanding of God's truth; we are only the recipients of God's grace. Our ministry of witness among people of other faiths presupposes our presence with them, sensitivity to their deepest faith commitments and experience, willingness to be their servants for Christ's sake, affirmation of what God has done and is doing among them, and love for them. Since God's mystery in Christ surpasses our understanding and since our knowledge of God's saving power is imperfect, we Christians are called to be witnesses to others, not judges of them. (World Council of Churches 1990, 32)

The conference came to two conclusions: 1) Christians are called to share their faith with persons of other faiths and invite them to be disciples of Jesus Christ; and 2) Christians should be open to the possibility of God's presence and work in people of other faiths. There was awareness that the conviction that witness to Jesus Christ can never be given up exists in tension with an affirmation of God's presence and work in people of other faiths. But, the conference affirmed, "we appreciate this tension, and do not attempt to resolve it" (World Council of Churches 1990, 33).

In all the world's major religions, there has been an almost simultaneous awakening in recent years to an awareness of their own identity and also, in many cases, to an awareness of their missionary responsibility. We have only to read the daily press to see the proliferation of ethnic conflicts with a strong religious content where fanaticism plays a destructive role. We are all too quick to recognize fanaticism when shown by some other religions, forgetting the sombre pages of our own Christian history and forgetting that sin, in the form of sectarian pride, lies in wait for us as a potential enemy to be exorcised.

The work of evangelism, therefore, demands that we search together with members of other faiths for a *modus vivendi*, a way of organizing society which will provide a degree of freedom in which we are all at liberty to convince and be convinced, but also where all can contribute to the establishing of a society that is enriched by these different contributions and that is not obliged to be in permanent conflict because of our different religious practices. This is becoming a very dangerous and serious problem in many areas of the world. It is a new global situation. Religions are here to stay.

What does it mean, then, for our evangelistic duty to proclaim the gospel to every creature, to call all nations to discipleship in Christ, to baptize and build Christian communities? We have a reality that invites to coexistence and to conviviality, which demands that we live side by side, and at the same time we have the imperative of the gospel to share the name of Jesus Christ with every creature. Proclamation in this new situation clearly demands a dialogical attitude. And that is, in fact, true of every situation. There is no way to share the gospel of God in Christ—offering himself on the cross, in total powerlessness, without any imposition, but appealing to the consciousness of the people contemplating him—with an imperial colonial superiority attitude that would contaminate our Christian attitude in relation to others. There is no way to proclaim the gospel of the crucified and risen Lord if it is not in an attitude of respect and consideration for the other. At the same time, no dialogue is such without an honest testimony of our faith allegiance. As the San Antonio conference said:

> Dialogue has its own place and integrity and is neither opposed to nor compatible with witness or proclamation. We do not water down our own commitment if we engage in dialogue; as a matter of fact, dialogue between people of different faiths is spurious, unless it proceeds from the acceptance and expression of faith commitment. Indeed, life with people of other faiths and ideologies is by its very nature an encounter of commitments. (World Council of Churches 1982d, paragraph 45) In dialogue we are invited to listen, in openness, to the possibility that the God we know in Jesus Christ may encounter us also in the lives of our neighbours of other faiths. On the other hand, we also see that the mutual sharing with people of other faiths in the efforts for justice, peace and service to the environment engages us in dialogue, "the dialogue of life." (World Council of Churches 1990, 32, 33)

Dialogue is not only or basically an intellectual exercise. It is a living side by side in an attitude of respect, learning and collaboration toward the construction of more human societies. Our challenge is to build societies where peoples of different religious loyalties will live side by side, giving testimony to their respective convictions and uniting forces in the building up of a common society.

Most of the religions, including Christianity, believe that their ultimate allegiance must permeate the life of society. While we do not have a model of society to call Christian, it is obvious from past Christian history that we have always assumed that the gospel values should permeate the whole of society. Other religious systems, especially Islam, do not distinguish between the civil society and the religious society. When we call for the building of secular societies where all religions will have the freedom to express themselves, they would affirm that a secular society is already based on the Christian premises of the relation between private individual and communal religion. The need, therefore, is for an expansion of our imagination, to discern a commonality of aims inside an obviously diverse presupposition of the nature of civil society as such. The search for common values and goals will provide the level of reciprocal trust where the testimony to our faith in Jesus Christ will have a far better chance to be understood.

The proclamation of Jesus Christ in this new religious atmosphere demands serious theological reflection on the significance of Jesus Christ for the whole of humankind and the significance of other religions in God's eschatological perspective, to combine, as Paul does in Romans 11, the passion for the sharing of the gospel with people of other religious convictions and the respect for the mystery of God in terms of his own eschatological recapitulation of all history.

In our evangelism, in our basic missionary attitude, we have let ourselves be led by negative judgment of the other instead of allowing ourselves to be guided entirely by contemplation of the crucified Christ and his loving service. Theologically it is clear that the gospel is by definition for others, but it is so as the expression and message of a nonsectarian love.

As we attempt to evaluate the role of other religious faiths in God's eschatological plan, we recall that when the Apostle Paul affirms his faith and hope in an eschatological understanding of the role attributed to Israel after the coming of Christ, he does so not as an excuse for not bearing witness to his people, but out of passionate concern that they should all come to know Jesus (Romans 9:1–3, 10:1). Nothing in our ecumenical experience in this matter of the role and place of other faiths questions the central tenet of our faith: that God was in Christ reconciling the world to God's own self. To accept the questions addressed to us by other religious faiths is to adopt the attitude urged by the Apostle Peter: "Always be prepared to make a defence to anyone who calls you to account for the hope that is in you."

## Mission in a Trinitarian Understanding

"The purpose of God according to Holy Scripture is to gather the whole of creation under the Lordship of Christ Jesus in whom, by the power of the Holy Spirit, all are brought into communion with God (Eph. 1)." So declared the Canberra assembly. It went on to affirm that:

> The Church is the foretaste of this communion with God and with one another. The grace of our Lord Jesus Christ, the love of God, and the communion of the Holy Spirit enable the one Church to live as sign of the reign of God and servant of the reconciliation with God, promised and provided for the whole creation. The purpose of the Church is to unite people in Christ in the power of the Spirit, to manifest communion in prayer and action and thus to point to the fulness of God in the glory of the kingdom. (World Council of Churches 1991a, 172)

The basic affirmation of the Great Commission is that Jesus has been given power over all creation on earth and in heaven. It is, in many ways, a tremendous pretension to proclaim this Jesus, but it is necessary for us to understand the event of Jesus Christ as going far beyond the conflicts with the authorities in Palestine, to see his triumph over sin and death as the promise of a new day for the whole of humankind and the beginning of a new relation with the whole of creation. We could speak of the eschatological frame of reference for the mission of the Christian church. We are not to call people to recognize in Jesus Christ only their saviour; they are invited to recognize in him the saviour of the world, the liberator of all creation. The kingdom of God is in the horizon of the mission of the church.

The assembly, in its work in Section I, reminds us that the biblical claim is

> that the redemptive work of Jesus Christ was renewal not only of human life, but of the whole cosmos. Thus we have hope that the covenant promises for the earth's wholeness can find fulfilment. In Christ, "the creation itself will be set free from its bondage to decay and will obtain the freedom of the glory of the children of God" (Rom. 8:21). In the whole of the Christian life, we take up the created things of this world and offer them to God for sanctification and transfiguration so that they might manifest the kingdom, where God's will is done and the creation glorifies God forever. (World Council of Churches 1991a, 57)

The sacraments of Christian worship use the elements of the created world to manifest the Triune God present among and in us. This sacramental Christian perspective influences our approach to the creation in general.

San Antonio expressed the same concern:

> Because the earth is the Lord's, the responsibility of the church towards the earth is a crucial part of the Church's mission. This mission brings the gospel of hope to all creation—a hope rooted in the resurrection of Christ. We are reminded that the early and undivided church stressed the deep unity between humanity and the whole of creation. In our church today we should share in prayer for the anxieties of this time. Our celebration of the Lord's table should affirm God's redeeming love for all creation, and the breaking of the bread together should empower us to share the gifts of the earth with one another. (World Council of Churches 1991a, 172)

Shalom, promised by the prophets in the Old Testament, is also an important point of reference. Especially in the Gospel of John, Jesus insists on the notion of peace as part of his messianic kingdom, of his promise that should be proclaimed and announced all over the world. The Canberra assembly insisted that "The calling of the church is to proclaim reconciliation and to provide healing, to overcome divisions based on race, gender, age, culture, colour, and to bring all people into communion with God" (World Council of Churches 1991a, 66).

The conviction of the presence of uncreated energies, of the action of the Holy Spirit awakening and calling nature and history to renewal, brings with it an evangelistic occasion. The Spirit of truth uncovers and reveals all truth. As we participate in the search for a new respect for nature and a new care for our neighbor, we point to God's scope and care for creation and humanity fully visible and manifested in Jesus Christ. As basic questions of value, meaning, purpose and priority confront humankind, to announce the creative activity of the Spirit is to call to a deeper dimension of reality and to an obligation to give account of the hope that is in us.

As we see the Spirit of Christ in the cross and resurrection breaking all human barriers and announcing the kingdom that is coming, we perceive the struggle for justice in the world as a spiritual struggle, where the Spirit points to Jesus as the full historical manifestation of redeeming love, creating energy and consoling presence. "There is an urgent need today for a new type of mission, not into foreign lands but into 'foreign structures.' By this term we mean economic, social and political structures which do not at all conform to Christian moral standards" (World Council of Churches 1991a, 66).

We have not yet been able to articulate together clearly the belonging of our historical commitments to the vision of the kingdom with our being the people of the Spirit, the body of Christ. However the Canberra assembly, with its main theme centered on the prayer to the Holy Spirit, obliged us to become very personal and to give testimony of the action of the Holy Spirit in the transformation of persons, church and world. In the New Testament, the Spirit is sent upon the whole community and upon each one of the members of that community. The Spirit creates *koinonia*, community with a purpose, to call all things to conversion and reconciliation in Jesus Christ; but inside that *koinonia*, the Spirit grants specific gifts for the building up of the body of Christ.

This personal transformation, this awareness of the action of the Spirit for sanctification, takes place inside the life of the Christian community, a community that is also being submitted to the sanctification activity of the Spirit and is being freed for service to God in the world. San Antonio, in stressing the integral quality of community in the Christian experience, affirmed:

> God in Trinity is a community of divine persons. Human beings are called to constitute life in the likeness of God, bound to one another in complete love. The unity/community which is God, established and maintained by love (agape), constitutes the plan for humanity. No individual person can constitute God's likeness as one. Just and loving interpersonal relationships are fundamental, for human life can reflect God's Trinitarian life—God's likeness—only in community, obedient to the will of God. And God's will is justice, the fullness of life for all God's children, of every nation, race and gender. (World Council of Churches 1991a, as of para. 18, pp. 44, 45)

The activity of the Spirit signifies a continuous process of transformation of the community and each of its members; the Spirit also works in the search for unity and reconciliation that is becoming more and more visible in the life of our churches.

The Holy Spirit challenges God's people to holy living, personally and corporately. Personal sanctification and corporate transformation belong together. At all times life is to be lived under and by the power of the Spirit. This continuous process of transfiguration, this ecclesiology of *koinonia* at the service of God's purpose to save and reconcile all in Christ, should become the commanding vision of the ecumenical movement and a challenge to our false dichotomies. How narrow is our ecclesiology when it centers on my salvation, forgetting the symbolic and sacramental service to be rendered to the whole of creation! But also how shallow is our social involvement when it misses the personal dimension of sanctification and eternal life and the communal ecclesial dimension of our faith!

To be possessed by the Spirit of God means internal, personal freedom produced by the action of that same Spirit. "The Holy Spirit is gloriously free and unbound (John 3) freeing and unbinding God's people from the structures and strictures of this world (Rom. 12). The challenge to God's people is to discover, accept and live in this freedom" (World Council of

Churches 1991a, 112). This freedom is the freedom to love and to serve; it is the freedom to invite all people and each individual to look beyond themselves to the love that God manifested to every creature and to make a commitment to be part of that all-embracing love.

## Notes

1. Editors' note: The perspective presented here, along with Dr. Castro's soft critique, is not supported by the editors of this volume. The inclusion of a reference to it, however, serves to show the urgency for continued dialogue and reflection in ecumenical theology of mission.

# 12

# From Vatican II to *Redemptoris Missio*

## A Development in the Theology of Mission

### THOMAS F. STRANSKY

### Vatican Council II (1962–1965)

Only by taking account of *all* the debates and resolutions of Vatican II can one understand the modern Roman Catholic Church (RCC), in particular for our purposes here, its understandings, motivations, practices, organization and even financing of missionary activities.

Pope John XXIII (1958-1963) intended the council of over 2,400 bishops from six continents to be the RCC's hope for "a new Pentecost," "a means of spiritual and apostolic renewal," "an updating (*aggiornamento*) of the church on the edge of a new era." After four two-month sessions, and with over 100,000 Latin words in sixteen documents, Vatican II covered every major biblical/theological/ ecclesiological issue, every major dimension of personal and communal renewal, of institutional life, of relationships to "Others" (whether other Christians, those of other world faiths, or of no explicit religious commitment), and of missionary and service outreach. The council directly faced marriage and the family, the development of culture, economic and social life, the political community, war and peace in the family of nations.

Vatican II used *the Church* as the fulcrum or vital center for all *aggiornamento* themes in its two longest synthetic documents: The Church (*Lumen Gentium* [LG], from its opening Latin words), and The Church in the Modern World (*Gaudium et Spes* [GS]). In their light the other fourteen

Thomas Stransky, Paulist, is the rector of the Tantur Ecumenical Institute for Theological Studies (Jerusalem), official consultor to the Pontifical Council for Christian Unity, and a member of the Joint Working Group between the Roman Catholic Church and the World Council of Churches. He is editor of the *Dictionary of the Ecumenical Movement* (1991).

statements bask. The central theological themes of the decree on the church's missionary activity (*Ad Gentes* [AG]) are derivative from LG and GS.[1]

As other Christian observers in the early 1960s, the Vatican II bishops were uncomfortably aware of a *Zeitgeist*, a mood that challenged the right of the church to be missionary. Such a mood was being fostered by advocates of a syncretistic union of all world religions, by internationalists who judged Christian mission to be an obstacle to peaceful coexistence between nations, by neonationalists who saw indigenous religion as an essential part of cultural heritage and identity which should be defended from "outside" Christian challenges, and Christians of a growing minority in a pluralistic one-world society who questioned if one had the right and responsibility to proclaim the explicit gospel to non-Christians. Were foreign missionaries but zealots who imposed a disturbing religious message among peoples who wanted to be left alone, and should be?

In this context, *Ad Gentes* intended to convince western Catholics to continue their support, by finance and personnel, of traditional foreign missionary activities as an ever vital function of the church.

## Post-Vatican II Developments (1966–1990)

The RCC as a whole, and each obediential member, were suddenly called to interiorize and carry out Vatican II's theological, pastoral and missionary demands. They were to do this in response to contradictory analyses of an elusively changing world, amid varied predictions about their consequences: for example, in relation to the decolonization process in the newly labeled "Third World" that was struggling through the first generations of new nationhood, blessed with new freedoms but cursed with new dependency syndromes. Only nostomania could expect the return of quiet seasons.

In hindsight, for the RCC, too much came too soon for too many. This future shock, this sudden disorientation of individual and collective consciousness and conscience, had much to do with post-Vatican II confusion and hesitations about the missionary nature and function of the church. It brought with it conflicting mission practices and an identity crisis within the traditional western missionaries' own lives, their sending organizations and supporters.

On the positive side, the very incarnate fidelities to Vatican II's challenges, including the risk of making mistakes, are causing holy tensions. Examples:

1. a movement of liberation theologies (initiated in Latin America) and a restructuring of local congregational life ("ecclesial basic communities"), so that the politically, socially and economically

oppressed and powerless have a voice in the very doing of theology in a faith that *does* justice

2. experiences of dialogue with peoples of other world faiths, especially in regions of Christian minorities (Asia), and of reflecting on the workings of God in those contexts

3. experiences of cooperation with "all people of good will" in building up a sane family of nations and societies within them, in the search for peace with justice

4. recognition of a soulless economic and technical development, especially in the West, that is now stimulating the search for truth about God, about the meaning of the human, of life itself

Nevertheless, some observers claim to hear the death gasps of traditional missions. Some are questioning the very validity of the biblical missionary mandate, or at least are asking for clearer whys. Has the content of that mandate been reduced to interreligious dialogue, works of human development, and socioeconomic, political and cultural liberations? Or since in the church's history the missionary drive has always been a sign of vitality, is its lessening ultimately a sign of a crisis of faith? of faith in the church? of faith in Jesus Christ? of faith in God?

## Official RC Responses and *Redemptoris Hominis*

By "official" I mean those teachings, directives, and guidelines which come from "the center"—the Holy See/Vatican, either directly from the pope or from his several offices within the Roman Curia. Such varied statements intentionally bear different degrees of authority or finality—a fact too often forgotten in their interpretations. An encyclical, such as John Paul II's *Redemptoris Missio* (RM, Dec.7, 1990), is a formal pastoral letter addressed to the universal RCC as a means of maintaining unity in faith and practice.[2]

The pope's mission encyclical, of burdensome length, reflects—sometimes strongly, sometimes weakly—official RC responses to an array of post-Vatican II positive and negative developments in the theology and practice of mission which during twenty-five years have been swirling within a world church of over 600 million adherents.

In this teaching task of both affirmation and correction, RM faces an almost no-win reception. On the one hand, RM tries to analyze church/world situations, and under the complex mission umbrella to synthesize with chosen emphases and nuances a massive RC theological heritage. On the other hand, RM raises realistic issues that leave room for biblicists, theologians and practitioners to debate and develop. Critics would prefer other emphases, or more detailed magisterial assertions on certain issues, or more open debate space on the same.

The pope sees a "new springtime of Christianity" but also "the waning of missionary activity specifically directed 'to the nations (*ad gentes*)' " at the very time when "God is opening before the church the horizons of a humanity more fully prepared for the sowing of the Gospel." He wants "to clear up doubts and ambiguities" in order to "commit all the church's energies to a new evangelization and to the mission *ad gentes.*" He sees the *urgency* of this: since Vatican II "the number of those who do not know Christ and do not know the Church . . . has almost doubled" in the world of 5.4 billion people (RM 1–3).

In short, the pope's very optimism in reading "the signs of the times" leads him to *exclude* those assertions of some biblicists, theologians and practitioners which go beyond the parameters of common RC teaching and, in his judgment, corrode "the permanent validity of the missionary mandate": in theology, in Christology, in ecclesiology, in soteriology (God's salvific ways), and ultimately, in missiology.

### Central Teachings

1. Excluded are *theologies* which deny the classic creedal understandings of the mystery of the Trinity. For the Christian, there can be no separation between theological reflection on the one God and on the triune God. This blunt insistence responds to claims that only a "theo-centric," a *non*-trinitarian approach, is amenable and understandable to those who are not Christian yet wish to find a common ground "in the one divine reality, by whatever name it is called" (RM 17). The God of the Christian faith to be proclaimed is the triune God, the God of salvation, the missionary God.

The ultimate ground for mission does not rest in the human desire for one's own or for others' salvation, or in our love for God and people, but in the trinitarian mystery of the "sending" God, centered in Christ, the Sent-One (Heb. 3:1), and in the Spirit, ("the principal agent of mission" [30]), who carry out the Father's saving plan: to build up the kingdom or reign of God.

Vatican II corrected the sharp RC tendency to co-extend the church with the reign of God. As Paul VI stated in 1975: "Only the Kingdom is absolute, and it makes everything else relative" (EN 27), even the church. God rules, the kingdom happens whenever and wherever God's will is fulfilled, within or outside the visible borders of the church.

Both the Bible and church tradition use different words and metaphors to describe and interpret this mission of God: building up, salvation, conversion, liberation, reconciliation, transfiguration, and so forth. None of them should be "reductive" of mission (RM 17). Reductive examples: *salvation* applies only to "souls," or only to those who are explicitly committed to Jesus Christ as Lord and Savior; *reconciliation*, only to human relationships; *liberation*, only to political, social or economic conditions; *transfigu-*

*ration*, only to persons (and not to all cultures, humanity itself, indeed the whole of creation). "The Kingdom of God is the manifestation and the realization of God's plan of salvation *in all its fullness*" (RM 15). It is not for us and our words to separate what the Father and the Spirit already hold together in the Word.

This movement of being divinely sent for kingdom building extends to the whole length and depth of ecclesial life in space and time. It transcends any and all of the church's specific tasks (e.g., initial evangelization, catechizing and preaching, worship, and loving service) and specific vocations within the church (e.g., the laity and the ordained). "The whole Church is missionary by its very nature" (RM 62) expresses that the church is called to become what it is.

2. Excluded are *Christologies* that deny Jesus Christ to be the fundamental, indispensable mediator between God and humankind, the sole mediator of salvation, redemption, justification, sanctification, and final reconciliation.

Jesus of Nazareth is the incarnate Word. To separate the Word from Jesus Christ, or Jesus from the Christ (a "Jesus of Nazareth" who is other than the "Christ of faith"), is "contrary to the Christian faith. . . . Jesus of Nazareth is the incarnate Word—a single and indivisible person." In him "the reign of God became present and was fulfilled." In him God wills all things to be united, in heaven and on earth [cf. Eph. 1:10]. Therefore, only in Jesus Christ is salvation, only through him comes salvation (18, 6).

This is the Good News—*holistic* salvation, best articulated by Paul VI: "As kernel and center of the Good News, Christ proclaims *salvation*, this great gift of God which is *liberation* from *everything* that oppresses man but which is, *above all*, liberation from *sin* and *the evil one*, in the joy of knowing God and being known by God, of seeing God, and of being turned over to God" (EN 9; RM 44).

3. Excluded are *ecclesiologies* that sever the relationship between the reign of God, the Christ, and his visible, structured community of disciples—the church.

The church is that part of humankind whom God has called explicitly to accept and live out the mission of building up, in word and deed, "the reign of Christ and of God among all peoples" (Eph. 5:5). "The kingdom of God cannot be detached from Christ or from the church" (RM 18), for the Church is "on earth the initial budding forth of God's kingdom" (LG 5), "the sign and instrument of this kingdom which is and is to come" (EN 59). "Distinct from Christ and the kingdom, but indissolubly united to both" (RM 19), the church is "not an end in itself, but fervently concerned to be completely of Christ, in Christ and for Christ, as well as completely of men and women, among them and for them" (EN 34; RM 19), so that the church can "open up for all men and women a free and sure path to full participation in the mystery of Christ" (AG 5). To say yes to Christ is to say yes to God's reign and to the Body of Christ, head and members, the church—

the icon of the presence in the world of God and of the kingdom.

Vatican official statements too often speak of "the Kingdom," "the Gospel," or "the Church" as if they exist in culturally disembodied forms, to which the cultures of peoples need to be "adapted" by being "purified," "elevated," "transformed," "perfected," or John Paul II's favorite word, "redeemed." But *Ad Gentes* imaged a particular church as the local incarnation of whatever in "the customs, traditions, wisdom, teaching, arts and sciences of the people could be used to praise the glory of the Creator, manifest the grace of the Savior, or contribute to the right ordering of Christian life." To be faithful to this image of earthing the church of the Gospel is to effect a profound *inculturation* in every sphere of ecclesial life: theology, ethics, primary evangelization, catechetics and preaching, religious life, formation of laity and clergy, liturgical worship, congregational life, ecumenical and interreligious relations, and canonical legislation (AG 19–22).

Thus, inculturation works dialectically in a "marvelous exchange": the transformation of a culture by the gospel, and the reexpression of the Gospel in terms of that culture. The church is to be completely at home among each people in the same authentic way that Jesus was at home in Nazareth. This is genuine catholicity.

RM stresses the first part of the process, even using an already heavily cultured word which is more than gospel, *Christianity*: "the intimate transformation of authentic cultural values through their integration in Christianity and the insertion of Christianity in the various human cultures" (52). In fact, it is an illusion to name an existing ideal culture called Christianity, certainly not Europe or North America. Even more in practice than in theory, Rome still hesitates to confront that second necessary part of the process—the reexpression of the Gospel: not only Africa christianized by the Christian faith but also the faith Africanized.

Two guiding principles are "compatibility with the gospel and communion with the universal church" (59), but in practice since Vatican II, Rome seems to display too much fear of possible overdomesticated gospels and too much anxiety of a potential diversified, culturally polycentric church unable to be held together in unity. Thus, this "particularly urgent" missionary objective of inculturation is for the pope a "gradual, slow journey" (RM 52).

So the questions remain to haunt: how do the *gentes* of the world become the *populus Dei* (people of God)? How much and what of their being *gentes* do they have to be freed *from* in order to be free *for* being mature member communities of the one yet diverse *Populus Dei*?

The church is a visible, structured family of local ("particular") churches, united in faith and sacraments and in governance through their overseers or bishops, with and under the bishop of Rome ("the servant of servants," responsible to maintain and foster the unity of the church in all its diversities). Together they bear missionary solicitude and direct responsibility for the whole church (RM 63). Through this family of local churches, the universal church and each particular church achieve growth in harmony through "authentic reciprocity" (64). Each should be generous and open to the needs of the others and share its spiritual and material goods. A local church is defective if it only receives or only gives, or worse, if it neither receives nor gives. "The evangelizing activity of the Christian community, first in its own locality, and then elsewhere as part of the church's universal mission, is the clearest sign of a mature faith." Thus, mission is not just *from* some countries, groups, races or cultures *to* others, but *in* and *to* all. Mission realizes the communion of churches in the church (48–49, 62–64).

But the one and only church bears historical divisions which contradict the will of Christ, scandalize the world, and damage the good news of reconciliation. Not yet fulfilled is the vocation of the church to be one, as Jesus is in the Father and the Father in Jesus, in order that the world may believe in the Sending God. Ecumenical and missionary activities are an inseparable duet. Even while the churches are divided, together they are called to common witness (50) by manifesting, especially through joint efforts, whatever divine gifts of truth and life they already share and experience together.

4. Excluded are *soteriologies* that claim that because God's universal love – God's self-communication through Christ – wills that every man and woman should be rescued from sin, death and judgment, every person *is* saved from the beginning to the end of God's salvation process, whether that person is explicitly Christian or not. Also excluded are soteriologies that restrict God's free initiative of salvation through undeserved grace, either by placing those initiatives only within the explicit Christian arena (e.g., explicit faith in Jesus Christ as Lord and Savior and explicit membership in the church), or by binding them to human intentions and efforts.

The old question of "the salvation of the unbeliever" finds a more developed answer in Vatican II and a more focused response in John Paul II's writings on Christian *anthropology* (the reality of grace in the human). In his first encyclical he states: "the human person – every person, without exception – has been redeemed by Christ; because Christ is in a way united to every human person, even if the individual may not realize this fact. Christ, who died and was raised up for all – for every human being and for all – *can* through his Spirit offer humans the light and the strength to measure up to his or her supreme destiny" (RH 14; RM 3). "The Spirit offers everyone the possibility of salvation through human cooperation, and works in everyone through 'seeds of the Word' found in human initiatives – including religious ones – and in human efforts to attain truth, goodness, and God himself" (RM 26, citing several Vatican II texts). Thus, a twofold respect dictates the church's relationship with other religions: "respect for man in his/her quest for the deepest questions of one's life, and respect for the action of the Spirit in man" (29). "Salvation, always a gift of the Spirit, requires man's cooperation, both to save oneself and to save others" (9). But the human person is free, and one can will rebellious fundamental no's.

If so, then "Why the church?" "Why be a Christian?" In "the one mystery of salvation" (9), all people are searching, albeit at times in a confused way" (11), and need the "communion of life, love and truth" which is the church, "the instrument of salvation for all" (9).

In short, everyone *can* be saved, but one *is* saved when "good faith," "sincere heart" and conscience-dictated deeds are present. God's undeserved, free initiating grace is always necessary, as *somehow* necessary is Christ's mediation, and *somehow* the church ("a mysterious relationship" [10]). "The somehows" and "the ways of God," the saving yes's and the damning no's to ever-present saving grace by free persons are left to theologians who, as did their predecessors, are developing the faith which seeks understanding.

5. Excluded are *missiologies* that so restrict the church's purposes and activities that the church need not try to offer all men and women, everywhere, their God-given right: a valid opportunity to be directly challenged by the explicit Gospel of explicit faith in Jesus Christ, the one Lord and Savior of all, and in his church. "The Church cannot fail to proclaim that Jesus came to reveal the face of God ... that true liberation consists in opening oneself to the love of Christ, 'our peace' (Eph. 2:14), and to his Church" (11).

In such proclamation the church should respect and foster the right of the person and of communities to social and civil freedom; that is, freedom from any coercion to act against conscience and prevention from expressing belief in teaching, worship, or social service. But more than that, proclamation should respect the gospel pedagogy of Christian witness and avoid whatever does not conform to the ways God draws free persons to respond to divine calls to serve God in spirit and in truth. Otherwise Christian witness is corrupted, becomes counter-proclamation, and thus proselytism (8).

Since Vatican II, *in practice* Roman Catholic and the wider ecumenical circles have become much more sensitive to the distinction between authentic witness and proselytism in proclamation and other missionary activities. They are rightly afraid of committing acts of spiritual violence (use Jesus as a club with which to herd people into salvation); or of being arrogantly disrespectful of others ("You are nothing in God's eyes and heart unless you explicitly believe in Jesus as Lord and Savior"); or of repeating past imperialisms (the presumed rights of God-squads prevail over "mere" human freedoms, including the right to be free from the manipulative hard sell). Thus irreplaceable initial proclamation is a permanent priority in the complex reality of mission among human communities (44).

### Mission *Ad Gentes*

RM develops *Ad Gentes'* threefold division of human communities. First are "peoples, groups and socio-cultural contexts in which Christ and his gospel are unknown, or which lack local Christian communities sufficiently mature to be able to incarnate the faith in their own environment and proclaim it to other groups." These arenas call for *mission ad gentes*, strictly speaking: primary or initial evangelization and founding or developing local churches. A second group includes those communities in which the already solidly established church functions normally: solid ecclesial structures, fervent faith in practice, "a sense of commitment to the universal mission." These communities call for *pastoral care*. The third group consists of those communities in areas with ancient Christian roots in which the baptized have lapsed in their faith and practice, becoming either nominal church adherents or *de*churched. These communities call for a *new* evangelization, a *re-evangelization* (33).

Unlike Vatican II's *Ad Gentes*, RM does not slight this third category, and it perceptively recognizes that one cannot detail a world, even a region, by a map with different designating colors of clear boundaries between missionary and pastoral and reevangelizing activities.

Furthermore, if an objective of mission *ad gentes* is "to found Christian communities and develop particular churches to their full maturity by "functioning normally in its local setting" (48), it is not clear where such churches are and when normal functioning begins.

True, every Christian is a missionary by baptism (71), but some—lay, religious and clergy—have "a special vocation patterned on that of the Apostles"—"a total commitment to evangelization," "one's whole person and life," "a radical self-giving without limits of energy and time," usually bonded together in mission institutes (65). The church will never become truly, fully missionary unless each particular church has missionaries *ad gentes* who radically exemplify what each Christian is and is called to become.

Because of so many new multicultural situations created by migrants, refugees and immigrant faiths, especially in burgeoning urban centers in all continents, in the final analysis no local church is so solidly "functioning normally" that it can eschew missionaries *ad gentes.* No culture exists that is definitively permeated by gospel values. Mission *ad gentes* remains in and to six continents.

## Conclusion

The above only shorthands some of the developments in official RC teaching, as expressed in *Redemptoris Missio*. It is only one example of the fundamental struggle of the RCC which tries not to be a self-centered, arrogant clan, but to be a selfless, humble servant-community that enters into profound solidarity with the experiences of human society, takes humanity seriously in the unfolding of its history, and *places the mystery of God within human history.*

One feels in the heart of RM those key creative tensions of the church's incarnating those gifts which it confesses according to the Nicene Creed (325): one, holy, catholic and apostolic. The tensions

a) between the necessary unity without uniformity of the church and legitimate, indeed necessary diversity without contradictions and divisions, during the transition of the RCC from the northern Atlantic center to a polycentric worldwide basis ("One")
b) between the fullness of Christian life and the perfection of love in adoring God in spirit and in truth and the embrace of a good yet sinful world, with choices, often ambiguous, of love of neighbor ("Holy")
c) between "the gospel message" to be proclaimed and its inculturations or integration of all that is authentically human ("Catholic")
d) between the one mission of ministry of teaching, worship and service inspired by the evangelical vision and teaching of the original apostles (Tradition), and the many traditions and ministries, always to be purified and renewed, by which it is effected ("Apostolic").

### Notes

1. See, e.g., A. P. Flannery, ed. (1975) in loco.
2. One should evaluate each encyclical and its sections on what is proposed and why, in the context of Vatican II teachings, of previous pronouncements from popes and the Curia, and of theological, biblical writings. RM is twinned with John Paul's first encyclical, *Redemptor Hominis* (The Redeemer of Humankind, March 4, 1979), in which he sets forth "the central commitment of my new ecclesial service . . . the relationship between the mystery of redemption in Jesus Christ and the dignity of man": "the church's fundamental function of every age, and particularly ours, is to direct man's gaze, to point the awareness and experience of the whole of humanity towards the mystery of Christ." And the pope supports his *Redemptoris Missio* with frequent quotes from Paul VI's *Evangelii Nuntiandi* (EN, Evangelization in the Modern World, 1975), itself a personalized meditation on the discussions and resolutions of the 1974 fourth Bishops' Synod—a postcouncil structure of representatives from each of the national or regional episcopal conferences; the 1974 theme—evangelization. Both EN and RM commemorate Vatican II's *Ad Gentes*: EN, the tenth anniversary; RM, the twenty-fifth.

Some sections of RM are all-too-brief summaries of John Paul's seven previous encyclicals, in particular, on the mercy of God (*Dives in Misericordia* 1980), on human labor (*Laborem Exercens* (1982), on the reevangelization of Greater Europe (*Slavorum Apostoli* 1985), and on social justice (*Sollicitudo Rei Socialis* 1988).

Furthermore, Vatican curial departments have issued careful teaching documents that more competently expand and nuance essential missionary themes in RM; in particular, those statements from the Congregations on Faith and Doctrine (e.g., liberation theologies); for the Eastern Churches; for Catholic Education; for the Evangelization of Peoples; the Council for Justice and Peace; for Christian

Unity; for Interreligious Relations; for the Laity; and for Culture.

And the Codes of Canon Law for the Western Church (1983) and the Eastern Catholic Churches (1989) include legislated missionary rights and responsibilities for different RC segments, structures, and institutions.

# PART FOUR

# EVANGELICAL CONCERNS

# Introductory Overview

The question is not whether Arthur Glasser is an evangelical, but it might be asked, "What kind of evangelical is he?" To be an evangelical in these days could mean being a fundamentalist or a charismatic or one who takes a variety of positions in between. It is such a ubiquitous term that evangelicals are in somewhat of a dilemma when describing themselves.

Ralph Covell's chapter is written around the current state of evangelicals. He refers to three classifications of evangelicals suggested by Paul Knitter. These are the fundamentalists, the conservatives and the ecumenicals. Art Glasser, being very much his own person, has an identity, in some ways, with all these categories. Beginning in the fundamentalist camp, he moved to a conservative ecumenical stance in later years. He has even objected, on occasion, to being called a conservative, as we shall mention below. The trajectories of his life have absolutely nothing to do with being wishy-washy. Art is too respectful of his own conservative tradition to be a classic ecumenic; while he is too respectful of the largeness of the body of Christ to be a classic conservative.

In fairness, we should refer to Art's own words to describe who he is as an evangelical. In the 1970s he was active in attendance at meetings of the CWME and the World Council. In reporting to the ASM about his reactions to the World Council Assembly at Bangkok (1974), he describes himself as an evangelical for the following reasons: his ground of religious authority is the Bible; all that Jesus said is normative for the church; and he is committed to certain apostolic emphases such as the new birth, holiness of life, and the biblical mandate to evangelize the world. Albeit, he preferred not to be called a "conservative" because of the term's close identity with an "obscurantist, anti-intellectual approach to biblical scholarship" (Glasser 1974).

Extremism, even on bedrock issues such as evangelism and the church, does invite error. Paul Hiebert and Ralph Covell both show that evangelicals are becoming more objective about their tendency to reductionism. With his own kind of humor, Art Glasser often says that some of his colleagues are still "working to make the world safe for Calvinism!" Hiebert's Mennonite perspective is wonderfully congruent with Glasser's way of thinking about the kingdom. Art could have written this chapter. Just as an exaggerated focus on evangelism produces flawed ecclesiology and can be excessively individualistic, so preoccupation with the church becomes institutionally self-serving, neglectful of mission, even humanistic. The kingdom paradigm needs the combination of evangelism and the church, along with a dynamic loyalty to the King.

Glasser's roots in China have given him appreciation for China missionary and scholar Ralph Covell. Covell is saying that evangelicals have come a long way. Of the many points of agreement between Glasser and Covell, one would be especially important to Art. What good is right doctrine if the attitude of the messenger is wrong? Covell's call for the "crucified mind," a relational spirit, and seeing Jesus in the people of every culture, fits Art Glasser. I'm sure Ralph would agree that Art has been a model of his vision of the future for evangelicals.

Arthur's association with J. Robertson McQuilkin, Jr., deserves special notice, since Art taught at Columbia Bible College during the early fifties. McQuilken freely recognizes the variety among evangelicals. He discusses the kingdom as a sort of catalytic theme which identifies "this worldly" from "other worldly" evangelicals. These men are brothers who have walked many of the same roads. They would have a memorable debate on *basileia* as "kingship" or "kingdom." Art would enthusiastically endorse McQuilkin's call for loyalty to the King as the highest evidence of kingdomship, but he would not agree that kingdom theology gives "co-equal status to social action and evangelism," and he would have to ask him what he means by "mainstream evangelicals."

D. S. G.

# 13

# Evangelism, Church, and Kingdom

## PAUL G. HIEBERT

Evangelism, Church and Kingdom of God–these are the three central themes in the modern missionary movement. How we define and relate them determines our mission paradigm and practice.

## Reductionism

One of the driving forces in modernity is the search for a Grand Unified Theory (GUT) that integrates a field of study using one system of explanation. For the most part, this search for unity has been achieved in the sciences by resorting to reductionism. One theory is used to explain reality, and other theories are seen as derivative. For example, the physical sciences explain reality in material terms and reduce biological processes to chemistry. Psychology accounts for humans in psychological terms and treats social and cultural phenomena as epiphenomenal.

Reductionism is also widespread in modern missiological circles. We try to integrate the mission vision by focusing on one central theme.

### Evangelism

Some missiologists emphasize the priority of evangelism (figure 1, model 1; see p. 154). Without this, they argue, there will be no visible church and no manifestations of the Kingdom in lands where the Gospel has never been preached.

Paul Hiebert served as a missionary in India, where he also grew up. He taught Anthropology and South Asian Studies at Kansas State University, the University of Washington, and Fuller Theological Seminary, before coming to Trinity Evangelical Divinity School where he is Chair of the Department of Mission and Evangelism, and Professor of Mission and Anthropology.

This conviction has motivated missionaries to go to "unevangelized" tribes and villages at the ends of the earth and to give their lives so that all might hear and believe the good news of salvation. The church around the world today is largely a product of their labors.

One example is the Student Volunteer Movement, with its motto, "The evangelization of the world in this generation." For Mott this meant that the salvation offered by Christ be "made known to all so that all might believe in him and be saved (Scherer 1987, 15). The task of discipling converts was secondary, and assigned to the church and its leaders.

This paradigm, however, is weak. First, it often leads to a shallow Christianity because there was little follow-up of new converts. For example, during the peak of the mission movement in India and Africa, sending agencies instituted comity to minimize duplication and competition. Under comity a missionary couple was assigned from two to four hundred villages which they alone were responsible to evangelize. The standard method was "touring." The missionary went from village to village holding one- or two-night evangelistic services in each. Converts were given a day or two of instruction and then turned over to "native" itinerant pastors who often had more than ten to twenty village gatherings to supervise. Many visited the new converts for a few hours once or twice a month. Many converts turned back to their old faith due to opposition, persecution, and lack of instruction and the support of a Christian community. Those who stood firm had little knowledge of biblical truth or life. The result was a shallow Christianity plagued by syncretism (Luke and Carman 1968).

Second, this approach has a flawed ecclesiology. Those who emphasize

**Figure 1**
**Reductionist Models of Missions**

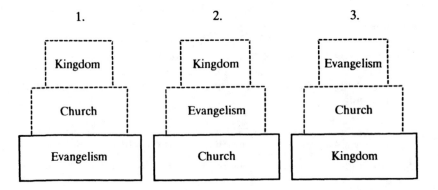

evangelism often give little attention to building churches into mature communities of faith and witness. Developing worship, fellowship, ministry, leadership, and Christian growth is left to others. These tasks are not seen as important as evangelism. In a sense, the church becomes a holding pen in which Christians wait until God takes them to heaven.

Third, salvation is defined in modern individualistic terms. It has to do with a person's relationship to God, not people. Faith is privatized and spiritualized. Success is measured by the number of converts, not transformed lives. Peace, justice and other social concerns are secondary tasks needed to keep the church busy until Christ returns. But an "individual gospel without a social gospel is a soul without a body and a social gospel without an individual gospel is a body without a soul" (Jones 1972, 40).

### Church

A second reductionism places priority on the church (figure 1, model 2) as the agent and goal of missions. Christ is preparing the church as a covenant community, and it gathers to worship God, strengthen the believers, and carry out evangelism. Our task in missions, therefore, is to build the church. To do so, we must organize congregations, train leaders, and nurture children in faith. It is the church that preserves the Gospel from generation to generation despite opposition and persecution.

The strength of this paradigm is its concern with worship, Christian community, and spiritual growth. It sees the church as God's light in this world.

One danger in this approach is that the Church becomes ingrown and self-serving and loses its sense of evangelism. There are so many needs in the church, and so little time and resources that urgency of evangelism is lost. Among the mainline denominations, this shift to church-centered missions is seen in the relationship between the International Missionary Council and the World Council of Churches. The Edinburgh (1910) Conference marked the high point of the modern western mission movement. Its very success, however, produced young churches around the world that wanted to join the global Christian community. The result was the formation of the World Council of Churches at Amsterdam (1948). The presence of young churches in largely unevangelized countries raised the question of who should do missions in these lands—foreigners or nationals. Given the growing anti-colonial ethos around the world, the answer increasingly was nationals. Missions became interchurch fellowship and interchurch aid. In the end, the WCC absorbed the IMC in New Delhi (1961). Lesslie Newbigin, then secretary of the IMC, warned that the merger could lead to a loss of mission vision (1958). This, in fact, took place. The missionary vision became diffused and fragmented in the mainline churches.

The evangelicals of North America continued to stress evangelism, but many of them became church-centered for another reason, namely by institutionalization. Churches, schools, and hospitals were built. In time these, like all institutions, demanded more resources and became self-centered (Weber 1968). Many evangelical churches maintained the rhetoric of evangelism, but in practice assigned their resources and best personnel to minister to the church. Evangelism became one among many of their projects.

A second danger is that this approach focuses on our human efforts. We come to believe that we build the church by planning, programs, and activities. We leave little place for prayer and God to work in extraordinary ways.

### Kingdom

A third group in missions focuses on the Kingdom of God as the central theme of missions (figure 1, model 3). Conversion and church, they point out, are not ends in themselves, but means to proclaim the Kingdom already come. This view was dominant at the Melbourne Conference of 1980, with its theme, "Your Kingdom Come." Krister Stendahl noted that the Lord's Prayer is "a sustained cry for the coming of the Kingdom" (Scherer 1987, 132). Ernst Käsemann said, "Christians and church communities are credible only as long as people hear issuing from them the passionate cry, 'Your kingdom come'" (1980, 61). Jesus himself came preaching the Kingdom and referred to it more than a hundred times. Our central task, therefore, is to proclaim justice and peace in a world full of oppression and wars. This is the good news of the gospel here and now.

The shift from a focus on church to that of Kingdom was seen in the WCC following the conference in Willingen. J. C. Hoekendijk criticized the church-centered missionary framework and called for a focus on the world and its needs. Mission increasingly was equated with bringing in the Kingdom (Scherer 1987, 107).

The strength of this paradigm is its concern for righteousness on earth and its encompassing view of the mission of the church. No narrow view here. Mission is not finished until the Kingdom has fully come and God's will is done on earth as it is in heaven. We must advance righteousness on earth (some add "by force, if need be").

One weakness of this view is that too often it loses sight of the lostness of human beings without Christ and the urgency of evangelism. Arthur Glasser pointed out in 1983 that "[The] church has never been so harassed and troubled by voices calling for the reduction or abandonment of [evangelism] — and for the reconceptualization of its message and mission in terms of social justice, international peace, racial integration, and the elimination of poverty" (1983, 30).

Another weakness is that the church becomes a political player in the arena of world politics. It is no longer a countercultural community on earth, a prophetic voice of the reign of God in the lives of his people. Or Christianity becomes a civil religion, used to justify democracy, capitalism, individual rights, and western civilization.

## Partial Integration

Many in missions have sought to counter the modern tendencies toward reductionism. They combine evangelism, church, and kingdom in various ways to develop a more complete paradigm of the church's missionary task (figure 2).

### *Evangelism and Church*

Early in the modern mission movement, leaders such as Henry Venn and Rufus Anderson tied evangelism to church planting (figure 2, model 1). They kept evangelism, but defined its goal as vital, autonomous, missionary churches. Roland Allen (1927), and later Donald McGavran (1980) made church planting the end of evangelism. They argued that evangelism is not complete until converts are incorporated into living churches. True churches must be defined in terms of their continuing growth and the multiplication of congregations.

The strength of this view is that it ties evangelism to the planting of churches. Evangelism without the church is incomplete. The church without evangelism is infirm. When we have both, we have a vital, growing church.

**Figure 2**
**Attempts at an Integrated Model of Missions**

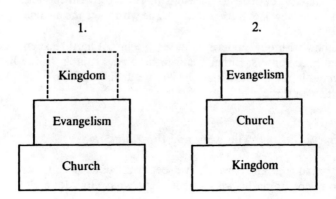

One weakness of this model is its human centeredness. Like all the paradigms we have surveyed so far, the focus is on what *we* do in missions. It is *we* who plan and carry out mission. If we fail, mission dies. This, indeed, is an arrogant view of mission.

Another weakness is its lack of concern for the poor and oppressed. E. Stanley Jones notes, "We made [the Kingdom] innocuous by reducing it to ecclesiasticism, the Church is the Kingdom; denominationalism, the particular denomination is the Kingdom; the nation is the Kingdom; the particular type of experience is the Kingdom; and so on" (1972, 30). We view ministry to human needs as secondary in view of the urgency of eternal salvation. In so doing, we have divorced spirit from body, future from present, and the Gospel from its fruits.

### Evangelism, Church, and Kingdom

Some attempts have been made to unite evangelism, church, and kingdom in a single paradigm. Here the emphasis is on God's Kingdom, which has come wherever people gather in Christ's name, and will come in its fullness with the return of Christ. Our mission, therefore, is to bring the lost into the church and the church into a prophetic ministry in the world.

There is much strength in this approach. It brings together the various strands of the mission task into a single cord. It has a broad enough view to avoid parochialisms. Above all, it sees missions as the work of God in which he calls his people to participate.

There are dangers, however. If we speak of missions as *missio dei* but do not define *dei*, we are free to equate the Kingdom with our own utopias—with Marxism, capitalism, and socialism. We can also unite with other religions that worship God to work for a heaven on earth and, in the process, deny the uniqueness of Christ and the Gospel. We end up weltering in conflicting relativisms of untethered ecumenism.

There is another danger, namely that we lose sight of the importance of evangelism and of the church. The focus is on the Kingdom on earth, rather than on the Gospel of Jesus Christ. This is captured in the phrase widely used after the New Delhi conference, "The world sets the agenda" (Scherer 1987, 107).

Somehow with our modern mind-set, we find it hard to keep a balance between three centers. Either evangelism, or the church, or the Kingdom is neglected in the implementation. We are unable to keep a burning commitment to all three.

### The King and the Kingdom

Our paradigms are flawed if we begin missions with human activity. Mission is not primarily what we do. It is what God does. But we must define *dei* in terms of the triune God of the Bible (figure 3).

As Arthur Glasser has constantly reminded us, we must begin with the work of the Father, who in creation made humans in his image for fellowship with him and who ever reaches out to save those who repent and return to him. We must focus on the work of Jesus Christ, who made salvation possible in his incarnation and opened the door for reconciliation and fellowship. Regarding this, Jones writes, "[A] rediscovery of the Kingdom without the rediscovery of the King would . . . be a half-discovery, for it would be a kingdom without a king . . . Jesus shows us what God is like and also shows us what the kingdom of God is like in operation. The kingdom of God is Christlikeness universalized" (1972, 34).

We must stress the work of the Holy Spirit, who works to bring us to repentance and to empower us in victorious Christian living.

With the King comes the Kingdom. The two are inseparably linked. When we preach Christ as Savior and Lord, we speak of his rule in the lives of his people.

Matthew makes it clear that Christ's coming was a threat to the established kingdoms of the earth. He was heralded as a king at birth (2:2). He made the Kingdom of God his message (4:17), and called it the Good News—the Gospel (4:23, Luke 4:43). He made it the first petition of the Lord's Prayer (6:10)—"Thy kingdom come (not thy church)" and defined it in the second—"Thy will be done."

In the end he was tried for treason by the Jewish and Roman courts and

**Figure 3**
**King, Kingdom, Church and Evangelism**

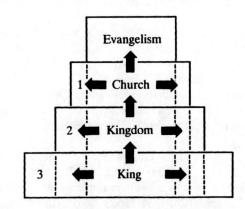

Key: 1 = church activities other than evangelism
    2 = God's rule outside the church
    3 = God's being outside of creation

killed as all insurrectionists were—on a cross (Yoder 1972). The high court in heaven found Jesus innocent, and Satan and humans wicked. It raised him from the dead and placed him on his lawful throne, and cast out the principalities and powers that had opposed him. Ironically, his death, which looked like defeat, was the means by which God wrought salvation for those who turn to him in repentance. In the end, every knee, in heaven and on earth, will bend before the King (Phil. 2:9–11). The implications of the King and the Kingdom for missions are far-reaching. First, God is at work in the affairs of nations to bring about his rule on earth. Moreover, he is at work in the lives of the people to whom we minister, long before we come and long after we leave. It is he that saves, not we. It is he that builds the church, not we.

Missions must be rooted, therefore, in prayer and the leading of God. We should make plans and use strategies, but these must always be open to sudden and total change as the Lord of the harvest issues his commands. The history of missions is full of the serendipities of God. We labor long and hard, and see little results. But suddenly there is a great harvest outside our program. A chance meeting here, an unexpected convert there lead to an explosion of the church in the most unlikely fields. As Art Glasser reminds us (1990b), the apparent failure of missions in China is turning into one of the greatest harvests in our century.

Second, a stress on the King and Kingdom gives us a sense of urgency. The King is returning to set up his Kingdom in person. We are preparing for his return. This eschatological dimension of mission keeps us from becoming too institutionalized in the church and too at home in this world. Mission always has a temporary spirit about it.

Third, a stress on the King and Kingdom keeps us from becoming self-centered as individuals and as churches. It points us to the world that is lost and broken outside the reign of Christ. Glasser points out,

> [T]he only acceptable response that can be made to God's gracious gift of the kingdom is to put oneself consciously and deliberately under Christ's rule and embrace this new pattern of values and services. This involves repentance, faith and submission. Those who do not "obey the gospel of our Lord Jesus . . . shall suffer the persecution of eternal destruction and exclusion from the presence of the Lord and from the glory of his might." (Glasser 1983, 38)

The Kingdom points us to the church. Here the King is worshiped, and here he delights to dwell. The church is the manifestation, however imperfect, of the Kingdom. It is to be a living example to the world of a covenant community of reconciliation that breaks down the human hostilities between races, classes, and genders. It is to be a servant community in which all care for one another.

The Kingdom motivates us to do evangelism, because we want to see

God's honor and rule extended to all people. Evangelism is the central task of the church on earth, because it is the one function the church can do better here than in heaven. Worship and fellowship, these it will do better in heaven.

*Kerygma* and *diaconia* — these two must go together because they are the witness of the Kingdom in a fallen world. We minister to the poor and oppressed because that is the character of the Kingdom. We actively invite people to enter the Kingdom because they are lost outside it.

Kingdom, Church, and Evangelism — we need all three to develop a biblical theology of mission. We need to get beyond the reductionisms of our western mind-set. But we must center these three on the person of Jesus Christ, God as missionary and Lord of Creation. Then we can keep evangelism, church and Kingdom in focus. This was the vision that Arthur Glasser gave to me.

# 14

# Jesus Christ and World Religions

## *Current Evangelical Viewpoints*

### RALPH COVELL

### Introduction

No doctrine is more important for the Kingdom of God than the unique person of its King and the obedience of his subjects to witness for him in all the world. To proclaim the message of this King to all the religions of the world demands not only inculturation but "inreligionization," an inside understanding of the "faith experience" of other peoples. How does God's Kingdom relate to the religious kingdoms? Has the King revealed himself in world religions? Does this revelation make it possible for people to be saved? If so, how? Is overt faith in Christ, the King, the only way for people to be saved? Is it just for God to condemn those who, by virtue of their birthplace and the neglect of his church, have never had a chance to hear the Gospel of the Kingdom? Is dialogue with adherents of world religions a help or hindrance in the task of world evangelization?

Evangelicals as a group have long neglected to analyze these issues. They are clear on the uniqueness of Christ and on God's will to save all humanity, but they face the dilemma that most of the people of the world are comfortable in the religion in which they were born. Christ is the unique, but apparently not the universal, savior. When crucial target dates appear— 1900 and 2000, for example—they mount new crusades to spread Christ's message universally, but without giving any new, creative thought to the relationship of these efforts to the nagging questions posed by world relig- ions.[1]

---

Ralph Covell was a missionary in China and Taiwan 1946-1966 and Professor of World Christianity at Denver Seminary 1967-1990 and dean 1979-1990. He was editor of *Missiology* 1982-1988 and has authored several books about mission in China.

For the most part, evangelical scholars from the time of the Wheaton Congress on Evangelism (1966) to the Lausanne II International Congress on World Evangelization (Manila 1989) have been satisfied with predictably repeating their basic proof texts on the finality of Christ. Disturbing biblical texts which might nuance their attitudes to other religious expressions are glossed over, put in footnotes, subsumed under traditional views, or placed in the last paragraph of an article.

### The Lausanne Covenant: One Evangelical Confession

How do American evangelicals understand world religions? It is difficult to be precise, for American evangelicals are *not* a unified group. In general, Paul Knitter (1985, 77) is right when he puts them into three groups: fundamentalists, conservative evangelicals, and ecumenical evangelicals. The latter two groups can be identified, at least informally, with the Lausanne Committee for World Evangelization (LCWE) and its doctrinal commitment. American evangelicals associated with the LCWE come largely from particular evangelical denominations belonging to the National Association of Evangelicals or from interdenominational churches. Some, however, are affiliated with mainline ecumenical denominations within the Protestant mainstream. The basic convictions of these evangelicals on Christianity and other faiths are found in the Lausanne Covenant in the section on the uniqueness and universality of Christ:[2]

> We affirm that there is only one Savior and only one Gospel, although there is a wide diversity of evangelistic approaches. We recognize that all men have some knowledge of God through the general revelation in nature. But we deny that this can save, for men suppress the truth by their unrighteousness. We also reject as derogatory to Christ and the Gospel every kind of syncretism and dialogue which implies that Christ speaks equally through all religions and ideologies. Jesus Christ, being himself the only Godman, who gave himself as the only ransom for sinners, is the only mediator between God and man. There is no other name by which we must be saved. All men are perishing because of sin, but God loves all men, not wishing that any should perish but that all should repent. Yet those who reject Christ repudiate the joy of salvation and condemn themselves to eternal separation from God. To proclaim Jesus as "the Savior of the world" is not to affirm that all men are either automatically or ultimately saved, still less to affirm that all religions offer salvation in Christ. Rather it is to proclaim God's love for a world of sinners and to invite all men to respond to him as Savior and Lord in the wholehearted personal commitment of repentance and faith. Jesus Christ has been exalted

above every other name; we long for the day when every knee shall bow to him and every tongue confess him Lord.

This statement, claiming the authority of Scripture as its sole basis, clearly declares:

1. God has revealed himself in a general way in nature.
2. This revelation is not salvific and only results in people rejecting the truth.
3. Jesus Christ, the God-man, is the only Savior from sin.
4. Christ is revealed in the Bible, but he does not speak through other religions and ideologies.
5. Christ is universal in the sense that he is available to all who hear his people's proclamation of the Gospel, but effective only to those who believe.
6. Those who reject Christ are eternally lost.
7. Other religions do not offer salvation in Christ.
8. That kind of dialogue which assumes that "Christ speaks equally in other religions" is to be repudiated.
9. Syncretism must be rejected.

### Post-Lausanne Reflections

Since this was not a church-originated confessional statement, many of the signators may not have been affirming their agreement with every jot and tittle. This, however, has been the basic parameter within which most evangelical theologians have worked. Some, however, both before and after Lausanne, have been bold enough to take some fresh initiatives.

First, a small number of evangelical writers affirm that the divine self-revelation (the illumination of the divine Logos plus the testimony of God's creation) is at least *potentially* salvific, and not merely judgmental in its intent. This general revelation is broad enough, they claim, to include a sense of God's kindness and mercy, as well as his claim on the human conscience. If the individual responds to this sense of need and gives oneself in "self-abandonment to God's mercy," then salvation is possible. Not operating on a large scale, this is what others have called "loophole" or "lifeboat salvation" (J. N. D. Anderson 1970; Cotterell 1988; Erickson 1975; Demarest 1982, 261).

Don Richardson (1984) appears to have opened the door for many more people to be saved through general revelation than has been the usual evangelical view. John Sanders and Clark Pinnock affirm that Christ's salvation is accessible to all humanity, either in this life or as a result of "eschatological evangelism," either at the time of or after death (Sanders 1992, 282–3). The more predominant belief among evangelicals continues to be that a positive response to God's general revelation prepares hearers to receive the Gospel message when they are later exposed to it through human agents.

Second, a corollary to this view is that such salvation does not depend on the hearer knowing specifically about the historical Jesus. The process is compared to those who were saved in the Old Testament period under the law by casting themselves on God's mercy, seen only dimly and partially through the sacrificial system. However, the only basis for this salvation, as for any of God's people, is the atoning death and resurrection of God's Son. Works of merit, so prominent in all religious systems, including Christianity, are specifically excluded as ways of reconciling humanity to God. Evangelicals find unacceptable, even as does an ecumenical theologian such as Carl Braaten, the theocentric model proposed by Paul Knitter that reduces and perhaps eliminates the definitive role of Christ in salvation (Braaten 1980, 16).

Third, within the evangelical tradition, an option for a few thinkers has been that human religious systems are both a response to and a suppression of God's personal and direct revelation. J. H. Bavinck commented:

In the night of the *bodhi*, when Buddha received his great, new insight concerning the world and life, God was touching him and struggling with him. God revealed Himself in that moment. Buddha responded to this revelation, and his answer to this day reveals God's hand and the result of human repression. In the "night of power" of which the ninety-seventh sutra of the Koran speaks, the night when "the angels descended" and the Koran descended from Allah's throne, God dealt with Mohammed and touched him. The great moments in the history of religion are the moments when God wrestled with man in a very particular way. (1966, 125)

The Christian missionary then does not bring God or Christ to another culture. *God* the Creator and Christ the Logos, who gives light to every person coming into the world, *has been working there long before the missionary arrived.* Cross-cultural communicators will be sensitive to this fact, both to the positive and negative, even as they proclaim God's love as revealed in the incarnate Christ.

Fourth, dialogue, except as the first step in the evangelizing process, is still a "dirty" word to many evangelicals. Many point out, probably correctly, that the broad evangelical community is gradually abandoning its conviction about the lostness of humanity, and that this was one reason for mainline denominations losing their motivation for world mission. If, however, God's self-revelation may be found in the world's religions, then there is every reason to engage in serious dialogue. This is no substitute for aggressive mission, including evangelism. The primitive church apparently did not specifically raise the issue, "How will those be saved who have never heard?" For them, to believe in Christ was to participate in his mission and to obey his call to "disciple the nations." It was assumed that the message would go everywhere—that everyone would have a chance to respond! Dialogue serves many necessary functions: it helps to sharpen understanding of Holy Scripture, it reveals how God's revelation in Christ is related to aspects of truth found in world religions, it gives new insight to human need and alternative responses to meeting it, and it establishes personal relationships with others in their unique situations. We are called to enter into dialogue confessionally and compassionately.

Even as some evangelicals have pushed their thinking to the parameters of their tradition, they are not prepared to give up the label of "exclusivists." This firm stance has disrupted dialogue with ecumenical theologians, one of whom has baldly stated that "exclusivism strikes more and more Christians as immoral. If the head proves it true, while the heart sees it as wicked, un-Christian, then should Christians not follow the heart? Maybe this is the crux of our dilemma" (W. C. Smith 1981, 202). If what evangelicals perceive as valuable is defined as "un-Christian," "immoral," and "wicked," dialogue has lost all meaning! Do these same theologians treat Buddhists and Muslims in dialogue with more respect?

Fifth, a few evangelical thinkers have developed more philosophical skills for presenting their case and no longer depend only on biblical "proof texts." Harold Netland, a missionary to Japan with the Evangelical Free Church of America, and who holds a Ph.D. from Claremont Graduate School under John Hick, argues persuasively that if people are to have a view of the relation among religions that is epistemologically sound and accurately portrays the values and beliefs of the respective religions, something like traditional Christian exclusivism is unavoidable (Netland 1987, 1988, 1991).

Evangelical scholars are not impressed by the academic rigor of the sociological or historical arguments used by some ecumenical and Roman Catholic scholars to void Acts 4:12 and other "exclusive" passages of any theological meaning. Gregory Baum's "survival language," Krister Stendahl's "confessional language, rather than propositional," (Anderson and Stransky 1981b, 15, 88) and John Gager's "cognitive dissonance" (Marty and Greenspahn 1988, 67–77) all fall in this category. These authors are apparently not comfortable with the narrow focus of these texts; neither are evangelical thinkers, but they have no liberty to evade them.

Sixth, evangelical theologians and missiologists have been more open to dialogue with Roman Catholics and conciliar ecumenists on issues of world religions. Informal discussions are well documented in Paul Knitter's *No Other Name?* (1985) as well as in the pages of many mission journals such as *Missiology,* the *International Review of Mission,* and the *International Bulletin of Missionary Research.*

The line between the more progressive evangelicals (whether we call them conservative or ecumenical evangelicals) and evangelical ecumenists not affiliated with the LCWE is often very thin. Where do we place Stephen

Neill, Hendrik Kraemer, or even Karl Barth? Lesslie Newbigin was certainly more evangelical in the celebration of the fiftieth anniversary of Tambaram than other ecumenical Protestant participants (Newbigin 1988). Gavin D'Costa (1986) lumps Neill, Newbigin, and J. N. D. Anderson in the camp of "neo–Kraemerians."

Valuable as informal dialogue may be, more is accomplished by formal structures that enable participants to interact with one another on specific topics over a period of time. Such was the Evangelical-Roman Catholic Dialogue on Mission (ERCDOM), which took place at three separate sites from 1977 to 1984. While the Roman Catholic participants were named by the Vatican Secretariat for Promoting Christian Unity and represented the official teaching of their church, the evangelicals represented only themselves and came from a variety of backgrounds and traditions.

The areas of agreement emerging from this extended interaction were indeed remarkable and encouraging. Participants reached a general consensus on the uniqueness and universality of Jesus Christ and on the reality of God's activity outside the Christian community. The basic point of disagreement was over the extent of salvation and the way it is mediated. Roman Catholics affirmed the view of Pope John Paul II's encyclical *Redemptor Hominis* that "every person, without exception, has been redeemed by Christ, and with each person, without any exception, Christ is in some way united, even when that person is not aware of that." In one place the document indicated that people must respond to God and be born anew to gain this salvation; another section indicated that most of humankind would receive God's mercy, unless they "specifically reject his offer."

*Redemptoris Missio*, issued by Pope John Paul II in December 1990, revealed the same ambivalence between faith in the incarnate Christ, who must be proclaimed to non-Christians and is the *raison d'être* for mission, and Christ who gives his grace for salvation to all who offer their "free cooperation" (Chapter 1:5, 10). Evangelicals, with a more radical sense of humanity's depravity, make a sharp distinction between those "in Christ" and those who are not. The salvific work of Christ is sufficient for all, but a personal decision must be made to receive him and to be transferred from the "kingdom of darkness" to the "kingdom of his beloved Son" (Col. 1:13).

## The Evangelistic Mandate

Because Protestant churches held to the uniqueness and universality of Jesus Christ, they sent missionaries to evangelize in all parts of the world. This was their answer to the question, "What about those who have never heard of Christ?" The message they proclaimed, at least until 1900, was in the evangelical tradition and would be well represented by the Lausanne

Covenant. As they aggressively presented this exclusive Gospel, they butted head-on with the classical religious traditions of many countries—Islam in the Middle East and portions of Asia, Buddhism in China, and Hinduism in India. Here their theoretical view of the unique Christ was tested in the crucible of what Eugene Nida calls the "socio-anthropological" context.

We must applaud with William Hutchison the creative efforts of many missionary pioneers: "The sensitivity that some missionary theorists brought to the dilemmas of cultural interaction was more than just enlightened for its time—often it was enlightened for any time, our own included" (1987, 205). Certain names stand out for China: James Legge, W. A. P. Martin, Timothy Richard, and Karl Reichelt. Unfortunately, for many missionaries, host-country cultural assumptions, the colonialist-era mentality, the burden of power, lack of anthropological insights, and superficial theological inter-pretations doomed them to relate inadequately to receptor cultures.

Early Protestant missionaries spoke disparagingly to the Chinese, as well as to their church supporters at home, concerning the pagan idols and "silly ceremonies" that made up Buddhism, whose traditions formed a large part of Chinese daily life. They passed out Christian tracts in Buddhist temple precincts and seldom sought to understand the function of Buddhism in society.

In Japan a mutual enmity existed between the Christian faith and Bud-dhism. To the newly arrived missionaries Japan was the land of "the gods and the Buddha," and the Buddhists referred to Christian missionary work as *sinnyu*, meaning "invasion," "intrusion," or "aggression." The mission-aries often referred to their work as the "occupation of Japan" and saw themselves as "religious invaders." Few indeed were the missionaries who tried to relate seriously to Buddhism (Thelle 1987, 7, 39).

Protestant missionaries in China did better with Confucian ideology, recognizing that this represented the warp and woof of Chinese society. In their preaching, writing, and training they tried, with varying degrees of success, to speak and write within a Confucian framework. In fact, their own mental grid of Scottish realism or "common sense," popularized widely in many American colleges through William Paley's *Natural Theology*, fitted nicely with Chinese "natural theology." Some missionaries, most notably those from the London Missionary Society, followed the path pioneered by the early Jesuit missionaries and affirmed that God's self-revelation was writ large on the pages of the ancient Chinese classics.

With a few exceptions, missionaries were fearful of converts who looked "too Confucian." Some, however, argued for "Confucius plus Christ," not-ing that a Chinese Christian who performed the Confucian rites "renounces nothing, nor is he supposed to accept any anti-Christian doctrine." No issue in Asia, whether in China or Japan, offended the sensitivities of the recep-tor cultures more than the attitude of Protestant missionaries toward the ancestral rites. These were viewed generally as religious idolatry, and little attempt was made to understand their social dimensions. As a result, they were rejected out of hand, and this proved to be an insurmountable obstacle to the reception of the Gospel message (Covell 1978, 1986). Evangelical missionaries are required to do better today. While almost compulsive about at least making major gains in world evangelization by 2000 A.D., if not actually completing this task, they often seem to be unaware of dramatic changes in the world. Pluralism, long present, is more apparent; the formal, colonial period has ended; in most areas of the world Christianity has lost or is losing its power base, and the world faces crucial problems, with many calling for less competition and more collaboration among religions. To penetrate into "no access" or "limited access" areas requires more than just a smattering of biblical education and a tip of the hat to complex cultures and world religions. Most important, it demands a radical change in attitudes.

Some evangelical theologians and missiologists are fine-tuning their theology. What can be said about the important area of *attitudes* and *practices*? When dialogue has occurred between evangelicals and other groups on relationships with other faiths, participants have been more disturbed with evangelical attitudes than with their theological stance. Critics have been willing to concede evangelical assertions on the Lordship of Christ and on his uniqueness and potential universality. They often agree that these doctrines lead logically to the exclusive nature of the Christian faith. What they object to is the way in which evangelicals load these conceptions with the historical and cultural baggage of American or European worldviews. Thus they accuse evangelicals, rightly in more instances than not, of triumphalism, a cocksure attitude, aggressiveness, cold and analytic logic, no sensitivity to people, and a continued colonialist mentality.

Not that there is no hope! During the last two decades some evangelicals have begun to turn the corner on these attitudes. Many are receiving in-depth training in cultural anthropology and have begun to give attention not merely to the message, but to the way in which it is perceived by receptor cultures. What changes are occurring?

1. Even as evangelicals continue to proclaim Christ as the only Savior, they see that this must be done, to use Kosuke Koyama's apt phrase, by "crucified minds, not a crusading spirit." The cross is not merely the center of the message of salvation; it is crucial for Christian living and ministry. They see the need to refuse power, privilege, and position and to walk in weakness and vulnerability. Ironically, this only returns them to square one: the pre-Constantinian church that, without any power base, presented its radical message in the marketplace of competing ideologies.

2. Evangelicals are beginning to think more relationally. They see the need to "proclaim the truth in love," to present Christ, not religious systems and programs. Particularly in Asian countries, truth must be tied closely with personal relationships, and neatly packaged and closely reasoned arguments will take second place. This demands that they come as learners and listen with empathy, that ability to stand in the shoes of people within the

receptor culture and understand inside needs as people see them.

3. Evangelicals recognize the difference between evangelism and proselytism. Adoniram Judson, unusual for his day, saw this clearly 150 years ago. He refused to use his scientific expertise to debunk indigenous ideas about eclipses, since he felt that this would enable him to manipulate his hearers into believing the Gospel. In today's world, the authority of money, cultural origin, political connection, knowledge, superior formal education, technology, and mission-agency clout must yield to the authority of Jesus Christ.

4. Evangelicals are learning to present the person and message of Christ within the context of local religious traditions. Don Richardson's use of "peace child" as a redemptive analogy for Jesus within the Sawi culture of Papua New Guinea is only one example of this.

5. Some evangelicals see the need in our chaotic world to live by the theology of presence. They have already recognized this need in hostile contexts where nothing else is possible. In some areas of the world where competing religious beliefs have produced extremely fragile intercommunity relationships, it may be wise, as well as Christian, to refrain from overt evangelism that would exacerbate this tension. Renewed community relationships may be the first priority. Evangelicals may be called upon to join with those of other religious affiliation to meet common needs related to poverty, injustice, and exploitation.

Even as evangelicals recognize the need for a theology of presence, they find it impossible to neglect evangelism. The poor and affluent, the refugees and those with homes, the oppressed and the oppressors, those in war and in peace, those who sin and are sinned against—they are all men and women who need to be reconciled to God through Jesus Christ, irrespective of what their traditional religion may be.

As the end of a millennium draws near, the number of evangelistic programs and strategies to reach all peoples is multiplying. The rhetoric and super "hype" that accompany these efforts may lead critics to conclude that we are mounting another crusade to return the world to the "Christendom" of old. But guilt from past mistakes in thinking and acting must not immobilize us. We need new, creative attitudes. We need to work as if all depended on us, and yet trust God's grace for those we cannot reach, confessing that God will deal justly and mercifully with them in ways beyond our ability to perceive.

## Notes

1. Four recent efforts have been made by J. Sanders (1992), Pinnock (1991), Netland (1991), and Taber and Taber (1992). Both Sanders and Pinnock opt for a thorough "wide-hope" position. Pinnock calls his belief "inclusive finality," and

Sanders refers to his view under the label of "inclusivism: universal accessible salvation apart from evangelization" (Sanders 1992, 215).

2. This covenant was signed at the International Congress on World Evangelization held at Lausanne, Switzerland, in 1974.

## 15

# An Evangelical Assessment of Mission
# Theology of the Kingdom of God

## J. ROBERTSON McQUILKIN

Is the Kingdom of God the overarching theme of Scripture?[1] Most evangelicals would not have thought to put it that way. If asked what the overarching theme of Scripture is, many would say, "Jesus Christ." Others would say, "Redemption. The Bible is salvation history." Some would see the comprehensive theme as God's revelation of himself in all his splendor, not focused primarily on his sovereign kingship. Others would call the Bible "Covenant Theology," encompassing the Old and New Covenants God made with certain people. Most evangelicals, nevertheless, would concede that the Kingdom of God is Christ's central theme and would concur that it is a central concept of Scripture. This acceptance would depend, of course, on how the Kingdom is defined and what implications are drawn from that thesis.

What, then, is the scope of common affirmation among evangelicals about the Kingdom of God?[2] What are the areas of divergence? How can the boundaries of agreement be extended? Most importantly for the issue at hand, what difference does it make to the fulfillment of the missionary mandate?

### Common Affirmations

That God's sovereign rule extends from eternity to eternity and encompasses all creation is never in question. Nothing is out of control: he is

J. Robertson McQuilkin, after serving as a pioneer church planter in Japan for 12 years, was President of Columbia Bible College and Seminary for 22 years. He has authored journal articles and books and is now Chancellor at CBC, ministering in church missions conferences and writing.

Lord of all. This is the ultimate reality, but there is a subplot in the cosmic story: Satan is described as the God of this world. So there is a temporal reality in which the unbelieving and disobedient within corporate Israel and the visible Church, as well as those outside the "household of faith," are under another dominion. Israel was a sphere in which God's kingship was acknowledged and made visible, and the Church is a sphere in which his kingship is acknowledged and made visible. His kingship, however, must be ratified by every member of the group who would be a true citizen of his eternal Kingdom (Rom. 2:28, 29; 4:12; 9:6–8). Thus the Kingdom of God is never coextensive with either Israel or the Church, and the proportion of true Kingdom citizens varies from church to church and from time to time. A further agreement is that there is coming a time when God's reign will be visible and universal, and this will be accomplished by God alone.

### Areas of Divergence

Formal differences may not be great, but emphases may result in wide divergence. First, there are differences among evangelicals as to the continuity of the Kingdom under the Old Covenant and the New. Most dispensationalists would see the Church as a parenthesis between the kingdom of ancient Israel and the kingdom of Israel yet to be, a mystery revealed by the Apostles. Some conclude that much of Jesus' teaching was not directed to the Church but was under the old regime, the law, and was for Israel past and future. This view has lost its strongest advocates in recent decades, but there is still a marked distinction between Israel and the Church made by some evangelicals, while others advocate a continuity or even identity between Israel and the Church.[3] Another area of difference is eschatological: will the visible, universal manifestation of the Kingdom take place on earth? If on earth, will it center in Israel or the Church?

Beyond these doctrinal differences, the implications drawn from them have proved very significant. Some have so emphasized the present internal and the future visible aspects of the Kingdom that they have not incorporated an emphasis on extending the influence of godliness beyond the personal and churchly. Others have incorporated the "salt and light" mandate for Kingdom citizens into the missionary mandate of the Church, weakening or even eclipsing evangelistic concern. In both instances, the critics have no doubt exaggerated the results of the opposing viewpoints, while advocates would deny the validity of the charges. But that there are some "otherworldly" and some "this worldly" evangelicals is apparent to most observers.

Evangelical advocates of "Kingdom Theology" take their mandate from the prayer our Lord taught his disciples, "Thy kingdom come, thy will be done on earth as it is in heaven." The task of the Church is to see that this prayer is answered, that his will in all respects is done on earth. They would not go along with liberation theology, which sees the Kingdom coming through God's activities in secular revolutionary forces. No, for them the Church is God's primary Kingdom task force in the Church era.[4] But the purpose of the church — its mission — is seen as focusing on promoting justice and mercy in society at large as much as on evangelism. With any tendency in this direction, most evangelicals take strong exception (see Beyerhaus 1971; Fife and Glasser 1962, 111–43; Glasser and McGavran 1983).

## Extending the Sphere of Agreement

Is there any way to bring evangelicals closer, to broaden the sphere of agreement? Perhaps not, but there is certainly hope for better communication. I suggest that we might find more common ground if we emphasized the fundamental meaning of *basileia*.

Biblical scholarship for some time has recognized that the root idea and dominant force of *basileia* is better expressed as kingship rather than kingdom (See K. Schmidt 1964, 579–90; Ladd 1952, 77ff.; Marshall 1977, 801–9). God's reign, not God's realm, is the focus.

Many conciliar evangelicals get exasperated when other evangelicals seem to restrict God's Kingdom to inner piety (as part of God's ultimate, invisible, universal Kingdom) or project it into some future era (as the manifestation of God's Kingdom on earth). Most nonconciliar evangelicals get exasperated when some of their colleagues seem to imply that the Church's role is to impose Kingdom values on an unregenerate society as part of God's universal Kingdom. Suppose both would move away from debating the *realm* of the King toward concentrating on the *reign* of the King and put a moratorium on using the term "Kingdom" to define relationships and responsibilities? God's kingly rule would become the focus.

Could we not reach agreement quickly that the two major tasks of those who acknowledge God's reigning authority in their lives are, in concert with other subjects of the King, to bring others to faith and obedience to the King (evangelism) and to endeavor to grow and help others grow in all dimensions of that faith and obedience (sanctification)?

Let me add a parenthetical word of explanation. "Sanctification" should not be artificially restricted to personal piety. Becoming like Christ as a model of Kingdom citizenship includes mercy and the pursuit of justice extended to those living outside the realm of the King. But neither should sanctification be incorporated into the definition of evangelism. Two tasks, not one: evangelism and sanctification. "Translation out of the Kingdom of Darkness into the realm of his dear Son" (Col. 1:13) must be followed by growth toward maturity as a subject of the King (2 Cor. 3:18; Eph. 4:11–16), and it is the task of the Church to pursue both of these goals.

I am suggesting a paradigm shift in emphasis from the extent of the realm to the quality of the reign. It is much easier to determine from scriptural data what obedience to the King entails than to define the boundaries of the Kingdom (who is inside the boundaries, in what sense the world is part of God's Kingdom). The debate would no longer concentrate on whether you have included too much territory or not enough territory in your Kingdom theology, but whether we are fully obedient to God's standards for evangelistic and ethical responsibility.

Assuming that this suggestion is not acceptable, that "Kingdom-Theology" rather than "Kingship" or "Lordship" theology is here to stay, I have a further suggestion. Proponents of Kingdom Theology, to win over mainstream evangelicals, will need to demonstrate compellingly that such a theology *of itself* demands equal billing for social action and evangelism in the mission of the Church toward the world. It would not be so difficult to prove that "mission" (meaning purpose) should incorporate both "cultural" and "evangelistic" mandates. But it would be a formidable task to prove that they are equal parts of missionary ("missions" in its traditional sense) responsibility or that social action is part of the *evangelistic* task.

## Mission of the Kingdom

Historically, mainstream Christians of evangelical persuasion have seen the task of missions as bringing people under the kingship of Christ in the fellowship of the Church, and one task of the Church as infusing the characteristics of the King into society as far as the Church's or its members' influence may extend. Missionary ministry to the physical and social needs of both citizens and noncitizens of the Kingdom has been pursued from varying motives. Some missionaries saw this as part of their ministry as transformed people, others as opening the door for evangelism, still others as the responsibility of the Church — the *result* of evangelism. But for whatever motive, it was a consistent concomitant of missionary evangelistic outreach.[5]

What mainstream evangelicals resist strongly, however, is giving *co-equal status* to social action and evangelism as parts of the *missionary* mandate of the church.[6] To change this will require more than an appeal to Kingdom Theology.[7] It will need demonstration from the New Testament data on the meaning of the Great Commission. This resistance to a redefinition of the missionary mandate is based on biblical, theological, and historical reasons.

There is a biblical, hermeneutical root to the issue. Evangelicals accept the historic view that we have a progressive revelation. The Old Testament must be understood through the teaching of Christ, and his message through the teaching of the Apostles he authorized to transmit the good news of his kingship. Though the Old Testament is authoritative and critical to understanding the missionary mandate, it will not do to give equal force, in defining the mission of the Church, to an Old Testament prophet and a New Testament Apostle if their focus differs.

The role of Israel in God's economy (Kingdom) was radically different from the Church. Though Old Testament prophets recognized that God's dominion extends far beyond the nation of Israel, they would never have said what Jesus said, "My kingdom is not of this world" (Jn. 18:36[8]; see also Jn. 17:14–16; Acts 1:6–8). In fact, apart from his eschatological references, Jesus' consistent emphasis was on his reign, his kingly rule, not its earthly, political manifestation. Once he had completed his redemptive mission, he met with the disciples over a period of more than six weeks, teaching about the kingship of God (Acts 1:3). In virtually every appearance, he came back to a single theme, what we call the great commission. To understand what he meant by this final mandate to the Church, we examine how those who heard it responded. The Acts of the Apostles and the New Testament letters make it very clear that Christ meant to extend his kingly reign in the hearts of people who would receive him and to gather them in a visible community which he called the Church, fulfilling his promise, "I will build my Church" (Mt. 16:18).

If Christ intended to include in that evangelistic mission a responsibility to redeem society, to restructure the unjust structures of the Roman Empire, he certainly failed to communicate that to those who were there. In fact, he remonstrated with the Apostles because they were hung up on that very vision of establishing the King*dom* at that time (Acts 1:6–8). The typical evangelical expects a theology of the mission of the Church to be developed primarily from the data found in Acts to Revelation, not primarily from the Old Testament or the teachings of Christ prior to his resurrection. Though God's purpose of worldwide redemption is clearly enunciated in all sections of Scripture and any legitimate theology of mission must be rooted in the Old Testament and expanded through the teachings of Jesus, the delineation of the specific task of the Church is found after the Church has come into existence. Revelation is progressive, and the earlier is to be understood in light of the latter.

Once a person or a group of people (a church) acknowledges Christ's kingship, however, they obligate themselves to obey all that Jesus commanded (Mt. 28:19, 20), and his commandments for showing mercy and promoting justice were in full harmony with the Old Testament prophets who burned with the fire of God's own compassion and indignation. As the sanctifying work of the Spirit in the lives of God's people, there is full authority to demand a faithful "salt and light" ministry in the community in which one finds oneself.[9]

But if one insists that the transformation of society is an equal part of the *missionary* mandate, that person will meet with resistance. The resistance is based on biblical understandings, but it is intensified by an historic sense: the near-at-hand, visible, earthly has always crowded out the geographically distant, invisible, spiritual. Once the two are given equal emphasis, commitment to the evangelistic task is gradually eroded and what the missionary does looks less and less like what the early Church and Paul the Apostle did in response to Christ's last great command.

Finally there is a theological reason for giving priority to the evangelistic mandate so far as the mission of the Church toward the world is concerned. It has to do with the character of God as Father (rather than King), with the nature of salvation and eternal destiny, with the purpose of God toward humankind. If all people on earth could prosper and be given a college education, full employment prevailed, all injustice and warfare ceased, and perfect health prevailed, but people remained alienated from God, his father-heart would still be broken. His *first* priority for alienated human beings is reconciliation to himself. The reason is not hard to find. Continued alienation in time means alienation for eternity. If utopia could be created for time but human beings were lost for eternity, the Father's heart could never be satisfied. So God's first priority is to bring lost sheep into the fold. Then follows another responsibility, distinct, but nevertheless important: growth in obedience to the Shepherd, likeness to Christ in every aspect of life. The historic erosion, in mainline churches, of the evangelistic mandate may have come more from a weakening of the theology of human destiny and salvation than from any major new understanding of human physical and social need.

There is another theological fact that is important. If it is hard to get regenerated people to obey the King, it is impossible to bring the unregenerate under the law of the Kingdom. First evangelism, then discipleship. True disciples are then enabled to reach out in evangelistic *mission* and *ministries* of social uplift. For example, the most successful evangelistic *and* transformational mission in Latin America has been the Assemblies of God. But the policy from the start, unlike most other missions, was to plant churches, not to build hospitals and schools (other than for theological training). Further, they refrained from political action. But now that people have been transformed, brought under the reign of the King, the churches are building major school systems and infusing Kingdom values into society through social action and church members elected to public office.

As a friendly outsider to Kingdom Theology advocates, then, I offer two suggestions. First, shift the emphasis from realm to reign, from Kingdom to kingship. Whether or not that is acceptable, pursue the debate on the nature of Church and mission with analysis of direct biblical instruction on the place of evangelism and social action in God's purposes for his Church. In this way we can broaden our understanding or, perhaps, even our range of agreement.

## Notes

1. See Glasser (1985), Gnanakan (1989, 102), and Verkuyl (1978, 203).
2. For a summary of various interpretations of the Kingdom, see Ladd (1974b).

3. See Ryrie (1965, 170-74), Pentecost (1964, 427-75), Showers (1990, 155-67). See also Scofield Reference Bible note at Mt. 6:33.

4. See Van Engen (1991a), especially chapter 7. But there is an emerging segment of Kingdom Theology advocates, especially among South American charismatics, that is virtually theonomistic and aims at establishing God's Kingdom in old-fashioned postmillennial terms of transforming society through political action. The more common view is advocated cogently by George Eldon Ladd (1959, 269).

5. See The Lausanne Covenant (1975, 4). Note the clear distinction between evangelism and social action.

6. For "Kingdom Theology" view, see Verkuyl (1978, 197-204), Glasser (1985, 11, 12).

7. See chapter 18, "Centrality of the Kingdom," in Hedlund (1991).

8. The force of Christ's words to Pilate is twofold: his Kingdom does not have its source in this world (*"from* this world," which OT prophets might well have said) *and* is not a worldly kingdom (*"of* this world," which an OT prophet could hardly say). See, e.g., Morris (1971).

9. See McQuilkin (1989), especially chapters 8, 9, 10.

# PART FIVE

# MISSIOLOGICAL ISSUES

# Introductory Overview

In this section the editors have somewhat arbitrarily chosen three important missiological topics. Each topic has ramifications for kingdom thinking that will take us well into the next century. Our concerns here are that we affirm the reasonableness of contextualization, distinguish between Christendom and the Kingdom and accept our missiological obligation toward the religions.

Arthur Glasser is not one to use the "in" words with too much enthusiasm. He has a gift for lengthening out traditional terms and expressions so they meet the demands of today. He enriches the older term "indigenous" until it says all that is required by the newer idea of "contextualization." Art is cautious of faddishness or being carried off by syncretism in the pursuit of relevance. For example, while the Old Testament meets human needs where they are, it also clearly shows "the abiding validity of non-negotiables," that are normative for "all people in all situations" (Arthur Glasser in Gilliland, 1989, 33).

Once setting these limits on the inculturation of the gospel, he is ready to talk about a wide range of contextualization issues. Art would heartily agree with Miriam Adeney that it is wrong for mission theorists to raise trivial controversies of doctrine in societies that are overwhelmed by poverty and injustice, or hassle over sectarian minutia where "poor Christians get smashed regularly by typhoons or political coups." Based on Philippine insights, Miriam's contribution models what is very close to Art's kingdom-heart.

Wilbert Shenk sees the idea of "Christendom" as a misrepresentation of the Church. This has been a severe handicap to the true mission enterprise and no more than a caricature of the Kingdom. Mission theologians must see how captive the Church has become to Christendom, how bound she is to the ethos and demands of secular culture and how inseparable she is from the clutches of the West. Shenk's view of the kingdom (*basileia*) is to truly incarnate the reign of God. Modernity has so blunted the sense of biblical kingdom that mission refers only to what happens "out there." The church, so heavily laden with Western baggage, must, herself, first encounter the gospel.

This will warm the Mennonite side of Glasser's heart. What is kingdom, says Art, but the servant community in submission to God's rule, which (must) live and worship in loving humility. Far from the secular rationalism of Christendom, kingdom people, once united in Christ lose the right to a separate existence.

Glasser will read what Gerald Anderson has written with hearty appreciation, especially on two points. For one, Art has always been a critic of the universalistic tendencies of the World Council of Churches. Secondly, even as this volume is being written, he is actively promoting relations with and evangelism among Jewish people.

Anderson shows that, regrettably, the ecumenical movement has so blurred the boundaries of truth that serious scholars are now writing about "relative absolutism." Art would agree with Gerald that the Chung presentation at Canberra showed how muddied the waters have become. The high priority Anderson gives to evangelism among the Jewish people will be resisted by some, but not by Arthur Glasser. When he reads that mission to the Jewish people is the "litmus test" for an adequate theology of religion, Art will smile and say, "Amen."

D. S. G.

# *16*

# Mission Theology from Alternate Centers

## MIRIAM ADENEY

What theological themes dynamize Christians from other cultures as they work in mission for Christ and his kingdom? And what could mainstream theologians and missiologists learn from these? The topic is boggling: vast in scope, sketchy in literature.[1] Possibly one underlying theme is holism: between the natural and the supernatural; between mind and body, theology and economy; between the individual and the group; between proposition and symbol; and between system and uncertainty.

Filipina theologian Melba Maggay gives a context for exploring this holism as she discusses four of these theme contrasts viewed from her "alternate center":

> The domination of Western theological formulations has led to a situation where in order to speak to their people, Christians in Asia and Africa are taught to answer questions raised by Greek sophists in the fourth century A.D.
>
> Filipinos who live in a culture still awed by the Power that can be clearly perceived in things that have been made are taught to start from the supposition that we are talking to post Christians long past the age of the mythical and therefore must belabor the existence of a supernatural God. We defend the Scripture as if we speak to the scientific rationalist, and not to people who have yet to see nature "demythologized," stripped of the wondrous and the magical.
>
> In a society overwhelmed by poverty and injustice and pressed by the constant threat of political instability, we learn to preoccupy ourselves with trivial theological controversies and such fine points as

Miriam Adeney holds a Ph.D. in anthropology and is the author of several books, including *God's Foreign Policy: Practical Ways to Help the World's Poor.* She is an Associate Professor at Seattle Pacific University, Adjunct Professor at Regent College, and frequent consultant to missions.

whether some scandalously miraculous gifts have ceased and whether in baptizing we ought to dunk or daintily pour.

Minds that would normally think in concrete wholes are painfully trained to make abstract distinctions between faith and works, Jesus as Lord and Jesus as Savior, the sphere of the "secular" and the sphere of the "holy."

Unable to cope with the fact that people are predestined to be saved and at the same time many freely will to damn themselves, Western theological traditions insist on presenting the sovereignty of God and human freedom as problematic, and this to an Oriental people happily able to live with the engaging perplexities of a paradox.

In a culture which puts a great deal of emphasis on interrelatedness, the offer of salvation continues to be cast in highly individualistic terms. Salvation is advertised as a purely private entrance into an otherworldly kingdom. The formula is to receive Jesus as "personal" Lord and Savior, as if He were merely one's own and no one else's, and as if the act concerned no one else but oneself. An act of commitment is thought to be more genuine if made against a backdrop of family hostility than if it were made against the more congenial environment of consensus. The call for repentance remains highly personal and pietistic, having to do almost exclusively with a beating of the breast over one's sins, and very rarely with one's participation in the collective guilt of unjust structures. Discipleship has been narrowed to evangelism and singing hymns to Jesus completely divorced from the witness demands of the larger community. God is said to be more deeply experienced in the rarefied heights of solitude, not in the warm and earthy explosion of togetherness. In effect, conversion in our culture has often meant a retreat into further isolation, not a flinging of arms wide open to meet the desolation of the world.

Because the Filipino evangelical church is for the most part made in the image of the American Bible belt, it has remained alienated from the surrounding culture. Instead of being scattered again in a deeper way among his people, a convert goes through a kind of cultural circumcision; he renounces an inherited culture of faith in favor of a more barren intellectualism in faith and worship; he learns to sing of summer and winter, springtime and harvest; quite unconsciously, he borrows the tastes and scruples of the missionary's Puritan conscience in matters of dress and lifestyle. If in the past he has burned deeply over the poverty of his people, he learns to temper his political opinions in a way that ceases to be offensive to the sedate politics of people raised in the soporific opulence of Middle America.

The result of all this is a continuing failure to speak to our people's needs, to discern the prophetic Word, God's message to this particular people at this particular time. (Maggay 1989, 55–57)

Maggay has highlighted several themes important not only for Filipino mission theologians, but for those from many cultures.

### Contemplative Confronters: Continuity between Spiritual and Material

NonWestern missionaries often participate in charismatic healings and exorcisms. They may quite naturally stop on a dike midway between two rice fields to pray for the crop. Quite a few have meditated on Christ, and then seen Him in a dream or vision. Both because of their need—many go out with little financial or logistical support—and because of their holism, they expect God's personal intervention frequently. Like the Apostle Peter they may say, "Silver and gold I do not have, but what I have I give you. In the name of Jesus of Nazareth, walk" (Acts 3:6). Like pioneer Western missionary William Carey, they "expect great things from God and attempt great things for God." Like a Muslim holy person, they bring with them God's *baraka*—God's power, God's grace, God's Spirit—when they enter a community.

Josue Fonseca, a Southern Baptist Chilean theologian, challenges foreign missionaries to a similar God-awareness:

For many years, foreign missionaries have been accused in Latin America of imposing cultural patterns of prayer and worship, being reluctant to promote native cultural forms to express adoration to God. However, in my opinion, what is behind this criticism is the failure of foreign missionaries to cultivate a personal commitment to spiritual life because of the technocratization of mission ... There is an increasing crisis of models among missionaries in spiritual life in Latin America, in part due to different factors: dualistic view of life, emphasis on doing rather than on being; functional character of mission; pragmatic rationalism; mass-culture and professionalization of Christian life. What mission needs at the present time, especially in Latin America, is wisdom and purity of character, and the presence of missionaries, either nationals or foreigners, who stimulate a profound sense of walking with God. (Fonseca 1990, 36)

To emphasize the kingdom more than the King: This is Christian professionals' perpetual temptation, as T. S. Eliot observes in his play on Thomas à Becket, murdered Archbishop of Canterbury:

Servant of God has chance of greater sin
And sorrow, than the man who serves a king.
For those who serve the greater cause may make the cause serve
  them,

Still doing right: and striving with political men
May make that cause political, not by what they do
But by what they are. (Eliot 1963, 45)


## Treasure Chests of Symbols: Continuity between Natural
## and Supernatural

This is seen not only in miraculous irruptions but also in God's creation
order. This order includes cultures. Endowed with God's image, endowed
with God-given creativity, people have developed cultures. Since people
are sinners, our cultures institutionalize patterns of idolatry and exploitation. Nevertheless, since we are also in God's image, our cultures as well
institutionalize patterns of beauty and wisdom and kindness. Viewed positively, cultures may be seen as treasure chests of symbols for exuberant
expression of the image of God (Adeney 1984, chapter 6; Niebuhr 1951).

Honoring local cultures includes developing ethnotheologies which
speak to local priorities and values through local thought categories and
symbol systems. This is the heart cry of many nonWestern missiologists.[2]
Mature study of the local great religions is an essential part of this.

On the other hand, just as Western missionaries find it hard to live out
the contextualization we affirm, so Chinese and Korean missionaries who
go to Southeast Asia struggle with their own ethnic and cultural imperialism. So do Russian missionaries among Kirghiz and Uzbeks. So do Latino
missionaries among tribal groups in Latin America. Often lacking solid
cross-cultural orientation, they may not even have categories through which
to understand the problem. Cross-cultural training which gives a theological
rationale for affirming and critiquing both their own culture and the culture
to which they go: This is a need of the decade.[3]


## The Beam in Our Eye: Continuity between Mind and Body,
## Theology and Economy

Poverty stalks the communities where many nonWestern missionaries
witness. Liberation theology has been a response in Latin America, Asia,
Africa, and among North American and European minorities—a call for
just liberation from exploitative structures perpetuated by richer countries
and local elites.[4] Some nonWestern Christian thinkers favor right-wing
development leading to modernization, however.[5] In either case, poverty is
so pervasive that it is the inescapable context of our missiology, even when
we work with the middle or upper class. The first conference of Evangelical
Mission Theologians from the Two Thirds World subtitled their published
papers: "Evangelical Cristologies from the Contexts of Poverty, Powerlessness, and Religious Pluralism" (Samuel and Sugden 1983a). As we drive

past clay hovels without electricity, nonWestern colleagues remind us of
our Lord:

> That glorious form, that light insufferable,
> And that far-beaming blaze of majesty . . .
> He laid aside; and here with us to be,
> Forsook the courts of everlasting day,
> And chose with us a darksome house of mortal clay.
>
> (Milton 1958, 456)

They ask us: What is the place of economic justice in our definitions of
mission?[6]

### "You Will Be Saved, and Your House": Continuity between Individual and Group

We Americans often do not know our friends' parents or children. Individualistic and self-reliant, we witness to people as though they were isolated in a social vacuum. By contrast, nonWestern Christians remember
that in the beginning God said it was not good for man to be alone; people
were created to live in communities of meaning. When they evangelize and
disciple, then, missionaries from such cultures think seriously about the
inquirer's family, kin group, and peer group.[7]

What Matheny writes about Muslims applies to many peoples:

(We) usually stress the benefits of salvation for the individual, but
Muslims may be more aware of the needs of society. Goldsmith tells
of a Muslim convert who became convicted of the truth of the claims
of Christ not because of personal need but because he was deeply
conscious of the needs of his people . . . "Might it therefore be right
to start our Christian witness in such societies with a message of what
Christ can do for a whole society rather than just for the individual
believer?" (Matheny 1981, 147–48)

### The Word in Pictures: Continuity between Propositions and Symbol

People who think in pictures need the whole Word of God as much as
anybody else does. NonWestern missionaries often transmit this through
song, metaphor, proverb, story, drama, debate, chanting, and memorization.
They recognize that the God who spoke propositionally through Paul in
the letter to the Romans is the same God who spoke to Balaam through
an ass, to Ezekiel through a vision of wheels within wheels, through John

in metaphor after metaphor, and through Jesus Himself in parable after parable.

Too often we give only snippets of God's Word to peoples who emphasize the right brain. Here a Christmas drama. There a short cassette course. Then our analytical teachers take over and we revert to sermons. We rejoice that they like to sing, but pay little attention to the thematic balance of their songs, because the songs are "worship," not "teaching."[8] As for the millions of Christians around the world today who never will learn to read well, we push them aside to second-class citizenship in the kingdom of God, even though media exist through which they could learn to retain much Scripture.

We ought to bring artists, songwriters, and dramatists to join forces with Bible scholars and curriculum specialists. We ought to pray for the Lord to raise up poets and composers and performers just as specifically as we pray for evangelists and teachers and medics.[9] We ought to sharpen our "teaching songs" and "teaching stories" through constructive criticism, and hold our creative artists to high standards of accountability. In short, we ought to learn from our nonWestern colleagues how to pour our Bible teaching into appropriate media.

### The Meek Will Inherit: Continuity between System and Uncertainty

This essay focuses on missionaries from cultures peripheral to the great centers of power. Being poor may not be their most important characteristic, however. People are not necessarily deprived because they have limited economic resources. Rather, they suffer cultural deprivation when the symbols associated with their culture begin to connote shame, or when there is restriction of economic opportunity in the face of an ideology which claims equal opportunity. Thus nonWestern missionaries may feel shamed alongside Western colleagues if they lack fax machines, or if they cannot afford to attend the right conferences, or to remain *au courant* with the latest theological books from Europe and North America. Minority missionaries may feel shamed alongside their majority-culture colleagues if they do not speak the majority language fluently.

Viewed differently, however, a simpler economic base may be associated with symbols that connote pride.[10] Furthermore, the weak often have weapons (Scott 1985). Slaves and women have been powerful forces in Christian history, working from beneath. Women missionaries have been able to penetrate where men would have been killed, because the women were seen as weak.[11] Evangelical minorities have provided a powerful "third way," whether in the England of the nineteenth century Clapham Sect (Pollock 1977; Bradley 1976), in Latin America[12] or in the Commonwealth of Independent States today.

In the world Church, this simple flexibility may be crucial. Rich Christians today approach mission through systems management, diagramming such strategy concepts as tentmakers, nonresident missionaries, multi-individual decision-making units, or criteria to distinguish unreached peoples. We are goal-oriented. Goals must be measurable. Imponderables do not fit our planning procedures. Hence uncertainty, ambiguity, and paradoxes get screened out. Poorer Christians, who get smashed regularly by typhoons or political coups, have learned to build and rebuild with the materials immediately at hand. They have learned how to move between being abased and abounding. This ability to cope, to make do, to bounce back, all the while "expecting great things from God," will serve the Church well in coming years as we face considerable destabilization because of problems such as pollution, population, the gap between rich and poor, nuclear proliferation, a populace of spectators, the erosion of logical thought, the technological invasion of privacy, and the spread of both New Age universalism and fundamental rigidities in nearly all the great religions.

## Notes

1. The author must plead her limits. She is neither a theologian nor the daughter of a theologian; but editor Charles Van Engen took her from among the anthropological kinship charts and said, "Go: Prophesy!" Indulgence is requested also for the use of the term "nonWestern" in reference to missionaries from "alternate centers." The fit is not exact.

2. A theological affirmation of their roots meets one of the greatest felt needs in poor countries. Where people struggle with low corporate self-esteem — "reverse ethnocentrism" — secular aid agents cannot tell them *why* their marginal culture is valuable. Marxists cannot. But Christians can: It is valuable because it is created by people in God's image, expressing God-given creativity. Poor people need not only methods but also meaning and motivation. A theological affirmation of their roots helps provide this.

To begin research on ethnotheology, the student might consult Dyrness (1990), which includes separate bibliographies on Latin American, African, and Asian theological works; several books published by the Asia Theological Association and edited by Bong Rin Ro (1984); Ferm (1986); and Samuel and Sugden (1983a). The last title contains the papers of the first conference of Evangelical Mission Theologians from the Two Thirds World.

3. Admittedly, Western Christian missionaries sometimes have not viewed individual cultures as gifts of God. Yet, by translating the Bible into local languages, missionaries de facto have affirmed local cultures and have given them a tool for revitalization, whether this was intended or not.

Today nonWestern as well as Western missionaries must check: Are we using the local language? Housed among the people? Buying locally? Living relatively simply? Traveling on public transportation? Finding our best field friends from among the local people? Getting spiritual nurture from local Christian leaders? Getting our news through their media? Relaxing through their sports, games, and music? Thinking about life through their values? Restraining our tendency to take over, even if we have the power to do so?

4. Ferm (1986), Costas (1982), bibliography on Latin American theologies by Dyrness (1990), and Bosch (1991b).

5. At the Lausanne II Conference in Manila in 1989, for example, one group of Latin American evangelicals worked on a strong statement for more liberationist emphasis, while another worked on a strong statement calling for less.

Bragg (1983, 37-96) discusses four alternative theoretical approaches to development: modernization theory; dependency and underdevelopment theory; global reformism: the New International Economic Order; and small-scale community self-reliance. He assesses the assumptions, strengths, and weaknesses of each.

6. Magalit (1979): "Please do not send us missionaries who insist on a dichotomy between evangelism and social concern. Missionaries who say that evangelism is our main, or even sole, concern; ministry to the temporal needs of people we will do also, but only as we have time, later, and as our limited resources allow. Such missionaries make it hard for us to refute the . . . charge that Christians . . . are but tools of American imperialism, desiring to perpetuate the pockets of privilege, and leaving the wretched to remain wretched."

Maggay (1991, 201): "The fact that most Christians are poor means that most Christian theology should be theology from the underside . . . Well-educated nonWesterners must decolonize their imaginations and learn to write from a position of powerlessness."

Costas (1982): "Any church, mission agency or theological institution that claims the whole world as its mission field and wants to proclaim faithfully the whole gospel must make a kerygmatic encounter with the structures that dominate and oppress human life a fundamental component of its agenda."

Escobar (1974): "I wonder sometimes if, taking into account the demonic forces at work behind racism, prejudice, oppression, corruption, and exploitation of the weak and the poor everywhere, and taking also into account evangelistic and missionary efforts which are totally unaware of these facts, the Lord would not tell us: 'Woe to you, zealous evangelists, hypocrites, for you traverse sea and land to make a single proselyte, and when he becomes a proselyte, you make him twice as much a child of hell as yourselves' (Mt. 23:15)."

7. The "homogenous unit" or "multiple-individual-decision-making-unit" associated with the church growth focus at Fuller Seminary has been criticized sharply, whether fairly or not, as monodimensional and racist (Padilla 1982; Verkuyl 1978). Nevertheless, nonWestern missionaries go right on reaching out to people along natural connections. Navahos now ministering to Mongolians stress their similarities: they both value horsemanship and sheep raising; they both have animistic backgrounds; they both like to eat liver with fat; they may have language similarities; they are of the same major race. Latin Americans now going to the Muslim world stress their similarities. Chinese ministering in Tahiti or British Guyana go first to the local Chinese, with whom they have the most in common.

The challenge, of course, is to keep extending our network. Twenty months ago, a woman named Fatimah came to faith in Christ. She was an African Muslim graduate student in Canada. Ever since then, three of my African Christian students and their wives and children have opened their homes unstintingly to Fatimah and her husband, Muhammad, extending their network to this Muslim family. In fact the couple has moved right in and lived with two of the families for periods. Throughout, there has been a sharing of families and a caring for family. The man who brought Fatimah to faith in Christ, Tanzanian Lutheran leader Justin Oforo describes the background of this corporate caring:

It is a miracle when a person is converted to Christianity in Africa. Yet it is even a bigger miracle when it happens in the West where the community support system is so weak. The concept of fatherhood of God in the Bible is easier to understand in my village of Mwaka than in Vancouver. The child in Mwaka grows up under the care, security, love and yet discipline of the father and community. This is a good basis for understanding God and grasping the nature of the care, love, and disciplining we get from our heavenly Father. In Vancouver the child may grow up in a single parent's home, or experience an abuse from the father, or suffer the pains of the separation of the parents. (Oforo 1991)

In Mwaka, God is assumed to be there, just as we read in Genesis 1:1, and the parents (whether Christian, Muslim or pagan) mention God in fear and awe. This is not so in places in Vancouver where teachers face the risk of being taken to court for teaching children the Lord's Prayer. Some of those who may not take such a hostile attitude toward God enjoy being agnostic. In Mwaka, where daily needs are difficult to provide for, people thank God for daily life and provision. In the materialistic West, it sounds stupid to associate the food on the table with God. Man is in control. His profession leads to a good income and with it he can buy whatever he needs.

    8. In the Solomon Islands, missionary anthropologist Allen Tippett recorded the doctrinal themes of church hymns sung over a number of months. In a highly Methodist area, themes on salvation and the Christian life predominated. Songs on God as Creator and Sustainer, and on the Holy Spirit, were rare. Shortly before the research period, a tragic, heretical schism had torn the denomination. In the new cult that developed, God as Creator and Sustainer and the Holy Spirit were prominent themes. These met felt needs, Tippett suggested. Had the orthodox church sung a more balanced hymnology, would it have helped prevent the heresy and new cult? Tippett believed it might have (Tippett 1967, 286-307).

    9. The importance of the poet as theologian has been explored in Schreiter (1985, 18).

    10. See Tanzanian Justin Oforo's praise of his village culture in note 7. See also Filipino William Girao's arguments against the "brain drain" quoted in Adeney (1984).

    11. Tucker and Liefeld (1987, 323): "If you had sent men, we would have killed them on sight ... But what could a great chief do with two harmless girls who insisted on calling him brother?" (Attributed to Chief Tariri of the Shapra people of Peru.)

    12. The "third way" provided by Protestants is a pervasive argument in D. Martin (1990b).

## 17

# The Culture of Modernity as a Missionary Challenge

## WILBERT R. SHENK

Although the culture of modernity has yet to be taken seriously as a subject of sustained missionary concern, my argument will be that this represents one of the most urgent frontiers facing the church in the twenty-first century. As always, "the past is prologue." Both church and culture today are products of a long historical process. The church of Christendom has been deeply implicated in the culture of modernity. Today we are hearing appeals for a fresh engagement by the church with modern culture. This calls for careful preparation. We need to sort through and get fresh perspective on the past as the first step into the future.

Over the past century there has been an undercurrent of uneasiness about the status of the church in the West. Survey after survey tells the same doleful story: the church of technocratic culture is in deep difficulty (e.g., Brierly 1991). The church's travail coincides with the deepening crisis of modernity as it phases into postmodernity. Here we shall use "modern culture" as the comprehensive term for modernity and postmodernity.

Modernity is the result of intellectual developments in European culture over a period of several centuries based on the influence of thinkers such as Bacon, Newton, Kepler, Galileo, and Descartes, who established the "scientific method" and laid the foundations in mathematics and physics for modern science. In the seventeenth and eighteenth centuries philosophers like Locke and Kant forged a new intellectual framework. The Enlightenment emphasized the potential of rational human reason to solve

Wilbert R. Shenk, missionary in Indonesia 1955-1959, has been director of Mission Training Center, Associated Mennonite Biblical Seminaries, Elkhart, Indiana, since 1990. He was vice-president of Overseas Ministries, Mennonite Board of Missions 1965-1990 and editor of *Mission Focus* 1972-1992.

problems, unaided by the supernatural, and radical skepticism as the hall-mark of all authentic intellectual pursuits.

Enlightenment culture put a premium on fact as that which can be tested in the laboratory—what is rational, objective, and verifiable. Public discourse was to be conducted on the basis of objective fact, what we can know with certainty. Values and religious beliefs were regarded as the realm of the superstitious and the subjective—that is, the unprovable—and thus must be relegated to the private sphere. Faith and knowledge were held to be nonreconcilable. This schism in modern culture has yet to be healed. The Enlightenment, which did so much to raise the dignity of the individual through a vision of human freedom and responsibility, has also produced profound alienation and anomie in the modern individual.[1]

Modern culture has been characterized by the triumph of science and technology. Scientific experimentation and technological innovation constituted the engine driving industrial development. By the nineteenth century the industrial revolution was well along. The scale and pace of industrialization forced on Western societies rapid restructuring as workers were drawn from the rural areas into factory towns. Urbanization brought new pressures to bear on civic and family life, raising novel questions about the meaning of human existence as the worker was perceived to be only a cog in the industrial machine.

Christendom was the dominant religious influence in the West[2] for fifteen hundred years. It arose in the fourth century when Christianity was first officially recognized by the emperor and gradually became the religion of state throughout Europe. The church viewed itself as the religious institution for society as a whole. At times this meant the church was actually the dominant power in society. Always the church had an unquestioned role alongside the social, political, economic and military institutions. By the time of the Protestant Reformation in the sixteenth century, there were signs that Christendom was beginning to crumble, but the breakdown was protracted, continuing into the twentieth century. Today vestiges of the old tradition remain in private, public, and religious spheres, but Christendom is a spent cultural force.

Nonetheless, the legacy of Christendom is crucial for understanding the missionary challenge of modern and postmodern culture because of the way the modern church is an extension of Christendom.

### The church of Christendom was a church without mission

Christendom politicized mission by making it an instrument of state policy. Once the tribes of Europe had been pacified and brought under control by church and state there was no further need for even this politicized mission. The notion of mission within the territory of Christendom contradicted the meaning of this new society.

Scholars have long debated whether the leading Protestant Reformers of the sixteenth century were advocates for missions.[3] It is a largely irrelevant exercise of forcing twentieth-century questions on the sixteenth century. Missions within Christendom were unthinkable, and Protestant Europe had not yet embarked on colonial expansion in the manner of the Catholic Portuguese and Spanish.

By the twentieth century, fundamental questions were being raised about the reality of Christendom because of its disturbing inertia in the face of dehumanizing spiritual and social conditions of the masses and its intellectual defensiveness. Two examples must suffice.

In the 1909 Bampton Lectures, Canon Walter Hobhouse canvassed the whole history of Christendom to develop his argument that the Church had been domesticated to fit political and cultural realities. Consequently, it was a Church without a mission to its world. Hobhouse urged that the Church reclaim its apostolic character as "a missionary Church, not only in heathen lands and among races which we are pleased to call 'inferior,' but in every country" (Hobhouse 1911, 320).

First as Archbishop of Rheims (1930–1940) and then of Paris (1940–1949), Cardinal Suhard was preoccupied with finding new answers to the social and spiritual conditions of modern society (Renard 1986, 350). He called for reevangelization. He encouraged the worker priest movement.[4] But the Vatican was negative on Mission de France, founded by Cardinal Suhard. Pius XII granted *provisional* approval on Suhard's deathbed in 1949.

Hobhouse and Suhard were voices crying in the wilderness. Hobhouse sent up a trial balloon that apparently attracted no attention. Suhard challenged the old assumptions that defined Christendom and promoted a missionary ecclesiology. With imagination he created new institutions and programs, only to meet resistance at the highest levels of the hierarchy. Christendom was deeply entrenched.

*The Christendom mentality inhibited the church from interacting critically, constructively and pastorally in the modern period when society was undergoing fundamental change*

Through the nineteenth century, the church was on the defensive in a culture dominated by science. Antagonists of the Christian faith played science off against religion in a successful effort to discredit the church in the popular mind. The church was also compromised by its reputation of being for the classes rather than the masses.[5]

Arthur Winnington-Ingram, who became Anglican bishop of London in 1901, observed that "it is not that the Church of God has lost the great towns: it never had them." Pius XI reportedly said that "The greatest scandal of the Church in the nineteenth century was that it lost the working class."[6] Although bishop and pope differed in emphasis, they were agreed that by the twentieth century the church had little credibility with the working masses.

By 1900 "working class" consciousness was fully formed and entrenched, including a distinctive attitude toward religion. The working class might continue to celebrate the rites of passage in the church, but otherwise they seldom attended services, and "many of them regarded the church and clergy with hostility" (McLeod 1980, 192). Whether Protestant or Catholic, the worker's attitude toward church was negative.

Throughout the modern period another process was at work that had important implications for the church. Dietrich Bonhoeffer spoke of humankind "coming of age." In the years following World War II, Europe was called a post-Christian society. The triumph of secularization was said to be inevitable and irreversible. In the 1960s theologians reinterpreted the Christian message in light of secularization. Harvey Cox caught the mood of the times in his bestseller, *The Secular City*: "Secularization rolls on, and if we are to understand and communicate with our present age we must learn to love it in its unremitting secularity" (Cox 1965, 4). The message was clear: any peace settlement between church and culture would be on terms set by secular culture.

Yet other careful observers found evidence of religious activity on all sides, including the places where there was supposed to be none, such as rapidly modernizing Japan. Secularization had to be redefined. Secularization was real; but a more nuanced understanding was required.

Because the church must live within the plausibility structure of its culture, it is always vulnerable to the temptation to conform to that structure. The modern plausibility structure sought to exclude religion altogether. Accommodation would assuredly spell trouble for the church, but there were theologians who advocated such a strategy. By contrast, a missionary stance vis-à-vis culture could have offered a constructively critical position from which to interact with modern culture. The Christendom inheritance militated against such a stance.

### Missiologists have reinforced the Christendom viewpoint with regard to mission

In no small measure due to the heroic exertions of Gustav Warneck, pioneer German missiologist, mission studies finally were admitted to the university late in the nineteenth century. Warneck insisted on a distinction between *missions* and *evangelization*.[7] Missions were efforts outside historic Christendom to establish the church. Evangelization was the action by which nominal Christians were called to actualize their latent faith. This formulation remained influential in mission studies until after 1945. No missiologist addressed the question of mission to the West; mission studies remained the servant of cross-cultural missions.

A conceptual shift was signaled by the slogan coming out of the meeting of the Commission on World Mission and Evangelism of the World Council of Churches in Mexico City in 1963: "Mission from six continents to six continents." The CWME followed this with a study in Europe and North America of "the missionary structure of the congregation," an initiative that never fulfilled its promise. At the same time the Second Vatican Council was forging a new position for Roman Catholics which emphasized the missionary responsibility of the whole people of God, but the conceptual shift was not translated into reforms—whether ecclesial, missiological, or in theological education.

The problematic had various dimensions. Two centuries of worldwide missionary exertions sponsored by Western churches largely failed to effect a fundamental reorientation in their ecclesial consciousness. Christendom remained a self-sufficient and insular reality. Church history and theology continued to be taught in the West as a largely Western affair. What happened "out there" was missions; what happened in the West was church. Owen Chadwick's two-volume *The Victorian Church*—the period when British missions had the largest missionary contingent of any nationality—contained not a single reference to this movement.[8] Few missiologists have challenged this state of affairs. Christendom assumptions and habits of mind furnished the conceptual framework even among those with an experience of global mission.

*Missionary encounter with modern culture requires that we hold together* **Basileia,** *as the content and goal, and* **Incarnation,** *as the essential strategy, as we listen carefully, respectfully, and compassionately to the modern world*

Various calls for missionary witness among the peoples of modernity have been made during the past two decades, including W. A. Visser 't Hooft, John Paul II, and Lesslie Newbigin. We can do no more than characterize briefly these three appeals.

W. A. Visser 't Hooft, founding general secretary of the World Council of Churches, having experienced Nazism firsthand, was deeply aware of the fundamental contradictions and demonic tendencies within modernity. In 1974 he addressed the new religiosity that was arising in reaction to secularization—which he diffidently termed "neo-paganism" (Rom. 1:25) (Visser 't Hooft 1974, 81–86; 1977, 349–60. Cf. Edgar 1983, 304–13; Spindler 1987, 8–11). Visser 't Hooft called first for a thorough "spring cleaning." Then we must go to the roots of modern culture as seen through philosophers, poets and novelists. It also meant the church itself must encounter the gospel afresh as the first step in discovering the Word for contemporary life.

In 1985 John Paul II appealed to all Catholics to participate in reevangelization/new evangelization: "I urge you in the name of the Lord Jesus Christ, to make yourselves proclaimers of the Gospel, to spread with all your might the saving Word."[9] The Pope's appeal has stirred both positive and negative reactions among Catholics. His critics hear a call to reestablish Christendom.[10] The Pope has emphasized the importance of culture for reevangelization and has created a new pontifical commission on culture.

The third voice is that of Lesslie Newbigin, missionary and bishop in India and ecumenical leader who returned to his homeland to retire. What struck him was an observable lack of hope in British society. For the past decade Newbigin has been preoccupied with the question, "Can the West be converted?" He has spelled out a program in a number of recent books (Newbigin 1983, 1986, 1989a, 1991). Newbigin insists that we must critically examine the fundamental presuppositions, the epistemological foundations on which modern culture rests. Only then will we know how the gospel as truth can heal the divisions and contradictions present in modern culture. The stance from which to understand modern culture is that of the missionary. The West needs to hear the gospel, the life-giving news of God's election of a people who live by the Word of God within this story.

These three leaders have not been alone in their concern. Throughout the twentieth century many initiatives have been taken to evangelize or reevangelize Western societies or bring renewal to the churches. What distinguishes these appeals is their insistence on going back to the roots of Western culture in order to understand it in terms of its origins and subsequent development.

The traditional distinction between mission and evangelism played on the assumption that the church *knows* its own culture profoundly. What remains is to employ certain techniques or methods in recruiting people back to the church. This stereotyping of evangelism had implications for both message and method. It had a reductionistic effect on both. In the West these techniques and methods are, of course, furnished by technocratic culture, and this suggests that evangelism itself has been secularized. The fact that the churches have for so long been defined by social categories indicates that, far from *knowing* the culture, the churches speak largely to their own segment within it. Secularized modes of evangelism are sources of alienation rather than means of personal and social reconciliation.

It is instructive that when our Lord began his public ministry, he stated his presupposition: "The time is fulfilled, and the kingdom of God is at hand; repent, and believe in the gospel" (Mark 1:15). The ministry of Jesus was set within the culture in which he was born and reared. With rare penetration he grasped the presuppositions on which his own culture was based—as suggested by the illuminating questions he put to people and the parables he told. His ministry was notable for the way he engaged the issues that mattered most to people.

The Palestine of Jesus' time was a culture in turmoil and under great strain. It was near the breaking point. Jesus modeled for us what it means to be in missionary encounter with one's culture. He was the outsider who became the insider without surrendering his outsider status. He never relaxed this bifocal stance. Jesus was recognizably "their own," but they refused to "own" him. He represented to his people *basileia*, a source of judgment and hope. In his person they knew they were encountering both God and themselves. In his incarnation Jesus held together his full identification with the human situation and his total commitment to *basileia*. This was the force field out of which his extraordinary mission was conducted. But every clue Jesus gave his disciples as to their own missionary vocation suggests that this is the authoritative model for them as well. Jesus left no general guidelines, formulae, or methods for his disciples to follow—only a demanding model.

Basing a missionary encounter with modern culture on *basileia* and incarnation will have several implications. First, this calls us to reject the Christendom notion whereby we claim a culture as being *Christian*. Every culture is incomplete without the gospel, but no culture is ever completely evangelized, for no culture is completely submitted to the reign of God. In every culture there are forces that contradict the reign of God. Because the church should know its own culture best, it has a special missionary vocation to that culture.

This leads to the second observation: the church's normal relationship to every culture is that of missionary encounter. The faithful church, living out God's reign, cannot feel completely at home in culture; yet in light of *basileia*, the church is responsible to every human society to witness to God's saving intention. This calls the church to a twofold action in relation to every culture. Incarnation signifies full identification, but it is incarnation in the service of disclosing God's love and will for humankind. This is the way marked by the cross.

Third, there is no biblical or theological basis for the territorial distinction between mission and evangelism. To accede to this dichotomy is to invite the church to "settle in" and be at home. The church is most at risk where it has been present in a culture for a long period so that it no longer conceives its relation to culture in terms of missionary encounter. The church remains socially and salvifically relevant so long as it is in tension with culture. The ongoing task of the church is to train its members to view "culture" through the critically constructive lenses of the missionary. This means, of course, learning to view a culture through kingdom categories in order to discern and expose those forces that bring death rather than life.

The culture of modernity is an unprecedented missionary frontier. It is the first culture which has had a long encounter with the Christian faith, but where vast numbers of people live post-Christian lives. The nonmissionary church of Christendom remains a dominant form of church in modern culture. This ecclesial reality can be made salvifically and socially relevant only if reshaped by *basileia* to become the means of incarnating the reign of God in modern culture.

## Notes

1. For a historical analysis, see Marty (1969). For a sociological interpretation, see Berger, Berger, and Kellner (1974). For a theological probe, see Gunton (1985).

2. "West" refers to the geographical-historical reality associated with Europe at least since Leo IX excommunicated the Eastern Church in 1052. North America and Australasia, by virtue of being settled by Europeans and having similar eco-

nomic and political systems, are included in the West. Latin America occupies a different position. Culturally it owes much to Europe; economically Latin America has never achieved parity with the West. Japan is a different sort of hybrid. It has preserved much of its cultural heritage but borrowed freely from the West as a part of its modernization starting in the late nineteenth century. Economically, Japan today ranks as one of the major industrial powers.

3. For an overview of these debates see Yoder (1984, 40-50).

4. The story of Abbe Godin, inspirer of the worker priest movement, is told in Ward (1949).

5. The story of religion in Europe is complex and the literature vast. Two accessible accounts of the recent period are Gilbert (1976) and McLeod (1981).

6. McLeod (1980, 191). Cf. the remark of Archbishop Lang that people "have never fallen from the church, for they were never within it" (cited by Hobhouse 1911, 323).

7. In his address to the Centenary Missions Conference in London in 1888 on the need for comity agreements, Warneck included this sentence: "Dear brethren in England and America, I believe that I speak in the name of all my German fellow-believers, if I urge upon you to cease from looking upon Germany, the land of Luther and Melanchthon, Arndt and Spener, Francke and Zinzendorf, Tholuck, Fliedner and Wichern, as a half heathen and rationalistic country" (Warneck 1888, 431-37).

8. Cited by Walls (1991, 146-55).

9. *Lumen Vitae* XLI:3 (1986), p. 246.

10. One example of critical reaction to John Paul's call is Luneau and Ladriere (1989).

*18*

# Theology of Religions and Missiology

## *A Time of Testing*

### GERALD H. ANDERSON

No issue in missiology is more important, more difficult, more controversial, or more divisive for the days ahead than the theology of religions.
This is the arena where conflicting truth claims among world religions challenge Christians to articulate their understanding of the relationship
between God's redemptive activity in Jesus Christ and people of other
faiths. Our understanding of the theological significance of other religious
traditions determines our attitude and approach to people of other faiths
in terms of mission, evangelism, dialogue, service, and other forms of Christian witness.

### Theological Neglect

Two primary factors account for the strategic importance of the theology
of religions in the 1990s and beyond. First is our situation of religious
pluralism. Christians in the West find themselves immersed in a context of
religious pluralism today that they are ill equipped theologically to deal
with. Some thirty years ago, in *The Theology of the Christian Mission*, I wrote,
"Christian theological endeavor has been more concerned with introspec-
tion, with intra-Christian relations, than with the interrelation of Christianity and other faiths. Too often those most interested in the nature of the
Christian faith have been those least interested in its relation to [people]
of other faiths" (Anderson, ed. 1961, 4). The result of this legacy is that,

Gerald H. Anderson is editor of the *International Bulletin of Missionary Research* and director of the Overseas Ministries Study Center in New Haven, Connecticut.

while there may be more consciousness of religious pluralism today, the churches in the West are not prepared to deal with it missiologically. The fruits of long missionary experience in the encounter with people of other faiths in other parts of the world have not been appropriated in the West. There is an assumption among Western Christians, says Andrew Walls, "that we are suddenly at Day One of the interreligious encounter, an assumption that bypasses the accumulated experience of many generations, and still worse, implicitly locks Christianity into a Western framework" (Walls 1991, 148).

The seriousness of the challenge to mission theology is hard to over-estimate. Max Warren, former general secretary of the Church Missionary Society in London, predicted in 1958 that "the impact of agnostic science will turn out to have been as child's play compared to the challenge to Christian theology of the faith of other men" (Quoted in W. C. Smith 1972, 121). Warren was absolutely right. This is *the* theological issue for mission in the 1990s and into the twenty-first century. Lutheran theologian Carl E. Braaten, writing about the situation in the 1990s, says, "The question whether there is the promise of salvation in the name of Jesus, and in no other name, is fast becoming a life-and-death issue facing contemporary Christianity. In the churches this issue will become the test of fidelity to the gospel, a matter of *status confessionis* more urgent than any other" (Braaten 1992, 89).

## Theological Relativism

A second critical factor confronting the theology of religions today is a rampant radical relativism. The most glaring example appears in *The Myth of Christian Uniqueness*, in which the authors propose a shift in Christian belief of such magnitude that they describe it as "the crossing of a theological Rubicon."[1] They propose that Christians should abandon claims about the uniqueness of Christ and Christianity, or about having any definitive revelation, and accept instead that there is a plurality of revelations and a parity of religions, with Christianity just one among many religions through which people may be saved.

Consider, for example, two of the essays in the above-mentioned volume: one by Gordon Kaufman, professor of divinity at Harvard Divinity School, and one by Langdon Gilkey, professor of theology at the University of Chicago Divinity School. The first surprise in reading their essays is that, where they are discussing issues of theological construction and authority, they never mention the Bible. Actually, Kaufman does allude to it once when he says, "In the biblical documents God is portrayed as a quasi-personal or agential reality—that is, the model in terms of which the notion of God is constructed is the human self or agent" (p. 10). But that is the sum total of attention to the Bible in these two essays. It is taken for granted, without discussion, that the Bible has nothing to contribute to the argument.

For Kaufman, Christian theology is not based on divine revelation, but on "human imaginative response," informed by "modern historical consciousness." This modern historical consciousness, he claims, liberates us from belief in divine inspiration and revelation, enabling us to see that our religious traditions are "the product of human imaginative creativity" (p. 8) and that our theological statements and claims are simply "the product of our own human study and reflection" (p. 12). The problem—as Lesslie Newbigin points out—is that Kaufman takes it for granted that the Christian Gospel is not true. He engages in a new form of idolatry, namely, a remarkably uncritical acceptance of the standpoint of "modern historical consciousness." Newbigin reminds us that " 'modern historical consciousness' is also a culturally conditioned phenomenon and does not provide us with a standpoint from which we can dispose of truth-claims of the Bible. . . . [It] provides no grounds upon which it is possible to deny that God might have acted decisively to reveal and effect the divine purpose for human history" (Newbigin 1989b, 50).

Langdon Gilkey, in his essay, is quite forthright in acknowledging that what the authors are doing in that volume represents "a monstrous shift indeed" (p. 39) from a belief that Christianity contains "the definitive revelation among other revelations to some sort of plurality of revelations" and a "rough parity" of religions, with "recognition of the co-validity and the co-efficacy of other religions" (pp. 37–39). This position, he says, "is *real* relativism" (p. 43); it "involves *all* theological doctrines, not just some of them" (p. 41), and it "has devastating theological effects," which he believes are desirable (p. 40). The problem, he admits, is that soon "we have no grounds for speaking of salvation at all, a situation of relativity far beyond asking about the salvation of *all*" (p. 44). However, he finds that a position of absolute relativity "seems to defy intellectual resolution" (p. 46), so he opts instead for "relative absoluteness"—with "one part absoluteness and two parts relativity" (p. 47).

As the center for theological understanding, Gilkey proposes "the absolute as *relatively* present in the relative—as the clue to the center of theological understanding" (p. 47). Lesslie Newbigin wryly observes, "I remain totally unconvinced by the idea of an absolute that is available on call when it is relatively necessary" (Newbigin 1989b, 52). It is hard to imagine that anyone would ever be converted or want to join the church on the basis of Gilkey's "clue to the center of theological understanding." Would anyone be willing to die for this? Would John Wesley have his heart "strangely warmed" by "the absolute as relatively present in the relative"?

Commenting on this viewpoint in the *International Bulletin of Missionary Research*, the editors stated that "the Christian world mission cannot afford to cross the theological Rubicon proposed by the authors of *The Myth* volume. Rather, we need to affirm again that unique 'Rubicon-crossing' event of twenty centuries ago: the redemptive entering of the Creator into human history in the person of Jesus Christ. Without the uniqueness of that person and that event, there is no gospel and no mission" (*International Bulletin of Missionary Research* 1989, 49).

## World Council of Churches

The World Council of Churches (WCC), through its Program on Dialogue with People of Living Faiths, is the arena where these issues have been addressed most consistently over the last twenty years. In the last three general assemblies of the WCC—at Nairobi in 1975, Vancouver in 1983, and Canberra in 1991—debate over issues about interfaith dialogue, religious pluralism, and syncretism were the most controversial and divisive subjects addressed by the assembly delegates. In each of these assemblies the delegates refused in the end (despite efforts by some staff, consultants, and delegates to the contrary) to approve any statement or report that appeared to deny the uniqueness of Christ or that placed dialogue in opposition to the evangelistic mission of the church. Nevertheless, the situation became so serious at the Seventh Assembly in Canberra that the Orthodox participants issued a statement in which they registered their "sincere concern" over "dangerous trends," such as an absence "from many WCC documents [of] the affirmation that Jesus Christ is the world's Saviour" and "a growing departure from biblically-based Christian understandings" ("Reflections of Orthodox Participants," in World Council of Churches 1991a, 279–82). In particular, the Orthodox indicated "a certain disquiet" about "developments of the WCC towards the broadening of its aims in the direction of relations with other religions," and they urged that a definition of theological criteria for these developments "must constitute the first priority of the WCC."

Some developments leading up to the Canberra Assembly that contributed to a crisis of confidence in the WCC were directly related to the theology of religions. In 1989 two veteran ecumenical missiologists expressed their deep dismay over a trend toward theological relativism in the council's Program on Dialogue. Lesslie Newbigin, a former director of the Commission on World Mission and Evangelism of the WCC, said that if the council went along with this trend, "it would become an irrelevance in the spiritual struggles that lie ahead of us" (Newbigin 1989b, 54). The distinguished Dutch missiologist Johannes Verkuyl predicted that the drift toward religious universalism and theological relativism in the dialogue program "will pose more and more serious questions not only about the credibility of the WCC, but even about its survival" (Verkuyl 1989, 55). A reaction led by Third World voices against the trend toward syncretism and theological relativism, along with a carefully balanced statement entitled "Witness Among People of Other Living Faiths," drafted in May 1989 by

David Bosch at the council's World Mission Conference in San Antonio, Texas, defused the crisis for a few months.

Then in January 1990 the Program on Dialogue held a consultation at Baar, Switzerland, in order "to move toward a more adequate theology of religions."[2] Twenty Orthodox, Protestant, and Catholic theologians (including Paul Knitter) and a number of council staff were invited to participate. They issued a statement entitled "Religious Plurality: Theological Perspectives and Affirmations" that echoed some of the same themes about a plurality of revelations and a parity of religions that were expressed in *The Myth of Christian Uniqueness*. The most that their statement affirmed about the importance of the Christ event was that it is "for us the clearest expression of the salvific will of God in all human history." Nowhere do they suggest, however, that it is essential for everyone even to hear about the salvific will of God revealed in Christ. Any exclusivist claims in the New Testament concerning the revelation of God in Christ (e.g., John 14:6; Acts 4:12) are ignored; and it urges "a need to move beyond a theology which confines salvation to the explicit personal commitment to Jesus Christ" (Baar Statement 1991, 49).

The controversy came to full view at the Canberra Assembly of the WCC in February 1991, with the keynote address on the Holy Spirit by Chung Hyun Kyung, a young Presbyterian theologian from South Korea (Chung 1991). In her address, Chung linked Christian theology with elements of popular religiosity in Korea. Many understood her to equate the Holy Spirit with the "spirits full of *Han*," associated in Korea with the wandering spirits of those who have died unjustly.

Another image of the Holy Spirit invoked by Chung was the Asian goddess *Kwan In*, a Korean Buddhist *bodhisattva* or enlightened being who is venerated by East Asian women's popular religiosity. Chung urged assembly participants, "This is perhaps the time we have to reread the Bible from the perspective of birds, water, air, trees and mountains. ... Learning to think like a mountain, changing our center from human beings to all living beings, has become our responsibility in order to survive." Prior to the assembly, Chung wrote, "My ... hope for the future direction of Asian women's theology is that it move away from the doctrinal purity of Christian theology and risk the survival-liberation centered syncretism" (Chung 1990, 113).

While her presentation at Canberra had a mixed reception, many observers felt that Chung had indeed tried to move the WCC away from its doctrinal basis toward a syncretistic theology of religions. There was widespread dismay among evangelicals, Orthodox, and others—including Asians—about the shamanistic overtones in her treatment of the relation between the Holy Spirit and other spirits. Raymond Fung of Hong Kong, who served several years as secretary for evangelism on the WCC staff, judged that Chung had "treated the subject in a most shabby manner" and that the presentation represented "a nonchalant attitude towards the spirit world which borders either on spiritual naivete or on manipulation and cynicism" (World Council of Churches, 1991a, 4.) To compound the problem, little was said at the assembly about Christian mission in terms of personal evangelism, conversion, and church growth (see Kerr 1991, 103).

Orthodox participants expressed "alarm" that in the presentations at the assembly, "some people tend to affirm with very great ease the presence of the Holy Spirit in many movements and developments without discernment. . . . We must guard against a tendency to substitute a 'private' spirit, the spirit of the world or other spirits for the Holy Spirit who proceeds from the Father and rests in the Son. . . . We find it impossible to invoke spirits of 'earth, air, water and sea creatures.' Pneumatology is inseparable from Christology or from the doctrine of the Holy Trinity confessed by the church on the basis of divine revelation" ("Reflections of Orthodox Participants," World Council of Churches 1991a, 281). After what they had seen and heard at Canberra, the Orthodox representatives said they were asking themselves, "Has the time come for the Orthodox churches and other member churches to review their relations with the World Council of Churches?" ("Reflections of Orthodox Participants," World Council of Churches 1991a, 282). Never before in the history of the ecumenical movement had an entire ecclesial tradition threatened to withdraw from the council, and the crisis was precipitated largely by issues of religious pluralism, interfaith dialogue, and syncretism—all related to the theology of religions.

## Two Traditions

In Scripture and in the history of Christian doctrine, there are two major traditions regarding the relationship of God's redemptive activity in Jesus Christ and people of other faiths.[3] One of these is the broad, inclusive tradition that emphasizes the *continuity* of God's activity in Christ with his activity among all persons everywhere. Jesus Christ in this view is crucial, normative, and definitive, but not exclusive. What is true of Jesus Christ in a focal way is pervasively true of the whole cosmos.

The other tradition is the narrow, particular, and exclusivistic tradition that emphasizes a radical *discontinuity* between Christian revelation, which is absolutely unique, and the whole range of non-Christian religious experience. According to this tradition, God has spoken to humanity only in the person of Jesus Christ and "there is salvation in no one else" (Acts 4:12). The tradition of discontinuity would emphasize Christ's saying in John 14:6 that "no one comes to the Father but by me."

In faithfulness to biblical revelation, both of these traditions must be affirmed and maintained, but this is difficult to do when some persons affirm continuity with doubtful uniqueness and others affirm uniqueness without continuity. What is needed in our theology of religions is uniqueness *with* continuity.[4]

## The Gospel and the Jewish People

The issues of uniqueness and continuity come into particularly sharp focus in the relationship of the Gospel and the Jewish people.[5] Initially Jesus saw himself as "sent only to . . . the house of Israel" (Matt. 15:24; cf. 10:5–6), and for St. Paul the pattern of mission was "to the Jew first" (Rom. 1:16). Christian mission thus began with the Jewish people, which is also where a theology of religions must begin. For while the relationship of the Gospel to the Jewish people is distinctive, it is not totally different or separate from the relationship of the Gospel to people of other faiths.

The relationship of the Gospel to the Jewish people is foundational for a theology of religions. If one's theological perspective on this issue is defective, it is likely that one's attitude and approach to people of other faiths will also be defective. Today if a Christian theologian says that the Jewish people do not need the Gospel, the same theologian very likely will also deny that people of other faiths need the Gospel, and we end up with a theological relativism that rejects the Christian mission to all people of other faiths. Mission to the Jewish people is the litmus test of an adequate theology of religions for missiology.

Today many Protestant and Catholic theologians maintain that Jews do not need the Gospel of Jesus Christ because—they say—Jews have their own covenant with God through Abraham, which renders faith in Jesus as the Messiah unnecessary. Allan R. Brockway, a former executive staff member of the WCC Program on Dialogue with People of Living Faiths, maintains that not only do Jews not need to profess faith in Jesus as the Messiah but that "by no stretch of the imagination can Jesus be understood as the 'Messiah of the Jews,' despite Christian belief. The most that can be claimed," he says, "is that Jesus was a failed messiah, as was bar [*sic*] Kokba" (Brockway 1988, 351).

It is ironic that whereas the first major controversy in the primitive church was whether anyone *other than* Jews should be discipled, today the controversy is just the opposite—whether Jews themselves should be discipled. Another irony is that whereas part of the original controversy was whether Gentiles had to become Jews in order to be Christians, today part of the controversy is whether Jews have to become Gentiles in order to be Christians.

Nothing in the New Testament suggests any exemption of Jews from the universal mission of the church to all nations and peoples. To the contrary, as indicated above, Jews were the original focus of mission. Jesus and all the apostles were Jews; the first church in Jerusalem probably consisted entirely of Jews, and all the churches mentioned in Acts presumably had

Jewish members. There are not two covenants with God, one for Jews and one for Christians. Rather God's covenant with Israel was fulfilled by Jesus, who proclaimed, "I have come not to destroy but to fulfill" (Matt. 5:17, anticipated in Jer. 31:31–33).[6]

Some mainline Protestant churches have compromised their position on mission to the Jews, and now favor dialogue only. But the Roman Catholic Church, the major Orthodox churches, the Lausanne Movement, and the World Evangelical Fellowship all affirm that everyone—Jews and Gentiles alike—needs faith in Jesus Christ. A theology of religions that is adequate for missiology must begin here and build upon it for our understanding of mission to people of other faiths.

These concerns have been at the heart of Arthur Glasser's work as a missiologist. He began his career as a missionary to the Jews and has retained a lifelong commitment to this work (Glasser 1990b, 112). He is a member of the Lausanne Consultation on Jewish Evangelism and is Coordinator for Judaic Studies at the School of World Mission, Fuller Theological Seminary. In his article "Mission in the 1990s" for the *International Bulletin of Missionary Research* (January 1989), he listed "witness to the Jews" as one of "two touchstone issues" on which "evangelicals will not waver or deviate" in the 1990s and beyond. The other issue, he said, is "the uniqueness of Christ in the midst of religious pluralism."[7] On both these issues—as on many others in missiology—Arthur Glasser is a colleague to be trusted and respected.

## Notes

1. Hick and Knitter (1987, viii). Subsequent page references to this volume are in the text.

2. Baar Statement (1991, 47-48). See also an account of the Baar meeting by Eck (1990).

3. See my articles "Continuity and Discontinuity" (Anderson 1971), "Religion as a Problem for the Christian Mission" (Anderson 1978), and "Response to Pietro Rossano" (Anderson 1981b).

4. This formulation was first suggested by Edmund Davison Soper (1943, 225-27).

5. I have written on this point at greater length, most recently in my chapter "Speaking the Truth in Love: An Evangelical Response [to Cardinal Jozef Tomko]" (Anderson 1990, 164-70). After this present essay was written, I was pleased to discover that Frederick Dale Bruner (my former missionary colleague on the faculty of Union Theological Seminary near Manila, Philippines), in volume two of his definitive commentary on Matthew, *The Churchbook: Matthew 13-28* (1990), had already stated a position on Jewish evangelism very similar to my own, when he concluded, "the litmus test today of whether one really believes that Jesus is the Savior of the world is the position one takes on the evangelism of the Jewish people" (742).

6. For a summary of conflicting viewpoints on these issues, see Gavin D'Costa (1990).

7. This article was reprinted under the title "The Evangelicals: Unwavering Commitment, Troublesome Divisions" (Anderson 1991a).

# PART SIX

# CONTEXTUAL CONSIDERATIONS

# Introductory Overview

There are various ways a volume of this kind can be brought to closure. In one sense, no manner of ending will properly conclude what is calculated to take us into a new millennium. In Part VI the editors chose to deal with kingdom/mission issues in several specific contexts. We decided that both the scholars and the subjects about which they write would have a special relationship to the honoree. By doing so, these particular areas of interest are but representative of the larger contemporary agenda. At the same time, by selecting writers who have personal connections to Arthur Glasser, we are aware that his broad integration of missiological interests will take us well into the future. In order to achieve this, the chapters had to be quite a bit shorter than those in Parts I to V. We appreciate our contributors' agreeing to this limitation, since in most cases what they have written is a summary of major research.

Evelyn Jensen received her Ph.D. from the School of World Mission and remembers Art as one who encouraged and supported her all along the way. Art, with his wife, Alice, are strong advocates for women. This side of Art's theology has been deeply appreciated, especially by women students who come from churches that take very conservative positions on women in ministry. Jensen emphasizes that women must be empowered both internally and externally if they are to achieve their God-intended roles in society and ministry.

Stuart Dauermann, who is Rabbi of the Ahavat Zion Messianic Synagogue, figures prominently in Art Glasser's life as friend and confidant. He is currently studying with Art for a Ph.D. in Missiology. Dauermann's contention is that through developing more fully the concept of *Keruv*, the Jewish tradition already has an inherent understanding of mission. The call to "bring near those who are afar off" must be accomplished in ways that are distinctly Jewish in theory and practice.

The 1980s will be remembered in the School of World Mission as Glasser's "Chinese period." During those years the Th.M. in Chinese Ministry was formed almost single-handedly by Art Glasser. It is a natural consequence of his years as missionary that he has endeared himself to Chinese people. Che Bin Tan, who headed the program until 1991, exposes the generally alien character of Chinese missions and shows that the theology of mission for Chinese must go beyond the "right message" to produce a better life in the traditional system.

*211*

Arthur has always been a scholar of European Christianity, and his ecumenical style has kept him in close touch with Church leaders on the Continent. It is fitting that a chapter should be contributed by one of his senior students who has ministered for years with an organization that grows out of German Pietism. Herman Buehler writes from a deep sense of mission to his Germanic roots. His conviction is that because of an almost exclusive emphasis on the second Person of the Trinity, a rediscovery of God as Father and Holy Spirit is urgently needed. This could lead to renewal in the Church.

African theologian Tite Tiénou came to Fuller while Art Glasser was still dean. He was the first African to receive the Ph.D. from the School of World Mission. After several years of teaching in the U.S.A., Tite has returned to West Africa to head a theological school in Côte d'Ivoire. This speaks to the commitment and contribution of students who have been shaped by Glasser. Fittingly, the burden of Tiénou's essay is the urgency for theological maturity in Africa, a call to change the shapes that have been configured by others into what is authentically and concretely African.

Dialogue with non-Christian religions has always held a fascination for Art. For years he taught the major course on Christian religious encounter. Saphir Athyal writes on theological issues relating to Hinduism. Athyal is well known in India's theological circles and in the Lausanne movement. Glasser and Athyal have worked together for years. Both see dialogue as very useful if carried out properly. Mutual respect and honesty are basic requirements. But this kind of mutuality is not without a price; it means being as candid about differences as about similarities.

As chief editor Van Engen opened this volume, and we decided he should bring our thinking full circle with a concluding chapter. He has done this by proposing that the touchstones of Kingdom mission theology are faith, love and hope, so providing both paradigm and spirit for mission today and tomorrow.

D. S. G.

# 19

# Women's Issues in Context

## EVELYN JENSEN

The theme of the contextualization of women's issues is by nature a very difficult one. It is difficult because, first of all as individuals, gender issues touch us at the deepest core of our identity, and second because, as a society, social systems and structures are frequently organized around gender beliefs and practices. It is also difficult because mission strategists must effectively avoid two main extremes: on the one hand, the exportation and imposition of western feminist ideology and theology on other cultures, and on the other hand, not allowing the gospel to be prophetic and counter cultural to the oppressive social, psychological and theological belief systems under which women exist.

In spite of these difficulties, the time has now come for mission strategists to give serious consideration to the contextualization of a biblical feminism. The devaluation and subsequent oppression of women is a universal phenomenon and varies only by degree and form from culture to culture. The Gospel's call for human dignity and justice is our foremost motivation for the task. In light of that call, the Church must ask, "What is the Good News for the women around the world who make up 50 percent of the world population and who are caught in disempowering value systems?"

The focus of this paper is the cross-cultural empowerment of women in family and church. More specifically, I will seek to understand the biblical basis of internal and external empowerment of women and to suggest some guidelines for the contextualization of women's empowerment.

### Internal Empowerment

Webster's dictionary defines empower to "give power, authority to someone." It also means "to give ability to someone or to enable someone." By

---

Evelyn Jensen, who holds a Ph.D. in Intercultural Studies, was a missionary to Ecuador under the Christian and Missionary Alliance. She is presently adjunct professor at Fuller's School of World Mission and at Canadian Bible College.

internal empowerment I am referring to that internal, personal sense of power which all of us must have in order to function in a healthy manner. It involves a sense of high self-esteem or self-image (McBride 1990, 22-26). A person who is internally empowered is one who has a sense of unique personal identity and value. This sense of worth and identity flows out of one's "beingness," not out of "doing." Internally empowered persons may be very aware of being strongly connected to a group or another individual, but will also have the ability to define themselves apart from others.

In my teaching experience, women from various cultures have frequently expressed that they feel profoundly flawed or just not "good enough." Some women describe the feeling of emptiness within as a deep hole at the center of their being. Even though some women hold very influential roles, they often feel like "second class" people. They feel ignored and not listened to, as if they were invisible and without a voice.

Speaking from a biblical perspective, I believe that the creation narratives in Genesis 1 and 2 and the Gospels present key universal theological principles regarding internal empowerment of women.[1] The first principle is that both men and women are created in the Image of God (Gen. 1:26–27). Of all the possible meanings of the Image of God, one thing is sure: women have the same Image of God imprinted in them as do men. In no way does a woman's reflection of this Image indicate a secondary, lesser or inferior Image of God.

The second principle is indicated in the mandate given to both the woman and the man: They were to rule over the rest of creation (Gen. 1:28). The woman was given equal responsibility with the man to have dominion over the whole earth. This chapter also teaches that creation of male and female was "very good" (1:31).

> The very nature of the female being and the normal, natural functions of her humanity were *good*! In many cultures around the world, women are valued less because it is thought that somehow their feminine bodily functions contaminate and defile them. But according to this creation account, women with all their bodily functions, such as conceiving, bearing and caring for children, are sacred and of great value and worth because they bear the imprint of the Triune God in their beings. (Jensen 1990)

The third principle relates to the special kind of relationship between the man and woman. The woman is created to be a "helper." The word "helper" appears 21 times in the Old Testament, 16 of which are used to describe the relationship of God as helper to his people. In Hebrew the word means "a suitable assistance," emphasizing the appropriateness or suitability of the assistance. The word in no way suggests an authority/subjection kind of relationship but rather the mutuality and reciprocity of the male/female relationship and the intrinsic unity of male and female in the human race.

According to Genesis 3, one of the major results of sin intruding into the human experience was the marring and damaging of the relationship between male and female. That which was created to be equal and mutual is now characterized by inequality, disunity and an authority/submission kind of relationship (3:16). It must be understood that verse 16 is *describing* the male/female relationship after sin came into the world but is not *prescribing* for all time a specific order in creation. This fallen condition can now only be redeemed through Christ's death and resurrection (Gal. 3:26–28).

Jesus then becomes our model for the contextualization of biblical feminism. Jesus' behavior and attitude toward women and his teachings about women were consistently counter-cultural in terms of the values and roles of women in Jewish society. Jesus called women to a radical discipleship (Mt. 12:49) and challenged them to new levels of spirituality (cf. John 8:1–11 with Luke 10:38–42 and John 11:30–32). Jesus showed his confidence in them by discussing profound theological issues with them (Mt. 15:19–21; 26:6–13; Lk. 10:38–42; Jn. 4:7–12; 11:20–32) and permitted them to be part of his itinerant band of disciples (Lk. 8:1–3). He used women as models of faith and as key characters in his illustrations and parables.[2]

It was probably in his teaching on divorce that Jesus most dramatically demonstrated a new system of values regarding women (Mt. 5:28–30). Instead of women being held responsible for men's lusting, "they were to be seen as valuable in their own right and treated with dignity. They were not to be seen as *objects* designed for the fulfillment of men's natural desires, but rather *subjects* whose intrinsic worth was not to be violated" (Jensen 1990, 40). For women this was indeed internal empowerment.

### External Empowerment

By external empowerment I am referring to the ability and skills of individuals to act upon the environment around them. It involves motivation and ability to have input into the decision-making process of a group, to have access to the resources of the group, and to share in the privileges of the group (McBride 1990, 22–26). The externally empowered person is one who can fully participate both in the private sphere of family and clan and the public sphere with skills and spiritual gifts which bring well-being to the individual and to the larger community.

Cross-cultural anthropological and sociological research abound with illustrations of how women are not empowered to function in the systems and structures of public institutions (Bernard 1987; Sivard 1985; Taylor 1985). Not the least of the social institutions to marginalize women in the public sphere has been the Church.

I believe the book of Acts and the Pauline Epistles give us ample instruction regarding the role of women in the Church. The book of Acts records that women continued to participate in the inauguration and expansion of the early Church. Not only did they wait and pray for the Comforter to come (ch. 1), it is significant that the women also were present for the outpouring of the Holy Spirit and received spiritual gifts, as had been promised (cf. Acts 2 with Joel 2:28–32). It is specially noted that women as well as men received the gift of prophecy, which was a very important spiritual gift in the early Church (cf. Acts 2:17; 21:8–9; 1 Cor. 14:39). Women were among the many early converts (5:14), were persecuted for their faith (8:3; 22:4), and were disciplined when necessary (5:1–11). Women served the Church by opening their houses for worship and prayer (12:12), serving the poor and needy (9:32–43), founding a church (cf. 16:11–40, and Phil 4:1–3), ministering through the gift of prophecy (21:8, 9), teaching as an itinerant missionary/teacher even to men (18:2, 18, 26) and leading congregations (Rom. 16:1, 2). Thus we see that women in the early Church had significant public roles in social work, teaching, evangelism, preaching, and church-planting ministries.

The Apostle Paul clearly taught that in Christ "there is neither Jew nor Greek, slave nor free, male nor female, for you are all one in Christ Jesus" (Gal. 3:28). Not only did he teach mutual and egalitarian principles between men and women, he also practiced them in his ministry. Paul mentions nine different women with whom he had ministered and calls them by the same titles as he called his male colaborers (Rom. 16:1, 3, 6, 7, 12; Phil. 4:2, 3) (Scholer 1983/84, 15). Thus we see that Paul empowered women for ministry in the Church in ways that challenged the culture.

The general thrust of Scripture affirms the internal and external empowerment of women. However, since we take the unity and inspiration of the whole Bible seriously, it cannot be ignored that Paul also seems to very strongly prohibit women from teaching or participating in certain congregations (1 Cor. 14:33–40; Eph. 5:21–33; 1 Tim. 2:8–15). Many scholars would agree that the apparent prohibitions of Paul must be put in their historical context and that these are not universal teaching for all times but rather counsel to be applied in very specific situations.[3]

## Toward Contextualization

Three factors are involved in the process of developing a critical contextualization model of the empowerment of women. First, it is necessary to do an "exegesis of the culture as one exercise and a fresh study of corresponding biblical themes as another."[4] Building upon the biblical hermeneutic concerning women's internal and external empowerment must be accompanied by a careful exegesis of the culture involved. The third factor to take into consideration is the change process. The following guidelines may move us toward a critical model of contextualization through change agency.

1. As kingdom people, we must have a strong commitment to the goal of equality and interdependence between men and women in Christ (Gal. 3:26–28). The working out of gender equality within the Church will be a sign to the surrounding culture of the power of the Gospel to heal damaged relationships.[5]

2. As kingdom people, we must be aware and sensitive to the inequities, exclusion, abuse and needs of women in the wider culture in which we minister, in order to be effectively counter-cultural.

3. The development of internal empowerment is a process, and every woman will move through different phases to realize it. The process will vary and be manifested in different forms according to the cultural setting. The main role of the missioner is to be a sensitive teacher and counselor to assist women to find internal empowerment.

4. In any given congregation the awareness level of gender issues must be raised in both men and women for long-term change and true consensus of the community to take place.

5. There seems to be a correlation between internal and external empowerment. That is, as a woman develops an increasing sense of self-worth and dignity, she will experience increasing security to claim and own her particular kind of external empowerment. The main role of the missioner is to be an advocate to open doors for the woman to use her gifts and skills for the benefit of the whole community or advocate for justice for the abused and neglected woman in the wider context.

6. In cultures where women's and men's worlds are very separate, it will be necessary to teach and train women separately until the women have a well-developed sense of internal and external empowerment. Otherwise, women have the tendency to become submerged in the agenda of the men's world.[6]

Since the contextualization of women's issues is a relatively new theme, much more study needs to be done. Nevertheless, let us hear the Gospel's call for the empowerment of all human beings, especially women.

### Notes

1. Examples of exegetical scholarship regarding women in ministry: Bilezikian (1989), Evans (1982), Richard and Catherine Kroeger (1981), Mickelsen (1986), Scholer (1983/84), Van Leeuwen (1990).

2. The following authors are of particular help regarding Jesus and women: Bilezikian (1989, 79-118), Evans (1982, 44-60), Scholer (1983/84, 15).

3. Besides the citations in note 2, the following are helpful: Cervin (n.d.), Kroeger (1979, 12-15), Scholer (1986, 193-219), Van Leeuwen (1986, 1988).

4. Gilliland (1989b, 317). See also Hiebert (1985a, 5-10; 1985b, 12-18; 1987, 104-11).

5. For more regarding the development of mutuality and partnership in cross-cultural situations, see Augsburger (1986, 214-43).

6. See Bernard (1987, 20-66) for a discussion of the pros and cons from a sociological perspective of training women separately.

## 20

# Let My People Go . . . into All the World

*Motivating for Mission in the Messianic Jewish Context*

## STUART DAUERMANN

### Introduction

Behind this chapter lies the conviction that the Messianic Jewish community needs to rethink its relationship to the mission task in order to once and for all recognize that doing mission does not require that we buy into someone else's *goyishe* (alien) agenda. Toward that end, I intend to demonstrate that doing mission is a very Jewish thing to do, and that indeed, ample materials, precedents and paradigms exist within our own culture to inform, shape and motivate Messianic Jewish mission.[1]

By "the Messianic Jewish community," I refer to the recent phenomenon of Jews who manifest a threefold allegiance to Yeshua as Savior and Lord, to one another as a community of faith, and to Jewish culture and ethnicity as an individual and corporate identity. Although, by extension, this community includes the spouses and children of its members, regardless of their faith commitment, plus a number of sympathetic and generally enthusiastic "fellow travelers" not born Jewish, the demographic heart of this community is ethnic Jews—those with one or both parents having been born Jews.

### The Messianic Movement—Something New, Yet Old

The phenomenon of Jews believing and embracing Yeshua as Savior and Lord is as old as the Bible. Still, historically, the Jewish presence in the

Stuart Dauermann is Rabbi of Ahavat Zion Messianic Synagogue in Beverly Hills, California, and Director of the Messianic Teaching Our Rituals And Heritage (TORAH) Institute. Dauermann served as a missionary and music director with Jews for Jesus from 1973 to 1989.

Body of Christ has been largely submerged, as Jewish believers have assimilated into the wider Gentile context. However, recent years have seen a vibrant and widely noted rebirth of self-awareness and communal cohesion on the part of Jewish disciples of the Nazarene.

As with other movements, the *terminus a quo* of this modern Messianic Jewish Movement is hard to determine dogmatically. People involved in the movement will choose different starting points depending upon their points of view and loyalties. Perhaps the best starting point would be the year 1973, when two seminal Messianic Jewish organizations were founded: Jews for Jesus and the Messianic Jewish Alliance. Both organizations sought to give expression to, and facilitate the widespread recognition of, the fact that self-respecting Jews could embrace Yeshua as Savior and also embrace their own Jewish identity. Their persistent and effective efforts have led to a continuing replication and modification of their approaches and emphases by other similar organizations.

Having broadly defined this community, we turn now to consider a hitherto unplumbed but missionally rich source of intracultural missional motivation in the Messianic Jewish context.

## The Mitzvah of *Keruv*: Judaism and Christianity Drinking from the Same Well

Perhaps the most intriguing argument for Messianic Jewish mission is that underlying the modern Jewish concept of the *mitzvah* of *keruv* (the religious obligation to draw others near). This rich concept, rooted in the Old Testament, flowers with rich missional content in the Mishnah, in the New Testament, and in Jewish practice.

### Isaiah 57:19: the Background of Keruv

Speaking God's mercy from out of the context of reflection upon the Exile, the prophet speaks words of comfort, stating, "I have seen his ways, but I will heal him; I will guide him and restore comfort to him, creating praise on the lips of the mourners in Israel. 'Peace, peace, to those far and near,' says the LORD, 'And I will heal them' " (Isaiah 57:18-19).

### The Targum's Interpretation of This Text

This "peace to those far and near" is interpreted by the Targum as applying to those who are obedient to the Torah (those near) and those who are not as yet obedient to Torah (those far).

### Rabbi Hillel's Missionary Mandate

The above Isaianic reference and its targum are echoed and transmuted wonderfully in a maxim of Hillel (first century B.C.E.), which, more than any other dictum, has become the watchword of Jewish missional efforts—whether in outreach to marginal Jews or in outreach to non-Jews. Recorded in the mishnaic tractate *Avot* (Chapter One, Mishnah 12), it states: "Be of the disciples of Aaron, loving peace and pursuing peace, loving mankind and bringing them nigh to the Law (better, 'Torah')." The juxtaposition of the reference to peace and the term "bringing them near" render it beyond dispute that the Isaianic reference is in Hillel's mind. He seems to go beyond the conservative restrictions of the Targum in his use of the general term *ha-beriyot* ("living beings, mankind") to describe the recipients of the peace-sharing efforts which he enjoins. In other words, Hillel appears to be extending the field of peace sharing beyond the confines of the Jewish community.

Philip Blackman, in his authoritative translation of the Mishnah, translates the passage with this universalistic thrust in mind, stating, "Hillel said, 'Be thou of the disciples of Aaron, loving peace, and pursuing peace, loving (thy) fellow-creatures and drawing them nigh to the Law.' "[2]

### Modern Jewish Responses to Hillel's Mandate

The term *keruv ha-rekhokim* ("drawing near those who are far away") is the term currently most in use to describe Jewish missional activity. Conservative Jewish scholars Joel Roth and Robert Gordis are among those who see in this principle a justification for outreach not only to the unaffiliated or marginal Jew but also to the non-Jew. However, they restrict their outreach to uninvolved Jews and to the non-Jewish spouses of Jews or the children of non-Jewish wives of Jewish men, who, in all branches of mainstream Judaism except Reform and Reconstructionist, would be regarded as non-Jews.[3]

Writing in the same issue of *Conservative Judaism* along with Roth and Gordis, Jacob B. Agus comments that all branches of modern Judaism are responding to the call of the *keruv* principle, noting missionary efforts such as the attempts of Lubavitch Hasidim to win marginal Jews to an observant life-style, the founding of institutes of learning and Jewish communal assimilation for *ba'alei teshuvah* (those newly returned to observant Judaism), and the loosening of formerly unbreachable strictures on the part of modern Orthodox leaders who seek thereby to not alienate those Jews who might otherwise drift away (Agus 1982, 36–7).

### The New Testament's Adoption of *Keruv* as a Missional Term

We are surely on safe ground if we assume that the apostles were familiar not only with Isaiah 57:19 but also with its Targumic interpretation with this statement of Hillel's. Apparently these formed the conceptual "soup" from which, under the inspiration of the Holy Spirit, they produced their own interpretations of what it means to offer or bring peace to those far and near.

### Peter's Use of the Term

On the Day of Pentecost, Peter borrowed this terminology when he spoke of the promise as being "for you and your children, and for all whom are far off — for all whom the Lord our God will call" (Acts 2:39). Especially when one considers Peter's earlier quotation from Joel concerning God's Spirit being poured out on all flesh, it seems clear that his reference includes the gathering of Gentiles into the fold of God's salvation, although he had not yet fully understood that these Gentiles would be coming into the fold *as Gentiles*.

### Paul's Use of the Term

It is Paul who unambiguously applies this concept to the non-Jew in his reference to how "in Christ Jesus, you [Gentiles] who once were far away [*huimeîs hoí pote óntes makron*] have been brought near through the blood of Christ" (*egenēthēte eggús en tō haímati toû Christou*) (Eph. 2:13).

It is by no means accidental that Paul speaks in the same context of how Christ has made of the two (Jew and Gentile) one new person, *"thus making peace."* Here again, we find a juxtaposition of "near and far" and of "peace" which makes the conceptual connection between this text and Isaiah 57:19 a certainty. It seems obvious, as well, that Hillel and the Targum are not far from the Apostle's mind either, as he makes mention in the same context of how Christ has abolished in his flesh the Law (Torah) with its commandments and regulations.[4]

### James's Use of the Term

In addition, when we examine the ruling of James at the Jerusalem Council (Acts 15), we can see the Jewish cultural value of *keruv ha-rekhokim* in operation in James' statement "we should not make it difficult for the Gentiles who are turning to God" (15:19). In the outworking of *keruv* in the Jewish community, one can trace from rabbinic times to the present a continuing debate concerning whether one is to make it difficult for the seeker to convert (thus weeding out the impetuous), or make it easy for them to do so. James is here lining up with the latter, more lenient position.[5]

### Toward a Messianic Jewish *Keruv*

*Mitzvah keruv* — the religious obligation to bring near those who are far off — is a concept which cries out to be developed, explored and implemented in the Messianic Jewish context. It seems to be irrefutably a major missional "word"—a thoroughly biblical and culturally appropriate term which must become incarnate in the actions of the Messianic Jewish community if we are to be faithful ambassadors of the Kingdom. In all of the contexts in which it is found, that of the Old Testament, the New Testament, and Judaism, the concept of *keruv* is clearly missional. It calls for the crossing of boundaries for the sake of that peace which God is offering to humanity. The concept needs to be explored and developed, and awaits ground-breaking research devoted to both theory and practice.

### The Priority of Recovering a Lost Sense of Missionary Vision

Sadly, one of the characteristics the Messianic Jewish community shares with the mainstream Jewish community is the loss of a missionary vision. As a leader in the movement, I must sadly admit that we Messianic Jews too often restrict our missional involvement to lip service and sporadic support of a handful of missionaries scattered throughout the world. Yet, one searches in vain for the kind of *passion* and *mobilization* for mission— either to our own people or to those others "who are not of this fold"— which ought to characterize our movement as it identifies itself so strongly with the first century church and the apostles.

I believe that the *mitzvah* of *keruv,* and other motivations for mission which historically have served the mainstream Jewish community, may well serve ours in fanning into flame the embers of Messianic Jewish mission.

### In Conclusion

Five broad avenues of endeavor suggest themselves by way of appropriate responses to this call for renewed missional effort in the Messianic Jewish community. First, much further research, discussion and experimentation needs to be done to discover, adapt and articulate contextually appropriate motivations and strategies for mission. Second, much needs to be done in the area of writing and publication—books, articles, monographs, magazines—if missional thought and action are to develop and disseminate in the Messianic Jewish community. Toward this end, I dream of the day when, perhaps in conjunction with the U.S. Center for World Mission or the School of World Mission at Fuller Seminary, someone will take the responsibility for developing and disseminating a missions magazine especially geared to the Messianic Jewish public. In addition to new literary "wineskins," the challenge remains for currently extant Messianic Jewish newsletters and publications to enter more fully into dialogue and discussion concerning Messianic Jewish mission. Only thus will our movement be catalyzed for missional ferment and creative change.

Third, Messianic Jewish congregational leaders themselves need to become informed, educated, trained, and motivated for mission. Workshops, seminars, and conferences need to be developed, and appropriate effort must be expended to design, initiate and sustain the kinds of formal, nonformal, and informal training programs that will lead to missional growth.[6]

Fourth, we must begin now to work toward the day when the Messianic Movement will have its own mission society, which I would suggest we call *B'nei Avraham v'Sarah* ("Children of Abraham and Sarah"), or perhaps *Or LaGoyim* ("A Light to the Nations"). After all, if even Rashi recognized that Abraham our father and Sarah our mother were missionaries, isn't it only right that we follow in their steps (ben Isaiah and Sharfman 1949)?[7]

Last, but actually first, we in the Messianic movement must *pray*. The kind of passion which God wants to characterize our movement comes ultimately from only one source—the work of God's Holy Spirit. Surely this is the kind of passion for God and for His concerns of which Yeshua spoke when he stated, "I have come to bring fire on the earth, and how I wish it were already kindled!" (Lk. 12:49). Even now He is raising up intercessors and prophetic spokespersons who will play a role in kindling and fanning that holy flame. Lord, let the fire come!

## Notes

1. As a working definition of mission, I offer the following modification of that supplied by Neill (1984) cited in Van Engen (1991a, 27). I define mission as "the intentional crossing of boundaries in order to inform and influence receptors toward responding to Christ and His gospel in saving faith." For the Messianic Jewish context, I broadly differentiate between intracultural missions to Jews (E-0 and E-1 evangelism), and intercultural mission to non-Jews (E-2 and E-3 evangelism).

2. Blackman (1964, 44). In footnotes to the text, Blackman comments that the term *fellow-creatures* implies "irrespective of race or creed," and the phrase *drawing them nigh to the Law* means "To an understanding of the existence of One God and the recognition and practice of His just moral laws" (1964, 44). In other words, he interprets Hillel's dictum as a call to drawing the non-Jew to ethical monotheism. I believe this is eisegetical on his part, reading into Hillel a mind-set not dictated by the text.

3. They state:

The principle of *keruv* is central to the ideals and aspirations of Judaism. We frequently cite as one of our most important goals the need to bring those who are only tangentially involved in things Jewish closer to the center of Jewish life and to make Judaism more central in their lives.

While the term *keruv* is most frequently invoked with regard to Jews, the same *attitude* might be of import with regard to non-Jews as well, provided that they indicate a desire to become part of the Jewish faith. The well-known aggadah about Hillel and the proselytes (B.T. *Shabbat* 31a) clearly deals with a case in which the non-Jews approached the Jewish community seeking conversion. The Jewish community did not proselytize.

In our day, however, we confront a situation that requires active attempts to convert non-Jews to Judaism. The extraordinarily high rate of intermarriages among Jews (encompassing members of all movements, including ours) demands our attention. Having failed to prevent these marriages or to convert the non-Jewish spouses to Judaism before marriage (if we indeed had the chance), we must now seek to ensure that these families remain a part of the Jewish people. Therefore, we must actively seek to convert the non-Jewish spouse, and, if the wife is not Jewish, then to convert the children born before the conversion as well. (Roth and Gordis 1982, 50-51)

4. I take the Apostle to be referring here not to the abolition of God's Law per se, but to the abolition of the restrictive use of the Law as it had been applied to denying Gentiles access to God and equality of status with the Jewish heirs of the covenants.

5. Roth and Gordis refer to these matters, stating:

When discussing the principle of *keruv* we would do well to remember another rabbinic dictum, *l'olam t'hi smol dukhah u-yamin m'karevet* (*Sotah* 47a, *Sanhedrin* 107b) [always let your left hand push (convert-inquirers) away and your right hand draw them near] . . . Of course, reasonable people can disagree as to what constitutes *vemin mekarevet,* or *semol dohah,* but in our opinion, the open invitation we have extended to non-Jewish members of these [mixed] marriages [in our congregations to have a circumscribed and limited role in congregational life] constitutes a strong *yemin mekarevet,* and the remainder of our efforts must be directed toward ensuring that until conversion, we have a *semol dohah* [denying to these people and to Jewish spouses roles which would either connote approval of the mixed marriage or blurring of the distinction between Jews/converts and those who are not].

The restrictions we have outlined do not stem from a lack of *ahavat beriyot* [that love of mankind spoken of in Hillel's dictum]. Rather, they stem from a desire to illustrate that the religion to which we seek to draw them is one based upon standards, with social and religious principles. We seek to explain through our actions that our tradition represents not an arbitrary set of social and religious distinctions, but a meaningful group of social and religious precepts, which we will strive always to maintain for the sake of God and His Torah. (Roth and Gordis 1982, 54)

In the same issue of *Conservative Judaism,* Seymour Siegel takes these authors to task for what he deems to be their offensive and overly hard-line stand. He comments:

The famous statement about *semol dohah* and *yemin mekaveret* was interpreted by one great preacher in the light of the fact that usually the right hand is stronger than the left one. Our pushing away should not be as harsh as our bringing close. (Siegel 1982, 57-58)

6. This equipping and motivational task is one of the long-term goals of *Hash-ivenu* (Cause us to Return) and the Messianic T.O.R.A.H. Institute (Teaching Our Rituals And Heritage), two interrelated organizations I am currently in the process of developing.

7. Reference is made here to Rashi's interpretation of Genesis 12:6, which states that when Abraham journeyed to Canaan, he took with him "Sarai his wife, and Lot, his brother's son, and . . . the souls they had gotten in Haran." Rashi interprets this reference to "the souls which they had gotten" as applying to the proselytes which Abraham and Sarah had won (ben Isaiah and Sharfman 1949, 103).

# 21

# Constructing a Theology of Mission for the Chinese Church

## CHE BIN TAN

Among the mission societies in China, the China Inland Mission was important because of the number of missionaries it involved and its deep and lasting impact. In terms of the place of origin of the missionary force, about half of the missionaries in China in the first half of this century were Americans. It is only appropriate that some reflections on mission to China should be done in a work honoring a veteran missionary and theologian of mission who was an American CIM missionary. The purpose of this short essay is to delineate some important issues in constructing a theology of mission in the light of Chinese cultural characteristics and the history of mission in China.

## The Kingdom of God and Its Political Implications

One of the major Chinese cultural characteristics is that it is pan-political. In the Chinese tradition, the imperial authority claimed that it was sanctioned by the mandate of heaven. The emperor and his officials were in charge of everything under heaven, and therefore all human phenomena were considered the business of the government. Religion was no exception. It was under the supervision and control of one of its departments. Against this background, perhaps it is no surprise that the first Chinese indigenous movement, heretical in the eyes of many, called the dynasty established in the middle of the eighteenth century by the name of *Tai Ping Tien Guo*,

Che Bin Tan is a Chinese theological scholar who taught in Singapore, Taiwan, Hong Kong, and Fuller School of World Mission for many years. Presently he is adjunct professor at Fuller's School of World Mission and senior pastor of two Chinese-American churches in greater Los Angeles.

the Tan, Heavenly Kingdom of Peace. The founder of this movement was a Confucian scholar who failed the civil examination and had only limited contacts with missionaries who were the teachers and interpreters of Christian faith at that time. Reading the Scripture from the Confucian perspective, the good news of Jesus Christ was interpreted as political in nature. Furthermore, as the Chinese emperor is called *Tien Zi*, the son of heaven, it is understandable that this founder called Jesus the elder brother and he himself another son of God.[1]

If this founder of the Tai Ping movement misunderstood the good news of Jesus because of ignorance, the efforts by missionaries such as Timothy Richards and W. A. P. Martin in introducing and promoting political reform at the end of nineteenth century definitely cannot be classified as acts of ignorance. Rather, it was because they came to realize through their own experience the all-powerful nature of Chinese government and its officials. This often had a negative impact on the lives of the people. The strong opposition against Christianity was often initiated by Confucian scholars closely related to the government or its officials.[2] In the twentieth century, political implications of the gospel are still an important issue. The question of Christianity and imperialism is an important, if not the most dominant, concern of the Three-Self Patriotic Movement, often known as the Opened Church, in China. In the discussion of the state of the church in China, a controversial issue is whether there are persecutions by the government. As is well known, the Chinese government repeatedly denied the presence of religious persecution. Perhaps this can be understood against the cultural background. For the Chinese government, all actions considered as uncooperative are antirevolutionary and therefore a serious political crime. In other words, what is seen as religious by some Christians is considered political in nature and punished as such.

The issue here is a two-pronged one. Here we have a situation faced by many other missionaries in cross-cultural situations: people read and understand the Bible from their own cultural perspective and can therefore misunderstand or distort its message. In relating to the Christian faith brought by missionaries from the West, non-Western people have difficulty understanding doctrinal formulations, in this case the separation of church and state, developed in the West. More importantly, in the Chinese context, a systematic presentation of the gospel which does not discuss what is classified as belonging to a discipline other than systematic theology—ethics for example—is seriously handicapped in achieving its purpose.

### Suffering and Oppression

It has been observed by the Chinese themselves that Chinese peasants, who make up about 80 percent of the Chinese population, are simply not interested in politics. The one common concern of the Chinese people is perhaps life here and now, especially a life free from suffering and oppression. Suffering and oppression are not modern phenomena in the Chinese soil. Yet it is fair to say the Chinese people have experienced them more intensely in the last two centuries. On the national level, foreign invasions, civil wars, internal struggles due to ideological differences and personal ambitions, in addition to a series of natural calamities, have all contributed to the loss of millions of human lives and tremendous emotional hurts.[3] China is also a poor country. It has been said that the only class distinction in China is the difference between the poor and the extremely poor. The June 4 Tienanmen Massacre in 1989, reflecting the oppressive nature of the government, was an incident that caught the attention of the world because of media exposure surrounding it; but by no means was it an isolated incident. As a result, there is pervasive alienation between the government and the people and between one person and another. The other side of the coin to suffering and oppression is the concern for life here and now, especially in terms of wealth and security. Again, this is not a new concern, but it is particularly pervasive in places where Chinese people consist of the majority of the population. In all these places, the governments are pushing for modernization and industrialization.

In the Chinese culture, the problem of suffering is addressed by the Buddhist and Daoist perspectives. In the opinion of this author, the message of the conservatives and fundamentalists in the Chinese church basically falls along this line. With emphasis on mental serenity and self-denial expressed in the form of acceptance of suffering and denial of material comfort, such a message brings about comforts to Christians who live in a world full of famine, flooding, and wars. Yet it does not address the mainstream Confucian concern for building a socio-political order. The biblical idea of redemption of God's creation through the resurrection of Jesus Christ, however, can provide a better option to address both problems of suffering and industrialization, because a basic problem with Confucianism is that it is not able to develop theoretical support for the pursuit of science, which is the basis of industrialization in the West.

## Peace and Reconciliation

In contrast to American culture, the Chinese core value is not individualistic but relational. Against the background of social upheaval and years of wars between states, the Confucian system sought to establish a socio-political order characterized by interpersonal harmony by assigning each person a proper place in such an order. Peace or harmony therefore is of extreme importance to the Chinese. To provide a basis for pursuit of such a harmonious, peaceful society, the Confucians led the Chinese people to believe in the inherent goodness of human nature. At the same time, they established a socio-political system organized on basis of the family model, which is hierarchical in structure and centered on ancestral worship. The system was enforced by social pressure through the concept of shame, education and penal laws. Such a system proved to be very powerful. It provided continuity for the Chinese culture for almost two thousand years. By the end of the eighteenth century, however, this system became stagnant and oppressive and began to break down under the impact of the West. The Chinese culture has been in the process of disintegration for the last two centuries. Chinese culture is in crisis.

Protestant missionary endeavor coincides with this whole process. Unfortunately, without fully understanding the Chinese culture and modern missiological and anthropological insights, Christianity crushed the Confucian system by condemning the ancestral worship which lay at the center of the whole Chinese socio-political structure. Preaching the doctrine of justification by faith in a strongly individualist frame, Christian mission tended to condemn all morally upright Chinese who believed in the inherent goodness of human nature. Worst of all, in their eagerness to convert the Chinese, the proclamation of the gospel was linked to imperialism because the missionaries, at least the majority of them, endorsed the use of military power by the West to force the Chinese to open their doors to the West. Thus the effort of evangelizing the Chinese took the posture of antagonism and opposition from an early date. Such an approach is in direct conflict with the Chinese mentality and value. More importantly, the doctrine of reconciliation is a better venue to address the Chinese longing for a harmonious relationship with the world and human beings.

This is not to say that no attempt has ever been made to address this basic Chinese issue. Watchman Nee, with his emphasis on a pure form of the local church, showed that he understood the Chinese need for the group. Wang Ming Dao, with his emphasis on repentance and Christian living, also had in mind the Confucian emphasis on morality. Yet both of them shied away from addressing social issues because they were influenced by the American fundamentalist fear of the social gospel. Nor should we deny the importance of justification by faith and the idea of guilt. If the idea of original sin is viewed through the concept of corporate headship, it is easily understandable by the Chinese by way of the idea of group responsibility. As to the doctrine of justification by faith, it can be used, as Paul did in Galatians and Ephesians, to tackle the issues of freedom from oppression, interpersonal harmony, the development of a new society (the Church) in which all human barriers are abolished, dignity of each individual respected, and equality of all believers affirmed. In other words, the doctrine of justification by faith as applied by the apostle Paul provides an important theoretical basis for the development of an ideal society longed for by the Chinese. It can be used to show how the ideas of guilt and law, ideas not congenial to the Chinese tradition, can lead to something which Confucianism cannot provide by its structural hierarchy. What is needed here is serious wrestling with the biblical text and the context, without compromising the biblical message.

### How Do I Know That Christian Faith Is the Only Truth?

Because of the fact that indigenization of theology was vehemently resisted by the conservative Chinese Christians in the 1920s and 30s, and because contextualization has been taken seriously by evangelical scholars only in recent years, Christianity remains largely foreign to most Chinese people. Although the basic Christian belief of monotheism is different from the Neo-Confucian belief of an impersonal heaven and from the popular polytheism, upon hearing of the good news of Jesus Christ, the initial reaction of a Chinese is not typically an epistemological query of the existence of God. As a matter of fact, Chinese philosophical thinking never begins with epistemology or ontology, for the Chinese mind-set is not interested in the abstract but in the concrete. As a result, the initial issue in the proclamation of the gospel is different from the West. But this does not mean that epistemological questions do not exist. They arise when a response to the message is required. Then they assume another form: for the Neo-Confucians, the question of knowing God is personal instead of impersonal; at the folk level, it is monotheism versus polytheism, questioning whether the Christian God is more powerful than others. At this point, intellectual argument is useful only if supported with evidence of the life-changing power of God. In other words, the life here and now of a Christian believer in flesh and blood is as important as, if not more than, intellectual persuasion.

### Concluding Remarks

People familiar with theological developments in the West and other parts of the world will certainly notice that the basic issues in constructing a Chinese theology of mission may look like those tackled by Liberation Theology, in that issues of political systems and moral theology and morality are emphasized. Yet a more careful look would also show that the final form or configuration of a theology of mission for the Chinese church will definitely be different, because each of the issues arises out of a particular Chinese background and poses specifically Chinese questions. The challenge of a Chinese theology of mission also goes beyond presenting a message that may be understandable in the traditional worldview. It involves introducing new yet important ideas that may help develop a better culture and socio-political system as the Chinese strive to attain the traditional ideal. It is our hope that this brief sketch may contribute to the evangelization of the Chinese people, a cause that is dear to the heart of Arthur Glasser and certainly the Triune God.

## Notes

1. Shih (1967) argues that this ideology can totally be explained by Confucian sources. He seems, however, to go too far because, for example, the idea of equality of man and woman for sure cannot be found in Chinese tradition.

2. Read, for example, Covell (1978).

3. For a general survey of Chinese history, read Fairbank (1986).

# 22

# Pietism's Most Challenging Task

*A Trinitarian Renewal*

## HERMAN BUEHLER

### Introduction

Germany's historic Pietism and its more recent evangelical offspring, the Fellowship Movement (*Gemeinschaftsbewegung*), face one of their most important challenges in today's reunited Germany: to bring spiritual renewal to Church and society. A revitalized church membership will effectively evangelize and disciple young and old within its context. It will bridge the stark differences between Germany's East and West, poor and rich, secular and religious. It will also provide the strong moral and spiritual base for a people who will share in a United Europe. Moreover, migrant populations attracted to this prosperous land will find it a true refuge and a blessing.

The privileged position of the pietists within Germany's Evangelical Churches provides them with excellent opportunities to share their dynamic, biblical faith with the many nominal, marginal, and alienated members distant from the living God and deeply dissatisfied with religious routine and authority. Many young people and educated professionals find the Church irrelevant to their life-style.

This most crucial hour demands a courageous, Luther-like affirmation of the Bible as the living Word of the Triune God. It calls for a powerful proclamation and demonstration of the living God Who revealed Himself as the loving Father, the gracious Savior, and the communing Holy Spirit.

Herman Buehler has been a member of a pietistic mission with German roots for the past 28 years, 15 of which he served in Micronesia. He is presently a Ph.D. candidate at the School of World Mission, Fuller Theological Seminary.

It requires a new biblical realism to challenge the rationalistically reduced world of the post-Enlightenment era, a view that has virtually eliminated the Triune God, the angels, and even Satan and his demonic host.

## Pietism's Contribution

It has been the historic Pietistic Movement that kept the essential Reformation heritage alive in the Evangelical Church of Germany (*Evangelische Kirche Deutschland*). It always emphasized a truthful Bible, a living and personal relationship with Jesus Christ, a holy walk expressed in prayer and witness — all nurtured in the small-group Bible studies, Spener's *collegia pietatis*, which have grown into the Fellowship Movement. This small-group approach clearly has provided the nonformal setting in which biblical Christianity was discovered and demonstrated. In the critical periods of church history, when this living faith was challenged by dead orthodoxy, deceptive Enlightenment, excessive rationalism, destructive liberalism, or syncretistic idealism, it was the pietists who kept their focus on the living Lord and His powerful Word, maintaining the essentials of biblical faith. They also were encouraged and enriched by revival and renewal movements (Methodism, Oxford, Moody) from other parts of the world (Beyreuther 1963, 1964; Bockmuehl 1985; Stoeffler 1965).

Early Pietism (about 1600–1800), with its roots deep in the Lutheran and Calvinist-Puritan concerns for personal salvation and piety, was promoted by pastors and teachers from within the Church. They desired to combine right living with right doctrines in the lives of church members. Initiated originally by Spener and developed further by men like Francke, Zinzendorf, and Bengel, Pietism became instrumental in making God and His Word real for many. It also produced the first missionaries who shared the Gospel with other nations.

Later Pietism (1800–1860s) faced times in which the churches were challenged by the Enlightenment's rationalism, idealism, and liberalism. Many outstanding scholars and pastors with a Pietistic heritage refused to let higher criticism radically alter the Word of God and the person of Jesus Christ. New mission organizations were formed, nobility and clergy were enlisted, and the common people were encouraged to share the Gospel within and without Germany.

The Fellowship Movement (1860s–present), Pietism's offspring and successor in the mid-nineteenth century, became most effective in evangelizing and discipling various regions of Germany. The movement was influenced by the revivals in the United States (Moody), England (Oxford), and Wales. It emphasized not only personal salvation through Christ but also personal piety through the Holy Spirit. It established many viable fellowship groups throughout Germany. These were united in 1888 to form the Gnadau Association of Fellowships (*Gnadauer Gemeinschaftsverband*), giving them an

organizational forum and theological leadership for dealing with ecclesiastical, theological, social and political issues. For example, it dealt with
the Pentecostal influence in Germany, issuing the Berlin Declaration in
1909 to warn of serious errors propounded by Pentecostals. During the
Nazi era, it refused to cooperate with the German Christian Movement
(Egelkraut 1983; Haarbeck 1956; Lange 1979; Sauberzweig 1959; Schmidt
1984).

## Pietism's Limitations

Since the Bible, untouched by higher criticism, has remained the primary
document of God's revelation for Pietists, the church's historic creeds, con-
fessions, and theological treatises have often been regarded with suspicion.
Without the benefits of evangelical, scholarly resources, this personalized,
subjective approach to biblical truth would result in a very narrow view of
reality (Aland 1970; Brown 1978; Fleisch 1912; Ohlemacher 1986).

Pietism's concentration on Jesus Christ has been its strength as well as
its weakness. On the one hand, a personal relationship to Him as Savior
has provided forgiveness of sin and peace with God. But on the other hand,
it caused a serious neglect of God the Father and God the Holy Spirit.
Concerned scholars reminded Pietists of the first and third articles of the
Apostles' Creed, while others spoke of the *Geistvergessenheit*, the "forgotten
Holy Spirit" in the life of the believers (Rienecker 1952; Dilschneider 1969).

Another area of weakness in contemporary Pietism is the biblical teaching on the encounter between the Kingdom of God versus the kingdom of
darkness. It seems that Luther's "two kingdom concepts" has partially
defused this tension, while the eschatological postponement of the kingdom
to the End has removed the conflict between the two realms. Moreover,
the subtle post-Enlightenment reduction of the supernatural to rational
views of reality has relegated Satan and his demons to the realm of mythol-
ogy (Arnold 1992; Ebeling 1970; Haarbeck 1956; Huntemann 1985; Kallas
1966; Oberman 1984; Otto 1938; Wendland 1934; Wenz 1975).

One of Pietism's strengths was expressed in its witness to the world, but
the primarily Christocentric focus on salvation of souls often overlooked
the trinitarian richness of the Father's creation and the Holy Spirit's presence and power. Entering other cultures in the name of the Triune God
would provide a greater biblical base for mission by way of a biblical view
of the *Missio Dei* (Bosch 1980; Newbigin 1978; Pflaum 1988; Schwarz 1980;
Vicedom 1965, 1975).

## Pietism's Need

A brief review of the biblical doctrine of the Triune God, the Kingdom
of God, and missions will be helpful.

## The Trinity

In recent years, biblical scholars, theologians, missiologists, and church leaders have reviewed the doctrine of the Trinity and its implications for the Christian life, worship, and mission of the Church (Braaten 1976; British Council of Churches 1989; Dilschneider 1969; Fortman 1982; Heron 1983; Moltmann 1991; Packer 1984). Some have called for an equal treatment of the articles of the Apostles' Creed. Others have reviewed the doctrine of the Trinity and related it to the worship, the kingdom, society, and missions (Bickersteth 1957; Boff 1988; British Council of Churches 1989; McGrath 1988; Moltmann 1981; Newbigin 1964; Philbert 1970; Vicedom 1965). Some scholars have come to view the Trinity from a social perspective (Boff 1988; Gruenler 1986; Moltmann 1981; Plantinga 1982, 1988, 1989). One notes:

> The holy Trinity is a divine society or community of three fully personal and fully divine beings: the Father, the Son, and the Spirit or Paraclete. These three are wonderfully unified by their common historical-redemptive purpose, revelation, and work . . . Father, Son, and Holy Spirit are "members one of another" to a superlative and exemplary degree. Indeed, their interpenetration, the *circumincession* or *perichoresis*, is so ineffable as to constitute the main trinitarian mystery and so powerful as to render the three one in a sense far deeper than mere generic or functional oneness. (Plantinga 1982, 190)

A recovery of the doctrine of God the Father could lead Pietists to praise and adore their heavenly Father. It would be a new experience for many (Luetgert 1984; Martin 1982). Paul and Peter opened some of their letters in praise and adoration of God the Father (2 Cor. 1:3; Eph. 1:3; 1 Peter 1:3). Jesus taught his disciples to pray to God the Father (Luke 11:2). Paul reminded the Ephesians that their prayer is to be addressed to the Father, through the Son, and in the Holy Spirit (Eph. 2:18), for "God (the Father) sent the Spirit of his Son into our hearts, crying, 'Abba, Father' " (Gal. 4:6).

Viewing God the Son from the trinitarian perspective gives His incarnation, death, resurrection, and ascension a much greater context. He came as the Father's gracious gift to lost humanity (John 3:16). He began his human life through the specific ministry of the Holy Spirit (Luke 1:35). He came to do the Father's will (John 4:30) and the work of the Father (17:4). He ministered under the guidance of the Holy Spirit (Mark 1:10–12). His present position is at the Father's right hand in heaven (Heb. 1:3).

A biblical recovery of the doctrine of God the Holy Spirit will bring a new appreciation of the commitment of the Triune God to redeem and restore human beings into the image of Jesus Christ. Ever since the day of

Pentecost, God the Holy Spirit has provided the presence and power of God for every Christian to live the victorious life (Acts 1:8).

## The Kingdom of God

The Bible teaches that the Kingdom of God is being established over the kingdom of darkness (Col. 1:13) now, while its glorious manifestation awaits the Second Coming of Christ (Rev. 11:15). Jesus demonstrated the presence of the Kingdom of God by casting out demons by the Spirit of God (Matt. 12:28). The object of the divine rule is the redemption of human beings and their deliverance from the powers of evil, even death (1 Cor. 15:23–28). The Kingdom of God is the redemptive rule of God in Christ defeating Satan and the powers of evil and delivering human beings from the sway of evil (Ladd 1964).

Pietists need to recognize that the post-Enlightenment era has not been helpful in recognizing the extent to which Satan and his demons are real and need to be dealt with in the authority of Jesus Christ conferred on his disciples via the Holy Spirit. The same school (Tübingen) that trained a Johann Christoph Blumhardt also produced David Friedrich Strauss. While the former victoriously proclaimed "Jesus as LORD over demons" (Zuendel 1954), the latter rationally dissected and demoted Jesus to the realm of the natural and human, leaving him powerless to save (Haegglund 1968).

Georg Vicedom noted that the Kingdom is larger than the Church and is established through the work of the Holy Spirit (Vicedom 1975, 81). Johannes Verkuyl sees the Kingdom of God as the "hub around which all mission work revolves" (Verkuyl 1978). Arthur Glasser has promoted the Kingdom focus in mission for many years, noting that in the person of Jesus Christ the Church and Kingdom of God are interrelated. Charles Van Engen also defines the Church in terms of the Kingdom of God, noting that it is the Community ruled by the King and it is the central locus of His reign. The Church's mission is to spread the knowledge of the rule of the King and thus becomes the sign of the Kingdom in the world, both to the seen and unseen realms (Van Engen 1991a).

## Missio Dei

Biblical mission affirms as its foundation and authority the Triune GOD. The concept of *Missio Dei* has been developed by missiologists from various nations and times (Bosch 1980, 239). They have come to a consensus that the biblical and theological basis of mission is the mission of the Triune God. David Bosch profoundly summarizes this concept of the *Missio Dei* when he notes:

> Mission has its origin . . . in God. God is a missionary. God . . . crosses frontiers toward the world. In creation God was already the God of

mission, with his Word and Spirit as "Missionaries" (Gen. 1:2–3). God likewise sent his incarnate Word, his Son, into the world. And he sent his Spirit at Pentecost. (Bosch 1980, 239)

Georg Vicedom (1965) described the larger work of the Triune God as *Missio Dei* in which his servants may enter and share. He further defined the Kingdom of God as His essential rule that is being established through the mission of the Church. It is the Triune God who is involved in every missionary endeavor and who through creation has prior claim on all peoples, tongues, tribes, and nations (Psalm 96:10). It is the Triune God, who by His Son has provided a way back for His alienated, rebellious creatures (John 14:6). It is the Triune God, who by His Holy Spirit selects, equips, and sends His servants to all nations (Acts 1:8).

### Conclusion

Pietists enriched by the doctrine of the Triune God can become instrumental in bringing a new attitude of worship and adoration of the heavenly Father to congregations who have lost the excitement. They will appreciate the gift of the Son from the midst of the Trinity, determined to redeem the lost. They will be thrilled by the ministry of the Holy Spirit, who shared with the other members of the Trinity in creation, salvation, and a holy life. They will rejoice in the hope of glory and the assurance of an eternal inheritance in the presence of the Triune God. Surely they will share this blessing as they lead others to a waiting Father in the Name of the Son by the power of the Holy Spirit.

# 23

# Themes in African Theology of Mission

## TITE TIÉNOU

### Introduction

The world of the last decade of the twentieth century differs from that of the end of the nineteenth century in many respects. In Africa, a significant aspect of this difference lies in the religious landscape of the continent. Christianity was unknown to most Africans at the end of the nineteenth century. Today, except for the northern regions of the continent, Christianity claims multitudes of adherents in Africa. In that sense, the churches of Africa are no longer outposts of foreign mission agencies. They have themselves become missionary churches (Karamaga 1990, 95). The growth and vitality of Christianity in Africa establish the immediate and general context for the development of themes in theology of mission from African perspectives.

The theology of Christian mission in Africa is also shaped by the history of Christian presence and ministry in the continent and current economic, political, social and religious realities. Consequently, in Africa, the themes of mission theology will rise out of the following four movements. First, African Christians must craft a theology that deals adequately with the need to consolidate and secure the gains of Christian mission. Second, African Christians must be liberated from the complexes associated with African identity so that they can participate fully in the mission of the crucified and risen Lord. Third, in an age of religious crisis and confusion in the continent, African mission theologians must articulate reasons for continued focus on expanding the Christian faith. Fourth, African Christians will need to establish solid theological bases for dealing with the

Tite Tiénou is Professor of Theology and Missiology at Alliance Theological Seminary, Nyack, New York, and President-Dean elect of the new Evangelical Theological Seminary of the Christian Alliance, Abidjan, Côte d'Ivoire.

staggering socio-economic and political crises of the continent.

The foregoing four movements provide the basis and context of the present reflections on African theology of mission. The themes sketched here are only illustrative of the kind of missiological reflection needed in Africa as we move into the third millennium. It should also be noted that they are not intended to present a coherent African theology of mission. Rather they offer one person's viewpoint on reflection on the good news of the Kingdom in an African setting.

### From Spreading the Seed to Securing the Foundations

Arthur Glasser expressed a fundamental fact of mission theory and practice when he wrote: "The Christian movement must focus on consolidation while reaching out in expansion" (1984, 726). In this double focus the first one, namely consolidation, is particularly needed in Africa as we enter the twenty-first century.

Ikenga-Metuh contends that in the third millennium, the emphasis of mission in Africa will need to "shift from 'primary evangelization' or 'extensive evangelization' to 'pastoral evangelization' or 'intensive evangelization'" (1989, 12). In Glasser's terminology, the focus will have to be on consolidation rather than expansion in Africa. This is not to suggest that expansion or the spreading of the seed of the gospel is no longer necessary in Africa. After all, the optimistic vision of Roland Oliver has not become reality. Oliver, noting the rapid growth of Christianity in Africa south of the Sahara desert since 1912, conjectured that "if things were to go at the same rate, there would be no pagans left in Africa after the year 1992" (1956, 8). Not only are there "pagans" left in Africa south of the Sahara, African Traditional Religions are currently showing signs of renewed vitality (Mbembe 1988). This fact and the missionizing zeal of other religions in the continent require that African Christians maintain "primary evangelization" as part of their mission involvement.

Yet the theological arguments for the priority of expansion are seldom more than statements of pragmatic strategies of Christian activism. For evangelicals especially, this kind of mission theology succeeds in introducing people to the gospel; but it neither nourishes them nor deepens their faith so that they can resist competing religions and ideologies and thus become themselves agents of propagation of the good news.

In Africa, expansion without consolidation has had disastrous consequences. Nominality has become a way of life for many, while thousands of more-or-less Christian religious movements have established themselves in the continent. African mission theologians therefore need to reverse these trends by developing a theology that seeks to permanently plant the Church of Christ in Africa and anchor the gospel deeply into current African cultures (Mushete 1989, 107). This kind of theology will help reduce the perception that the Christian gospel is foreign to Africa and Africans. It will also secure a basis for Africans to become joyfully and unashamedly active in mission. African ownership of the gospel is critical for African participation in mission.

## From Identity Crisis to Liberated Participation in Mission

Contemporary analysts commonly describe Africa as a continent in crisis. Of all the crises Africans face today, perhaps none is as devastating as the crisis of identity. Culturally, many Africans are alienated from themselves and have become foreigners in their own countries. This reality which Mushete calls "anthropological poverty" (1989, 103), robs Africans of their selfhood. It causes them to define their identity in relationship to foreigners, particularly Europeans. Africans perceive themselves and are often perceived as either assimilated Europeans or as the exact opposite of Europeans.

This is not the place to examine the causes of the Africans' identity crisis. Whether "the missionary enterprise produced what can be called an African Christian identity problem" (Bediako 1983, 88) or not, the fact is that the question of African identity relates directly to issues of mission theology in the continent. For instance, does adherence to the gospel imply mindless westernization? Do all calls for specific African appropriations of the gospel necessarily mean rejection of the truth once and for all delivered? If the answer to either question is affirmative, then why should thinking Africans embrace such an alienating gospel or become agents of its propagation?

An alien Christianity produces, at best, numerical adherence and superficial vitality. Such a Christianity derives its real strength from outside Africa and is unable to deal with problems that are genuinely African. African adherents to this kind of Christianity tend to be preoccupied more with what happens abroad than with crucial issues of their context. They are sometimes more focused on fighting alien theological battles than on boldly nourishing the faithful and proclaiming the good news.

If the African identity crisis is as important and serious as outlined above, then African mission theologians must show how, biblically and theologically, being African is neither a curse nor a shame. This is a necessary step because, more than any other race on earth, a theology of curse has been used as a basis for evangelizing the black race (Mbembe 1988, 40-42). African Christians therefore need to be restored in full humanity by the Lord, Creator and Redeemer. Thus liberated by the good news of the Kingdom, African Christians will be able to participate fully in the mission of the crucified and risen Lord.

### Boldness in the Face of Religious Confusion and Crisis

Religious pluralism is alive and well in contemporary Africa. Countless religions compete vigorously for the hearts, minds and souls of Africans. This religious competition creates confusion and provides the breeding ground for opportunists of all kinds. This has prompted analysts such as Achille Mbembe to claim that religious identity no longer exists in Africa. Rather, he observes, Africans tend to weigh the offers made by the religious merchants and decide in favor of the ones which bring the best immediate practical benefits (1988, 69).

Competition for Africa is particularly fierce between Christianity and Islam. It is clear that "the two religions continue to compete for the soul of Africa" (Mazrui 1990, 257). Yet African Christian mission theologians should not pessimistically resign themselves to the prospect of Islam once again uprooting Christianity in Africa. They should not let themselves be carried by the optimism of people like Mazrui, who thinks that Africa will become a laboratory for religious and ideological cooperation. In other words, they should not allow the possibility of conflict with Islam or other religions to determine their agenda for mission theology and practice. Rather they must seize the reality of religious competition as a challenge for them to articulate ways of bold and humble proclamation of the gospel of Jesus the Christ.

Denigration, conquest and triumphalism have too frequently been ingredients of Christian missionizing in Africa. They must be discarded in the present climate of religious competition and crisis affecting the continent. One need not denigrate the followers of other religions in order to magnify Christ and his gospel. Likewise, conquest and triumphalism may produce short-term gains, but they are destructive in the long term. Consequently, the way forward is to produce a theology of Christian mission which convincingly demonstrates that the gospel can be proclaimed boldly and without compromise, denigration or conquest. This is one of the most urgent themes for reflection by African mission theologians in the years to come.

### Good News in the Face of Socio-Economic and Political Crisis

In articulating a theology of mission, African theologians will have to deal with issues related to the goal of mission. In what sense is the gospel good news, given the general social, economic and political crises affecting Africa? For what purpose should a person choose to become a participant in the gospel? Are the promises of the gospel purely otherworldly, or should the gospel be used exclusively as a manual for curing present ills?

Given the fact that "reconstruction is the new priority for African nations in the 1990s," "the churches and their theologians will need to respond to this new priority in relevant fashion, to facilitate this process of reconstruction" (Mugambi 1991, 36). Many African Christians who are fully committed to the gospel of Jesus Christ agree with the idea that "preaching Jesus Christ in Africa cannot be reduced to a simple appointment for the hereafter. [Preaching] is a formal invitation to total salvation in respect of all domains of African life" (Chipenda and Karamaga 1991, 26). They realize, however, that such ideas can easily be misinterpreted to mean that the gospel is more about material well-being than spiritual restoration. That is why they insist, with Pénoukou, that the quality of an individual's life is evaluated more in terms of his or her being than in relationship to possessions (1984, 91). Consequently, the gospel is about transforming the very nature of human beings so that they can live and practice compassionate service and justice in their societies.

Mission theologians in Africa must wrestle seriously with the human situation of mission in the continent. To do so they need to begin with the recognition that "mission . . . [is] to be contextual, holistic and liberating" (Arias 1992, 30). They cannot afford to let themselves be trapped in the sterile debate on the relationship between evangelism and social responsibility. Rather they will derive guidance from the conviction that "religion that God our Father accepts as pure and faultless is this: to look after orphans and widows in their distress and to keep oneself from being polluted by the world" (James 1:27). They will neither forsake the importance of calling people to conversion to Christ and personal piety nor abandon the focus on urging Christ's disciples to engage in costly service.

## Conclusion

During the 1990s and into the next millennium, the African continent will present a laboratory for testing Glasser's agenda for mission theology in the nineties. The foregoing reflections, cast in four categories, have indicated major themes for African mission theology as we enter the twenty-first century. There are encouraging signs that many people have begun reflecting on the issues outlined here. My personal hope is that in the near future Africans will cease being only consumers of mission theologies produced elsewhere. May God grant that African Christians become contributors to global mission theology.

# 24

# A Theology of Mission in Relation to Hinduism

## SAPHIR P. ATHYAL

The problem of mission in relation to Hinduism has a wider implication and broader relevance than the context of India. Most nonrevelatory religions, those other than Judaism, Islam and Christianity, bear a strong resemblance to the Hindu system of belief.

Adherents of Hinduism, both Indian Hindus overseas and converts to the faith, are scattered throughout the world. In addition to the 700 million Hindus who live in India, a significant number of people in nations like Nepal, Sri Lanka, Fiji, Marielus, and Singapore are Hindu. Yoga, Transcendental Meditation, the Hare Krishna movement, and the teachings of many Hindu gurus have become rapidly popular in Western countries with widespread acceptance since the 1960's and 1970's.

In recent years, the Hindu worldview and teachings have penetrated mainstream thought and life in the West through the guise of the New Age movement. All the fundamental teachings and practices of the New Age movement have their origin in Hinduism. The central New Age doctrine is that all in existence is one and that this oneness is the only reality. This is the central precept of the Hindu faith. The subtle way Hinduism has permeated all parts of the world and especially western society through this movement is alarming. Many people in the West who fancy themselves as Christians could in fact be called "anonymous Hindus."

### All-Inclusive Nature of Hinduism

A basic problem one faces in the issue of mission in relation to Hinduism is the fact that it is not a coherent religious system but rather a complex

---

Dr. Saphir P. Athyal served as the President of Union Biblical Seminary at Pune, India, the founder and chairman of the Asia Theological Association, the Deputy Chairman of the Lausanne Committee and the Program Chairman of Lausanne II in Manila, 1989. He teaches at Fuller Seminary every spring as a guest professor.

jumble of religions that often are inconsistent with one another. It lacks a clean identity. It is generally recognized that the word "Hindu" is most likely derived from the ancient word for river. Therefore the term Hinduism describes the religious beliefs, traditions and practices that developed over three millennia among the people who lived in the region of the Indus River.

Hinduism has no founder, no one creed or system of beliefs nor one normative scripture to which all Hindus subscribe. Elements of polytheism, henotheism, monotheism, manism and atheism are found within it. On the one hand it has superstitions and worship of idols and evil spirits, but on the other hand, some of the most sublime reflections on religious truths and philosophical speculations on the nature of the ultimate reality are seen in Hinduism.

Hinduism has many sect groups and subgroups with their own separate gods and traditions. So also it has different forms, such as the animistic or primitive, the popular, the mystical, the philosophical, the militant and the secular peoples. Yet there are some common elements in most segments of Hinduism, such as the denial of the material as real, each one belonging to a caste, the concept of *karma*, transmigration of soul, and self-realization as one's ultimate goal.

With its heterogeneous and complex nature, Hinduism claims itself as *satana dharma*, the eternal religion that is sufficient to meet the fundamental needs of all peoples. It affirms that it contains within itself the best elements of all other faiths. Generally, Hindus are not exclusivists, but rather tolerant of other religions. However, militant Hindu fundamentalism is rapidly growing, with its strong opposition to Christianity and other faiths, despite the avowed secularism of India.

In addition to believing that their faith contains the best in all religions, many Hindu thinkers hold fast to the concept of the unity of all religions. They claim that all religions are at different levels of development in an ascending order, just as the steps of a ladder; with, of course, Hinduism at the top of the ladder. To them, other faiths are valid and useful as the preparatory stages in people's spiritual journey to that *summmum bonum*.

Still another Hindu attitude is that all religions are equally valid in their respective historical and cultural contexts, but that none is universally normative. We see in Hindu theology of religions that one can recognize all three main schools found in present-day Christian writers, namely: exclusivism, which is becoming increasingly popular in India; inclusivism, with religions playing the role of school masters; and pluralism, or the parity of all religions. Viewed from any of these three positions, Hindus find no need for conversion from Hinduism to Christianity or any other religion.

## Pluralism: Hindu and Christian

The cornerstone of a true theology of Christian mission is the affirmation that the revelation of God through Jesus Christ is unique, final and universally normative. There is "no other name" than his through which one can be saved. But in recent years this foundational truth has been questioned and set aside by many Christian theologians in India and around the world.

This is of particular concern for mission in India. The concept that all religions involve equally valid cultural and historical responses of people to God has been the classical position of Hinduism for ages. Hinduism has had its own varieties of Ernst Troeltsch, John Hick and Paul Knitter for many centuries.

One may speak of the varied theologies of religions of the Hindu thinkers, as described above. But it is clear that Hinduism's notion of God as the Oneness of all things, the knowledge of whom is through one's intuition, should logically lead us to the conclusion that all different religions and paths ultimately reach the same God or Reality. The dictum that describes the stance of most Hindu leaders is, "Truth is One; the sages call It by different names." Several key leaders like Gandhiji, rightly or wrongly, interpreted the Hindu position as one that holds all religions as not only true in their own right, but also as equally true. The most faithful western commentary on this age-old Hindu concept of pluralism is found in the writings of John Hick, who elaborated the position for his western audience.

In Hinduism no religion is universally normative and authoritative. Each faith is valid in its own particular context. The best path to God is the faith into which one is born, directed by one's previous life.

Because of the general Hindu notion of the parity of all religions, pluralistic Christian thinking creates a crisis in the theology of mission in India. Pluralists claim that all religions are equally valid responses to God's diverse but relevant revelations to different peoples. Because Christ is only one of those revelations or decisive events, we are told that our approach should be "theocentric" rather than "Christocentric." Christ is moved from the center to the "leading edge."

To try to understand the nature of the Deity through Hinduism leads us into a chaotic state. In Hinduism it is possible that God is, and more logically speaking he is not; he is a person but very likely not a person; he is one and possibly he is many; and indeed the worshiper himself is the deity worshiped.

Christian pluralists assume there is God, one God, who has certain characteristics such as holiness, love, wisdom and justice. They attribute to him an interest in people and their salvation. These and the other assertions they make about God derive from their Christian upbringing and understanding of God as revealed in Christ. Then they assume that people of any other religion can come to the same basic notions. It is like a person who discovers a star through a powerful telescope and gains some knowledge about its position and nature, and then throws away the telescope, claiming that everybody everywhere knows the star in their own respective ways.

What is theocentrism when the totality of all is in fact God and there is no question of a center? When God-consciousness is Self-consciousness, the concept of God becomes people's subjective fancies of different types. If the different understandings of Deity in Hinduism and other faiths are all valid, then in the God-head there should be diversity, or more logically, there should be many gods. There is only a foggy line between pluralism and polytheism.

Because there is immense greatness and mystery in the Godhead, humankind needs a concrete and particular expression or self-revelation of him as in Jesus Christ. Otherwise we cannot have even an approximate notion of who he is.

Pluralism, whether in Hinduism, in the New Age movement, or in the writings of certain Christians, is the grain of the present day. It denies anything absolute, considers exclusivism as the greatest offense, and claims that everything that brings self-fulfillment is valid and true. Truth is what one feels good about. Hinduism warmly welcomes the Christian gospel if Christ can be considered one of the great sages and the concept of "no other name" is abandoned.

### Hindu-Christian Dialogue

The term "interreligious" dialogue in the general sense of the word describes the interaction and the mutual sharing of life and ideas between people of different faiths. In India above 80 percent of the population are Hindus and less than 3 percent (the unofficial figure is nearly 5 percent) Christian. Naturally where we live as neighbors, an unstructured sharing of experiences and thoughts always takes place as we participate in common struggles and community issues. Mutual influences are inevitable, even in the areas of religious concepts and worship practices. But any deliberate dialogue on religious matters and beliefs is often consciously avoided.

There are several centers in India for dialogue, and leading churches have commissions on dialogue. Many books have been written on the subject. Yet actual dialogue in an atmosphere of mutual respect, frankness and earnestness is very rare. The Roman Catholic Church in India has made more progress in this area than other denominations.

When dialogue takes place, it tends to be at a philosophical or academic level, and not at the personal spiritual level. Hindus who participate do so as a concession to their Christian friends or for a better academic understanding of Christianity. As they constitute the predominate majority of the nation's population, unlike the Christians who are a small minority, they do not feel a need for acceptance and recognition from others. They also often are suspicious of the motives of the Christians in their interest in dialogue.

What is the value and use of dialogue? At one extreme there are those who understand dialogue as a common search by people of different faiths for the ultimate Truth or Reality which is manifold and inexhaustible. At the other extreme there are those who use the occasion of dialogue for apologetics or polemics.

Dialogue done in the spirit of genuine respect for and openness to one another will prove to be beneficial and meaningful to those who participate. It clears prejudices and misunderstandings. It clarifies questions about one another's faith. It creates mutual acceptability and rapport between different religious groups and a better atmosphere for tackling social issues and problems of multireligious communities.

Dialogue highlights the truth and values in religions by which one can build bridges of understanding with others. It can enrich the participants in certain areas of their own religious lives. If it is done at the level of honest sharing of innermost personal search and experience of God, dialogue could be very useful for our understanding of how God works among Hindus. All of these could prepare the ground for the sharing of the gospel of Jesus Christ.

### Nonnegotiable Basics: Hindu and Christian

A Christian trying to understand with sincerity and openness the nature of God's dealings with Hindus may find several elements of "continuity" between Hinduism and Christianity at certain levels. But radical "discontinuity" is evident in the areas of the most fundamental teachings and basic doctrines of the two faiths. Let me mention only a few examples.

First, there is discontinuity between the Hindu and Christian views of the character of God. Hinduism's position is pantheistic monism. Oneness of all things is the only Reality or God, and it is impersonal. It is called Brahman, Cosmic Consciousness, *Shoonya* (nothingness), or Self. It cannot be defined in terms of qualities of personality. Any concept of the Deity as a person, whether in Christianity or in any religion, is considered an elementary level of understanding of God. For example, Hinduism's very popular *Bhakti* movement, in which God is viewed as a person, finds many points of contact with Christianity, but the *Bhakti* movement is regarded as a preliminary stage in a spiritual pilgrimage.

Christians cannot accept this. Personality is the highest quality of being that we know of as distinguished from animals, plants and the material world. Freedom to reflect, change, create and direct our own destiny is the highest feature we have. To deny the personal character of God is to scrap everything Christians know of him, his qualities, his activities and his personal relationship with humankind.

Second, there is discontinuity between the Hindu and Christian views of the nature and means of salvation. Where there is no concept of a personal God, there cannot be a serious view of sin and consequently no valid understanding of salvation. In Hinduism salvation is deliverance from all the limitations put on one as a person. Each one is in a prison of the body, the will, the senses and "gross consciousness." Therefore sin is ignorance, *avidya*, not realizing that we are the Cosmic Self, but thinking of ourselves as separate individuals. When we achieve "Pure Consciousness" and merge with the Cosmic Self, our identity is lost, like a drop of rain falling into an ocean and losing its separate existence.

But what is done about all the evils and injustice we committed against God, others and ourselves? Hinduism gives no answers. Forgiveness is seldom mentioned, as the concept has no place in Hindu theology. So also it follows that if there is no God who is separate from humankind, then we are each responsible for our salvation, whether by works, devotion or knowledge, as in Hinduism.

Third, there is discontinuity between the Hindu and Christian views of the nature of the world and society. In Hinduism, despite all its different interpretations, the general notion about the world is that what is seen is not real but is illusion or *maya*. It is like a person in the dark seeing a rope on the road and thinking that it is really a snake.

There are at least three serious implications of this view to a Christian. One has to do with history. In Hinduism, history belongs to the realm of the unreal, without purpose or direction. In Christianity, however, God is the Lord and guide of history and history is the scene of God's self-revelation and salvation deeds.

Another issue is the reality and value of other individuals and our relationship with them. In Hinduism there is no teaching similar to the Christian concept of corporate worship, fellowship and the importance of belonging to one another as different organs of one body.

Still another issue is that of sacrificial service to others, which is an inherent component of Christian mission. In Hinduism, except in some of the recent reform movements, the concept of service plays no role except that it adds merit to the one who renders service. In the Christian faith, loving our neighbor as ourselves cannot be divorced from loving God.

In these radical discontinuities and in many other teachings, the Christian faith finds no common ground with Hinduism.

Paul's sharing of the gospel of Christ with his Gentile audience at Athens (Acts 17:16–34) provides a good model for our approach to Hindus. He had a clear understanding of their religious convictions, literature and philosophies. He met them at their best, accenting some of the truths and good values in their beliefs. He built all possible bridges with them, starting where they were. Yet he made starkly clear the differences between his concept and theirs, all of which are very pertinent to the context of Hinduism. Paul continues with a call to repentance and proclaims to them with authority the way of salvation provided in Jesus Christ by a God whom they had confessed as "The Unknown God."

# CONCLUSION

# 25

# Faith, Love, and Hope

## A Theology of Mission On-the-Way

### CHARLES VAN ENGEN

In this time-between-the-times we live in the stressful dialectic of the Kingdom of God, a Kingdom that has already come in Jesus Christ, yet is still coming (Cullmann 1951). This reality becomes even more poignant when focused on the last decade of the last century of a millennium.

The already-and-not-yet character of God's rule means that the Church and its mission constitute an interim sign. In the power of the Spirit, the Church points all humanity backward to its origins in God's creation and forward to the present and coming Kingdom in Jesus Christ.[1] (Verkuyl 1978, 203; Arthur Glasser 1985, 12; 1990a, 250; and Glasser and McGavran 1983, 30–46.)

Looking into the next millennium, we are filled with awe and no little fear. In *Transforming Mission*, David Bosch laid out the broad parameters of our agenda for doing theology of mission into the foreseeable future. In doing so, he attempted to describe for us what he considered to be some of the most important "Elements of an Emerging Ecumenical Missionary Paradigm" (1991b, 368ff).[2] It will take a number of years and a host of conversations to find a way to deal with, and cohesively integrate, the many diverse elements Bosch offered us. Although we reason like children and "see through a glass, darkly" (1 Cor. 13:11–12), yet we can at least look over the horizon and search for a road map of what may lie ahead. At the risk of being simplistic, partial, and too general, I would offer the following thesis: Going into the next millennium we need a trinitarian theology of mission that:

- emanates from a deeply personal, biblical, and corporate *faith* in Jesus Christ (the King);

- is lived out in the Body of Christ as an ecumenical fellowship of *love* (the central locus of Christ's reign);
- and offers *hope* for the total transformation of God's world (as a sign of the present inbreaking of the coming Kingdom of God).

In offering this thesis, I have borrowed an organizing framework from the Apostle Paul. As if it were a kind of signature, Paul salted his letters with references to a significant triad of missiological ideas: *faith, hope and love*. Mixing their order and interweaving them with other contextual agendas, Paul's triad gives us a glimpse of what might be called the "habitus"[3] or integrating idea of his mission theology.[4] In what follows, the order of Faith, Love, and Hope is used to give a sense of movement on the road to God's future. The first principle in the triad is faith.

### Faith: The Holy Spirit Motivates the Church's Participation in God's Mission

Roland Allen (1962) and Harry Boer (1961), among others, emphasized the fact that the coming of the Holy Spirit at Pentecost brought a radically new and deeply personal relationship with Jesus Christ that is essential to mission. The traditional Pentecostal Movement since the turn of the century (and the Wesleyans before that), the Charismatic Movement of the last thirty years, and the Orthodox traditions in their participation in the World Council of Churches have continually emphasized the role of the Holy Spirit, personal faith, and deep spirituality as foundational for Christian mission. In this vein, there is substantial agreement between, say, Section I of *The San Antonio Report* (WCC 1990), *The Manila Manifesto* (LCWE 1989), and *Evangelii Nuntiandi* and *Redemptoris Missio*. This being the case, faith plays a crucial role with reference to some of the most critical issues of our time. Six considerations center on faith as we look across the horizon of a new millennium.

First, in certain circles, faith, as trust in God's revelation in Jesus Christ, enscripturated in the Bible and witnessed to by the Holy Spirit, is sometimes questioned, and even at times rejected. But mission that is not based on biblical revelation, the text that declares the uniqueness of Jesus Christ and offers a new birth through the Holy Spirit, may be church expansion or colonialist extension or sectarian proselytism—but it is not God's mission (cf Gnanakan 1992, 195ff).

God's mission emanates from the power of the resurrection (Eph. 1), in "the power of the Spirit."[5] This also means that God's mission should be tested and tried. As John suggested, "Every spirit (and every enterprise of mission) that acknowledges that Jesus Christ has come in the flesh is from God, but every spirit that does not acknowledge Jesus is not from God" (1 Jn. 4:2–3). A theocentric pluralist perspective that disavows the uniqueness of Jesus Christ may be polite conversation or even compassionate cooper-ation, but it is not the apostolate of Jesus Christ. For when we are involved in God's mission, then we are participating in Jesus' mission: "As the Father has sent me, I am sending you" (John 20:21) (see Glasser 1976, 3). Jesus calls us to be ambassadors, calling the world to be reconciled to God through faith in Jesus Christ—and such reconciliation is impossible apart from personal and corporate faith in Jesus Christ (2 Cor. 5).

Secondly, mission that derives from faith will take seriously the centuries of reflection by the People of God concerning their faith as revealed by God in the Scriptures and as understood by the community of faith since Abraham. This means that systematic and historical theology need to be given their appropriate places in filling out the meaning, scope, and impli-cations of mission. But it also means that there can be no truly biblical development of systematic or historical theology unless these are thoroughly saturated with missional questions, intentions, and dimensions.[6]

Thirdly, mission from faith means that conversation with people of other faiths will occur at the deepest levels of shared convictions. This entails a radical differentiation between religion and culture, faith and worldview. To confuse religion and faith on the one hand with culture and worldview on the other too often means that once one affirms cultural relativity, one must immediately take the next step and accept religious pluralism. Such a confusion is quite evident in the writings of Wilfred Cantwell Smith, Karl Rahner, John Hick, John Cobb, Paul Knitter, and Wesley Ariarajah. One of the future tasks of theology of mission will be to more clearly distinguish these two aspects of human experience.[7]

Further, it will also be important to distinguish between the Holy Spirit (as a unique part of the triune God) and the spirits (be these pantheistic, animistic, spiritist, New Age, or materialist). The lack of such a distinction was part of the issue that arose at Canberra. This would also help us differentiate the Holy Spirit from human spirituality—a crucial issue related to the difference between *God's* mission and our own expansionist agendas.

Fourth, mission from faith will mean a continued search for ways in which our faith may be *public* faith, based on the facts of revelation. Espe-cially in the West, this involves wrestling with the straitjacket of the Enlight-enment that has wanted to force the concept of faith into a privatist mold of individual taste, as Lesslie Newbigin has so aptly demonstrated (New-bigin 1986, 1989a).[8] Missionary faith inevitably, rightly, and powerfully must be a public faith, interested in the inner, spiritual conversion of the person as part of a larger social, economic, political, and global reality. Each per-son's conversion on the micro-scale has implications for the transformation of society on the macro-scale, and vice versa. No longer can we maintain a dichotomy between these two. Mission theology into the next millennium must find a way to speak to both these aspects as part of the same reality. This means that missiology must find a way to integrate spirituality, psychology, anthropology, and sociology in a wholistic understanding that more closely approximates reality.

Fifth, mission from faith will mean we are deeply concerned about four billion people and thousands of unreached people groups who have not yet experienced the transformation of the Spirit through faith in Jesus Christ. Our hearts will ache for them (Rom. 9:1–3), we will consider ourselves their debtors (Rom. 1:14), and we will yearn deeply to see them touched by the Holy Spirit and converted to Jesus Christ (Van Engen 1981). This is a mission theology that cannot stop short of committed plans and action, a mission theology that understands that it exists for the sake of those who have not yet become part of the People of God. As Johannes Verkuyl has said it, "Missiology may never become a substitute for action and participation ... If study does not lead to participation, whether at home or abroad, missiology has lost her humble calling" (Verkuyl 1978, 6).[9]

Lastly, mission from faith through the Holy Spirit will not only use the gifts of the Spirit for ministry in the world; it will occur when the *fruits* of the Spirit emanate through the lives of the People of God (Gal. 5:22–26). Down through the history of mission, one would wish that the motivations, means, and goals of mission had been more thoroughly washed with love, joy, peace, patience, kindness, goodness, faithfulness, gentleness, and self-control. For the Church to be believable, it will need to conduct its mission as an expression of the *fruit* of the Spirit, conscious of Christ's lordship in the midst of God's People. This brings us to our second major word in Paul's triad: love.

## Love: Jesus Christ Activates His Body's Participation in God's Mission

"By this all (people) will know that you are my disciples, if you love one another" (Jn. 13:35). Jesus calls for agape love as the supreme quality of the fellowship of missionary disciples. As never before, the Church of Jesus Christ must discover what it means to be a fellowship of love—especially now that the Church circles the globe and its center of gravity has shifted from North and West to South and East. Never before in the history of humanity has the Christian faith been adhered to by people of so many cultures. Today we can empirically observe what we implicitly knew: that the Gospel was infinitely "translatable" into all human cultures (Sanneh 1989). The theological implications of this fact are staggering. Only three can be highlighted.

In the first place, a multicultural world church calls for a new paradigm that more closely relates church, unity, and mission. When we say "church," for example, we need to carefully balance the local and the universal, as the Orthodox tradition so often reminds us. No longer can we mean *only* the older denominations with roots in Western Europe, nor even their daughter churches in Africa, Asia, and Latin America, as in the phrase, "World Council of *Churches*." New religious movements in Asia, indigenous independent churches in Africa, new ecclesial groups in Latin America, new denominations all over the world, meta-churches of hundreds of thousands that are denominations in their own right—all these have developed since the 1960s, and they have given a whole new meaning to the word "church" (Walls 1976).

We need a new paradigm of ecumenicity. The July 1992 issue of *International Review of Mission* provides an excellent starting point for discussing this matter.[10] Mission in love must first mean that we learn to love, understand, listen to, and be corrected by one another in the Christian Church (cf. Van Engen 1990).[11]

This involves more than tolerance as the highest value and more than the celebration of total diversity with little commonality. Mission-in-love is also deeper than "Learning About Theology from the Third World" (Dyrness 1990), although it clearly begins with such learning. Rene Padilla has said it well.

> From the perspective of wholistic mission, there is no place for the polarization between an ecumenical outlook and an evangelical one. To be an ecumenical Christian is to be a Christian who conceives of the whole oikoumene (the inhabited world) as the place of God's transforming action ... To be an evangelical Christian is to be a Christian who conceives of the gospel as good news of the love of God in Jesus Christ, the living Word witnessed to by the Bible, the written Word of God. It is to confess and to live out the gospel of Jesus Christ as Lord of the whole of life in the power of the Holy Spirit. It is to work together in the proclamation of the gospel to all the peoples of the earth ... and in the formation of local Christian congregations that nurture and share the faith. (Padilla 1992, 381– 82)

Mission-in-love will hold tightly to the truth of the gospel as revealed in the Scriptures and hold loosely to the provincial agendas of one's own particular Christian tradition, be that evangelical, ecumenical, Roman Catholic, Orthodox, pentecostal, or charismatic.[12]

Secondly, mission-in-love will affect the way we do theology on a global, multi-worldview scale into the next millennium. The basis on which we do theology of mission, the data we incorporate, the methodologies we use, the people we listen to, and the issues we address will probably undergo considerable change. World conferences, their pronouncements, and the studies and papers emanating from such conferences, will probably become less important for theology of mission. Instead, we will need to listen carefully to the People of God in local contexts, and then strive to find ways in which local theologizing may impact the world church, and vice versa.

If the Church is the loving Body of Christ, a community of faith-in-love that exists for and in mission for the world, then neither local theolog*ies* nor a monolithic supercultural theology are viable for a theology of mission that goes "beyond anti-colonialism to globalism" (Hiebert 1991, 263). Rather, we must find ways to affirm *both* the local and the universal (see H. Berkhof 1985, 71–73). Following Augustine (as well as the Vincentian Canon), truth is considered to lie in "what has everywhere, always, by all been believed" (cf. Van Engen 1981, 200–11). As William Dyrness rightly observes,

> If it is true that theology that matters will be a theology of the majority of Christians, then "theology in the Third World is now the only theology worth caring about." If theology is to be rooted in the actual lives of Christians today, increasingly it will have to be from the poor to the poor, in Africa, Latin America, and Asia. And theology done in the West, if it is not to become increasingly provincial, [Walls] notes, will have to be done in dialogue with the theological leaders in the Third World. (Dyrness 1990, 13; quoting Walls 1976, 182)

If this way of theologizing were given its place in the world Church, more weight might need to be ascribed to the theological principle of acceptance or reception, an idea articulated, for example, by Gamaliel in Acts 5:33–39. This principle calls for all new theological ideas to be tested by the People of God who over time (sometimes centuries) will determine whether the idea should ultimately be accepted or rejected by the Church.

A third implication of mission in love has to do with nuancing our Kingdom of God theology to include the strong covenantal perspectives found in Scripture. Kingdom thinking tends to support concepts of hierarchy and order. Covenant, on the other hand, tends to empower the weak and strengthen them through new relationships. The biblical idea of covenant is impossible without the broader concept of the reign of God in Jesus Christ. But we may discover that the "kingdom of God" perspective is best worked out through covenantal relationships that especially pick up the feminine images of God's care: giving birth, embracing, loving, self-giving, providing, and protecting.

Thus a covenantal/kingdom mission theology would take seriously the role of refugees, women, the poor, the marginalized, the weak, and the foolish in understanding a biblical hermeneutic of the Church's participation in God's mission. What is needed is a missiological theology that arises from and speaks to the entire community (see Hauerwas and Willimon 1991; Mary Motte 1991). This is the mission wisdom of Hagar, Ruth, Esther, Daniel, and the widow of Sarapheth (see, e.g., Luke 4 and Matt. 15:21–28). This is mission from weakness and foolishness (1 Cor. 1:18–31). The third millennium may bring us back to a situation reminiscent of the early Church, where our mission will necessarily be from weakness, foolishness, and poverty. This would entail a radical paradigm shift in mission theology. Neither option makes it more or less true. Truth can only be judged in terms of "centered sets" that examine our proximity or distance from Jesus Christ (Hiebert 1978). However, the shift would dramatically change the way we do mission.

This shift may not be optional. The drastic ecological, economic, political, social, religious, demographic, and other changes happening on our small globe are presenting us with a new reality that will call for a new paradigm of theology of mission. This shift in paradigm leads to the third dimension of Paul's triad: hope.

### Hope: God's Mission Is to Create a New Heaven and a New Earth

First Peter places our evangelistic confession in the context of a missional encounter of Church and world; hope is the central motif. "But in your hearts set apart Christ as Lord. Always be prepared to give an answer to everyone who asks you to give the reason for the *hope* that you have. But do this with gentleness and respect . . . " (3:15-16).

Hope is possibly the most explosive concept that missiology has to offer today. Oscar Cullmann recognized it thirty years ago.

> The genuine primitive Christian hope does not paralyze Christian action in the world. On the contrary, the proclamation of the Christian Gospel in the missionary enterprise is a characteristic form of such action, since it expresses the belief that "missions" are an essential element in the eschatological divine plan of salvation. The missionary work of the Church is the eschatological foretaste of the Kingdom of God, and the Biblical hope of the "end" constitutes the keenest incentive to action. (Cullmann 1961)

Today we are a long way from the unbelievable optimism of a hundred years ago regarding Western civilization, technology, and culture-Protestantism. These proved themselves to be empty and misguided, precisely because they were centered on faith in technology and civilization rather than on Jesus Christ.

But such a recognition should not blind us to the influence that hope and hopelessness can have on the way people participate in God's mission. For example, during the exile, the Israelites seem to have wavered between hopelessness and hope — and the difference entailed a radically distinct hermeneutic of God's mission and their part in it. On the one hand, they were prone to moan, "How can we sing a song in a foreign land?" (Ps. 137:4). But some followed the lead of Daniel, Esther, and others. Theirs was a hope-filled approach that even the weeping prophet Jeremiah advocated.

> Build houses and live in them; plant gardens and eat their produce. Take wives and have sons and daughters . . . multiply there, and do not decrease. But seek the welfare of the city where I have sent you into exile, and pray to the Lord on its behalf, for in its welfare you will find your welfare. (Jer. 29:6–7)

Here is a perspective that offers, precisely in its hopefulness, the possibility of reconciliation in a deeply biblical sense.[13] It represents a mission paradigm that Sunday Aigbe of Nigeria has called the "prophetic mandate" (1991).

The last couple years have convinced me that hope is probably the most important single concept that the Church of Jesus Christ has to offer the world of the next millennium. There was a particular period of about twenty-six days when for the first time in my life I thought we might actually live in a world of peace. The Berlin wall was coming down, Eastern Europe was changing, negotiations were going on in the Middle East, Latin America was beginning to find its way politically and economically, South Africa was beginning its tortuous process of change, Asia was exploding economically and technologically, China was on the move to new things, and African nations were beginning to find new paths. But the hiatus was short-lived.

Today as I sit and write these lines I am reminded of cities in which I have experienced the most terrible tragedy of all: the nearly total loss of hope. Be it São Paulo, Sarajevo, or Mexico City, Kuwait City after the war, Los Angeles after the riots, or Miami after the hurricane—what I keep hearing is an almost complete loss of hope. Especially in Latin America, the demise of Marxism as a viable approach, along with the failure of democratization to offer anything new for the welfare of the poor masses, have brought a spirit of hopeless resignation that deeply concerns me. When I was a child growing up in Southern Mexico, there was always a degree of optimism. Tomorrow, next week, the next governor, the next president, more education, and better organization would eventually change things. That hope seems to have died.

A missiology of hope[14] is central to Paul's missiological praxis.[15] This hope is neither breezy escapism, empty optimism, blind conformism, nor unrealistic utopianism: all of which can be found in the missiologies of this century. Rather, Paul's missiology of hope includes at least the following three components.

First, a missiology of hope means that Christians care, and care so deeply that they will risk hoping for the new. They dare hope because they know that, in Christ's Kingdom, God's grace through faith brings about a radical and total transformation. "Therefore, if anyone is in Christ, (that one) is a new creation; the old has gone, the new has come!" (2 Cor. 5:17).

Secondly, a missiology of hope means that Christians dare to believe that together they can change the world (cf. Barrett 1983, 51). This is at the heart of mission. But we must remember the not-yet-ness of God's Kingdom, along with its already-ness. We of the "baby-boomer" generation of the United States believed we could change the world on our own. We followed J. C. Hoekendijk in his pessimism about the Church and thought we could change the world by ourselves through Lyndon Johnson's "great society," through the Peace Corps, and through computer technology. As a result, many of us today are indelibly marked with pessimism and cynicism. We discovered that we could not change even the cities in which we created Christian communes, much less the world. We missed the mark by failing to realize our own sinfulness and the true extent of the Fall, by failing to grasp that we can neither bring in the Kingdom nor create the utopias envisioned by the ideologues. Rather, as we participate in God's mission, God's reign comes when people accept Jesus as Lord—and in obedience begin to see God's will being done "on earth as it is in heaven" (Matt. 6:10). This involves structural and societal change as well as personal transformation. It involves the whole person, not only the spiritual aspects. It involves all of life, not only the ecclesiastical.[16]

Third, a missiology of hope means that Christians profess certainty in that which they do not see (Heb. 11:1). It means participating with Jesus in being a "light to the Gentiles" (Acts 13:47–49; Luke 2:32; 4:18–21). Living in the time between Ascension and Parousia, we recognize the presence of God's Kingdom, live out its ethics (Matt. 5–8), and call people and structures to be reconciled with creation, with themselves, with each other, and with God (2 Cor. 5:18–21). This missiology of hope is deeply and creatively transformational, for it seeks to be a sign of the present and coming Kingdom of God. Through it we recognize our profound commitment to radical transformation when we pray, "Your Kingdom Come" (Matt. 6:10).

Yet at the same time we will remember that the Kingdom is present and coming only as the King comes. Our mission does not hasten Christ's coming, nor does it create the Kingdom. Rather, the Kingdom of God defines our mission (Costas 1979, 8–9), for only Jesus the King can bring the Kingdom. Our mission, like that of Jesus, is to "preach the good news of the Kingdom of God to other towns also, because that is why (we have been) sent" (Luke 4:43; Acts 13:46–49). "Even so, come, Lord Jesus" (Rev. 22:20).

In this time-between-the-times, our participation in God's mission into the next millennium awaits us like an adventure, a journey in the midst of, and moving toward, the present-and-coming reign of God, a running forward to discover what we already know: Jesus Christ is King.

## Notes

1. David Bosch (1991b, 368-93; 1980, 75-83, 239-48) has provided an excellent overview and critique of the *missio Dei* concept, especially as it was misused and

unbiblically reshaped in the missiology of the World Council of Churches from 1965 to 1980. See, among others, Norman Goodall (1953, 195-97); James Scherer (1987, 126-34); Lesslie Newbigin (1977, 63-68; 1978, chapters 4, 8, and 9); Wilhelm Andersen (1961); R. C. Bassham (1979, 33-40, 67-71, 168-69); and J. Verkuyl (1978, 2-4, 197-204).

The Kingdom of God (and a biblical perspective of the *missio Dei* within that) has become a major point of consensus in global missiology. See, for example, Esther and Mortimer Arias (1980); Mortimer Arias (1984); C. Van Engen (1981, 277-307; 1991a, 101-18); William Dyrness (1983); Robert Linthicum (1991, 80-108)—along with J. Blauw (1962); Hans Küng (1971, 46ff.); G. E. Ladd (1974b); John Bright (1953, 216, 231-38); Karl Barth (1958, 655ff.); H. N. Ridderbos (1962); G. Vicedom (1965); W. Pannenberg (1969); C. René Padilla (1985); Orlando Costas (1979, 5-8; 1989); Donald Senior and Carroll Stuhlmueller (1983, 141-60); Dempster, Klaus, and Petersen (1991, 1-58); Emilio Castro (1985, 38-88); WCC (1980); George Peters (1981, 37-47); Edward Pentecost (1982); Paul Pomerville (1985); Ken Gnanakan (1989); C. Peter Wagner (1987, 35-55, 96-112); Gailyn Van Rheenen (1983, 1-20); and William Abraham (1989).

2. Bosch mentions Mission as: the Church-With-Others, *missio Dei*, Mediating Salvation, the Quest for Justice, Evangelism, Contextualization, Liberation, Inculturation, Common Witness, Ministry by the Whole People of God, Witness to People of Other Living Faiths, Theology, and Action in Hope.

3. Cf. Van Engen (1987, 524-25), Bosch (1991b, 489).

4. See, for example, Rom. 5:1-5; Rom. 12:9-13; 1 Cor. 13:13; Gal. 5:5-6; Eph. 1:15; Col. 1:3-6; 1 Thes. 1:3, 5:8; 2 Thes. 1:3 with 2:13-17; 1 Tim. 4:9-12; 2 Tim. 1:5, 13-14; Philemon 5-6; and—however we deal with its authorship—Hebrews 6:9-12.

5. Moltmann (1977).

6. Cf. Ray S. Anderson (1991).

7. See Van Engen (1991b, 189-90).

8. The October 1991 issue of *Missiology* is an excellent introduction to some of these issues.

9. Some people seem to be using the year 2000 as an instrument of urgency and promotion, making rather frantic claims that the world must be evangelized by 2000. I wonder if this perspective allows one to trust in faith that the God of history may have plans for the human race beyond the year 2000. To affirm that all people must be evangelized by 2000 goes far beyond the limits of the "Watchword" of Edinburgh, 1910: "the evangelization of the world in this generation." John R. Mott, J. H. Oldham and others never meant the phrase to mean that all people would become Christians in their generation. Christ wills that no one should perish, but Scripture also recognizes the Fall and knows that "all we like sheep have gone astray." Many will choose not to respond to God's invitation.

10. See also Saayman (1990) and Bosch (1991b, 457-67).

11. See also *Mission and Evangelism: An Ecumenical Affirmation* (NCCC/DOM: 1983, 9).

12. Cf. Myers (1992).

13. See Schreiter (1992b).

14. Although Jürgen Moltmann and others developed a theology of hope in the 1960s, the concept did not emanate in new missiological directions. A *missiology* of hope is at once individual, social, and structural; and it derives from a deep sense

of identity, purpose, and the *missio Dei.* This needs further exploration. Cf. Bosch (1980, 234-38).

15. Cf., e.g., Eph. 1:18; Col. 1:5, 23, 27; Eph. 2:12; 1 Thes. 1:3; 2:19; 4:13; 2 Thes. 2:16. See also Prov. 13:12; 29:18; Heb. 6:18; 10:23; 1 Pet. 1:3; 3:15.

16. The papers and declaration of the Consultation on the Church in Response to Human Need held in Wheaton in 1983 are a good place to begin one's reflection on these issues. See Samuel and Sugden (1983b).

# Works Cited

Abraham, William J.
  1989    *The Logic of Evangelism*. Grand Rapids, Mich.: Eerdmans.
Achtemeier, Paul J.
  1983    "An Apocalyptic Shift in Early Christian Tradition: Reflections on Some Canonical Evidence." *The Catholic Biblical Quarterly* 45:231–48.
*Ad Gentes* (AG).
  1965    "Vatican Council II. Decree on the Church's Missionary Activity." In A. Flannery, ed. *Vatican Council II: The Conciliar and Post-Conciliar Documents*. Collegeville, Minn.: The Liturgical Press, 1981, 813–56.
Adeney, Miriam.
  1984    *God's Foreign Policy: Practical Ways to Help the World's Poor*. Grand Rapids, Mich.: Eerdmans Publishing Co.
Advisory Committee on the Theme of the Second WCC Assembly at Evanston (1954) ["Christ—the Hope of the World"].
  1954    "Report of the Advisory Commission on the Main Theme of the Second WCC Assembly: Christ—the Hope of the World." *Ecumenical Review* 6:430–65.
Agus, Jacob B.
  1982    "The *Mitzvah* of *Keruv*." *Conservative Judaism* 35 (4), Summer: 33–38.
Aigbe, Sunday.
  1991    "Cultural Mandate, Evangelistic Mandate, Prophetic Mandate: of These Three the Greatest Is . . . " *Missiology* 19 (1) (January): 31–43.
Aland, Kurt.
  1970    *Pietismus und die Bibel. Arbeiten zur Geschichte des Pietismus*, Band 9. Witten: Luther Verlag.
Allen, Roland.
  1927    *The Spontaneous Expansion of the Church and the Cases Which Hinder It*. London: World Dominion Press.
  1962    *The Spontaneous Expansion of the Church*. Grand Rapids, Mich.: Eerdmans.
Amaladoss, Michael.
  1990a   *Making All Things New: Dialogue, Pluralism and Evangelization in Asia*. Maryknoll, N.Y.: Orbis Books.
  1990b   "Mission: From Vatican II Into the Coming Decade." *International Review of Mission* 79: 211–20.
Andersen, Wilhelm.
  1961    "Further Toward a Theology of Mission." In G. H. Anderson, ed. *The Theology of the Christian Mission*. New York: McGraw–Hill, 300–13.

Anderson, Gerald H.
1971    "Continuity and Discontinuity." In *Concise Dictionary of the Christian World Mission*. Stephen Neill, Gerald H. Anderson, and John Goodwin, eds. London: Lutterworth Press; Nashville: Abingdon Press, 1971, 146–47.
1978    "Religion as a Problem for the Christian Mission." In *Christian Faith in a Religiously Plural World*. Donald G. Dawe and John B. Carman, eds. Maryknoll, N.Y.: Orbis Books, 106–7.
1981    "Response to Pietro Rossano." In *Christ's Lordship and Religious Pluralism*. Anderson and Stransky, eds. Maryknoll, N.Y.: Orbis, 113–14.
1989    "The Truth of Christian Uniqueness." *International Bulletin of Missionary Research* 13 (2) 49.
1990    "Speaking the Truth in Love: An Evangelical Response [to Cardinal Jozef Tomko]." In *Christian Mission and Interreligious Dialogue*. Paul Mojzes and Leonard Swidler, eds. Lewiston, N.Y.: Edwin Mellen Press, 164–70.
1991a   "The Evangelicals: Unwavering Commitment, Troublesome Divisions." In *Mission in the 1990s*. Gerald H. Anderson, James M. Phillips, and Robert T. Coote, eds. Grand Rapids, Mich.: Wm. B. Eerdmans Publishing; New Haven, Conn.: Overseas Ministries Study Center.
1991b   "Mission Research, Writing, and Publishing: 1971-1991." *International Bulletin of Missionary Research* 15, no. 4. (October): 165-72.
Anderson, Gerald H., ed.
1961    *The Theology of the Christian Mission*. New York: McGraw-Hill.
Anderson, Gerald H. and Thomas Stransky, eds.
1981a   *Faith Meets Faith*. Mission Trends No. 5. Grand Rapids, Mich.: William B. Eerdmans Publishing Company.
1981b   *Christ's Lordship and Religious Pluralism*. Maryknoll, N.Y.: Orbis Books.
Anderson, J. N. D.
1970    *Christ and Comparative Religion*. Downers Grove, Ill.: InterVarsity.
Anderson, Ray.
1991    *The Praxis of Pentecost: Revisioning the Church's Life and Mission*. Pasadena, Calif.: Fuller Theological Seminary.
Arias, Mortimer.
1984    *Announcing the Reign of God: Evangelization and the Subversive Memory of Jesus*. Philadelphia: Fortress Press.
1992    "My Pilgrimage in Mission." *International Bulletin of Missionary Research* 16, 1 (January): 28–32.
Arias, Mortimer, and Esther Arias.
1980    *The Cry of My People: Out of Captivity in Latin America*. New York: Friendship.
Arnold, Clinton E.
1992    *Powers of Darkness—Principalities & Powers in Paul's Letters*. Downers Grove, Ill.: InterVarsity Press.
Augsburger, David.
1986    *Pastoral Counseling Across Cultures*. Philadelphia: Westminster Press.
Aus, Roger.
1971    *Comfort in Judgment: The Use of Day of the Lord and Theophany*

*Traditions in Second Thessalonians 2*. New Haven, Conn.: Yale University Press.

1976      "The Relevance of Isaiah 66:7 to Revelation 12 and 2 Thessalonians." *Zeitschrift für die neutestamentliche Wissenschaft* 67:252–68.

1977      "God's Plan and God's Power: Isaiah 66 and the Restraining Factors of 2 Thess. 2:6–7." *Journal of Biblical Literature* 96:537–53.

Baar Statement.

1991      "Religious Plurality: Theological Perspectives and Affirmations." *Current Dialogue*, no. 19 (January): 47–49.

Badaracco, Claire.

1992      "Can the Church Save Women? Public Opinion, The U.N. and the Policy Gap." *America*, March 14, 217.

Bailey, John A.

1979      "Who Wrote II Thessalonians?" *New Testament Studies* 25:135–45.

Bakke, Ray.

1989      "A Theology as Big as the City." *Urban Mission* 6, no. 5 (May): 8-19.

Barbour, Ian.

1974      *Myths, Models and Paradigms*. New York: Harper & Row.

Barnouin, M.

1976/77   "Les Problemes de traduction concernant II Thess. ii. 6–7." *New Testament Studies* 23:495f.

Barrett, C. K.

1962      *From First Adam to Last: A Study in Pauline Theology*. London: Adam & Charles Black.

Barrett, David.

1980      *Christian Witness to Large Cities – The Thailand Report: Lausanne Occasional Paper No. 9*. Wheaton: Lausanne Committee for World Evangelization.

1983      "Silver and Gold Have I None: Church of the Poor or Church of the Rich?" *International Bulletin of Missionary Research* 7, no. 4 (October): 146–51.

1986      *World-Class Cities and World Evangelization*. Birmingham: New Hope.

1992      "Annual Statistical Table on Global Mission: 1992." *International Review of Missionary Research* 16, no. 1 (January 1992): 27.

Barth, Karl.

1933      *The Epistle to the Romans*. London: Oxford University Press.

1958      *Church Dogmatics*. Edinburgh: T & T Clark.

Bassham, Roger.

1979      *Mission Theology: 1948–1975 Years of Worldwide Creative Tension Ecumenical, Evangelical, and Roman Catholic*. Pasadena, Calif.: William Carey Library.

Bassler, Jouette M.

1991      *God and Mammon: Asking for Money in the New Testament*. Nashville: Abingdon Press.

Bauer, W.

1957      *A Greek-English Lexicon of the New Testament and Other Early Christian Literature*. Trans. from the 4th German edition by W. F. Arndt and F. W. Gingrich. Chicago: University of Chicago Press.

Bavinck, J. H.
  1949    *Religieus Besef en Christelijk Geloof* (Religious Awareness and Christian
          Faith). Kampen: Kok.
  1966    *The Church Between Temple and Mosque*. Grand Rapids, Mich.: William
          B. Eerdmans Publishing Company.
Beaver, R. Pierce, ed.
  1967    *To Advance the Gospel: Selections from the Writings of Rufus Anderson*.
          Grand Rapids, Mich.: Eerdmans.
  1980    *American Protestant Women in World Mission: History of the First Fem-
          inist Movement in North America*, 2nd ed. Grand Rapids, Mich.: Eerd-
          mans.
Bediako, Kwame.
  1983    "Biblical Christologies in the Context of African Traditional Relig-
          ions." In *Sharing Jesus in the Two Thirds World*. Vinay Samuel and Chris
          Sugden, eds. Grand Rapids, Mich.: William B. Eerdmans Publishing
          Company, 81–121.
Beker, J. Christiaan.
  1980    *Paul the Apostle: The Triumph of God in Life and Thought*. Philadelphia:
          Fortress Press.
  1982    *Paul's Apocalyptic Gospel: The Coming Triumph of God*. Philadelphia:
          Fortress Press.
ben Isaiah, Abraham and Benjamin Sharfman, trans.
  1949    *The Pentateuch and Rashi's Commentary: A Linear Translation into Eng-
          lish*. New York: S. S. and R. Publishing Company. (In collaboration
          with Harry M. Orlinsky and Morris Charner.)
Benjamin, Don.
  1983    *Deuteronomy and City Life*. Lanham, Md.: University Press of America.
Berger, Peter L., Brigette Berger, and Hansfried Kellner.
  1974    *The Homeless Mind: Modernization and Consciousness*. Harmondsworth:
          Penguin Books.
Berkhof, Hendrikus.
  1966    *Christ and the Meaning of History*. Trans. from the 4ᵗʰ Dutch edition by
          L. Buurman. Grand Rapids, Mich.: Baker Book House.
  1985    *Introduction to the Study of Dogmatics*. Grand Rapids, Mich.: Eerdmans.
Berkhof, Hendrikus, and Philip Potter.
  1964    *Keywords of the Gospel*. London: SCM.
Bernard, Jessie.
  1987    *The Female World from a Global Perspective*. Bloomington, Ind.: Indiana
          University Press.
Betz, O.
  1963    "Der Katechon." *New Testament Studies* 9:276–91.
Beyerhaus, Peter.
  1971    *Missions: Which Way? Humanization or Redemption?* Grand Rapids,
          Mich.: Zondervan.
Beyreuther, Erich.
  1963    *Der Geschichtliche Auftrag des Pietismus in der Gegenwart*. Stuttgart:
          Calwer Verlag.

1964     "Pietismus." *Evangelisches Kirchelexikon.* Goettingen: Vandehoeck & Ruprecht.

Bickersteth, Edward Henry.
1957     *The Trinity.* Grand Rapids, Mich.: Kregel Publications.

Bilezikian, Gilbert.
1989     *Beyond Sex Roles.* Grand Rapids, Mich: Baker Book House.

Blackman, Philip, ed.
1964     *Tractate Avotho.* New York: The Judaiaca Press.

Blanton, R. E.
1976     "Anthropological Study of Cities." *Annual Review of Anthropology* 5: 250.

Blauw, Johannes.
1962     *The Missionary Nature of the Church.* Grand Rapids, Mich.: Eerdmans.

Block, Daniel.
1988     *The Gods of the Nations.* Jackson, Miss.: Evangelical Theological Society.

Bockmuehl, Klaus.
1985     *Die aktualitaet des Pietismus Theologie und Dienst,* Heft 45. Giessen: Brunnen Verlag.

Boer, Harry.
1961     *Pentecost and Mission.* Grand Rapids, Mich.: Eerdmans.

Boff, Leonardo.
1988     *Trinity and Society.* Theology and Liberation Series. Maryknoll, N.Y.: Orbis Books.

Boff, Leonardo and Clodovis Boff
1987     *Introducing Liberation Theology.* Maryknoll, N.Y.: Orbis Books.

Borowitz, Eugene R.
1980     *Contemporary Christologies: A Jewish Response.* New York: Paulist Press.

Bosch, David J.
1978     "The Why and How of a True Biblical Foundation for Mission." In Jerald D. Gort, ed. *Zending Op Weg Naar de Toekomst: Essays Aangeboden Aan Prof. Dr. J. Verkuyl.* Kampen, J. H. Kok, 33–45.

1980     *Witness to the World.* London: Marshall, Morgan and Scott; Atlanta: John Knox Press.

1983     "The Structure of Mission: An Exposition of Matt. 28:16–20." In *Exploring Church Growth.* Wilbert R. Shenk, ed. Grand Rapids, Mich.: Eerdmans, 218–48.

1991a     "Church Perspectives on the Future of South Africa." In Alberts and F. Chikane, eds. *The Road to Rustenburg: The Church Looking Forward to a New South Africa.* Cape Town: Struik Christian Books, 129–39.

1991b     *Transforming Mission: Paradigm Shifts in Theology of Mission.* Maryknoll, N.Y.: Orbis Books.

Bosch, David J., and Oscar Cullmann.
1959     *Die Heidenmission in der Zukunftsschau Jesu. Eine Untersuchung zur Eschatologie der synoptischen Evangelien.* Zurich: Zwingli Verlag.

Braaten, Carl E.
1976     "A Trinitarian Theology of the Cross." *The Journal of Religion* 56:113-21.

1977    *The Flaming Center*. Philadelphia: Fortress Press.
1980    "Who Do We Say That He Is? On The Uniqueness and Universality of Jesus Christ." *Missiology* 8 (1):13–30.
1992    *No Other Gospel! Christianity Among the World's Religions*. Minneapolis: Fortress Press.

Bradley, Ian.
1976    *The Call to Seriousness: The Evangelical Impact on the Victorians*. New York: Macmillan Publishing Co., Inc.

Bragg, Wayne.
1983    "Beyond Development." In Tom Sine, ed. *The Church in Response to Human Need*. Monrovia, Calif.: MARC.

Branick, Vincent P.
1985    "Apocalyptic Paul?" *The Catholic Biblical Quarterly* 47:664-75.

Branson, Mark Lau, and C. Rene Padilla, eds.
1986    *Conflict and Context: Hermeneutics in the Americas*. Grand Rapids, Mich.: Eerdmans.

Braybrooke, Marcus
1992    *Pilgrimage of Hope: One Hundred Years of Global Interfaith Dialogue*. New York: Crossroad.

Bria, Ion.
1991    *The Sense of Ecumenical Tradition: the Ecumenical Witness and Vision of the Orthodox*. Geneva: World Council of Churches.

Brierly, Peter, ed.
1991    *"Christian" England: What the English Census Revealed*. London: MARC Europe.

Bright, John.
1953    *The Kingdom of God*. Nashville: Abingdon.

British Council of Churches.
1989    *The Forgotten Trinity*. Vol. 1. Report of the BCC Study Commission of Trinitarian Doctrine Today. London: British Council of Churches.
1989    *The Forgotten Trinity*. Vol. 2. A Study Guide. London: British Council of Churches.

Brockway, Allan R.
1988    "Learning Christology through Dialogue with Jews." *Journal of Ecumenical Studies* 25, no. 3:351.

Brown, Dale.
1978    *Understanding Pietism*. Grand Rapids, Mich.: Wm. B. Eerdmans Publishing Company.

Bruce, F. F.
1977    *Paul: Apostle of the Free Spirit*. Exeter: Paternoster Press.
1982    *1 and 2 Thessalonians*. Waco, Tex.: Word Books.
1985    *The Letter of Paul to the Romans. An Introduction and Commentary*. 2nd ed. Leicester: InterVarsity Press.

Bruner, Frederick Dale
1990    *The Churchbook: Matthew 13-28*. Dallas: Word.

Burrows, W. R.
1986    "Decree on the Church's Missionary Activity." In T. E. O'Connell, ed. *Vatican II and Its Documents: An American Reappraisal*. Wilmington, Del.: Michael Glazier, 180–96.

Campbell, Barbara E.
1983    *United Methodist Women in the Middle of Tomorrow,* 2nd ed. New York: Women's Division, General Board of Global Ministries, the United Methodist Church.

Carriker, C. Timothy.
1987    "A Review of J. Christiaan Beker's Thesis in Light of 1 Thessalonians 4:13–5:11 and 1 Corinthians 15:20–28." Unpublished Ph.D. seminar paper presented at Fuller Theological Seminary.

Castro, Emilio.
1985    *Freedom in Mission: The Perspective of the Kingdom of God, an Ecumenical Inquiry.* Geneva: World Council of Churches.

Cervin, Richard.
n.d.    "Does *kephale* ('head') Mean 'Source' or 'Authority' in Greek Literature?" Unpublished paper, Urbana, Ill.: University of Illinois.

Chareonwongsak, Kriengsak.
1990    "Hope of Bangkok: A Visionary Model of Church Growth and Church Planting." *Urban Mission* 7, no. 3 (January): 25-35.

Chilton, E. F.
1880    "Woman's Work." *Woman's Missionary Advocate* 1 (July): 13.

China Centenary Missionary Conference Records.
1907    Shanghai. New York: American Tract Society.

Chipenda, José, and André Karamaga, eds.
1991    *The Right Time for Change: What Hope for Crisis-Stricken Africa?* Nairobi: All-Africa Conference of Churches.

Cho, Paul Yonggi.
1991    "Cho: 'Church Growth Begins in the Pastor's Heart.' " Interview by Joyce Wells Booze. *The Council Today,* August 9.

Chopp, Rebecca S.
1986    *The Praxis of Suffering: An Interpretation of Liberation and Political Theologies.* Maryknoll, N.Y.: Orbis Books.

Chung Hyun, Kyung.
1990    *Struggle to Be the Sun Again.* Maryknoll, N.Y.: Orbis Books.
1991    "Come, Holy Spirit—Renew the Whole Creation." *Signs of the Spirit, Official Report.* Geneva: WCC, 37–47.

Coggins, James, and Paul Hiebert, eds.
1989    *Wonders and the Word.* Winnepeg and Hillsboro, Kans.: Kindred Press.

Conn, Harvie M.
1984    *Eternal Word and Changing Worlds: Theology, Anthropology and Mission in Trialogue.* Grand Rapids, Mich.: Zondervan.
1985    "Lucan Perspectives and the City." *Missiology* 12 (4), October: 409–19.
1987    *A Clarified Vision for Urban Mission.* Grand Rapids, Mich.: Zondervan Publishing House.
1992a   "Genesis as Urban Prologue." In *Discipling the City.* Roger Greenway, ed. Grand Rapids, Mich.: Baker Book House.
1992b   *Eternal Word and Changing Worlds.* (1984). Phillipsburg, N.J.: Presbyterian and Reformed Publishing Company.
1992c   *Evangelism: Doing Justice and Preaching Grace.* (1982). Phillipsburg, N.J.: Presbyterian and Reformed Publishing Company.

Cook, Guillermo.
1985    *The Expectation of the Poor: Latin American Basic Ecclesial Communities in Protestant Perspective.* Maryknoll, N.Y.: Orbis Books.

Coppens, J.
1970    "Les deux Obstacles au Retour glorieux du Sauveur (ii Thess. II, 6–7)." *Ephemerides Theologica Lovanienses* 46:383–89.

Costas, Orlando.
1979    *The Integrity of Mission: The Inner Life and Outreach of the Church.* San Francisco: Harper and Row.
1982    *Christ Outside the Gate: Mission Beyond Christendom.* Maryknoll, N.Y.: Orbis Books.
1989    *Liberating News: A Theology of Contextual Evangelization.* Grand Rapids, Mich.: Eerdmans.
1990    "Evangelical Theology in the Two-Thirds World." In *Earthen Vessels.* Joel Carpenter and Wilbert Shenk, eds. Grand Rapids, Mich.: William B. Eerdmans Pub. Co.
1991    *Christ Outside the Gate.* Maryknoll, N.Y.: Orbis Books.

Cotterell, Peter.
1988    "The Unevangelized: An Olive Branch from the Opposition." *International Review of Mission* 77 (1):131–35.

Covell, Ralph.
1978    *W. A. P. Martin, Pioneer of Progress in China.* Washington, D.C.: Christian University Press.
1986    *Confucius, the Buddha, and Christ.* Maryknoll, N.Y.: Orbis Books.

Cox, Harvey.
1965    *The Secular City.* London: SCM.

Cragg, Kenneth.
1956    *The Call of the Minaret.* New York: Oxford University Press; Maryknoll, N.Y.: Orbis Books, 1984.
1959    *Sandals at the Mosque.* New York: Oxford University Press.

Cross, Dale.
1989    "An Evaluation of Approaches for Urban Mission: Discovering Indicators of Effectiveness." Unpublished D.Min. project, Westminster Theological Seminary.

Cullmann, Oscar.
1936    Le caractère eschatologique du devoir missionaire et de la conscience apostolique de S. Paul. Étude sur le *katechon (-ōn)* Thess.2:6-7." *Revue d'Histoire et de Philosphie Religieuses* 16:210–45.
1938    "Quand viendra le Royaaume de Dieu." *Revue d'Histoire et de Philosophie religieuses* 18:174–86.
1951    *Christ and Time.* London: SCM; Philadelphia: Westminster.
1956    "Eschatology and Mission in the New Testament." In *The Background of the New Testament and Its Eschatology.* W. D. Davies and D. Daube, eds. Cambridge: Cambridge University Press.
1961    "Eschatology and Missions in the New Testament." In Gerald Anderson, ed. *The Theology of the Christian Mission.* New York: McGraw-Hill, 42–54.
1963    "The Connection of Primal Events and End Events with the New Testament Redemptive History." In *The Old Testament and the Christian Faith: A Theological Discussion.* B. W. Anderson, ed. New York: Harper and Row.
1967a   *Christ and Time.* Philadelphia: Westminster, 66ff.

1967b    *Salvation in History*. Trans. from the German by S. G. Sowers, et al. London: SCM Press.

Cullmann, Oscar, and David J. Bosch.

1959    *Die Heidenmission in der Zukunftsschau Jesu. Eine Untersuchung zur Eschatologie der synoptischen Evangelien*. Zürich: Zwingli Verlag.

D'Costa, Gavin.

1986    *Theology and Religious Pluralism*. Oxford: Basil Blackwell.

1990    "One Covenant or Many Covenants? Toward a Theology of Christian-Jewish Relations." *Journal of Ecumenical Studies* 27, no. 3: 441–52.

1991    *Christian Uniqueness Reconsidered*. Maryknoll, N.Y.: Orbis Books.

de Gruchy, John W.

1986    *Evangelical Witness in South Africa*. Dobsonville: Concerned Evangelicals.

1991    *Liberating Reformed Theology*. Grand Rapids, Mich.: Eerdmans.

de Groot, A.

1964    *De Bijbel over het Heil der Volken*. Roermond: Romens.

Delaney, Joan.

1987    *The Relationship of the Roman Catholic Church to the Commission on World Mission and Evangelism of the World Council of Churches*. Verbum SVD, vol. 28, 82–88.

Demarest, Bruce.

1982    *General Revelation*. Grand Rapids, Mich.: Zondervan.

Dempster, Murray, Byron Klaus, and Douglas Petersen.

1991    *Called & Empowered: Global Mission in Pentecostal Perspective*. Peabody, Mass.: Hendrickson.

de Ridder, Richard.

1971    *Discipling the Nations*. Grand Rapids, Mich.: Baker.

Dilschneider, Otto.

1969    *Glaube an den Heiligen Geist*. Wuppertal: Theologischer Verlag Rolf Brockhaus.

Donfried, K. D.

1985    "The Cults of Thessalonica & the Thessalonian Correspondence." *New Testament Studies* 31:342ff.

Douglas, Ian T.

1992    "A Lost Voice: Women's Participation in the Foreign Mission Work of the Episcopal Church, 1920-1970." *Anglican and Episcopal History* 61 (March).

Douglas, J. D., ed.

1975    *Let the Earth Hear His Voice*. International Congress on World Evangelization, Lausanne, Switzerland, 1974. Minneapolis, Minn.: World Wide Publications.

1990    International Congress on World Evangelization, Second, 1989, Manila, Philippines.
        *Proclaim Christ Until He Comes: Calling the Whole Church to Take the Whole Gospel to the Whole World*. Minneapolis, Minn.: World Wide Publications.

Duerr, J.

1947    *Sendende und Werdende Kirche in der Missions-theologie Gustav Warneck*. Basel: Basler Missionbuchhandlung.

du Plessis, J. G.
   1990    "For Reasons of the Heart: A Critical Appraisal of David Bosch's Use of Scripture in the Foundations of Christian Mission." *Missionalia* 18, no. 1 (April): 75–85.

Dyrness, William.
   1983    *Let the Earth Rejoice: A Biblical Theology of Holistic Mission.* Pasadena, Calif.: Fuller Seminary Press.
   1990    *Learning About Theology from the Third World.* Grand Rapids, Mich.: Zondervan Publishing House.

Eames, Edwin, and Judith Goode.
   1977    *Anthropology of the City.* Englewood Cliffs, N.J.: Prentice-Hall, Inc.

Ebeling, Gerhard.
   1970    *Luther—An Introduction to His Thought.* Philadelphia: Fortress Press, 175-91.

Eck, Diana L.
   1990    "On Seeking and Finding in the World's Religions." *Christian Century,* May 2, 454–56.

Edgar, William.
   1983    "New Right—Old Paganism." *Nederlands Theologisch Tijschrift* 37:4.

Egelkraut, Helmut.
   1983    "Pietismus und Reformation." *Luther und der Pietismus.* Giessen: Brunnen Verlag.

Eliot, T. S.
   1963    *Murder in the Cathedral.* New York: Harcourt, Brace and World.

Ellul, Jacques.
   1970    *The Meaning of the City.* Grand Rapids, Mich.: William B. Eerdmans Publishing Company.

Erickson, Millard J.
   1975    "Hope For Those Who Haven't Heard? Yes, but—." *Evangelical Missions Quarterly* (2):122–26.

Escobar, Samuel.
   1974    "Evangelism and Man's Search for Freedom, Justice and Fulfillment." In *Let the Earth Hear His Voice.* J. D. Doublas, ed. Minneapolis, Minn.: World Wide Publications, 303–26.
   1987    *La Fe Evangelica y las Teologias de la Liberacion.* El Paso, Tex.: Casa Bautista de Publicaciones.
   1990    "From Lausanne 1974 to Manila 1989: The Pilgrimage of Urban Mission." *Urban Mission* 7, no. 4 (March): 724–27.

*Evangelii Nuntiandi* (EN).
   1975    *Pope Paul VI. Apostolic Exhortation on Evangelization in the Modern World.* Washington, D. C.: United States Catholic Conference, 1976.

Evans, Mary J.
   1982    *Woman in the Bible.* Downers Grove, Ill.: InterVarsity Press.

Fairbank, John K.
   1986    *The Great Chinese Revolution: 1800–1985.* New York: Harper & Row.

Ferm, Deane William.
   1986    *Third World Liberation Theologies: A Reader.* Maryknoll, N.Y.: Orbis Books.

Fernando, Ajith.
    1987    *The Christian's Attitude Toward World Religions*. Wheaton, Ill.: Tyndale
        House.
Fife, Eric S., and Arthur F. Glasser.
    1962    *Missions in Crisis: Rethinking Missionary Strategy*. London: InterVarsity.
Flannery, A. P., ed.
    1975    *Documents of Vatican II*. Grand Rapids, Mich.: Eerdmans.
Fleisch, Paul.
    1912    *Dis Moderne Gemeinschaftsbewegung in Deutschland*. Leipzig: Verlag
        von H. G. Wallmann.
Fonseca, Josue.
    1990    "Foreign Evangelical Mission Societies in Latin America: Cross-Cul-
        tural Adjustments for a New Decade." Unpublished manuscript.
Fortman, Edmund J.
    1982    *The Triune God: A Historical Study of the Doctrine of the Trinity*. Grand
        Rapids, Mich.: Baker Book House.
Frick, Frank S.
    1977    *The City in Ancient Israel*. Missoula, Mont.: Scholars Press.
Fung, Raymond.
    1991    (Letter) *Monthly Letter on Evangelism* 6/7 (June/July): 1.
Ganz, Herbert.
    1962    *The Urban Villagers*. New York: The Free Press.
Georgi, Dieter.
    1992    *Remembering the Poor: The History of Paul's Collection for Jerusalem*.
        Nashville: Abingdon Press.
Getty, Mary Ann.
    1983    "An Apocalyptic Perspective on Rom 10:4." *Horizons in Biblical The-
        ology* 5:79–131.
Giblin, C. H.
    1967    *The Threat to the Faith: An Exegetical and Theological Reexamination of
        2 Thessalonians 2*. Analecta Biblica 31. Rome: Pontifical Bible Institute.
Gilbert, Alan D.
    1976    *Religion and Society in Industrial England*. London: Longman.
Gilliland, Dean S.
    1983    *Pauline Theology and Mission Practice*. Grand Rapids, Mich.: Baker.
    1989a   "New Testament Contextualization: Continuity and Particularity in
        Paul's Theology." In *The Word Among Us: Contextualizing Theology for
        Mission Today*. Dean S. Gilliland, ed. Dallas, Tex: Word Publishing
        House, 52–73.
Gilliland, Dean S., ed.
    1989b   *The Word Among Us: Contextualizing Theology for Mission Today*. Dallas,
        Tex: Word Publishing House.
Glasser, Arthur F.
    1972    "Salvation Today and the Kingdom." In *Crucial Issues in Missions
        Tomorrow*, D. McGavran, ed. Chicago: Moody Press.
    1973    "Salvation—Yesterday, Tomorrow and Today." *Evangelical Missions
        Quarterly* 9 (July): 144–49.
    1974    "Bangkok: An Evangelical Evaluation." *Themelios* 10, no. 1: 26–32.
    1976    "The Missionary Task: An Introduction." In Glasser, Hiebert, Wagner,

and Winter, eds. *Crucial Dimensions in World Evangelization*. Pasadena, Calif.: William Carey Library, 3–10.

1978    "Can This Gulf Be Bridged? Reflections on the Ecumenical/Evangelical Dialogue." *Missiology: An International Review* 6, no. 3 (July): 275–82.

1979    "Conference Report on Muslim Evangelization." In *The Gospel and Islam: A 1978 Compendium*. Don McCurry, ed. Monrovia: MARC, 38–57.

1984    "Missiology." In *The Concise Evangelical Dictionary of Theology*. Walter A. Elwell, ed. Grand Rapids, Mich.: Baker Book House, 724–27.

1985    "The Evolution of Evangelical Mission Theology Since World War II." *International Bulletin of Missionary Research* 9, no. 1 (January): 9–13. This was reprinted in Harvie Conn, ed. *Practical Theology and the Ministry of the Church 1952–1984*, (Philadelphia: Presbyterian & Reformed, 1990), 235–52.

1989    "Old Testament Contextualization: Revelation and Its Environment." In *The Word Among Us: Contextualizing Theology for Mission Today*. Dean Gilliland, ed. Dallas: Word, 32–51.

1990a   *Kingdom and Mission: A Biblical Study of the Kingdom of God and the World Mission of His People*. Unpublished course syllabus. Pasadena, Calif.: Fuller Theological Seminary.

1990b   "My Pilgrimage in Mission." *International Bulletin of Missionary Research* 14, no. 3 (July): 112–15.

Glasser, Arthur F., and Donald McGavran.

1983    *Contemporary Theologies of Mission*. Grand Rapids, Mich.: Baker.

1990    *Kingdom and Mission: A Biblical View of God and the World Mission of His People*. Unpublished course syllabus. Pasadena, Calif.: Fuller Theological Seminary.

Glover, Robert.

1946    *The Bible Basis of Mission*. Los Angeles: Bible House of Los Angeles.

Gnanakan, Ken R.

1989    *Kingdom Concerns: A Biblical Exploration Toward a Theology of Mission*. Bangalore: Theological Book Trust.

1992    *The Pluralist Predicament*. Bangalore: Theological Book Trust.

Goldingay, John.

1989    "The Bible in the City." *Theology* 92, no. 745 (January): 5–15.

Goodall, Norman, ed.

1953    *Missions Under the Cross*. London: Edinburgh House; New York: Friendship.

Gort, J. D., ed.

1978    *Zeveling Op Weg Naar de toekomst, Essays Dungeboden A an Prof. J. Verkuyl*. Kampen: Kok.

Grant, Robert M.

1986    *Gods and the One God*. Philadelphia: The Westminster Press.

Greenway, Roger.

1990    "Reflections on Lausanne II." *Urban Mission* 7, no. 3 (January): 3–7.

Greenway, Roger, ed.

1976    *Guidelines for Urban Church Planting*. Grand Rapids, Mich.: Baker Book House.

Greenway, Roger, and Timothy Monsma.
1989    *Cities: Missions' New Frontier*. Grand Rapids, Mich.: Baker Book House.
Grigg, Viv.
1990    *Companion to the Poor*. Monrovia: MARC.
Gruenler, Royce Gordon.
1986    *The Trinity in the Gospel of John: A Thematic Commentary on the Fourth Gospel*. Grand Rapids, Mich.: Baker Book House.
Gulick, John.
1989    *The Humanity of Cities*. Granby, Mass.: Bergin and Garvey Publishers, Inc.
Gunton, Colin.
1985    *Enlightenment and Alienation*. Grand Rapids, Mich.: William B. Eerdmans Co..
Gutiérrez, Gustavo.
1974    *A Theology of Liberation*. Maryknoll, N.Y.: Orbis Books.
1982    "The Irruption of the Poor in Latin America." In Sergio Torres and John Eagleson, eds. *The Challenge of Basic Christian Communities*. Maryknoll, N.Y.: Orbis Books, 108.
1985a   *The Power of the Poor in History*. Maryknoll, N.Y.: Orbis Books.
1985b   *The Kairos Document—A Challenge to the Church*. Braamfontein: The Kairos Theologians.
1987    *Towards A Relevant Pentecostal Witness*. Available from P.O. Box 45244, 4012 Chatsglen, South Africa.
Haarbeck, Hermann, ed.
1957    *Flugfeuer Fremden Geistes*. Offenbach: Gnadauer Verlag.
Haarbeck, Theodor.
1956    *Die Bibel Sagt*. Werkbuch Biblischer Glaubenslehre. Giessen: Brunnen Verlag.
Haegglund, Bengt.
1968    *History of Theology*. Trans. by G. J. Lund from Swedish. Saint Louis: Concordia Publishing House, 360–77.
Hahn, Ferdinand.
1984    "Biblische Begründung der Mission." *Warum Mission?* St. Ottilien: EOS Verlag, 265–88.
Haight, Roger.
1985    *An Alternative Vision: An Interpretation of Liberation Theology*. New York: Paulist Press.
Hassey, Janette.
1986    *No Time for Silence*. Grand Rapids, Mich.: Academie Books.
Hauerwas, Stanley, and William Willimon.
1991    "Why Resident Aliens Struck a Chord." *Missiology* 19, no. 4 (October): 419–29.
Hedlund, Roger E.
1991    *The Mission of the Church in the World: A Biblical Theology*. Grand Rapids, Mich.: Baker.
Helmore, Kristin.
1985    "The Neglected Resource: Women in the Developing World." Reprint. *The Christian Science Monitor*.

Hengel, Martin.
  1983    *Between Jesus and Paul. Studies in the Earliest History of Christianity.* Trans. by John Bowden. Philadelphia: Fortress Press.
Heron, Alasdair I. C.
  1983    *The Holy Spirit.* Philadelphia: The Westminster Press.
Hick, John, and Paul Knitter, eds.
  1987    *The Myth of Christian Uniqueness.* Maryknoll, N.Y.: Orbis Books.
Hiebert, Paul.
  1978    "Conversion, Culture and Cognitive Categories." *Gospel in Context* 1, no. 3 (October): 24–29.
  1985a    "Epistemological Foundations for Science and Technology." *TSF Bulletin* (March–April): 5–10.
  1985b    "The Missiological Implications of an Epistemological Shift" *TSF Bulletin* (May–June): 12–18.
  1987    "Critical Contextualization." *International Bulletin of Missionary Research* (July), 104–11.
  1989    "Form and Meaning in Contextualization of the Gospel." In *The Word Among Us: Contextualizing Theology for Mission Today.* Dean Gilliland, ed. Dallas, Tex.: Word, 101–20.
  1991    "Beyond Anti-Colonialism to Globalism." *Missiology* 19, no. 3 (July): 263–82.
Hill, Patricia
  1985    *The World Their Household: The American Woman's Foreign Mission Movement and Cultural Transformation, 1870-1920.* Ann Arbor: University of Michigan Press.
Hobhouse, Walter.
  1911    *The Church and World in Idea and History.* London: Macmillan.
Hodges, Melvin.
  1977    *A Theology of the Church and Its Mission: A Pentecostal Perspective.* Springfield, Mo.: Gospel.
  1978    *The Indigenous Church and the Missionary.* Pasadena, Calif.: William Carey Library.
Hoekendijk, Johannes.
  1950    "The Call to Evangelism." *International Review of Missions* 39: 162–75.
  1952    "The Church in Missionary Thinking." *International Review of Missions* 41: 324–36.
  1966    *The Church Inside Out.* Philadelphia: Westminster.
Hoover, Theressa
  1983    *With Unveiled Face: Centennial Reflections on Women and Men in the Community of the Church.* New York: Women's Division, General Board of Global Ministries, the United Methodist Church.
Hunsberger, George R.
  1991    "The Newbigin Gauntlet: Developing a Domestic Missiology for North America." *Missiology* 19, no. 4 (October): 391–408
Huntemann, Georg.
  1985    *Ideologische Unterwanderung in Gemeinde, Theologie, Und Bekenntnis.* Bad Liebenzell: Verlag der Liebenzeller Mission.
Hutchison, William.
  1987    *Errand to the World: American Protestant Thought and Foreign Missions.* Chicago: University of Chicago Press.

Ikenga-Metuh, Emefie.
1989    "Contextualization: A Missiological Imperative for the Church in Africa in the Third Millennium." *Mission Studies* 12, vol. 2: 3–16.
*International Bulletin of Missionary Research*
1989    "The Truth of Christian Uniqueness." *International Bulletin of Missionary Research* 13, no. 2 (April): 49.
International Missionary Council.
1939    "The Place of the Church in Evangelism." *The World Mission of the Church*. Findings and Recommendations of the International Missionary Council, Tambaram, Madras, India, December 1938. London & New York: IMC.
Jensen, Evelyn.
1990    "Women in Ministry and Mission." *World Christian*: Summer Reader.
Jewett, Robert.
1986a    *The Thessalonian Correspondence: Pauline Rhetoric and Millenarian Piety*. Philadelphia: Fortress Press.
1986b    "The Law and the Coexistence of the Jews and Gentiles in Romans." *Interpretation* 39:xiii, 93f.
John Paul II, Pope.
1986    *Dominum et Vivificantem (DeV)*. Vatican City: Vatican Polyglot Press.
1986    *Lumen Vitae*. World Mission Day Message, October 1985, XLI:3, 246.
Jones, E. Stanley.
1972    *The Unshakable Kingdom and the Unchanging Person*. Nashville: Abingdon Press.
Judge, E. A.
1974    "St. Paul as a Radical Critic of Society." In *Interchange* no. 16. Sidney, Australia: AFES, 191.
Kallas, James.
1966    *The Satanward View—A Study in Pauline Theology*. Philadelphia: The Westminster Press, pp. 133–52.
Karamaga, André.
1990    *L'Evangile en Afrique: Ruptures et continuité*. Yens/Morges, Switzerland: Editions Cabédita.
Karp, David, Gregory Stone, and William Yoels.
1991    *Being Urban: A Sociology of City Life*. New York: Praeger Publications.
Käsemann, Ernst.
1980    *Commentary on Romans*. Trans. from the German by G. W. Bromiley. Grand Rapids, Mich.: Eerdmans.
Keck, Leander E.
1984    "Paul and Apocalyptic Theology." *Interpretation* 38:229–41.
Kelsey, D. H.
1975    *The Uses of Scripture in Recent Theology*. Philadelphia: Fortress.
Kemper, Robert.
1991    "Trends in Urban Anthropological Research." *Urban Anthropology* 20, no. 4 (Winter): 383.
Kerr, David A.
1991    "Come Holy Spirit—Renew the Whole Creation": The Canberra Assembly and Issues of Mission. *International Bulletin of Missionary Research* 15: 98–103.

Kirk, Andrew.
  1987    *God's Word for a Complex World: Discovering How the Bible Speaks Today.* London: Marshall Pickering.
Kline, Meredeth.
  1983    *Kingdom Prologue, Vol. II.* Class syllabus printed privately by the author.
Knitter, Paul.
  1985    *No Other Name?* Maryknoll, N.Y.: Orbis Books.
Knox, John.
  1964    "Romans 15:14–33 and Paul's Conception of His Apostolic Mission." *Journal of Biblical Literature* 83: 1-11.
Kraft, Charles.
  1989    *Christianity with Power.* Ann Arbor, Mich.: Servant Publications.
Kramm, Thomas.
  1979    *Analyse und Bewährung theologischer Modelle zur Begründung der Mission: Entscheidungskriterien in der aktuellen Auseinandersetzung zwischen einem heilgeschichtlich-ekklesiologischen und einem geschichtlich-eschatologischen Missions verständnis.* Aachen: missio aktuell Verlag GmbH.
Kroeger, Catherine C.
  1979    "Ancient Heresies and a Strange Greek Verb." *The Reformed Journal* 29, no. 3 (March): 12–15.
Kroeger, Catherine, and Richard Kroeger.
  1981    "Women Elders–Sinners or Servants?" New York: Council of Women and the Church, The United Presbyterian Church, U.S.A.
  1992    *I Suffer Not a Woman.* Grand Rapids, Mich.: Baker Book House.
Krupat, Edward.
  1985    *People in Cities: the Urban Environment and Its Effects.* Cambridge: Cambridge University Press.
Kuhn, Thomas S.
  1962    *The Structure of Scientific Revolutions.* Chicago: University of Chicago Press.
  1977    *The Essential Tension: Selected Studies in Scientific Tradition and Change.* Chicago: University of Chicago Press.
Küng, Hans.
  1971    *The Church.* London: Search Press.
Küng, Hans, and David Tracy, eds.
  1989    *Paradigm Change in Theology.* New York: Crossroad.
Ladd, George Eldon.
  1952    *Crucial Questions About the Kingdom of God.* Grand Rapids, Mich.: Eerdmans.
  1959    *The Gospel of the Kingdom: Scriptural Studies in the Kingdom of God.* Grand Rapids, Mich.: Eerdmans.
  1964    *Jesus and the Kingdom: The Eschatology of Biblical Realism.* Waco, Tex.: Word Books.
  1974a   *A Theology of the New Testament.* Grand Rapids, Mich.: Eerdmans.
  1974b   *The Presence of the Future: The Eschatology of Biblical Realism.* Grand Rapids, Mich.: Eerdmans.
Lakatos, Imre.
  1978    "Falsification and Methodology of Scientific Research Programmes." In *The Methodology of Scientific Research Programmes.* Philosophical

Papers, vol. I. John Worrall and Gregory Currie, eds. Cambridge: Cambridge University Press, 8–10.

Lange, Dieter.
1979     *Eine Bewgung Bricht Sich Bahn*. Giessen: Brunnen Verlag.

LaRondelle, Hans K.
1983     "Paul's Prophetic Outline in 2 Thessalonians 2." *Andrews University Seminary Studies* 21:61–119.

Latin America.
1992     Special issue on "Columbus and the New World: Evangelization or Invasion." *Missiology* 20, no. 2 (April).

Lausanne Covenant, The, section 5.
1975     *Let the Earth Hear His Voice*. Minneapolis, Minn.: World Wide Publications.

Lausanne II in Manila, 1989.
1990     *Proclaim Christ Until He Comes: Calling the Whole Church to Take the Whole Gospel to the Whole World*. ICOWE, 1989. Minneapolis: World Wide Publications.

Laverdiere, E.
1991     "Redemptoris Missio: An Introduction and Brief Presentation." *Omnis Terra*, no. 221 (September–October): 372–87.

Leenhardt, Franz J.
1961     *The Epistle to the Romans. A Commentary*. London: Lutterworth Press.

Lewis, C.S.
1952     *The Chronicles of Narnia*. New York: Macmillan.

Lewis, Gordon.
1964     "Mission to The Athenians Part IV: The Response of Athens and the Christian Mission." *Seminary Study Series*. Denver, Colo.: Denver Seminary, 1–9.

Liebow, Eliot.
1967     *Tally's Corner*. Boston: Little, Brown & Co.

Liégé, P. A.
1956     "Encyclique." In G. Jacquemet, ed. *Catholicisme: Hier, Aujourd'hui, Demain*. Vol. IV. Paris: Lehouzey et Ané.

Linthicum, Robert C.
1991     *City of God, City of Satan: A Biblical Theology of the Urban Church*. Grand Rapids, Mich.: Zondervan.

Love, Richard D., II.
1992     "The Theology of the Kingdom of God: A Model for Contextualization and Holistic Evangelism Among the Sundanese, with Special Reference to the Spirit Realm." Unpublished D.Min. project. Westminster Theological Seminary.

Luetgert, Wilhelm.
1984     *Schoepfung und Offenbarung*. Giessen: Brunnen Verlag.

Luke, P. Y., and J. Carman.
1968     *Village Christians and Hindu Culture: Study of a Rural Church in Andhra Pradesh, South India*. London: Lutterworth Press.

Luneau, Rene, with Paul Ladriere, eds.
1989     *Le Reve de Compostelle: Vers la Restauration d'une Europe Chretienne?* Paris: Centurion.

McBride, Martha C.
  1990    "Autonomy and the Struggle for Female Identity: Implications for
          Counseling Women." *Journal of Counseling and Development* 69: 22–
          26.
Macdonell, R. W.
  1928    *Belle Harris Bennett: Her Life and Work.* Nashville: Board of Missions,
          Methodist Episcopal Church, South.
McGavran, Donald A.
  1980    *Understanding Church Growth.* Rev. ed. Grand Rapids, Mich.: William
          B. Eerdmans Publishing Company.
McGrath, Alister.
  1988    *Understanding the Trinity.* Grand Rapids, Mich.: Zondervan Publishing
          House.
Mackay, John A.
  1928    "The Power of Evangelism." *Addresses and Other Records.* Report of
          the Jerusalem Meeting of the International Missionary Council, March
          24–April 8, 1928. Vol. 8. Humphrey Milford: Oxford University Press.
  1942    *A Preface to Christian Theology.* London: Nisbet.
McLeod, Hugh.
  1980    "The Dechristianisation of the Working Class in Western Europe
          (1950–1900)." *Social Compass* 27:2–3.
  1981    *Religion and the People of Western Europe, 1789–1970.* London: Oxford
          University Press.
McQuilkin, J. Robertson.
  1989    *An Introduction to Biblical Ethics.* Wheaton, Ill.: Tyndale House.
Magalit, Isabelo.
  1979    "The Messenger's Qualifications." Urbana Missionary Convention,
          Urbana, Illinois, December.
Maggay, Melba.
  1989    "Theology, Context, and the Filipino Church." In *Communicating
          Cross-Culturally: Towards a New Context for Missions in the Philippines.*
          Quezon City, Philippines: New Day Publishers.
  1991    "Christian Literature and Society in the 1990s," *Evangelical Review of
          Theology* 15: 201.
Marshall, I. H.
  1977    "Kingdom of God, Of Heaven." *The Zondervan Pictorial Encyclopedia
          of the Bible.* Vol. 3. Grand Rapids, Mich.: Zondervan.
Martin, David.
  1990a   "The Hidden Fire." Interview by Tim Stafford. *Christianity Today*, May
          14, 23–26.
  1990b   *Tongues of Fire.* London: Blackwell.
Martin, Ralph P.
  1982    *The Worship of God: Some Theological, Pastoral, and Practical Reflec-
          tions.* Grand Rapids, Mich.: Wm. B. Eerdmans Publishing Company.
Marty, Martin E.
  1969    *The Modern Schism: Three Paths to the Secular.* New York: Harper and
          Row.
Marty, Martin E., and Fred Greenspahn, eds.
  1988    *Pushing the Faith: Proselytism and Civility in a Pluralistic World.* New
          York: Crossroad.

Matheny, Tim.
1981      *Reaching the Arabs: A Felt Need Approach*. Pasadena, Calif.: William
          Carey Library.
Mazrui, Ali A.
1990      *Cultural Forces in World Politics*. London: James Currey Ltd.
Mbembe, Achille.
1988      *Afriques indociles*. Paris: Editions Karthala.
Mearns, Christopher.
1981      "Early Eschatological Development in Paul. The Evidence of 1 and 2
          Thessalonians." *New Testament Studies* 27:137–57.
Meeking, Basil.
1984      "After Vatican II." *International Review of Mission* 73: 57–65.
Meeking, Basil, and John Stott, eds.
1986      *The Evangelical-Roman Catholic Dialogue on Missions, 1977-84—A
          Report*. Grand Rapids, Mich.: Eerdmans.
Messer, Donald E.
1992      *A Conspiracy of Goodness: Contemporary Images of Christian Mission*.
          Nashville: Abingdon.
Michaelis, Wilhelm.
1968      "prōton." In *Theological Dictionary of the New Testament*, vol. 6. Ed. by
          G. Friedrich and trans. by G. W. Bromiley from the German edition.
          Grand Rapids, Mich.: Eerdmans, 868–70.
Mickelsen, Alvera, ed.
1986      *Women, Authority and the Bible*. Downers Grove, Ill.: InterVarsity Press.
Míguez Bonino, José.
1975      *Doing Theology in a Revolutionary Situation*. Philadelphia: Fortress.
Milton, John.
1958      "On the Morning of Christ's Nativity." In Robert Pratt, et al. eds.
          *Masters of British Literature*. Boston: Houghton Mifflin Co.
Minear, Paul.
1971      *The Obedience of Faith: The Purpose of Paul in the Epistle to the Romans*.
          London: SCM Press.
*Missionary Obligation of the Church, The.*
1952      Willingen, Germany. London: Edinburgh House Press.
"Missio Dei."
1971      *Concise Dictionary of the Christian World Mission*. S. C. Neill, et al., eds.
          Nashville: Abingdon, 387.
1991      *Dictionary of the Ecumenical Movement*. N. Lossky, et al., eds. Geneva:
          WCC, 687–89.
Moltmann, Jürgen.
1977      *The Church in the Power of the Spirit*. London: SCM.
1981      *The Trinity and the Kingdom: The Doctrine of God*. New York: Harper
          & Row Publishers.
1991      *Der Geist des Lebens: Eine Ganzheitliche Pneumatologie*. Muenchen:
          Chr. Kaiser Verlag.
Montefiore, Hugh, ed.
1992      *The Gospel and Contemporary Culture*. London: Mowbray.
Montgomery, Helen Barrett.
1910      *Western Women in Eastern Lands: An Outline Study of Fifty Years of
          Woman's Worth in Foreign Missions*. New York: MacMillan.

Morris, Leon.
  1971    *Commentary on the Gospel of John*. Grand Rapids, Mich.: Eerdmans.
  1988    *The Epistle to the Romans*. Leicester: InterVarsity Press.
Mott, John R.
  1946    *The Student Volunteer Movement for Foreign Missions*. Addresses and
           Papers of John R. Mott. New York: Association Press.
Motte, Mary.
  1991    "The Poor: Starting Point for Mission." In Gerald Anderson, James
           Phillips, and Robert Coote eds. *Mission in the 1990s*. Grand Rapids,
           Mich.: Eerdmans, 50–54.
Mueller-Vollmer, Kurt, ed.
  1989    *The Hermeneutics Reader*. New York: Continuum.
Mugambi, J. N. K.
  1991    "The Future of the Church and the Church of the Future in Africa."
           In *The Church of Africa: Towards a Theology of Reconstruction*. José B.
           Chipenda, et al., eds. Nairobi: All-Africa Conference of Churches.
Müller, K.
  1987    *Mission Theology: An Introduction*. Sankt Augustin, Germany: Steyler
           Verlag.
Muller, Richard A.
  1991    *The Study of Theology: From Biblical Interpretation to Contemporary For-
           mulation*. Grand Rapids, Mich.: Zondervan.
Murphy, Nancey.
  1990    *Theology in the Age of Scientific Reasoning*. Ithaca, N.Y.: Cornell Uni-
           versity Press.
Mushete, A. Ngindu.
  1989    *Les thèmes majeurs de la théologie africaine*. Paris: Editions L'Harmat-
           tan.
Mutiso-Mbinda, John.
  1991    *Mission and Unity*: Perspectives From the WCC Seventh Assembly in
           Canberra. Unpublished.
Myers, Bryant.
  1992    "A Funny Thing Happened on the Way to Evangelical Ecumenical
           Cooperation." *Missiology* 81, no. 323 (July): 397–407.
NCCC/DOM.
  1983    *Mission and Evangelism: An Ecumenical Affirmation*. New York: NCCC.
Neill, Stephen S.
  1976    *Salvation Tomorrow*. Nashville: Abingdon.
  1984    "How My Mind Has Changed About Mission." Video recording pro-
           duced by Overseas Ministries Study Center. Cited in Charles Van
           Engen, *God's Missionary People: Rethinking the Purpose of the Local
           Church* (Grand Rapids, Mich.: Baker, 1991), 27.
Netland, Harold.
  1987    "Exclusivism, Tolerance and Truth." *Missiology* 15 (2):77–95.
  1988    "Toward Contextualized Apologetics." *Missiology* 16 (3):289–304.
  1991    *Dissonant Voices, Religious Pluralism and the Question of Faith*. Grand
           Rapids, Mich.:William B. Eerdmans Publishing Company.
Newbigin, Lesslie.
  1958    *One Body, One Gospel, One World: The Christian Mission Today*. London
           and New York: International Missionary Council.

1963    *The Relevance of a Trinitarian Doctrine for Today's Mission*. London: Edinburgh House.

1964    *Trinitarian Faith and Today's Mission*. Richmond, Va.: John Knox Press.

1969    *The Finality of Christ*. Richmond,Va.: John Knox Press.

1977    *The Good Shepherd: Meditations on Christian Ministry in Today's World*. Grand Rapids, Mich.: Eerdmans.

1978    *The Open Secret: Sketches for a Missionary Theology*.Grand Rapids, Mich.: William B. Eerdmans Publishing Company.

1983    *The Other Side of 1984*. Grand Rapids, Mich.: William B. Eerdmans Co.

1986    *Foolishness to the Greeks: The Gospel and Western Culture*. Geneva: World Council of Churches.

1988    "A Sermon Preached at the Thanksgiving Service for the Fiftieth Anniversary of the Tambaram Conference of the International Missionary Council. *Missiology* 78 (July): 325–331.

1989a   *The Gospel and Pluralist Society*. Grand Rapids, Mich.: William B. Eerdmans Co.

1989b   "Religious Pluralism and the Uniqueness of Jesus Christ." *International Bulletin of Missionary Research* 13, no. 2 (April): 50–55.

1991    *Truth to Tell*. Grand Rapids, Mich.: William B. Eerdmans Co.

Niebuhr, H. Richard.

1951    *Christ and Culture*. New York: Harper and Row.

Nyquist, J. W.

1991    "The Uses of the New Testament as Illustrated in Missiological Themes Within Selected Documents of the Second Vatican Council." Unpublished D. Miss. Dissertation. Trinity Evangelical Divinity School, Deerfield, Ill.

Oberman, Heiko A.

1984    "Thesen zur Zwei-Reiche-Lehre." *Luther und die Politische Welt*. Historische Forschungen, Band 9. Stuttgart: Franz Steiner Verlag Wiesbaden GMBH, 27–34.

Oforo, Justin.

1990    Unpublished manuscript. Vancouver, B.C.: Regent College.

Ohlemacher, Joerg.

1986    *Das Reich Gottes in Deutschland Bauen* — Ein Beitrag zur Vorgeschichte und Theologie der Deutschen Gemeinschaftsbewegung. *Arbeiten zur Geschichte des Pietismus*, Band 23. Goettingen: Vandenhoeck & Ruprecht.

Oliver, Roland.

1956    *How Christian is Africa?* London: The Highway Press.

Orchard, R. K., ed.

1958    *The Ghana Assembly of the IMC*, Accra, Ghana, 1958. London.

1964    *Witness in Six Continents: Records of the CWME of the WCC*, Mexico City, 1963. London: Edinburgh House Press.

Otto, Rudolf.

1938    *The Kingdom of God and the Son of Man*. Trans. F. V. Filson and B. Lee Woolf. London: Lutherworth Press.

Packer, J. I.

1984    *Keep in Step with the Spirit*. Old Tappan, N.J.: Fleming H. Revell Company.

Padilla, C. Rene.
  1980    "Hermeneutics and Culture—A Theological Perspective." In John R.
          W. Stott and Robert Coote, eds. *Down to Earth: Studies in Christianity
          and Culture*. Grand Rapids, Mich.: Eerdmans.
  1982    "The Unity of the Church and the Homogenous Unit Principle." *Mis-
          sion Between the Times: Essays on the Kingdom*. Grand Rapids, Mich.:
          Eerdmans Publishing Co.
  1985    *Mission Between the Times: Essays on the Kingdom*. Grand Rapids,
          Mich.: Eerdmans.
  1992    "Wholistic Mission: Evangelical and Ecumenical." *Missiology* 81, no.
          323 (July): 381–82.
Padilla, C. Rene, et al.
  1975    *El Reino de Dios y America Latina*. El Paso: Casa Bautista de Publi-
          caciones.
Palen, J. John.
  1987    *The Urban World, 3rd ed*. New York: McGraw-Hill Book Company.
Pannell, William.
  1992    *Evangelism from the Bottom Up*. Grand Rapids, Mich.: Zondervan Pub-
          lishing House.
Pannenberg, Wolfhart.
  1969    *Theology and the Kingdom of God*. Philadelphia: Westminster.
Pasquariello, Ronald, et al.
  1982    *Redeeming the City*. New York: Pilgrim Press.
Paul VI.
  1975    *Evangelii Nuntiandi*. Washington, D.C.: U.S. Catholic Conference.
Pénoukou, Efoé-Julien.
  1984    *Eglises d'Afrique: propositions pour l'avenir*. Paris: Editions Karthala.
Pentecost, Edward C.
  1982    *Issues in Missiology: An Introduction*. Grand Rapids, Mich.: Baker.
Pentecost, J. Dwight.
  1964    *Things to Come*. Grand Rapids, Mich.: Zondervan.
Peters, George W.
  1981    *A Theology of Church Growth*. Grand Rapids, Mich.: Zondervan.
Pflaum, Lienhard.
  1988    "Gnadau und die Aeussere Mission." *Dem Auftrag Verpflichtet—Die
          Gnadauer Gemeinschaftsbewegung*. Dillenburg: Gnadauer Verlag.
Philbert, Bernhard.
  1970    *Der Dreieine: Anfang und Sein—Struktur der Schoepfung*. Stein: Chris-
          tiana-Verlag.
Pinnock, Clark.
  1991    *A Wideness in God's Mercy*. Grand Rapids, Mich.: Zondervan.
Plantinga, Cornelius.
  1982    The Hodgson-Welch Debate and the Social Analogy of the Trinity.
          Unpublished Ph.D. dissertation. Princeton Theological Seminary.
  1988    "The Threeness/Oneness Problem of the Trinity." *Calvin Theological
          Journal* 23(1):37–53.
  1989    "Social Trinity and Tritheism." *Trinity, Incarnation, and Atonement*.
          Library of Religious Studies. Notre Dame, Ind.: University of Notre
          Dame Press.
Pollock, John.
  1977    *Wilberforce*. London: Lion Publishing.

Pomerville, Paul A.
  1985     *The Third Force in Mission: A Pentecostal Contribution to Contemporary Mission Theology*. Peabody, Mass.: Hendrickson.
Pontifical Council for Interreligious Dialogue and Congregation for the Evangelization of Peoples.
  1991     "Dialogue and Proclamation." *Origins* 21, no. 8 (July 4): 121–35.
Press, Irwin, and Estellie Smith, eds.
  1980     *Urban Place and Process*. New York: Macmillan.
Ramsay, Richard B.
  1992     "A Vision for Church Growth in Chile: A Study of Growth Factors in Protestant Churches in Chile, with an Analysis of the Relationship between Numerical Growth and Integral Ministry." Unpublished D.Min. project, Westminster Theological Seminary.
Ranson, C. W., ed.
  1948     *Renewal and Advance: Christian Witness in a Revolutionary World*. London: Edinburg House, 1948.
Read, William R., Victor M. Monterroso, and Harmon A. Johnson.
  1969     *Latin American Church Growth*. Grand Rapids, Mich.: William B. Eerdmans Publishing Company.
*Redemptoris Missio* (RM).
  1990     *Pope John Paul II. Encyclical Letter on the Permanent Validity of the Church's Missionary Mandate*. Washington, D. C.: United States Catholic Conference. Also published in *Catholic International* 2 (1991): 252–92.
Renard, Pierre.
  1986     "Cardinal Suhard and the New Evangelization: A Review Essay." *Lumen Vitae*, XLI:3.
Richardson, Don.
  1984     *Eternity in Their Hearts*. Ventura, Calif.: Regal.
Ridderbos, Herman.
  1962     *The Coming of the Kingdom*. Philadelphia: Presbyterian and Reformed.
  1975     *Paul: An Outline of His Theology*. Trans. J. R. DeWitt. Grand Rapids, Mich.: Eerdmans.
Rienecker, Fritz.
  1952     *Biblische Kritik am Pietismus Alter und Neuer Zeit*. Offenbach am Main: Gnadauer Verlag.
Ro, Bong Rin.
  1984     *The Bible and Theology in Asian Contexts*. Taichung, Taiwan: Asia Theological Association.
Rohrbaugh, Richard L.
  1991     "The City in the Second Testament." *Biblical Theology Bulletin* 21(2), Summer: 71.
Roth, Joel, and Robert Gordis.
  1982     "*Keruv* and the Status of Intermarried Families." *Conservative Judaism* 35(4), Summer: 50–55.
Rowley, H. H.
  1955     *The Missionary Message of the Old Testament*. London: The Carey Kingsgate Press.

Ryrie, Charles Caldwell.
  1965    *Dispensationalism Today*. Chicago: Moody Press.
Saayman, Willem.
  1990    "Bridging the Gulf: David Bosch and the Ecumenical/Evangelical
           Polarisation." *Missionalia* 18, no. 1 (April): 99–108.
  1992    "Biblical Insights on New Creation and Mission in Power and Faith."
           Unpublished paper read at the International Association for Mission
           Studies meeting in Hawaii, August.
Samuel, Vinay, and Chris Sugden, eds.
  1983a   *Sharing Jesus in the Two-Thirds World: Evangelical Christologies from the
           Contexts of Poverty, Powerlessness, and Religious Pluralism*. Bangalore:
           Partnership in Mission—Asia.
  1983b   *The Church in Response to Human Need*. Grand Rapids, Mich.: Eerd-
           mans.
  1987    *The Church in Response to Human Need: The Wheaton 1983 Consulta-
           tion*. Grand Rapids, Mich.: Eerdmans. Oxford: Regnum.
Sanders, E. P.
  1983    *Paul, the Law, and the Jewish People*. Philadelphia: Fortress Press.
Sanders, John.
  1992    *No Other Name*. Grand Rapids, Mich.: William B. Eerdmans Publishing
           Company.
Sanneh, Lamin.
  1989    *Translating the Message: The Missionary Impact on Culture*. Maryknoll,
           N.Y.: Orbis Books.
Sauberzweig, Hans von.
  1959    *Er Der Meister Wir Die Brueder*. Geschichte der Gnadauer Gemein-
           schaftsbewegung 1888–1958. Offenbach: Gnadauer Verlag.
Scherer, James A., and Stephen Bevans.
  1987    *Gospel, Church, & Kingdom: Comparative Studies in World Mission The-
           ology*. Minneapolis, Minn.: Augsburg.
  1992b   "Mission Statements: How They Are Developed and What They Tell
           Us." *International Bulletin of Missionary Research* 16, no. 3 (July): 98-
           104.
Scherer, James A., and Stephen Bevans, eds.
  1992a   *New Directions in Mission and Evangelization 1: Basic Statements 1979*.
           Maryknoll, N.Y.: Orbis Books.
Schmemann, Alexander.
  1961    "The Missionary Imperative in the Orthodox Tradition." In G. H.
           Anderson, ed. *The Theology of Christian Mission*. New York: McGraw-
           Hill, 250–57.
  1979    *Church, World, Mission: Reflections on Orthodoxy in the West*. Crestwood,
           N.J.: St. Vladimir's Seminary Press.
Schmidt, Karl Ludwig.
  1964    In *Theological Dictionary of the New Testament, Vol. 1*. Gerhard Kittel,
           ed. Geoffrey W. Bromiley, trans. and ed. Grand Rapids, Mich.: Eerd-
           mans.
Schmidt, Martin.
  1984    *Der Pietismus als Theologische Erscheinung Arbeiten zur Geschichte Des-
           pietismus*, Band 20. Goettingen: Vandenhoeck & Ruprecht.

Schneider, E. E.
   1963      "Mysterium Iniquitis." *Theologische Zeitschrift* 19:113–25.
Schoeps, H. J.
   1961      *The Theology of the Apostle Paul in the Light of Jewish Religious History*.
             Trans. H. Knight. Philadelphia: Westminster Press.
Scholer, David.
   1983/84   "Women in Ministry." In *The Covenant Companion*, vols. 72 and 73.
   1986      "I Timothy 2:9–15 and the Place of Women in the Church's Ministry."
             In A. Mickelsen, ed. *Women, Authority and the Bible*. Downers Grove,
             Ill.: InterVarsity Press.
Schreiter, Robert J.
   1985      *Constructing Local Theologies*. London: SCM Press; Maryknoll, N.Y.:
             Orbis Books.
   1992a     *Reconciliation: Mission and Ministry in a Changing Social Order*. The
             Boston Theological Institute Series. Vol. 3. Maryknoll, N.Y.: Orbis
             Books.
   1992b     "Reconciliation as a Missionary Task." *Missiology* 20, no. 1 (January):
             3–10.
Schwarz, Gerold.
   1980      *Mission, Gemeinde und Oekumene in der Theologie Karl Hartenstein*.
             Stuttgart: Calwer Verlag.
Scott, James C.
   1985      *Weapons of the Weak: Everyday Forms of Peasant Resistance*. New
             Haven, Conn.: Yale University Press.
Sege, Irene.
   1992      "The grim mystery of world's missing women." *Boston Globe*, February
             3, 23, 25.
Segundo, Juan Luis.
   1976      *The Liberation of Theology*. Maryknoll, N.Y.: Orbis Books.
Senior, Donald, and Carroll Stuhlmueller.
   1983      *The Biblical Foundations of Mission*. Maryknoll, N.Y.: Orbis Books.
Shaw, R. Daniel.
   1988      *Transculturation: The Cultural Factors in Translation and Other Com-
             munication Tasks*. Pasadena, Calif.: William Carey Library.
Shenk, Wilbert.
   1983      *Henry Venn — Missionary Statesman*. ASM Series No. 6. Maryknoll, N.Y.:
             Orbis Books.
   1991      "Missionary Encounter With Culture." *International Bulletin of Mis-
             sionary Research* 15: 104–9.
Shih, Vincent Y. C.
   1967      *The Taiping Ideology*. Seattle: University of Washington.
Shorter, Aylward.
   1991      *The Church in the African City*. Maryknoll, N.Y.: Orbis Books.
Showers, Renald E.
   1990      *There Really Is a Difference! A Comparison of Covenant and Dispensa-
             tional Theology*. Bellmawr, N.J.: The Friends of Israel Gospel Ministry.
Siegel, Seymour.
   1982      "Comments on the Statement '*Keruv* and the Status of Intermarried
             Families'." *Conservative Judaism* 35(4), Summer: 56–58.

Sinclair, Maurice.
   1988      *Ripening Harvest: Gathering Storm*. Monrovia, Calif.: MARC, 20.
Sivard, Ruth Leger.
   1985      *Women . . . A World Survey*. Washington, D.C.: World Priorities.
Smedes, Lewis B., ed.
   1987      *Ministry and the Miraculous*. Pasadena, Calif.: Fuller Theological Sem-
            inary.
Smith, Fred.
   1992      "Encounter with God: the Guayaquil Model." *Urban Mission* 9, no. 3
            (January): 6-13.
Smith, Wilfred Cantwell.
   1972      *The Faith of Other Men*. 1963. New York: Harper Torchbook.
   1981      "An Attempt at Summation." In Anderson and Stransky, eds. *Faith
            Meets Faith*. Mission Trends No. 5. Grand Rapids, Mich.: William B.
            Eerdmans Publishing Company.
Sookhdeo, Patrick, ed.
   1978      *Jesus Christ The Only Way*. Exeter: Paternoster Press.
Soper, Edmund Davison.
   1943      *The Philosophy of the Christian World Mission*. Nashville: Abingdon-
            Cokesbury Press.
Spindler, Marc R.
   1987      "Europe's Neo-Paganism: A Perverse Inculturation." *International Bul-
            letin of Missionary Research* 11:1 (January): 8-11.
Stackhouse, Max L.
   1972      *Ethics and the Urban Ethos*. Boston: Beacon Press.
   1988      "Contextualization, Contextuality, and Contextualism." *One Faith,
            Many Cultures*. Ruy O. Costa, ed. Maryknoll, N.Y.: Orbis Books; Cam-
            bridge, Mass.: Boston Theological Institute.
Stair, Tim, ed.
   1988      *Urban Task Force Report: Surveys and Profiles of Urban Mennonite Con-
            gregations*. Inter-Mennonite Home Ministries Council.
Stendahl, Krister.
   1977      *Paul Among Jews and Gentiles*. London: SCM.
Stoeffler, Ernst F.
   1965      *The Rise of Evangelical Pietism*. Leiden: E. J. Brill.
Stott, John.
   1975a     *The Lausanne Covenant: An Exposition and Commentary*. Wheaton, Ill.:
            Lausanne Committee on World Evangelization.
   1975b     *Christian Mission in the Modern World*. Downers Grove, Ill.: Inter-
            Varsity.
Stott, John R., and Robert Coote, eds.
   1980      *Down to Earth: Studies in Christianity and Culture*. Grand Rapids, Mich.:
            Wm. B. Eerdmans Pub. Company.
Strack, Hermann L. and Paul Billerbeck
   1924      *Kommentar zum Neuen Testament aus Talmud und Midrasch*. Vol. II,
            588ff., Vol. III, 640ff. Mhunchen: Beck.
Stransky, Thomas.
   1991      Evangelical-Roman Catholic Dialogue on Mission. *Dictionary of the
            Ecumenical Movement*. Geneva: World Council of Churches.

Stravinskas, P. M. J., ed.
1991      "Encyclical." *Our Sunday Visitor's Catholic Encyclopedia*. Huntington, Ind.: Our Sunday Visitor Press, 353.
Sundkler, Bengt.
1965      *The World of Mission*. Grand Rapids, Mich.: Eerdmans.
Suttles, Gerald.
1968      *The Social Order of the Slum*. Chicago: University of Chicago Press.
Taber, Charles R., and Betty J. Taber
1992      "A Christian Understanding of 'Religion' and 'the Religions.' " *Missiology* 20 (1):69–78.
Taylor, Debbie, et al.
1985      *Women: A World Report*. New York: Oxford University Press.
Thelle, Notte R.
1987      *Buddhism and Christianity in Japan: From Conflict to Dialogue, 1854–99*. Honolulu: University of Hawaii Press.
Tippett, Allen R.
1967      *Solomon Islands Christianity*. London: Lutterworth.
Tomko, J.
1991      "Proclaiming Christ the World's Only Savior." *Osservatore Romano*. English Weekly Edition (April 15): 4.
Toulmin, Stephen.
1977      "The Structure of Scientific Theories." In *The Structure of Scientific Theories*, F. Suppe. ed. Champaign, Ill.: University of Illinois Press, 600–14.
Towns, Elmer.
1990      *Ten of Today's Most Innovative Churches*. Ventura, Calif.: Regal Books.
Townsend, John T.
1980      "II Thessalonians 2:3–12." In *Society of Biblical Literature 1980 Seminar Papers*. Paul Achtemeier, ed. Chico: Scholar's Press, 233–51.
*Tractate Avoth*.
1964      Philip Blackman, ed. New York: The Judaica Press.
Tucker, Ruth A.
1988      *Guardians of the Great Commission*. Grand Rapids, Mich.: Academie Books.
Tucker, Ruth, and Walter Liefeld.
1987      *Daughters of the Church: Women and Ministry from New Testament Times to the Present*. Grand Rapids, Mich.: Zondervan Publishing House.
Ukpong, Justin S.
1992      "Christian Mission and the Recreation of the Earth in Power and Faith: A Biblical Christological Perspective." Unpublished paper delivered at the International Association for Mission Studies meeting in Hawaii, August.
U.S. Catholic Mission Association/Division of Overseas Ministries National Conference of Churches of Christ (USCMA/DOM-NCCC).
1987      Divided Churches/Common Witness: An Unfinished Task for U. S. Christians in Mission. Offset.
Van Engen, Charles.
1981      *The Growth of the True Church. An Analysis of Church Growth Theory*. Amsterdam: Rodopi.

1987    "Responses to James Scherer's Paper from Different Disciplinary Perspectives: Systematic Theology." *Missiology* 15, no. 4 (October): 524–25.

1989    "The New Covenant: Knowing God in Context." In Dean Gilliland, ed. *The Word Among Us*. Dallas, Tex.: Word, 74–100.

1990    "A Broadening Vision: Forty Years of Evangelical Theology of Mission, 1946–1986." In Joel Carpenter and Wilbert Shenk, eds. *Earthen Vessels: American Evangelicals and Foreign Mission, 1880–1980*. Grand Rapids, Mich.: Eerdmans, 203–4.

1991a   *God's Missionary People: Rethinking the Purpose of the Local Church*. Grand Rapids, Mich.: Baker.

1991b   "The Effect of Universalism on Mission Effort." In William Crockett and James Sigountos, eds. *Through No Fault of Their Own: The Fate of Those Who Never Heard*. Grand Rapids, Mich.: Baker, 183–94.

Van Leeuwen, Mary Stewart.

1986    "The Christian Mind and the Challenge of Gender Relations." *The Reformed Journal* 37 (September): 17–23.

1988    "Christian Maturity in Light of Feminist Theory." *Psychology and Theology* 16, no. 2 (Summer): 168–82.

1990    *Gender and Grace*. Downers Grove, Ill.: InterVarsity Press.

Van Rheenen, Gailyn.

1983    *Biblical Anchored Mission: Perspectives on Church Growth*. Austin, Tex.: Firm Foundation Pub.

Verdesi, Elizabeth Howell.

1973    In *But Still Out: Women in the Church*. Philadelphia: Westminster.

Verkuyl, Johannes.

1978    *Contemporary Missiology: An Introduction*. Dale Cooper, trans. and ed. Grand Rapids, Mich.: William B. Eerdmans.

1989    "Mission in the 1990s." *International Bulletin of Missionary Research* 13, no. 2: 55–58.

Vicedom, Georg F.

1965    *The Mission of God: An Introduction to the Theology of Mission*. G. A. Thiele and D. Hilgendorf, trans. St. Louis: Concordia Publishing House, from German original (1957).

1975    *Actio Dei–Mission und Reich Gottes*. Muenchen: Chr. Kaiser Verlag.

Visser 't Hooft, W. A.

1963    *No Other Name*. Philadelphia: Westminster Press.

1974    "Evangelism in the Neo-Pagan Situation." *International Review of Mission* vol. 63, no. 249 (January): 81-86.

1977    "Evangelism among Europe's Neo-Pagans." *International Review of Mission* vol. 66, no. 264 (October): 349-60.

Vos, Geerhardus.

1949    *The Pauline Eschatology*. Princeton, N.J.: Princeton University Press.

Wagner, C. Peter.

1987    *Strategies for Church Growth: Tools for Effective Mission and Evangelism*. Ventura, Calif.: Regal.

1988a     *How to Have a Healing Ministry Without Making Your Church Sick.* Ventura, Calif.: Regal Books.

1988b     *The Third Wave of the Holy Spirit.* Ann Arbor, Mich.: Servant Publications.

1991     "Spiritual Power in Urban Evangelism: Dynamic Lessons from Argentina." *Evangelical Missions Quarterly* 27, no. 2 (April): 130-37.

Walls, Andrew F.
1976     "Toward an Understanding of Africa's Place in Christian History." In J. S. Pobee, ed. *Religion in a Pluralist Society.* Leiden: Brill, 180-89.

1991     "Structural Problems in Mission Studies." *International Bulletin of Missionary Research* 15, no. 4 (October): 146-52, 154-55.

Walsh, J. P. M.
1987     *The Mighty From Their Thrones: Power in the Biblical Tradition.* Philadelphia: Fortress Press.

Walzer, Michael.
1966     *The Revolution of the Saints. A Study in the Origins of Radical Politics.* London: Weidenfeld and Nicolson.

Ward, Maisie.
1949     *France Pagan? The Mission of Abbe Godin.* London: Sheed and Ward.

Warneck, Gustav.
1888     "The Mutual Relations of Evangelical Missionary Societies." In James Johnson, ed. *Report of the Missionary Conference on Protestant Missions of the World.* London: James Nisbet and Co.

Warren, Max.
1951     *The Christian Mission.* London: SCM Press, 78.

Warren, Max, ed.
1971     *To Apply the Gospel: Selections from the Writings of Henry Venn.* Grand Rapids, Mich.: Eerdmans.

Weber, Max.
1968     *On Charisma and Institution Building.* Chicago: University of Chicago Press.

Wendland, Heinz-Dietrich.
1934     *Reichsidee und Gottesreich.* Jena: Eugen Dietrich Verlag.

Wenz, Helmut.
1975     *Theologie des Reiches Gottes — Hat Jesus sich Geirrt?* Hamburg: Herbert Reich Evangelischer Verlag.

Werner, Dietrich.
1991     "Missionary Structure of the Congregation." In *Dictionary of the Ecumenical Movement.* N. Lossky, et al., eds. WCC, 699-701.

Whiteman, Darrell L.
1990     Editorial. *Missiology* 18: 394.

Wiedemann, L.
1963     *Mission und Eschatologie. Eine Analyse der neueren deutschen evangelischen Missiontheologie.* Druckerei Paderborn: Verlag-Bonifacius.

Wielenga, B.
1992     "The Bible in a Changing South Africa: The Quest for a Responsible Biblical Hermeneutic in Mission." *Missionalia* 20: no. 1 (April): 28-37.

Wieser, Thomas, ed.
  1966    *Planning for Mission: Working Papers on the New Quest for Mission Communities*. London: Epworth.
Williams, Don.
  1989    *Signs, Wonders and the Kingdom of God*. Ann Arbor, Mich.: Servant Publications.
Willing, Jennie Fowler.
  1869    "Under Bonds to Help Heathen Women." *Heathen Woman's Friend* I (August).
Willis, Wendell, ed.
  1987    *The Kingdom of God in 20th-Century Interpretation*. Peabody, Mass.: Hendrickson.
Wilson, Samuel.
  1990    "Opportunities and Obstacles to Joint Missionary Witness." *Missiology* 18: 449–61.
Wimber, John.
  1985    *Power Evangelism*. London: Hodder and Stoughton.
Wolterstorff, Nicholas.
  1983    *Until Justice and Peace Embrace*. Grand Rapids, Mich.: Eerdmans.
World Council of Churches.
  1967    *The Church for Others and the Church for the World: A Quest for Structures for Missionary Congregations*. Geneva: World Council of Churches.
  1968a    "Renewal in Mission." *The Uppsala Report 1968*. Norman Goodall, ed. Geneva: World Council of Churches.
  1968b    *Sources for Change: Searching for Flexible Church Structures*. Commission on Stewardship and Evangelism of the Lutheran World Federation. Geneva: World Council of Churches.
  1975    "Confessing Christ Today." Report of Section I. *Breaking Barriers: Nairobi 1975*, 43–57. Geneva: World Council of Churches.
  1980    *Your Kingdom Come: Mission Perspectives*. Report on the World Conference on Mission and Evangelism, Melbourne, Australia, 13–25 May, 1980. Geneva: World Council of Churches/CWME.
  1982a    *Baptism, Eucharist and Ministry*. Faith and Order Paper no. 111. Geneva: World Council of Churches.
  1982b    *Common Witness: A Study Document of the Joint Working Group of the Roman Catholic Church and the World Council of Churches*. Geneva: World Council of Churches.
  1982c    *Your Kingdom Come*: Report on the World Conference on Mission and Evangelism, Melbourne Australia. Geneva: World Council of Churches.
  1983a    *Mission and Evangelism: An Ecumenical Affirmation*. Geneva: World Council of Churches.
  1983b    *Gathered for Life: Official Report, VI Assembly*. David Gill, ed. Geneva: World Council of Churches; Grand Rapids, Mich.: Eerdmans.
  1986    *Go Forth in Peace: Orthodox Perspectives on Mission*. Ion Bria, ed. WCC Mission Series No. 7. Geneva: World Council of Churches.
  1987    *Current Dialogue*. Geneva: World Council of Churches.
  1990    *The San Antonio Report: Your Will be Done—Mission in Christ's Way*. Frederick R. Wilson, ed. Geneva: World Council of Churches.

1991a    *Signs of the Spirit: Official Report, World Council of Churches Seventh Assembly*. Michael Kinnamon, ed. Geneva: World Council of Churches; Grand Rapids, Mich: Eerdmans.

1991b    *Monthly Letter on Evangelism* 6/7 (June/July): 1.

World Council of Churches/CWME.

1989    *Mission From Three Perspectives*. Geneva: WCC/CWME.

Yoder, John Howard.

1972    *The Politics of Jesus*. Grand Rapids, Mich.: Eerdmans.

1984    "Reformation and Mission: A Bibliographic Survey." In Wilbert R. Shenk, ed. *Anabaptism and Mission*. Scottdale, Pa.: Herald Press.

Zuendel, Friedrich.

1954    *Johann Christoph Blumhardt*. Giessen: Brunnen Verlag.

# Scripture Index

# Author/Subject Index

Abraham, 206, 224, 226, 255
Abraham, William, 262
Accommodation, 195
Acts, 40, 46, 48, 57, 60, 66, 78, 99, 144, 166, 176, 185, 204-206, 216, 222, 228, 237-238, 249, 258, 261
*Ad Gentes Divinitus*, 28, 38-39, 43, 108, 138, 140, 142, 144-146
Adeney, Miriam, 181, 183, 186, 191
Africa, 89, 94, 96, 101, 113, 117-118, 142, 154, 183, 186, 191, 212, 239-243, 257-258, 260
African Traditional Religion, 240
Africanized, 142
Africans, 239, 241-243
Agape, 135, 256
Aggiornamento, 137
Agnostic, 191, 201
Agus, Jacob B., 221
Aigbe, Sunday, 260
Aland, Kurt, 235
Alien, aliens, 61, 94, 128, 211, 219, 241
Allen, Roland, 60, 157, 191, 254
Alliance, 89
Almsgiving, 62-63
Amaladoss, Michael, 121-122, 124
Ambassador, ambassadors, 54-55, 78, 223, 255
Amen, 182
America, 34, 56-61, 65-66, 71, 93, 96, 101, 110, 114, 116-117, 120, 138, 142, 156, 166, 177, 184-186, 188, 195, 198-199, 257-258, 260
American, Americans, 47, 26, 29-30, 56, 58, 60, 65, 71, 91, 109-113, 116-117, 119, 163, 168-169, 178, 184, 186-187, 189-190, 227, 229-230
American Society of Missiology (ASM), 6, 7, 107, 119, 151
Amsterdam, 155
Anabaptist, Anabaptists, 69, 89, 92-95
Ancestral, 168, 230
Ancient Near East, 99-100
Andersen, Wilhelm, 262

Anderson, Gerald, 28, 80, 166, 182, 200, 207-208
Anderson, J.N.D., 45, 164, 167
Anderson, Ray S., 262
Anderson, Rufus, 82, 157
Angel, angels, 47, 165, 234
Anglican, 4, 194
Anglo-Saxon, 101
Animistic, 190, 245, 255
Anomie, 193
Anonymous Christians, 244
Anonymous Hindus, 244
Anthropological, 34, 97, 104, 168, 189, 215, 230, 241
Anthropologist, 191
Anthropology, 32, 69, 104, 143, 169, 256
Antichrist, 4, 47-48
Antichristian, 168
Anticolonial, 155
Anticolonialism, 258
Antioch, 61
Antithesis, 5, 47
Antiurban, 101-102
Antiutopian, 95
Apartheid, 92
Apocalyptic, 26, 45-55
Apologetics, 248
Apostles, 78, 145-146, 173, 175-176, 206, 221, 223, 235-236
Apostleship, 52
Apostolate, 63, 255
Apostolic, 26, 47, 49, 58, 64, 87-88, 128, 137, 146, 151, 194
Appleton, George, 79
Arana, Pedro, 58
Archaeology, 100
Argentina, 59
Ariarajah, Wesley, 255
Arias, Mortimer, 243, 262
Arnold, Clinton E., 235
Ascension, 236, 261
Asia, 96, 101, 110, 118, 139, 168, 183, 186, 189, 257-258, 260